Lecture Notes in Artificial Intelligence   4908

Edited by J. G. Carbonell and J. Siekmann

Subseries of Lecture Notes in Computer Science

Mehdi Dastani   Amal El Fallah Seghrouchni
Alessandro Ricci   Michael Winikoff (Eds.)

Programming Multi-Agent Systems

5th International Workshop, ProMAS 2007
Honolulu, HI, USA, May 15, 2007
Revised and Invited Papers

 Springer

Series Editors

Jaime G. Carbonell, Carnegie Mellon University, Pittsburgh, PA, USA
Jörg Siekmann, University of Saarland, Saarbrücken, Germany

Volume Editors

Mehdi Dastani
Utrecht University, The Netherlands
E-mail: mehdi@cs.uu.nl

Amal El Fallah Seghrouchni
University of Paris VI, France
E-mail: amal.elfallah@lip6.fr

Alessandro Ricci
Università di Bologna, Cesena, Italy
E-mail: a.ricci@unibo.it

Michael Winikoff
RMIT University, Melbourne, Australia
E-mail: michael.winikoff@rmit.edu.au

Library of Congress Control Number: 2008924793

CR Subject Classification (1998): I.2.11, I.2, C.2.4, D.2, F.3, D.3

LNCS Sublibrary: SL 7 – Artificial Intelligence

ISSN   0302-9743
ISBN-10   3-540-79042-X Springer Berlin Heidelberg New York
ISBN-13   978-3-540-79042-6 Springer Berlin Heidelberg New York

This work is subject to copyright. All rights are reserved, whether the whole or part of the material is concerned, specifically the rights of translation, reprinting, re-use of illustrations, recitation, broadcasting, reproduction on microfilms or in any other way, and storage in data banks. Duplication of this publication or parts thereof is permitted only under the provisions of the German Copyright Law of September 9, 1965, in its current version, and permission for use must always be obtained from Springer. Violations are liable to prosecution under the German Copyright Law.

Springer is a part of Springer Science+Business Media

springer.com

© Springer-Verlag Berlin Heidelberg 2008

Typesetting: Camera-ready by author, data conversion by Scientific Publishing Services, Chennai, India
Printed on acid-free paper   SPIN: 12253067   06/3180   5 4 3 2 1 0

Preface

These are the post-proceedings of the International Workshop on Programming Multi-Agent Systems (ProMAS 2007), the fifth of a series of workshops that is attracting increasing attention from researchers and practitioners in multi-agent systems.

Multi-agent systems (MAS) constitute a promising software development paradigm for complex and distributed applications. The aim of the ProMAS workshop series is to promote and contribute to the establishment of MAS as a mainstream approach to the development of industrial-strength software. In particular, ProMAS aims to address the technologies that are required for implementing multi-agent systems designs or specifications effectively. We promote the discussion and exchange of ideas on principles, concepts, requirements, techniques, and tools that are essential for programming approaches and technologies specifically devised for MAS.

The idea of organizing the first workshop of the series was first discussed during the Dagstuhl seminar "Programming Multi-Agent Systems Based on Logic", where the focus was on *logic-based approaches*. It was felt that the scope should be broadened beyond logic-based approaches, thus giving the current scope and aims of ProMAS.

After four very successful editions of the ProMAS workshop series, which took place at AAMAS 2003 (Melbourne, Australia), AAMAS 2004 (New York, USA), AAMAS 2005 (Utrecht, The Netherlands), and AAMAS 2006 (Hakodate, Japan), the fifth edition took place on May 14 in Honolulu, Hawai'i, in conjunction with AAMAS 2007, the main international conference on autonomous agents and MAS. ProMAS 2007 received 17 submissions. These were reviewed by members of the Program Committee, and 11 papers were accepted.

At the workshop, in addition to the papers being presented, Jörg Müller gave an invited talk on business applications of agent technologies. Subsequently, Jörg was invited to prepare an invited paper for the post-proceedings. The resulting paper (written with Bernhard Bauer and Stephan Roser) examines the trade-offs involved in selecting an architecture for business process modelling and enactment.

The proceedings also contain an invited paper by Ralph Rönnquist describing a new agent platform, GORITE, which we hope will be of interest to the ProMAS community. GORITE ("GOal oRIented TEams") is a Java-based framework that provides facilities for implementing agent teams and goals. The aim of GORITE is to offer the team programming view and concepts dressed up in a standard Java solution, and thereby make the benefits of the paradigm accessible to a wider audience.

All but one of the 11 regular papers in these proceedings fall into one of three themes. The first paper by Keiser et al. is the exception. It looks at adding accounting features to the JIAC agent platform, motivated by the maxim that "objects do it for free, agents do it for money." The three themes that the remaining papers fall into are "Environment and Interaction", "Agent Programming Languages", and "Analysis of MAS".

Environment and Interaction

The paper by Aldewereld et al. develops a method for deriving interaction protocols from norms using landmarks. Their procedure can be used to systematically derive concrete protocols that can be used by agents in norm-governed electronic institutions, and ensure that the norms of the institution will be fulfilled.

The paper by Santos et al. presents a way of interoperating Bayesian network knowledge amongst agents using an ontology-based approach.

The paper by Ricci et al. builds on their A&A (Agents and Artifacts) principles which argue that *artifacts* play a critical role in activities. The paper presents the CARTAGO platform and shows how it can be integrated with existing MAS programming frameworks, using the *Jason* platform as an example.

Agent Programming Languages

The paper by Dastani and Meyer presents the agent-oriented programming language 2APL ("A Practical Agent Programming Language"), a successor to the well-known 3APL language. The syntax and semantics of 2APL are presented.

The paper by Dennis et al. presents an intermediate language for BDI-style programming languages. The intermediate language aims to be a low-level "lingua franca" for existing high-level languages, ultimately enabling a generic model checker to be developed. The semantics of the language are presented, focussing on plan processing and intentions.

The paper by Novák and Dix proposes a mechanism for modularity which works by extending the syntax of the language using the concept of a mental state transformer. Formal semantics and a concrete syntax are presented.

The paper by Hindriks also tackles the issue of modularity in agent programming languages. Hindriks' solution, developed in the context of the GOAL language, views modules as policy-based intentions which can be activated when their context condition is true. Modules also allow the agent to "focus" its attention, thus reducing the inherent non-determinism in GOAL and similar languages.

Analysis of MAS

The paper by Mermet et al. proposes the use of goal decomposition trees (GDTs) to model agent behavior, and shows how properties of GDTs can be proven.

The paper by Vigueras and Botía proposes the use of causality graphs to visualize the behavior of a multi-agent system. They argue that causality graphs make the behavior of an MAS easier to follow than simple sequence diagrams, and give an algorithm for building causality graphs.

The paper by Furbach et al. shows how a multi-agent system can be modelled using a combination of UML state-charts and hybrid automata. The proposed modelling notation is suitable for real-time systems with continuous variables. By exploiting existing model checkers for hybrid automata these systems can be model checked.

Agent Contest 2007

The proceedings also contain papers relating to Agent Contest 2007 (http://cig.in.tu-clausthal.de/AgentContest2007/). While the first two editions of this contest were organized within the Computational Logic in Multi-Agent Systems workshop series (CLIMA 2005 and CLIMA 2006), the organizers (Mehdi Dastani, Jürgen Dix and Peter Novák) felt that ProMAS is an ideal environment for such a contest. For this edition the actual contest took place in April/May with the results announced at ProMAS 2007. The winner of the ProMAS 2007 Agent Contest was the JIAC IV team from the DAI-Labor, Technische Universität Berlin, Germany. The second team was the microJIAC team, from the same institute, followed by the Jason team. These proceedings contain a detailed report about the contest by the contest organizers, as well as five papers describing the MAS that were accepted for Agent Contest 2007.

One of the driving motivations behind the ProMAS workshop series (and all associated activities) was the observation that the area of autonomous agents and MAS has grown into a promising technology offering sensible alternatives for the design of distributed, intelligent systems. However, the success of MAS development can only be guaranteed if we can bridge the gap from analysis and design to effective implementation. This, in turn, requires the development of fully fledged and general purpose programming technology so that the concepts and techniques of MAS can be easily and directly implemented. Only by advancing our understanding of the key issues in the development of large-scale MAS will we see a paradigm shift, with MAS techniques becoming, as the AAMAS community predicted, the predominant approach to the development of complex distributed systems that are able to operate in dynamic and unpredictable environments. We hope that the work described in this volume takes us a step closer to this goal.

Finally, we would like to thank all the authors, the invited speaker, the author of the second invited paper, the Program Committee members, and additional reviewers for their outstanding contribution to the success of ProMAS 2007. We are particularly grateful to the AAMAS 2007 organizers for their technical support and for hosting ProMAS 2007.

November 2007

Mehdi Dastani
Amal El Fallah Seghrouchni
Alessandro Ricci
Michael Winikoff

Organization

Organizing Committee

Mehdi Dastani,   Utrecht University, The Netherlands
Amal El Fallah Seghrouchni   University of Paris VI, France
Alessandro Ricci   Università di Bologna a Cesena, Italy
Michael Winikoff   RMIT University, Australia

Steering Committee

Rafael H. Bordini,   University of Durham, UK
Mehdi Dastani,   Utrecht University, The Netherlands
Jürgen Dix   Clausthal University of Technology, Germany
Amal El Fallah Seghrouchni   University of Paris VI, France

Program Committee

Matteo Baldoni   Università degli Studi di Torino, Italy
Juan A. Botía Blaya   Universidad de Murcia, Spain
Lars Braubach   University of Hamburg, Germany
Jean-Pierre Briot   University of Paris 6, France
Keith Clark   Imperial College, UK
Rem Collier   University College Dublin, Ireland
Yves Demazeau   Institut IMAG - Grenoble, France
Frank Dignum   Utrecht University, The Netherlands
Michael Fisher   University of Liverpool, UK
Jorge Gómez-Sanz   Universidad Complutense de Madrid, Spain
Vladimir Gorodetsky   St. Petersburg Institute for Informatics and
     Automation, Russia
Shinichi Honiden   NII, Tokyo, Japan
Jomi Hübner   Universidade Regional de Blumenau, Brazil
João Leite   Universidade Nova de Lisboa, Portugal
Jiming Liu   Hong Kong Baptist University, Hong Kong
John-Jules Meyer   Utrecht University, The Netherlands
Toyoaki Nishida   Kyoto University, Japan
Andrea Omicini   Università di Bologna a Cesena, Italy
Juan Pavon   Universidad Complutense de Madrid, Spain
Alexander Pokahr   University of Hamburg, Germany
Chris Reed   Calico Jack Ltd., UK
Birna van Riemsdijk   Ludwig Maximilians University, Germany

Sebastian Sardina	RMIT University, Australia
Nathan Schurr	University of Southern California, USA
Paolo Torroni	University of Bologna, Italy

Additional Reviewers

Koen Hindriks, Marc-Philippe Huget

Table of Contents

Agent Contest Competition

Decentralized Business Process Modeling and Enactment: ICT Architecture Topologies and Decision Methods

Bernhard Bauer[1], Jörg P. Müller[2], and Stephan Roser[1]

[1] Programming Distributed Systems Lab
University of Augsburg
Universitätsstrasse 14, D-86135 Augsburg, Germany
{bauer,roser}@ds-lab.org
[2] Department of Informatics
Clausthal University of Technology
Julius-Albert-Str. 4, D-38678 Clausthal-Zellerfeld, Germany
joerg.mueller@tu-clausthal.de

Abstract. Multiagent systems have been proposed in the literature as a suitable architectural and implementation approach for cross-enterprise collaboration, due to their support for decentral decision-making and peer-to-peer coordination, loosely coupled interaction, modeling support for the notion of electronic institutions, and built-in adaptability mechanisms. While we agree with this general view, we argue that different application domain and different market constellations require different types of architecture. In this paper we look at the specific problem of selecting an information and communication technology (ICT) architecture for cross-enterprise business process (CBP) design and enactment. Therefore we identify three important architectural patterns for CBP enactment. We then propose a decision method for architecture selection based on the analytic hierarchy process (AHP) approach. Finally we illustrate the method by applying it to two application scenarios with differing characteristics. Robustness of the decision method is analyzed by performing a sensitivity analysis.

1 Introduction

Under the pressure of globalization, companies are urged to constantly adapt to new market situations and and competitors innovations. Focusing on their core business and core competencies, they engage in cross-enterprise business processes (CBPs) with new partners all over the world in ever changing constellations. Companies are organized into global networks and outsource those activities that can be performed quicker, more effectively, or at lower cost, by others.

These developments create new challenges for enterprise information and communication technology (ICT), requiring ICT systems to support constantly changing enterprise collaboration relationships and to create application systems

M. Dastani et al.(Eds.): ProMAS 2007, LNAI 4908, pp. 1–26, 2008.
© Springer-Verlag Berlin Heidelberg 2008

that support or automate business process enactment starting from business level descriptions and models of CBPs.

Multiagent systems [18] have been proposed in the literature as a suitable architectural and implementation approach for cross-enterprise collaboration [19,20], due to their support for decentral decision-making and peer-to-peer co-ordination, loosely coupled coordination, modeling support for the notion of electronic institutions [14], and built-in adaptability. However, while we agree that the distributed and sometimes decentral topologies require some kind of multiagent organization principles, we argue that different application domains and different market constellations require different types of system architecture.

Let us look at the following example of collaborative product development in the automotive sector (see [35]). The scenario (see Figure 1) describes the interaction between an automotive Original Equipment Manufacturer (OEM) and its supplier network consisting of multiple tiers of suppliers, during the process of Strategic Sourcing. Strategic Sourcing is an early step within Cooperative Product Development, where OEMs set up strategic partnerships with the larger (so-called first-tier) suppliers with the aim of producing specific subsystems (e.g., powertrain, safety electronics) of a planned car series. In the use case considered for this paper, the OEM shares Requests for Quotations with its first-tier suppliers (1). First-tier suppliers serve as gateways to the supplier network; specifications are reviewed and conditions negotiated with second-tier suppliers (2), and feasibility of the requests are checked. First-tier suppliers then issue quotes or suggest changes to the OEM (3). This cycle is repeated until all parties agree on a feasible specification. Finally, first-tier suppliers submit quotes to the OEM.

Figure 1 gives a high-level (business-level) model of the cross-enterprise business processes involved in this scenario. Trying to map this model into an executable ICT model, several non-trivial questions need to be answered regarding the ICT architecture. In particular, the question that we address in this paper is the following: What is the most appropriate architectural choice to model the interactions between the OEM and the 1st tier suppliers? A decentral, peer-to-peer

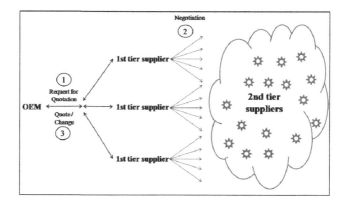

Fig. 1. Application example: Collaborative product development

messaging architecture where each role in each process instance is mapped into an agent-like entity to run and control it? An architecture with a central broker (e.g. located at the OEM) that centrally enacts and controls the cross-enterprise business processes? Or a mixture of both, a decentral broker architecture where each enterprise provides a publicly visible instance (agent) to control and coordinate their business process roles while hiding other, private, elements.

Thus, we can see using this scenario that there are different architectural choices / paradigms possible for underlying information and communication technology (ICT) system design. Intuitively, none of these choices is per se better than any other; making the right decision depends on a number of environmental characteristics (called contingencies in [10]). In this paper we propose a model for decision support suitable for enterprise architects to derive an appropriate supporting architecture paradigm for a given use case / application domain. Assuming some model-driven design paradigm [17,4], we start from business level models and (semi-automatically) transforms these models into (platform-independent) ICT models (so-called PIMs); these PIM models are then subject to further transformation via platform-specific models (PSMs) down to the code-level.

In this paper, we address the problem of selecting a suitable ICT architecture at the PIM level, thus resulting in an architecture-driven approach to CBP modeling and enactment. The contribution of this paper is fourfold: First, we identify three important architectural patterns for CBP enactment; second we propose a decision method for architecture selection based on the analytic hierarchy process (AHP [31]); third, we show the applicability of the method by applying it to application scenarios with differing characteristics; fourth, we investigate the robustness of the decision method by performing a sensitivity analysis.

The paper is structured as follows: In Section 2, we provide the background on service-oriented architecture, model-driven engineering, and decision methods. Section 3 presents three ICT-level architecture patterns for CBPs. The decision method is proposed in Section 4; Section 5 analyzes the applicability of our method to two application scenarios. The paper ends with a discussion and outlook in Section 6.

2   Background

2.1   Model-Driven Engineering

Software engineering currently witnesses a paradigm shift from object-oriented implementation towards model-driven implementation. This carries important consequences on the way information systems are built and maintained [4]. Model-driven Engineering (MDE) treats models as first class artifacts, which are used for modeling and code generation. This raises the level of abstraction at which developers create and evolve software [16] and reduces complexity of software artifacts by separating concerns and aspects of a system [17]. Thus MDE shifts the focus of software development away from the technology domain towards the problem domain. Largely automated model transformations refine (semi-)automatically abstract models to more concrete models or simply describe mappings between models of the same level of abstraction. In particular, transformation engines and generators are used to generate code and other target domain artifacts with input from both modeling experts and domain experts [32]. MDE is an approach to bridge the semantic gap that exists between domain-specific concepts encountered in modern software applications and standard programming technologies used to implement them [6].

Two prominent representatives of MDE are the OMG's Model Driven Architecture (MDA) and the software factory initiative from Microsoft.

In MDE, models and model transformations, which can be also treated as models, embody critical solutions and insights to enterprise challenges and hence are seen as assets for an organization [21]. Assets are artifacts that provide solutions to problems, should be reusable in and customizable to various contexts.

2.2   Service-Oriented Multiagent Architectures

In recent years, a new generation of integration solutions has been developed under the service-oriented paradigm, which lends itself to develop highly adaptable solutions and to reuse existing applications. In a service-oriented world, sets of services are assembled and reused to quickly adapt to new business needs. However, service-orientation does not provide an integration solution by itself. Service-oriented integration introduces the concept of service (which can be implemented through Web Services) to establish a platform-independent model with various integration architectures. Service-oriented architecture (SOA) can be realized by an agent-oriented architecture. However, agents have additional features, services usually not have, like high-level, speech-act based communication, pre-defined interaction protocols (e.g. the ContractNet protocol or auction mechanisms) and goal-oriented composition of agents. In other words, agents are more sophisticated services. See also [33].

Service. While, from an economic point of view, a service is the non-material equivalent of a good sold to a costumer, we use the term service from an ICT point of view, where a service is seen as a business or technical functionality. We define service *"as a well-defined, self-contained function that does not depend on the context or state of other services"* [5]. Service-orientation is based on this concept of service.

Agents. Software agents are computer systems capable of flexible autonomous action in a dynamic, unpredictable and open environment [18]. These characteristics give agent technology a high potential to support process-centered modeling and operation of businesses. Consequently, starting with ADEPT [19], there have been various research efforts of using agent technology in business process management. However, the focus of ADEPT was on communication and collaboration in business process management. It was not geared to being a directly usable business process support platform. Migrating agent technology successfully to business applications requires end-to-end solutions that integrate with standards, that preserve companies' investment in hardware, software platforms, tools, and people, and that enable the incremental introduction of new technologies. The OMG has set up a new standardization effort called *UML Metamodel and Profile for Service* (UPMS). The UPMS RFP requests a services metamodel and profile for extending UML with capabilities applicable to modeling services using a SOA[1]. Within this standardization effort a new RFP is prepared for the integration of agent technology in a service-oriented world. This can provide a first step towards solving this problem.

2.3 Cross-Enterprise Business Processes

Many people and organizations participate in the construction of a software system, and impose different concerns and requirements on the system, in particular in CBPs. Business considerations determine non-functional qualities that must be accommodated in the system architecture. Quality attributes like availability, modifiability, performance, security, testability, usability, or business qualities are orthogonal to functional attributes describing the system's capabilities, services, and behavior. Since quality attributes are critical to the success of a system, they must be considered throughout design, implementation and deployment. Beyond these quality attributes, costs e.g. for hardware, software licences, and software development have to be considered when choosing the right architecture. In our work we investigate how service-oriented or agent-oriented architecture of software systems for CBPs can be derived from business level descriptions. The architecture variants and model transformations we describe are independent of functional attributes, since they can be applied to (nearly) any models describing CBPs. We investigate how three architecture variants for realizing CBPs in service-oriented software systems can be derived from business level descriptions and how to evaluate the right architecture for different contexts, thus supporting the enactment of high-level CBP specifications.

Orchestration & Choreography. Orchestration and choreography describe two complimentary notions of a process. In orchestration a central entity coordinates the execution of services involved in a higher-level business process. Only the coordinator of the orchestration is aware of this composition. Choreography describes the interactions of collaborating entities (e.g. services or agents), each of which may have their own internal orchestration processes. These interactions are often structured into interaction protocols to represent the conversation between the parties. [27] An important distinction between orchestration and choreography is the fact that orchestration is generally owned and operated by a single organization while in a choreography no organization necessarily controls the collaboration logic [11].

Process Modeling. In process modeling it is common to distinguish between an internal and an external view of business processes. Depending on the viewpoint, a process is described either as an executable, abstract, or collaborative process:

---

[1] see http://adtf.omg.org/adptf_info.htm

The internal view models the 'how' of a business process from the modeler's view. As the flow of an *executable process* [26] is described from the viewpoint of a single process coordinating its sub-processes, this is often referred to as process orchestration. *Abstract processes* model the external view on and the 'what' of a business process. Each process specifies the public interactions it performs in relation to its roles in collaborations. A *collaborative process* describes the collaboration between abstract processes in the case of process choreography. The collaborations between the involved parties are modeled as interaction patterns between their roles from the viewpoint of an external observer.

2.4 ICT Architecture Variants for CBP Enactment

Service-oriented integration solutions can be categorized by their topology (see Figure 2). In a purely decentralized MAS topology services of the participating organizations implicitly establish the collaborative process through direct message exchange; this is a realization of choreography. In a hierarchical topology a controller service defines the steps necessary to achieve the overall goal and maps these steps to services provided by the contributing organizations; this is kind realization of orchestration. However, in many cases, a mixture of hierarchical and decentralized MAS topology, i.e. a heterogenous topology, is used to realize complex multipartner collaborations [23].

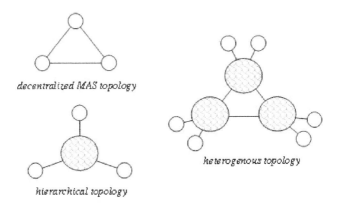

Fig. 2. Coordination topologies

2.5 Architecture Evaluation and Decision Methods

Architecture Evaluation. Scenario-based ICT architecture evaluation is used to determine quality of software architecture. In architecture evaluation methods like ATAM, SAAM, or ARID [1,8] quality attributes are characterized by scenario descriptions.

Quality attributes are part of the non-functional requirements and therefore properties of a system. They can be broadly grouped into two categories [9]. Qualities like performance, security, availability, and usability are observable via execution at *run-time*, and qualities like extensibility, modifiability, portability, or reusability, which are not observable via execution [3].

According to Bass et al. [1], scenario descriptions consist of a *stimulus* (a condition that needs to be considered when it arrives at a system), a *source of stimulus* (some entity that generates the stimulus) , an *environment* (the stimulus occurs within certain conditions), an *artifact* (the part of the system that is stimulated), a *response* (the response is the activity undertaken after arrival of the stimulus) and a *response measure* (defines how the result of the response is measured). General scenarios [2] are applicable to many software systems and have architectural implications; they establish sets of scenarios which are configured to the respective application domain (for which evaluation is performed) by varying the expected response value scales of the scenarios.

To be able to decide how good a quality attribute or a scenario is supported by a software architecture pattern and to compare architecture patterns, it is crucial to understand how an architecture influences quality attributes. According to Bass et al. [1] architects use so-called tactics to achieve quality attributes. A tactic is a design decision that influences the control of a quality attribute. The software architecture patterns described in this article make use of the following tactics (non-exclusive list; for detailed description see also [1] p.99ff): *Maintain semantic coherence, anticipate expected changes, generalize module, restrict communication paths, use an intermediary, maintain existing interfaces,* and *hide information*.

Tactics are used by an architect to create a design using design patterns, architectural patterns, or architectural strategies. An architect usually chooses a pattern or a collection of patterns designed to realize one or more tactics. However, each pattern implements multiple tactics, whether desired or not. The following list provides an overview of architecture patterns, design patterns, and design principles used to realize the above described tactics (non-exclusive list compiled from [1], [12], [11], and [13]): *Wrapper, broker, abstraction, loose coupling,* and *orchestration*.

Analytic Hierarchy Process. The Analytic Hierarchy Process (AHP) [31] is a decision making approach, which decomposes a decision problem into a hierarchical network of factors and subfactors. Factor decomposition establishes a hierarchy of first level and second level factors cascading from the decision objective or goal. AHP applies pairwise comparisons to the factors and the alternatives in the decision making process. Pairwise comparisons lend themselves to solving problems with limited number of choices, where each choice has a number of attributes and it is difficult to formalize some of those attributes. Finally the ratings of the second level factors are aggregated to first level factors and the final rating.

Contingency Theory. The contingency theory for organizations [10] is used to rationalize how the various aspects of organizations' environment (called *contingency factors*) influence organization structure. It suggests, that there is no unique or best way to organize an organization, but the design of an organization and its systems must 'fit' with its environment. The *"organizational effectiveness results from the fitting characteristics of the organization, such as its structure, to contingencies that reflect the situation of the organization"* [10, p.1]. *"Contingency theory (...) sees maximum performance as resulting from adopting, not the maximum, but rather the appropriate level of the structural variable that fits the contingency. Therefore, the optimal structural level is seldom the maximum, and which level is optimal is dependent upon the level of the contingency variable"* [10, p.4]. Translating this into the terms of companies and their business systems, a maximum of centralization, decentralization, or some of the ICT system architectural qualities like modifiability, security, etc., will seldom yield maximum performance of an ICT system for the overall business goals.

3   Architecture Paradigms for CBPs

In Sections 2.4 and 2.2 we have introduced the abstract topologies for CBP enactment and described how service-orientation and agents fit together. Now we have a closer look at these coordination architectures and how they can be applied to realize service-oriented integration solutions. These architectures are used to control the conversation flow between the participating organizations. In an agent world this is comparable to interaction protocols. For the description of the coordination architecture we assume, that each organization willing to participate in a cross-organizational collaboration supported by ICT systems, has a set of *elementary services (ES)*, which are as far as possible realized by agents. These elementary services are application, business, or hybrid services. In our descriptions we also assume without loss of generality, that the elementary services are realized as process services, so that we can use the distinction between executable and abstract process. Nevertheless, elementary services could be realized by arbitrary code fragments. An elementary service can only be a controller service with regard to the organizations' internal service composition, but not with regard to the collaboration process. *Cross-organizational business*

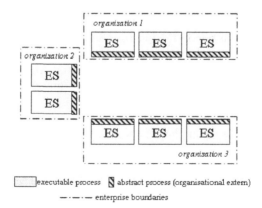

Fig. 3. Brokerless architecture

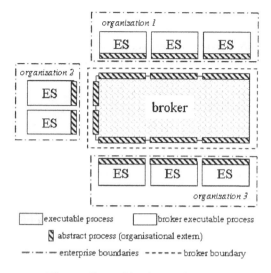

Fig. 4. Central broker architecture

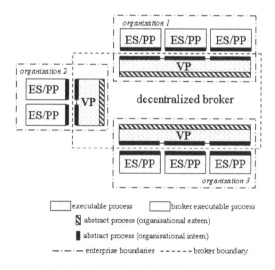

Fig. 5. Decentral broker architecture

processes (CBPs) represent the conversation flow and message exchange between the organizations participating in the collaboration (in particular in an agent communication language).

- *Brokerless architecture*: A brokerless coordination architecture (see Figure 3) can be used to realize the decentralized MAS topology, where messages are exchanged directly between the elementary services of the participants as usual in an agents world. Due to the mutual exchange of messages the elementary services depend on each other. Control flow logic of CBPs is realized by the executable process of the participants' elementary services. Changing the business protocol would result in changing multiple elementary services, i.e. their executable processes. Further, the abstract process of the elementary services are directly exposed to the collaboration space and therefore are directly accessible by entities outside enterprise boundaries.

– *Central broker architecture*: Figure 4 depicts the central broker coordination architecture. Messages are no longer exchanged directly between the elementary services, but over a central broker component, which is realized by a controller service. The controller service is a process that orchestrates the elementary services of the participating organizations. It acts as a global observer process coordinating the partners as well as making decisions on the basis of data used in the CBP. In the case of a change to the CBP protocol's messages and semantics, only the broker process needs to be modified. Since the broker process is not necessarily owned by one of the participating partners, organizations may hide their elementary services from their collaborators. However, they have to reveal them to a third party instead.

– *Decental broker architecture*: The *decentralized broker architecture* introduces elements of the decentralized MAS topology in the hierarchical topology of the central broker architecture. It splits the single broker component into several controller processes jointly providing the broker functionality (note the boundaries in Figure 5). Each organization provides one controller service, also called *view process (VP)*, which orchestrates the organization's internal elementary services. Messages across organizational boundaries are only exchanged by the view processes, which encapsulate the elementary services. In this architecture the elementary service can be seen as kind of *private processes (PP)*.

4 A Method for Evaluation of ICT Architecture Applicability

This section presents an evaluation and decision method that helps to select appropriate ICT architectures for CBPs enactment. The evaluation method takes into account the trade-offs between coordination structures, which are implemented by the ICT system architectures in terms of coordination costs and vulnerability costs (see [24]). As visualized in Figure 6 the evaluation model distinguishes between quantitative factors, that are measurable by concrete figures (objective factors), and qualitative (subjective factors), which are difficult or impossible to measure. Coordination costs to establish and maintain communication links between collaborating patterns are included as quantitative factors in terms of software, hardware, and labor in the evaluation model. Coordination costs like costs for exchanging messages between collaborating partners are taken into account by qualitative factors. Vulnerability costs, which are "the unavoidable costs of a changed situation that are incurred before the organization can adapt to a new situation" [24], are qualitative factors in the evaluation model.

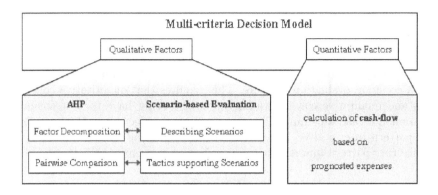

Fig. 6. Multi-criteria decision model for ICT architectures

To be able to compare the architectural CBP approaches in the face of architectural decisions, it is necessary to get a quantitative measure from qualitative actors. Thus, we apply, extend and customize the multi-criteria decision model of Ghandforoush et al. [15], which is a modified version of Brown and Gibson's model [7]. As it is a quantitative model, it is useful for selecting one alternative from a given set of alternatives based on quantitative and qualitative factors. Figure 6 depicts the design of our multi-criteria decision model developed to evaluate ICT architectures for CBP enactment. The rating of the quantitative factors is determined by the means of cash-flow analysis of the predicted costs. For rating the qualitative factors we combine AHP and scenario-based software architecture evaluation methods. First, based on the AHP, the factors, which have to be considered in the evaluation, are determined by decomposing the evaluation problem and arranged in a hierarchy decomposition tree. The factors are described by the means of quality attributes and scenarios. Rating the scenarios and the alternatives is done by pairwise comparison. The ratings, i.e. the pairwise comparisons, are based upon how good the alternatives realize tactics supporting the respective scenarios.

4.1   Multi-criteria Evaluation and Decision Model

The multi-criteria evaluation and decision distinguishes between objective (quantitative) factors and subjective (qualitative) factors.

- *Objective factors* are evaluated in monetary terms, and as such are easily quantifiable. Our quantification is based on the cash flow approach and therefore on the discounted present value. The evaluation model considers costs for software, hardware and labor.[2]

---

[2] The focus of the evaluation model is on the viewpoint of an integrator. The integrator takes into account purchase, licensing, set up, and maintenance costs for hardware and integration and maintenance costs for software. Development of software itself plays a secondary role, since the service or agent software has to be developed independent of the chosen architecture.

– *Subjective factors* are characterized by the fact that they are qualitative measures that typically cannot be quantified. When evaluating software architecture, quality attributes and scenarios are measures in qualitative terms.

The underlying principle of the model is to combine the two evaluation factors into a common evaluation measure. This requires that quantitative considerations and qualitative considerations, where the latter have to be transformed in common measurable units. The model allows to select one software architecture pattern from a given set of alternatives. Following [15], for each software architecture pattern i an architecture evaluation measure AEM_i is defined:

$$AEM_i = X \cdot OFM_i + (1 - X) \cdot SFM_i \tag{1}$$

where

AEM_i = architecture evaluation measure, $0 \leq AEM_i \leq 1$

OFM_i = objective factor measure, $0 \leq OFM_i \leq 1$ and $\sum_{i=1}^{n} OFM_i = 1$

SFM_i = subjective factor measure, $0 \leq SFM_i \leq 1$ and $\sum_{i=1}^{n} SFM_i = 1$

X = weight assigned to the objective factor, $0 \leq X \leq 1$

n = total number of software architecture patterns evaluated, $1 \leq i \leq n$

AEM_i is a measure between 0 and 1 for a particular software architecture pattern, where software architecture patterns with a higher measure score better than patterns with a lower measure. The measure depends to large extend on the choice of the weight X assigned to the objective factors OFM_i and the subjective factors SFM_i. This parameter can be used for sensitivity analysis.

Objective factors are quantified in terms of monetary units. In order to make them comparable to subjective factors, the objective factors have to be converted to a dimensionless index, i.e. an index with the dimension of one:

$$OFM_i = \frac{1}{OFC_i \cdot \sum_{i=1}^{n} \left(\frac{1}{OFC_i}\right)}, i = 1, 2, \ldots, n \tag{2}$$

where

OFC_i = total objective factor costs for software architecture pattern i

Brown and Gibson [7] ensure through three principles that the objective factor measure is compatible with the subjective factor measure: the software architecture pattern with the highest cost will have the minimum OFM_i, the relationship of OFC_i for each pattern relative to all other patterns is preserved, and the sum of all OFM_i is equal to 1.

The subjective factors can be grouped into a hierarchy of factors. A first level factors is an aggregation of a set of second levels factors. Within one first level factor the relative importance of a second level factor is rated by assigning a weight SSW_{k_j} to each of the second level factors. Similar the weight SFW_j specifies the relative importance of one first level factor to the other first level factors. Both factors weights depend on the *organizational context and the collaboration* for which the software architecture patterns are evaluated. The factor weights are independent of software architecture patterns, and can also be used for sensitivity analysis. The subjective factor measure SFM_i is defined as follows:

$$SFM_i = \sum_{j=1}^{m} \left(SFW_j \cdot \sum_{k=1}^{o_j} \left(SSW_{k_j} \cdot SAW_{ik_j} \right) \right) \tag{3}$$

$$SFW_j = \frac{SFW'_j}{\sum_{j=1}^{m} SFW'_j} \tag{4}$$

$$SSW_{k_j} = \frac{SSW'_{k_j}}{\sum_{k=1}^{o_j} SSW'_{k_j}} \tag{5}$$

$$SAW_{ik_j} = \frac{SAW'_{ik_j}}{\sum_{i=1}^{n} SAW'_{ik_j}} \tag{6}$$

where

SFW_j = normalized weight value of first level factor j

SFW'_j = weight of first level factor j to each first level factor

SSW_{k_j} = normalized weight value of 2nd level factor k_j for one 1st level
      factor j

SSW'_{k_j} = weight of second level factor k_j to all second level factors
      in first level factor j

SAW_{ik_j} = normalized rating of architecture variant i for subjective factor k_j

SAW'_{ik_j} = rating of architecture variant i for subjective factor k_j

m = total number of first level factors among the subjective factors

o_j = total number of second level factors in a specific first level factor j

All, the first level factor weight SFW_j, the second level factor weight SSW_{k_j}, and the architecture variant rating SAW_{ik_j} are normalized measures and sum up to one. Thus also the subjective factor measure SFM_i sums up to one and is represented in the same numerical scale as the objective factors. SFW_j, SSW_{k_j}, and SAW_{ik_j} are defined as follows:

4.2   Measuring Qualitative Factors

The part of the evaluation and decision model concerned with measuring qualitative factors is supposed to deal with two main challenges. First it has to provide concepts to evaluate software architecture patterns with respect to organizations' demands. Second the model has to provide means to support people using the model by rating factors and alternatives in order to achieve reasonable and consistent measurements throughout the evaluation process.

We use scenario-based evaluation for software architecture patterns, which is a good way to determine quality attributes of software architecture. The AHP [31] first decomposes a decision problem into a hierarchical network of factors and subfactors before it aggregates second level factors to first level factors. In scenario-based evaluation, first level factors are represented by quality attributes and second level factors are represented by scenario descriptions.

Since it is problematic to provide sensible scales for measuring the response value of our high level software architectural patterns, we make use of pairwise comparison (see AHP [31]) to rate the qualitative factors and the evaluated software architecture patterns. The decisions for the comparisons are made on the basis of which tactics the evaluated software architecture patterns support and the contingency factors influencing organizations and the collaboration.

Scenario-Based ICT Architecture Evaluation. Scenario-based ICT architecture evaluation is used to determine quality of software architecture. Hence desired architectural quality attributes are refined by general usage scenarios. These allow a detailed rating of how good quality attributes are supported by software architecture pattern. Quality attributes and scenarios descriptions are used to determine the qualitative factors measure.

Quality Attributes. Our evaluation model considers the strategic quality attributes modifiability, privacy, reusability and interoperability. For the quality attribute privacy we evaluate the privacy of corporate data and knowledge, which has to be exposed by the enterprises due to the applied software architecture pattern. We do not consider execution related topics like intrusion, denial of service attacks, etc. In the case of interoperability, which can be observed both at execution and build time, we only consider strategic issues like change and reuse of functionality or interaction protocols; we do not consider e.g. conversion of message data at runtime. Furthermore, the evaluation model addresses some more run-time related issues like efficiency and manageability of process execution.

Scenario Descriptions. The evaluation model is supposed to be suitable for a diversity of systems supporting businesses collaborations. Thus, general scenarios have to be developed, which can be applied to classes of systems rather than to one concrete system. Scenarios represent the characteristics of quality attributes and are used to determine how good quality attributes can be satisfied by systems realizing certain software architecture patterns. The following list gives an overview of the quality attributes (printed in boldface) and the associated scenarios defined for our evaluation and decision model.

- *Modifiability*
  - *Scenario 1:* Modification of CBPs
  - *Scenario 2:* Change of partners in CBP
  - *Scenario 3:* Incremental development of CBPs
  - *Scenario 4:* Change of elementary services

- • *Scenario 5:* Development of CBP variants
- **Privacy**
  - • *Scenario 6:* Privacy of internal ESs related data
  - • *Scenario 7:* Privacy of internal CBPs realizations
- **Reusability**
  - • *Scenario 8:* Reuse of CBPs
  - • *Scenario 9:* Reuse of elementary services
- **Interoperability**
  - • *Scenario 10:* Change of CBP protocol specification
  - • *Scenario 11:* Change of ES's interfaces
- **Efficiency**
  - • *Scenario 12:* Bottle-neck
  - • *Scenario 13:* Security overhead
- **Manageability**
  - • *Scenario 14:* Versioning
  - • *Scenario 15:* Monitoring

Table 1 depicts the description of the *'Modification of CBPs'* scenario. Descriptions of the other scenarios can be found in [28].

Factor Decomposition and Pairwise Comparisons. Factor decomposition and pairwise comparisons of our evaluation model are based on the Analytic Hierarchy Process (AHP) [31].

Factor decomposition. Factor decomposition establishes a hierarchy of first level and second level factors cascading from the decision objective or goal. The hierarchy for our decision method is structured as follows (see Figure 7): At the top level one can find the overall goal to have the best *architecture quality*. At the first level contains quality attributes like *modifiability, privacy, reuse*, etc., which

Table 1. Scenario 1 – Modification of CBPs

Scenario 1 – Modification of CBPs	
Source	Management
Stimulus	Due to the constant and rapid change in business existing CBPs have to be adapted to the new business models.
Environment	Design-time
Artifact	Cross-organizational business process
Response	The necessary changes in order to enact the new CBP affect a minimal number of existing modules. Necessary change of existing modules should have no side-effects on other processes (e.g CBPs).
Response Measure	Without broker: up to n ESs of the partners are affected Central broker: the central broker is affected Decentral broker: VPs of the respective partner(s) are affected

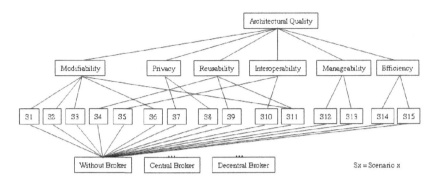

Fig. 7. AHP decomposition rree for CBP evaluation model

contribute to the quality of an architecture. The scenarios are used at the second
level to give a more detailed description of how the quality attributes have to
be established. At the bottom level we can find the architectural variants which
have to support the scenarios.

Pairwise Comparisons. AHP uses pairwise comparison for both determining the
priority for the subjective factors and rating the architectural alternatives.

Weighting the Subjective Factors. To determine the weights for subjective factors,
i.e. which scenarios or quality attribute is more important than another, pairwise
comparisons are conducted between the first-level factors and the second-level factors. Therefore the factors are arranged in a matrix a and the evaluators have to
determine the ratings a_{ij} of the factors by pairwise comparisons. They use a scale
to measure relative importance ranging from one to nine (one means that both
factors are equally important; nine means that one factor is extremely more important than another). To calculate the ratios of the factors v_i, the entries of the
matrix a_{ij} have to be normalized to $\overline{a_{ij}}$. Then the normalized matrix entries $\overline{a_{ij}}$ of
each row are summed up and divided through the number factors, i.e. the average
value of the normalized matrix entries for each row is determined.

$$v_i = \frac{\sum_{j=1}^{n} \overline{a_{ij}}}{n} = \frac{\sum_{j=1}^{n} \frac{a_{ij}}{\sum_{i=1}^{n} a_{ij}}}{n}$$

As a result, v_i is the weight for the respective SFW'_j or SSW'_{k_j} for the first
and second level factors. It holds that $SFW'_j = SFW_j$ and $SSW'_{k_j} = SSW_{k_j}$
since the weights of the factors v_i are already normalized. The aggregation of
the factor weights is achieved by multiplying the second level factor weight with
the respective first level factor weight.

Rating the Scenarios. To rate the scenarios, our decision method applies a relative measurement, which based on a scale (see above) to express preference of
one alternative over another. For example, one can say that to support a scenario under certain contingencies, alternative a_1 is strongly favored instead of

alternative a_2. For each scenario an evaluation matrix is established, in which the alternatives are compared. To determine the rating of the alternatives (i.e. the priority vector), we apply the 'ideal mode' which should be used in cases where one alternative shall be chosen [30,29]. The 'ideal mode' solves the rank reversal problem, where the number and kind of alternatives might influence the decision. The matrix is constructed analogous to the matrix for weighting the scenarios. Only the calculation of the priority vector's values differs, since we apply the 'ideal mode' and not the 'distributive mode'. One obtains the values of the priority vector in ideal mode v_i^{id} by dividing v_i by the maximal value of v: $v_i^{id} = \frac{v_i}{max(v_i)}$; v_i^{id} corresponds to the rating of the architecture variant SAW'_{ik_j}.

The measurement values of how good ICT coordination architectures support the scenarios is specific to organizational and collaboration context, i.e. the contingencies. It is possible that under certain contingencies one alternative is the best for supporting a scenario, while under different contingencies this alternative may be less appropriate to support the same scenario.

Rating the ICT Architecture Alternative. To compare the ICT coordination architectures one needs to know how good these architectures support architecture quality attributes and scenarios. Therefore it is necessary to understand by which means an architect influences the quality attributes of an architecture. As described in [1], software architects use so-called tactics to achieve quality attributes (see Section 2.5).

In the case of *scenario 1* the architect applies tactics that reduce the number of modules and processes (*response of scenario 1*) that are affected by changes to processes (*stimulus of scenario 1*). Through the *maintenance of semantic coherence* the architect ensures that the responsibilities among the services in a CBP work together without excessive reliance on each other. To *anticipate expected changes* reduces the services that need to be modified in case of certain changes. *Generalized services* allow to compute a broader range of functions based on the same input. An architect can apply these three tactics to CBP architectures by using the patterns *abstraction, loose coupling*, and *orchestration*.

With this information it is, in general, possible to decide whether one architecture variant supports a scenario better than another one. Having a look at *scenario 1* (cp. Table 1), the decentral broker architecture incorporates the patterns *abstraction, loose coupling*, and *orchestration* for *CBPs*, which is the artifact of the scenario description. Thus it realizes the tactics *maintain semantic coherence, anticipate expected changes*, and *generalize module*. The architecture without broker instead, realizes none of these patterns and tactics for the artifact (CBPs) of scenario 1. Thus we can infer that the decentral broker architecture better supports scenario 1 than the architecture without broker. The remaining question is, how contingencies influence the ratings and the distance between the ratings of the evaluated architectures.

Contingencies. In our decision method we consider contingencies within the collaboration network (internal contingencies) and outside the collaboration network (external contingencies). Internal contingencies characterize the collaboration model and the organizations participating in the collaborations. These are: the *collaboration topology*, that takes into account the distribution of influence and power among the partners; the complexity and specificity of the *products* developed by the collaborating organizations; the *service flow* that is characterized by the amount of data and the number of messages exchanged; aspects related with the *process* itself like length of the process or the estimated number of process instance during execution. External contingencies are external factors that highly influence organizations' decision and strategies, and therefore impact also the choice of an ICT coordination architecture: *standardization* considers the existence of industry-specific, national, or international standards; *maturity* takes the existence of commonly accepted processes, protocols, etc., into account; *business semantics* considers the availability of standards and their maturity with regard to defining semantics of a specific domain; *legislation* comprises the regulations which impose special requirements regarding security, monitoring, and other aspects of the collaboration. [22]

If we assume for example a high degree of standardization to rate scenario 1, the decentral broker architecture is not much better than or even equal to the architecture without broker. Standardized parts of the CBP and the ESs can be reused and combined in arbitrary ways adapting to the change in business (stimulus of scenario 1). Necessary changes affect about the same number of modules (cp. response and response measure of scenario 1 in Table 1) in both coordination architectures.

Of course there exist other contingencies, which are also relevant for the decision about an ICT coordination architecture. For example, the dynamics of the collaboration (internal contingency) and the industry dynamics (external contingency) both address the aspect of change. Since change is already covered by the scenario descriptions, this aspect has to be considered by weighing scenarios and quality attributes. Change is not addressed a second time in rating the scenarios.

4.3   Measuring Quantitative Factors

In the decision method quantitative factors are evaluated in monetary terms on the basis of the discounted cash flow approach.[3] The discounted present value of the future cash flows FV_i^D, which corresponds to the objective factor measure OFC_i for a software architecture pattern i, is defined as follows:

$$OFC_i = \sum_{j=1}^{m} FV_{i_j}^{D} = \sum_{t=0}^{N-1} \frac{FV_{i_{j_t}}}{(1+d)^t} \tag{7}$$

where

$FV_{i_j}^{D}$ = discounted present value of the future cash flow (FV) for factor j

$FV_{i_{j_t}}$ = nominal value of a cash flow amount in a future period t for factor j

---

[3] The description of the quantitative factors is quite short, since we focus on the qualitative factors and contingencies in this paper.

$$d = \text{discount rate}$$
$$N = \text{number of discounting periods}$$
$$m = \text{total number of objective factors}$$

The decision model considers costs for software (*purchasing costs* and *annual licences*), hardware (*purchasing costs* and *annual leasing fees*) and labor (*costs to set up the systems, maintenance costs*, and *costs to develop and deploy new and modified processes*).

5 Applying the Evaluation Method

As described in the introduction, companies organize themselves into global networks and outsource those activities that can be performed quicker, more effectively, or at lower cost, by others [34]. However, outsourcing and interacting in global networks also increases overhead costs for collaboration, coordination, and intermediation. One approach to describe the influence of organizational structure on these overhead costs is the transaction cost model [37,38]. In today's economies, transactions for example make up more than 30% of the total costs of an automobile [36]. Transaction costs heavily depend on the capabilities of business systems to keep up with constantly evolving business relationships and cross-organizational value chains. However, in the comparison to transaction costs, IT costs are much less than transaction costs (in the Automotive example this is about 6% of the overall costs [36]).

In this section, we apply the evaluation method to two scenarios: a virtual enterprise scenario (Section 5.1) and to a scenario with collaborating SMEs (Section 5.2). In doing so, the goal is to identify the collaboration architecture which best supports the cross-organizational value chain and helps to reduce transaction costs. The trade-off between reducing transaction costs (qualitative factors) and reducing of IT cost (quantitative factors) through the choice of a collaboration architecture is discussed in a sensitivity analysis.

5.1 Virtual Enterprise Scenario

This scenario deals with virtual enterprises that collaborate in big, long-running CBPs (approx. 90 processing steps). The OEM and the big first-tier suppliers introduced in the automotive scenario in Section 1 together form a virtual enterprise, which builds a temporary network of independent companies, suppliers, customers. They are linked by information technology to share costs, skills, and access to one another's markets. The services the partners provide to the CBP are to 50% legacy applications, which will be replaced within the next five years. The services, their interfaces, and data types are not standardized, so that interoperability is an important issue. About 30% of the CBP are standardized and it may be necessary to provide variants of the CBP. The privacy of the enterprises' services is only medium important, since the enterprises make their profit through economy of scale. Hence, they also participate with their elementary services in other CBPs.

Determining the Qualitative Measure

Weighting the subjective factors. To determine the weight of the quality attributes and the scenarios pairwise comparison are applied like described in Section 4.2.

Table 2. Priority comparison matrix for the first level factors

	mod.	pri.	reuse	int.	eff.	man.	v_i
modifiability	1	7	3	$\frac{1}{3}$	3	3	0.21
privacy	$\frac{1}{7}$	1	$\frac{1}{4}$	$\frac{1}{9}$	$\frac{1}{5}$	$\frac{1}{5}$	0.03
reuse	$\frac{1}{3}$	4	1	$\frac{1}{5}$	1	1	0.10
interoperability	3	9	5	1	5	5	0.45
efficiency	$\frac{1}{3}$	5	1	$\frac{1}{5}$	1	1	0.10
managability	$\frac{1}{3}$	5	1	$\frac{1}{5}$	1	1	0.10

Table 2 depicts the weighting of the first level factors, i.e. the quality attributes, for the virtual enterprise scenario. Modifiability is considered more important than privacy and reuse but less important than interoperability. The column of the priority vector v_i depicts the weighting of the quality attributes.

Table 3. Priority comparison matrix for the second level factor modifiability

modifiability	sc.1	sc.2	sc.3	sc.6	sc.11	v_i
scenario 1	1	3	7	$\frac{1}{5}$	$\frac{1}{3}$	0.14
scenario 2	$\frac{1}{3}$	1	5	$\frac{1}{5}$	$\frac{1}{5}$	0.08
scenario 3	$\frac{1}{5}$	$\frac{1}{7}$	1	$\frac{1}{9}$	$\frac{1}{9}$	0.03
scenario 6	5	5	9	1	3	0.47
scenario 11	3	5	9	$\frac{1}{3}$	1	0.27

Table 3 depicts the weighting of the scenarios are used to describe the modifiability attribute in the virtual enterprise scenario. The scenarios are analogously compared as the other quality attributes in Table 2. The column of the priority vector v_i depicts the weighting of the scenarios.

Rating the Scenarios. The scenarios are rated by pairwise comparing the architecture alternatives. The decisions are based on how good the architectures support the scenarios via tactics and patterns). The rating, i.e. the values decision, also depend on the characteristics of the contingency factors of the application scenario for which the evaluation is performed.

Table 4 depicts the rating matrix for scenario 1. As described in Section 4.2 the central broker alternative supports scenario 1 better than the brokerless alternative. Relevant contingencies for scenario 1 are the grade of standardization and the maturity of the CPB and the services. Since both contingencies are rather low in the virtual enterprise scenario, the architectural quality is important for the support of this scenario, which leads to the comparison value 7 between the

Table 4. Rating scenario 1

scenario 1	Wo-Br.	Cen-Br.	Dec-Br.	v_i^{id}
Wo-Br.	1	$\frac{1}{7}$	$\frac{1}{7}$	0.14
Cen-Br.	7	1	1	1.00
Dec-Br.	7	1	1	1.00

central broker and without broker architecture. The central and decentral broker architecture are rated equally important with the value 1. The column of the priority vector v_i^{id} depicts the weighting of the scenarios.

Overall Subjective Measure. The overall subjective measure is computed on the basis of the factor weights and the scenario ratings. Table 5 depicts the relevant data. In row two one can find the weighting of the quality attributes from Table 2. The weighting of the scenarios that describe the quality attributes are specified in row four. The scenario ratings can be found in the columns of the respective scenarios. For example the rating, i.e. priority vector values v_i^{id}, for scenario 1 can be found in column 2 row 5-7. The overall subjective measure is calculated with the formula (3) and can be found in the last column.

Table 5. Overall subjective measure

	Modifiability					Sec.		Reuse			Int.op.		Eff.		Man.		SFM_i^{id}	SFM_i
	0.21					0.03		0.10			0.45		0.10		0.10			
	S1	S2	S3	S6	S11	S7	S8	S4	S9	S11	S5	S10	S12	S13	S14	S15		
	0.14	0.08	0.03	0.47	0.27	0.17 0.83		0.43 0.43 0.14			0.17 0.83		0.50 0.50		0.50 0.50			
Wo-Br.	0.14	0.11	0.08	0.16	0.08	0.30 0.20		0.30 0.17 0.08			0.14 0.17		1.00 0.17		0.12 0.11		0.202	0.121
Cen-Br.	1.00	0.44	0.30	0.46	0.30	0.11 0.20		0.12 0.59 0.30			1.00 0.41		0.33 1.00		1.00 1.00		0.545	0.327
Dec-Br.	1.00	1.00	1.00	1.00	1.00	1.00 1.00		1.00 1.00 1.00			1.00 1.00		1.00 0.41		0.60 0.44		0.920	0.552

Determining the Quantitative Measure

Overall Objective Measure. The objective measure is calculated on the basis of the cash flow of the costs for software, labor, hardware. For the virtual enterprise scenario with four collaborating enterprises we have estimated the following costs. It is important to understand, that the scale (euro, dollar, etc.) is not important for the overall objective measure, since the scale is transformed into an dimensionless index. In Table 6 one can see that for the architecture without broker 5075 thousand cost units were estimated (OFC_i). The overall objective measure OFM_i can be found in the last column.

Sensitivity Analysis and Interpretation. The architectural evaluation measure AEM_i for each architecture variant is determined on the basis on the objective factor measure OFM_i and the subjective factor measure SFM_i (see formula (1)). The measure depends on the weight X assigned to the objective and subjective factor. This weight lends itself also for sensitivity analysis.

Table 6. Overall subjective measure

	Software	Hardware	Labour	OFC_i	OFM_i
Wo-Br.	45K	75K	4955K	5075K	0.127
Cen-Br.	69K	95K	1200K	1364K	0.471
Dec-Br.	118K	135K	1367K	1620K	0.399

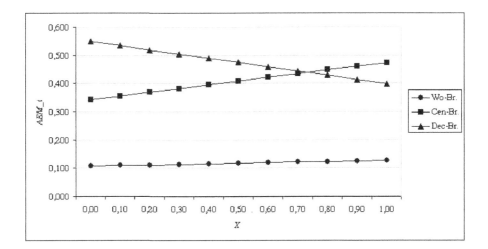

Fig. 8. Sensitivity analysis chart

Figure 8 depicts the sensitivity analysis chart for the virtual enterprise scenario. The x-axis represents the importance of the objective factors measure and the y-axis the architecture evaluation measure for the respective architecture variant.

On the basis of this evaluation result we can conclude, that either the central broker or the decentral broker architecture variant should be selected. The variant without broker gets significantly lower rating values for all X than the other ones. The decentral broker architecture scores better for the qualitative measurement (especially for $X = 0$), while the central broker architecture is better in terms of IT costs. A feasible estimation of X is to consider the relationship between the percentage of transaction costs and IT costs of the total costs. In the automotive industry IT costs (6%) are low in comparison to the transaction costs (30%) (cp. [36]). This leads to an estimation of $X \approx 0.2$ for the virtual enterprise scenario applied to the automotive industry. Thus, we would suggest to select the decentral broker architecture in the virtual enterprise scenario. Even if transaction costs and IT costs got equally important ($X = 0.5$), the architecture evaluation measure of the decentral broker variant would be still be a bit better than the central broker variant.

5.2 SME Scenario

This scenario represents the CBPs between the second-tier (or even third- and fourth-tier suppliers) of the automotive scenario from Section 1. The second-tier suppliers are SMEs that manufacture parts, which can be largely standardized and can be reused in many cars or other application domains. The SMEs produce for example screws, fuses, circuit boards, etc.. They support rather short processes with approx. 20 processing steps. The specificity of the service is low. Smaller and equal partners (SMEs) frequently join and leave the collaborations and most SMEs also participate in other similar collaborations. Participating partners have similar interfaces, data types, etc., and the services and CBPs are de-facto standardized (e.g. already formulated in ebXML). Hence, interoperability is not so an important issue to these organizations. Also changes to the existing CBPs are rare (up to three times a year). However, about 50% of the service offer by the SMEs are legacy applications, which will be partially replaced within the next five years.

Determining the Qualitative Measure. The overall subjective measure can be found in Table 7.

Table 7. Overall subjective measure

	Modifiability 0.16					Sec. 0.04		Reuse 0.25			Int.op. 0.06		Eff. 0.25		Man. 0.25		SFM_i^{id}	SFM_i
	S1	S2	S3	S6	S11	S7	S8	S4	S9	S11	S5	S10	S12	S13	S14	S15		
	0.05	0.59	0.05	0.21	0.11	0.50	0.50	0.45	0.45	0.09	0.20	0.80	0.83	0.17	0.17	0.83		
Wo-Br.	0.39	0.36	0.50	0.20	0.40	1.00	1.00	1.00	0.17	0.40	0.17	0.40	1.00	0.50	0.30	0.17	0.529	0.293
Cen-Br.	1.00	0.50	1.00	1.00	1.00	0.64	1.00	1.00	0.30	0.41	0.64	0.41	0.64	0.12	1.00	1.00	0.589	0.326
Dec-Br.	1.00	1.00	1.00	1.00	1.00	1.00	1.00	0.55	1.00	1.00	1.00	1.00	0.40	1.00	0.50	1.00	0.688	0.381

Determining the Quantitative Measure. The overall objective measure can be found in Table 8.

Table 8. Overall subjective measure

	Software	Hardware	Labour	OFC_i	OFM_i
Wo-Br.	100K	100K	100K	300K	0.453
Cen-Br.	124K	120K	195K	439K	0.310
Dec-Br.	197K	180v	198K	575K	0.237

Sensitivity Analysis and Interpretation. Figure 9 depicts the sensitivity analysis chart for the SME. One can clearly see how the contingencies standardization and short processes influence the architecture evaluation measure. Although the partners in the collaboration frequently change the architecture variant without broker scores very well. For most X, the brokerless architecture has the highest evaluation measure and even for low X its measure is hardly

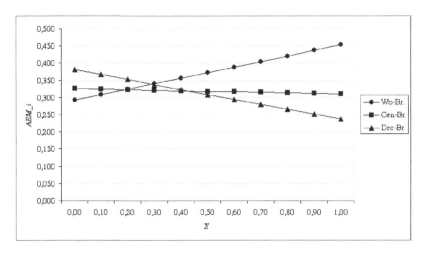

Fig. 9. Sensitivity analysis chart

lower than the measure for the broker architecture. However, if contingencies change, like new monitoring requirements from the government, the intersection point of the curves would be at a higher X (it would move to the right). This would make the broker architectures more interesting to realize the SMEs scenario.

6 Discussion and Outlook

The contribution of the work reported in this paper is fourfold: First, we identified three important architectural patterns for CBP enactment: brokerless architecture, decentral broker architecture, and central broker architecture. Second, we proposed a decision method for architecture selection based on the analytic hierarchy process (AHP, see [31]). This method targets ICT architects and promises a systematic way to evaluate and compare ICT level architecture variants for a certain application scenario, based on pairwise comparison of alternatives. Third, we showed the applicability of our method by applying it to two application scenarios with differing characteristics: A virtual enterprise scenario (comparable to the relationship between the OEM and the selected first-tier suppliers discussed in Section 1) and an SME network scenario (similar to the second-tier network part of the example in Section 1). Finally, we investigated the robustness of the decision method by performing a sensitivity analysis.

An area for future work is the examination and deeper evaluation of the decision method. One aspect concerns the choice of making pairwise comparisons between alternatives as described in Section 4. Our experience so far indicates that pairwise comparisons reduce the amount of information that is necessary for decisions. Since people can only deal with information involving simultaneously a small number of facts (seven plus or minus two) [25], pairwise comparisons help evaluators to make better judgements compared to methods where more information needs to be considered. Though pairwise comparisons require more complex calculations than other rating approaches, they promise to provide more exact results. The AHP method involves also redundant comparisons to improve validity, recognizing that participants may be uncertain or make poor judgements in some of the comparisons. Further investigation are needed to achieve a more fundamental understanding of the trade-offs involved in redundant pairwise comparisons and possible alternatives.

A second area concerns the question how decision methods as the one described in this paper can be built into existing enterprise modeling frameworks and model-driven IDEs, to support process modelers and ICT architects in their task of creating and managing executable CBP specifications from business level models. Also, more fine-grained models and extensions of our decision method need to be developed to support this process down to the platform-specific and code levels.

References

1. Bass, L., Clements, P., Kazman, R.: Software Architecture in Practice. Addison-Wesley, Reading (2003)
2. Bass, L., John, B.E.: Linking Usability to Software Architecture Patterns Through General Scenarios. Journal of Systems and Software 66, 187–197 (2003)
3. Bennett, D.W.: Designing Hard Software - The Essential Task. Prentice Hall, Englewood Cliffs (1997)
4. Bézivin, J.: On the unification power of models. Software and System Modeling 4, 171–188 (2005)
5. Birman, A., Ritsko, J.: Preface to Service-Oriented Architecture. IBM Systems Journal 44, 651–652 (2005)
6. Booch, G., Brown, A., Iyengar, S., Rumbaugh, J., Selic, B.: An MDA Manifesto. MDA Journal (2004)
7. Brown, P.A., Gibson, D.F.: A quantified model for facility site selection application to multiplant location problem. AIIE transactions: industrial engineering research and development 4, 1–10 (1972)
8. Clements, P., Kazman, R., Klein, M.: Evaluating Software Architecture. Addison-Wesley, Reading (2002)
9. Dolan, T.J.: Architecture assessment of Information-System Families. PhD thesis, Technische Universiteit Eindhoven (2001)
10. Donaldson, L.: The Contingency Theory of Organizations. SAGE Publications, Inc., Thousand Oaks (2001)
11. Erl, T.: Service-Oriented Architecture: Concepts, Technology, and Design. Prentice Hall International, Englewood Cliffs (2005)
12. Erl, T.: Service-Oriented Architecture: A Field Guide to Integrating XML and Web Services. Prentice Hall International, Englewood Cliffs (2004)
13. Gamma, E., Helm, R., Johnson, R.E.: Design Patterns. In: Elements of Reusable Object-Oriented Software, Addison-Wesley Longman, Amsterdam (1995)
14. Garcia-Camino, A., Noriega, P., Rodriguez-Aguilar, J.: Implementing Norms in Electronic Institutions. In: Fourth International Joint Conference on Autonomous Agents and Multiagent Systems (AAMAS 2005), pp. 667–673. ACM Press, New York (2005)
15. Ghandforoush, P., Huang, P.Y., Taylor, B.W.: A mulit-criteria decision model for the selection of a computerized manufacturing control system. International Journal of Production Research 23, 117–128 (1985)

16. Greenfield, J., Short, K., Cook, S., Kent, S.: Software Factories: Assembling Applications with Patterns, Models, Frameworks, and Tools. Wiley Publishing Inc., Chichester (2004)
17. Hailpern, B., Tarr, P.: Model-driven development: The good, the bad, and the ugly. IBM Systems Journal 45, 451–461 (2006)
18. Jennings, N.R., Sycara, K., Wooldridge, M.: A Roadmap of Agent Research and Development. Journal of Autonomous Agents and Multi-Agent Systems 1, 7–38 (1998)
19. Jennings, N.R., Faratin, P., Norman, T.J., O'Brien, P., Odgers, B.: Autonomous Agents for Business Process Management. Int. Journal of Applied Artificial Intelligence 14, 145–189 (2000)
20. Jennings, N.R., Faratin, P., Norman, T.J., O'Brien, P., Odgers, B., Alty, J.L.: Implementing a Business Process Management System using ADEPT: A Real-World Case Study. Int. Journal of Applied Artificial Intelligence 14, 421–465 (2000)
21. Larsen, G.: Model-driven development: Assets and reuse. IBM Systems Journal 45, 541–553 (2006)
22. Legner, C., Wende, K.: Towards an Excellence Framework for Business Interoperability. In: 19th Bled eConference "eValues", Slovenia (2006)
23. Leymann, F., Roller, D., Schmidt, M.T.: Web services and business process management. IBM Systems Journal 41, 198–211 (2002)
24. Malone, T.W.: Modeling Coordination in Organizations and Markets. Management Science 33, 1317–1332 (1987)
25. Miller, G.A.: The Magical Number Seven, Plus or Minus Two: Some Limits on our Capacity for Processing Information. The Psychological Review 63, 81–97 (1956)
26. OASIS: Web Services Business Process Execution Language Version 2.0. wsbpel-primer (2007)
27. OMG: Business Process Definition MetaModel (BPDM), final submission. bmi/2006-11-03 (2006)
28. Roser, S.: Designing and Enacting Cross-organisational Business Processes: A Model-driven, Ontology-based Approach. PhD thesis, University of Augsburg, (2008)(forthcoming)
29. Saaty, T.L.: Decision Making for Leaders. 3rd edn., RWS Publications (1999)
30. Saaty, T.L.: How to make a decision: The Analytic Hierarchy Process. Interfaces 24, 19–43 (1994)
31. Saaty, T.L.: The Analytic Hierarchy Process. McGraw-Hill, New York (1980)
32. Schmidt, D.C.: Guest Editor's Introduction: Model-Driven Engineering. Computer 39, 25–31 (2006)
33. Singh, M., Huhns, M.: Service Oriented Computing: Semantics, Processes, Agents. John Wiley & Sons, Chichester, West Sussex, UK (2005)
34. Snow, C.C., Miles, R.E., Coleman, H.J.: Managing 21st Century Network Organizations. Organizational Dynamics 20, 5–20 (1992)
35. Stäber, F., Sobrito, G., Müller, J., Bartlang, U., Friese, T.: Interoperability challenges and solutions in Automotive Collaborative Product Development. In: Gonçalves, R., Müller, J., Mertins, K., Zelm, M. (eds.) Enterprise Interoperability II: New Challenges and Approaches, pp. 709–720. Springer, Heidelberg (2007)
36. Strassmann, P.A.: Is Outsourcing Profitable? In: Lecture at George Mason University (2006)
37. Williamson, O.E.: Markets and Hierarchies: Analysis and Antitrust Implications. Free Press, New York (1975)
38. Williamson, O.E.: Transaction Cost Economics. In: Handbook of Industrial Organization, vol. 1, pp. 135–182 (1989)

The Goal Oriented Teams (GORITE) Framework

Ralph Rönnquist

Intendico Pty Ltd
Melbourne, Australia

Abstract. Goal Oriented Teams (GORITE) is a Java framework for implementation of Goal Oriented Process Models in a Team Oriented Paradigm. The GORITE concept combines a Team Oriented view of software systems with Goal Oriented process modelling, and offers an effective approach to complex and large-scale software. A Java developer would use GORITE for implementing their Team Oriented design, and whilst the framework makes this a straight-forward task, it relies on the Java developer utilising background skills in Team and Goal Oriented Programming to form the design. The Goal Oriented Programming side of GORITE provides a BDI (Belief - Desire - Intention) style execution machinery for goal oriented process models. Technically the goal hierarchies, which define how goals are achieved by means of achieving sub goals, are data structures that are interpreted in order to carry out the process steps that achieving the goals require. The Team Oriented Programming paradigm takes systems design to a new level. As design concept it extends the Agent Oriented Programming paradigm by including explicit modelling of the organisation of agents that comprise an application, whilst allowing for openness in actual composition. This paper is a presentation of the GORITE framework, with a primary focus on illustrating how the GORITE elements are used for capturing Goal Oriented Teams designs, and with less focus on the methodological philosophy underpinning this style of programming.

1   Introduction

This is a "white paper" on the Goal Oriented Teams (GORITE) framework. We present the framework in fair detail, and we describe how a developer must think in order to make best use of the framework. The start-point and general argument for considering to use GORITE is that it reduces the difficulty in programming a complex system, which it does by perpetuating the Team Programming analogy, that the software mimics the work of a human organisation.

The GORITE emphasis is that of developing a software system with complex behaviour by using the analogy to human organisation as a design technique, and thus form a software architecture that in concept is based on autonomous organisational units. But in the software, as opposed to a human organisation, the autonomous reasoning is represented and carried out at all levels. Through this, the system behaviour is designed at all levels, and although the behaviour

M. Dastani et al.(Eds.): ProMAS 2007, LNAI 4908, pp. 27–41, 2008.
© Springer-Verlag Berlin Heidelberg 2008

may be too complex to predict, it is engineered behaviour with a high degree of repeatability, which brings significant gains in terms of performance, simplicity and maintainability of the software.

In [3], Horling et al makes the point that "real-time control has become increasingly important as technologies are moved from the lab into real world situations. The complexity associated with these systems increases as control and autonomy are distributed, due to such issues as precedence constraints, shared resources, and the lack of a complete and consistent world view." For instance, as discussed by Landre et al in [5], the complexity of the problems call for solutions that can provide delegated autonomy at the architectural level, which is the essence in Team Programming.

As noted by Kaminka et al in [2], one can separate team work from task work, and provide domain independent support for team work at an architectural level, using team work models. This may be pursued at an agent level, resulting in reasoning components aimed at making agents participate effectively in teams. In this context however, GORITE is similar to the JACK framework [4], in representing teams as concrete entities that are attributed with reasoned behaviour. It means to apply an organisation-oriented engineering perspective, similar to [6], and use team work models to model autonomous organisational units.

A Java developer would use GORITE for implementing their Team Oriented design, and whilst the framework makes this a straight-forward task, it relies on utilising background skills in Team and Goal Oriented Programming. In this paper we discuss the central concepts of this paradigm in terms of their realisations as GORITE elements.

- The Goal Oriented Programming side of GORITE provides a BDI [1] (Belief - Desire - Intention) execution machinery for goal oriented process models. Technically the programming is done by creating goal hierarchies, which define how goals are achieved by means of achieving sub goals, and these are data structures that are interpreted in order to carry out the process steps that achieving the goals require.
- The Team Oriented Programming side of GORITE is based on the notion that a software system is conceived as an organisation of cooperating agents, or recursively, as a team of sub teams, which operate together so as to provide the system function. There is a loose analogy with human organisations in this, such that the overall functions are understood as the fruits of (business) processes that coordinate the efforts of the individuals. In the Team Oriented design, the behaviour of organisational units are defined separately from the behaviour of their sub units. Unit behaviour is expressed as an orchestration of the services that sub units provide.

The overall design stance is an organisation oriented engineering perspective: At first we regard the system as a whole as a performer although comprised of sub units, and we design a top layer of system processes that coordinate efforts of the organisational sub units. Thereafter we focus on each sub unit in turn, regard it a performer although comprised of sub units, and design its processes that coordinate efforts of its sub units, and so forth.

The GORITE framework simply maps this perspective onto Goal Oriented Team Programming: A team is an organisational unit, which operates autonomously according to its defined business processes in order to fill its function as sub unit of a larger team. In other words, a team is a performer for the larger team (or teams) it belongs to, while its own behaviour typically is defined as a coordination of the performer it consists of. The team concept is recursive in this way; that a team consists of sub teams. From the "above", the team is seen as a performer in itself, and from "below" it has members that are performers.

The layout of this paper is as follows: In section 2, we introduce the GORITE elements by means of an expanded example. In section 3, we look at the execution machinery in more detail, and follow the single-thread execution through multiple, concurrent chains of reasoning. Section 4 contains some concluding remarks.

2   GORITE Example

This example has been called the "Hello World" application for Team Programming. It is a toy application to simulate a spacecraft with Martians flying to Earth to greet the Earthlings. A Martian spacecraft is flown in a particular way, which requires a *pilot* to fly the spacecraft and a *crew* to look out for the destination. When "at the destination" is reported by the crew, the pilot stops flying, and a Martian who is selected for the *greeter* role, greets the Earthlings.

The point is that the advantage with Team Programming only shows up if there is some complexity to the problem, and in particular, it requires some small amount of *organisational structure* in order for the team concept to make good sense. Although the example is quite artificial, we can find a number of similar more serious applications. For example, without straining things too much, this kind of application could be a mobile data collector for a sensor network. Such a unit would include similar kinds of separate functions, to deal with mobility, sensing and mission objective in an effective orchestration. Of course in that case the modelling might not stop at the data collection units, but extend across the sensor network, with, perhaps, sensors organised according to geography, function, data etc., and more complex organisation dynamics.

For the "Hello World" example, we draw up the central process model in GORITE for a "visit a planet" goal through a code snippet like the one below. A reader not quite familiar with Java might still make some sense from the code by knowing that the phrase form "new Goal [] { A, B, ... }" simply means an aggregate (an array) of goals A, B, etc. The code snippet, which is actual GORITE code, shows a Java statement using GORITE elements to represent the process model of how to achieve the specified "visit a planet" goal. It is a Goal Oriented process model expressed as a goal hierarchy where a goal is achieved by means of achieving sub goals.

```
addGoal( new Goal( "visit a planet", Sequence, new Goal [] {
    new Goal( "fly to destination", Parallel, new Goal [] {
        new Goal( "pilot", "fly spacecraft" ),
        new Goal( "arrived", Control, new Goal [] {
            new Goal( "crew", "look out" )
        } )
    } ),
    new Goal( "greeter", "greet" )
} ) );
```

The goal hierarchy is formed by using <u>Goal</u> objects, where the top and inner hierarchy nodes represent composite goals that are achieved by means of achieving their sub goals in certain ways. In the snippet above, the top level goal "visit a planet", has two sub goals, "fly to destination" and for the "greeter" to "greet", to be achieved in sequence. The first of them, "fly to destination", has two parallel sub goals: for the "pilot" to "fly spacecraft", and the "arrived" goal of ending "fly to destination" with success when the "look out" goal performed by "crew" succeeds. (The Control type goal has process model semantics beyond success and failure, namely, to force an enclosing parallel goal execution to succeed. See section 3 for details)

The leaf level nodes in a goal hierarchy are task goals with respect to the modelled process. This simply means that they are defined elsewhere and not within the process model at hand. The leaf goals in the code snippet refer to organisational roles, and they declare that the fillers of the indicated roles should achieve the indicated goals; when the process model is executed and the role filler goals arise, the role fillers are free to chose their methods to achieve their goals, which they do by referring to their own capabilities.

In words, the "visit a planet" process model is set out as follows:

1. First the <u>Performer</u> that fills the "pilot" role is asked to achieve a "fly spacecraft" goal, and in parallel, the <u>Performer</u> that fills the "crew" role is asked to fill the "look out" goal.
2. Eventually, when the "crew" "look out" goal succeeds, the "pilot" "fly spacecraft" goal is interrupted, and the "fly to destination" succeeds.
3. Then the <u>Performer</u> that fills the "greeter" role is asked to achieve the "greet" goal.
4. When all is achieved in that way, then the "visit a planet" goal has been achieved.

The word <u>Performer</u> is highlighted because it names the GORITE class that is used for representing the entities that fill roles and have capabilities to achieve goals. There is a <u>Team</u> class and a <u>Performer</u> class, both of which are used to, in an object oriented way, define the organisational potential, i.e. the *types* of entities that the desired organisation involves. The particular organisation is formed by instantiating the appropriate organisational units, and link them into the organisational structure. Conceptually, a <u>Team</u> is an organisational unit that may *have* sub units, and it is also a <u>Performer</u>, which is an organisational unit that may *be* a sub unit.

2.1   A SpaceCraft Team

Organisational modelling in GORITE has five aspects: two aspects that concern the organisational potential or which types of entities an application make use of, and three aspects that concern the actual formation and deployment of performers for performing goals. This section and the next illustrate these aspects for the example application.

For our example, we are looking a defining a SpaceCraft Team type with a "flight staff" TaskTeam to deploy for the "visit a planet" goal. The code snippet below outlines the SpaceCraft Team type definition. It defines SpaceCraft as a type of Team, which when created, is set up with a "flight staff" TaskTeam that consists of "pilot", "crew" and "greeter" roles, and a process model for achieving a "visit a planet" goal.

```
public class SpaceCraft extends Team {
    public SpaceCraft(String name) {
        super( name );
        setTaskTeam( "flight staff", new TaskTeam() {{
            new Role( "greeter", new String [] { "greet" } ),
            new Role( "pilot", new String [] { "fly spacecraft" } ),
            new Role( "crew", new String [] { "look out" } )
        }} );
        addGoal( new Goal( "visit a planet", Sequence, new Goal [] {
            deploy( "flight staff" ),
            new Goal( "fly to destination", Parallel, new Goal [] {
                new Goal( "pilot", "fly spacecraft" ),
                new Goal( "arrived", Control, new Goal [] {
                    new Goal( "crew", "look out" )
                } )
            } ),
            new Goal( "greeter", "greet" )
        } ) );
    }
}
```

We note that the "visit a planet" goal hierarchy includes the initial step to deploy the "flight staff" task team for performing the goal. This additional step establishes which particular performers of the team to use for the particular execution; it dynamically defines the local meaning of the role references "pilot", "crew" and "greeter" in the goal execution.

The types of entities to define include the Team and Performer extensions that represent the organisational unit types. Further it includes defining which *groups of roles* a team has, to deploy for performing its goals. This is called *task team*, and is represented by a TaskTeam class, which is instantiated and filled with Role objects in order to represent a role group in a Team. Depending on the complexity of a Team, there will be one or more TaskTeam definitions, and these may be declared up front or be formed dynamically to deploy for particular goals.

As shown in the code snippet, the "flight staff" TaskTeam includes three roles, and each role is defined to require a filler of a particular ability in terms of goals. Thus, to fill the "pilot" role, a performer must be able to achieve the "fly spacecraft" goal, the "crew" role requires the "look out" goal and the "greeter" must be able to "greet". This is an interface declaration that links the "visit a planet" orchestration with the particular abilities it exercises of its performers.

We note that the code snippet is a complete definition of the SpaceCraft Team type. The example application needs to create one instance of this type for representing one particular spacecraft, and it needs to ask that spacecraft to achieve a "visit a plant" goal.

2.2   Defining the Martians

The SpaceCraft Team is attributed with an orchestration plan to achieve the "visit a plant" goal by means of coordinating the Martians in the roles of "pilot", "crew" and "greeter". To this end, the Martians need to be able to perform the functions their roles require.

GORITE includes a Capability class that is used for composing abilities into functional units. For this example, we invent the capabilities SpaceCraftFlying, SpaceGazing and Greeting to cater for the required abilities of the three roles. The following code snippet presents a simple Greeting capability definition, where the "greet" goal is defined as a *task goal* that is achieved by means of making a line of console output.

The code snippet is also an illustration of the transition from GORITE goal processing to application Java code, which is done by means of re-implementing the "execute" method of the Goal class. We discuss goal processing in more detail later in section 3.

```java
public class Greeting extends Capability {
    public Greeting() {
        addGoal( new Goal( "greet" ) {
            public States execute(Data d) {
                System.out.println( "Hello " + d.getValue( "destination" ) );
                return PASSED;
            }
        } ) );
    }
}
```

The Greeting Capability above is quite simple. In general a capability may include any number of goal hierarchies of any complexity as well as sub capabilities of any complexity, and further, as a Java class, it may include any methods and members that might be needed in order to implement the desired function or functions. Generally speaking, this is where the functional design gets mapped into implementation concepts, which at the end of the day is a collection of capability type definitions. (Capabilities may also be built dynamically, in which case they exist as particular un-named competences rather than types)

Continuing the example, the reader may imagine the three capabilities Space-CraftFlying, SpaceGazing and Greeting being properly defined. If we then would be short of time, we could use them to create an application in the following way.

```
public class Main {
    public static void main(String [] args) {
        Team t = new SpaceCraft( "explorer" );
        t.addPerformers( new Performer [] {
            new Performer( "ralph" ) {{
                addCapability( new SpaceCraftFlying() ); }},
            new Performer( "dennis" ) {{
                addCapability( new SpaceGazing() ); }},
            new Performer( "jacquie" ) {{
                addCapability( new Greeting() ); }}
        } );
        ...
    }
}
```

By that code snippet, which is an application "main" method, three individual performers with individual capabilities are created, and these are added to the "explorer" SpaceCraft. (The ellipsis indicates that there is some code omitted, which includes asking the team to perform the "visit a planet" goal). The three performers are set up as members of the SpaceCraft Team, and these are the ones considered for populating the "flight staff" TaskTeam, where they will be selected to fill roles on the basis of their abilities.

An alternative, more well-designed approach is to define a Martian Performer type, as illustrated by the following code snippet.

```
public class Martian extends Performer {
    public Martian(String name) {
        super( name );
        addCapability( new SpaceCraftFlying() );
        addCapability( new SpaceGazing() );
        addCapability( new Greeting() );
    }
}
```

In that definition, a Martian type is introduced as a well-trained Performer that can take on any of the three "flight staff" roles. The corresponding application "main" method would create and add Martian instances to the "explorer" SpaceCraft Team. This is illustrated in the following code snippet.

```
public class Main {
    public static void main(String [] args) {
        Team t = new SpaceCraft( "explorer" );
        t.addPerformers( new Performer [] {
            new Martian( "ralph" ),
            new Martian( "dennis" ),
            new Martian( "jacquie" )
        } );
        ...
    }
}
```

We note that in the second modelling alternative, the "flight staff" TaskTeam can be populated in many different ways; any Martian can perform any of the roles. Though, by the default population method, the roles will be filled distinctly by different performers.

2.3   Organisational Modelling Notes

As noted above, the GORITE Organisational Modelling involves five aspects, which are:

- to define types of *organisational units*, which is done by defining Java classes that extend Team or Performer;
- to define groups of roles, or *task teams*, within teams, which is done by using the TaskTeam and Role classes;
- to build the *organisational structure*, which is done by adding performers to teams;
- to *populate task teams*, which as in the example, may be done by utilising the default task team population function, or it may be done be explicitly declaring performers to fill roles; and finally,
- to *establish the role fillers* in goals being performed, which as in the example, may be done be means of the "deploy" utility method.

Only the first aspect is strictly a compile-time definition in GORITE, while the other four are made in run-time structures, and the last aspect in particular, which is to deploy a particular task team to achieve a particular goal, typically occurs as part of that goal processing. The diagram below presents a concept map for GORITE with respect to organisational modelling:

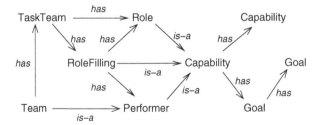

The RoleFilling class is generally not used explicitly, but indirectly as part of populating a TaskTeam, where it represents an individual role filling. We note that role filling includes the notion of *multi-filled role*, where there are multiple fillers to a role. In that case, the fillers are treated as one in the eyes of the team, and goals directed to the role are achieved by all fillers in parallel. This is discussed further in section 3.1.

The right-hand side of the concept map above shows how the organisational modelling ties in with the process modelling by virtue of the organisational units being capabilities, i.e. having methods for achieving goals. In that way each unit contains the process models by which it operates.

This manner of software design applies an analogy to a human organisation, using the concept of *team* to represent an organisational unit that on the one hand is regarded as a *performer* in processes spanning multiple units, and on the other hand achieves its goals through its internal coordination of its sub units.

3   GORITE Goal Processing

Teams, performers and roles are attributed with *plans* of how to achieve goals. These are expressed as goal hierarchies that define how goals are composed of sub goals, and a typical design combines goal hierarchies into capabilities as a way of structuring the software. In GORITE, a team is a performer, and there is a common execution machinery for goal processing regardless of whether goals are team goals or performer goals. A role is a capability that augments a team with *protocol plans* that are focused on a particular role filling.

The process modelling of GORITE is Goal Oriented, which means that processing is casted in terms of achieving goals. Thus, the process models for a team are like statements or paragraphs that explain how the team achieves its goals by means of achieving sub goals and performing tasks. At some points in the goal hierarchy, sub goals are deferred to team members, which deploy their own processes to achieve these goals. The team level process is primarily concerned with the coordination of member activity rather than how the detailed tasks are performed.

In practice, a goal hierarchy is created by instantiating Goal objects, and then for each goal tell its *name*, its *type*, and its *sub-goals*. The goal name is that which identifies the goal. The names of the inner nodes of a goal hierarchy are not semantically significant, whereas the top level name identifies which goal a hierarchy achieves, and the leaf goal names of BDI type goals identify which goals to look up methods for. The goal type declares how a goal is processed, and ties a particular execution semantics to the goal. Inner nodes of a goal hierarchy have types Sequence, Parallel, Condition, Loop, Repeat, End, Control or Fail, and leaf nodes have types Task or BDI. By combining the different types of goals, one can express any kind of procedural semantics in a goal hierarchy, which thus constitutes a plan for reasoned behaviour.

The detailed execution semantics for the various types of goals are as follows.

Sequence. A Sequence goal is achieved by achieving its sub goals one by one in sequence, and it fails immediately when a sub goal fails.

Condition. A Condition goal is achieved by attempting to achieve its sub goals one by one in sequence and succeed immediately when a sub goal succeeds. The Condition goal fails if all its sub goals fail.

Fail. A Fail goal is achieved by attempting to achieve its sub goals one by one in sequence, and succeed immediately when a sub goal fails. The Fail goal fails if all its sub goals succeed.

Loop. A Loop goal is achieved by repeating its sub goals as a Sequence goal again and again until somewhere in a sub goal hierarchy an End goal breaks the loop. The Loop goal fails immediately if a sub goal fails, and it succeeds when an inner End goal breaks the loop.

End. An End goal has a loop control semantics in addition to normal success and failure. If all its sub goals succeed when attempted one by one in sequence, like a Sequence goal, then the End goal breaks an enclosing Loop goal. Otherwise, when a sub goal fails, then the End goal succeeds without breaking the loop. An End goal never fails.

Parallel. A Parallel goal is achieved by achieving its sub goals in parallel, and it fails immediately when a sub goal fails. Further, if a sub goal fails, all other sub goals are cancelled.

Repeat. A Repeat goal is achieved in the same way as a Sequence goal, but by instantiating it over a multi-valued data element, so that each instantiation gets a separate data context focusing on one of the values for that data element. The instantiations are processed as parallel branches, and the Repeat goal succeeds when all branches have succeeded. If a branch fails, then the Repeat goal fails, and all other branches are cancelled.

Control. A Control goal has a control semantics similar to End goal, but for parallel goal executions. Its sub goals are performed in sequence, and if all succeed, then the Control goal causes the enclosing parallel execution to cancel all branches and succeed. The parallel executions include the Parallel goal, the Repeat goal and the implicit parallel branches of a multi-filled role.

Task. A Task goal is achieved by referring to its "execute" method, which contains Java code, and returns an execution state, which is one of PASSED, FAILED, STOPPED or BLOCKED.

BDI. A BDI goal is processed in a more complex way that implements the BDI plan selection and re-posting on failure. Generally a BDI goal is achieved by selecting a goal hierarchy for the nominated goal and achieve that, and it fails if all alternatives fail.

The goal hierarchies that represent process models for achieving a BDI goal are also called *plans*, and a BDI goal is achieved by means of trying all the alternative plans one by one until one succeeds. The GORITE Plan class extends the Goal class to allow a *context predicate* that identifies instantiation variants of a plan relating to the situation at hand, and a *precedence value* that guides the selection of which alternative to try next. The instantiation variants arise by the context predicate being true for different combinations of bindings for the variables involved, and each such combination of bindings defines an applicable variant of the plan. The precedence value is then used to partially order alternatives, and allow programmed control of the order to try the alternatives in. This is discussed further in section 3.3.

3.1 Coordination Goals

Team plans involve *coordination goals*, which are BDI goals that refer to roles. An ordinary BDI goal, i.e., without a role, is a goal for the current performer, whereas a coordination goal, i.e., a BDI goal that nominates a role, is a goal for the fillers of that role. The "visit a planet" example in section 2 is a team plan with such coordination goals.

The GORITE role filling concept includes a protocol layer where plans are attributed to roles. Such plans are used to handle coordination goals, and are performed by the team with a focus on a particular role filling. These plans typically define meta-level team activity related to a role filler activity such as monitoring the performer progress relative to other performers, and perhaps make amendment notes to the performer.

The following is a code example where the "crew" role filling is changed so that the performer goal merely means to look out for the next planet, while the decision step to determine whether that planet is the destination, is attributed to the Role object:

```
new Role( "crew", new String [] { "look for next planet" } ) {{
    addGoal( new Goal( "look out", Loop, new Goal [] {
        new Goal( "crew", "look for next planet" ),
        new Goal( "end if destination", End, new Goal [] {
            new Goal( "is destination?" ) {
                public States execute(Data d) {
                    if ( d.getValue( "planet" ).equals( d.getValue( "destination") ) )
                        return PASSED;
                    return FAILED;
                }
            }
        } )
    } ) );
}}
```

By the revised code, the "crew" filler is unaware about the longer term role objective of finding a particular planet, and it merely keeps achieving the simpler goal to be on look-out for the next planet. The simpler goal involves naming the planet in the data element "planet", before succeeding. However the team keeps asking the "crew" to "look for next planet" until the destination is reached.

The snippet above illustrates a plan attributed to a role as way of augmenting a performer ability into a compound activity, and lift out the decision making step to be a team level reasoning step; it's not for the "crew" to decide that the destination is reached.

A semantically more complex variation would be to make the decision step a responsibility of the "greeter" role, in which case the "crew" plan would refer to the "greeter" role to achieve the "is destination?" goal. The notion might be extended further into a design where we embed all the "visit a planet" coordination within role plans. For instance, we might say that "visit a planet" is something a "greeter" does, within the context of the task team. It then will ask the "pilot" role to "fly to destination", and this, as before, requires a "crew" to "look out". We might end up with the following definition of the "flight staff" TaskTeam:

```
setTaskTeam( "flight staff", new TaskTeam() {{
    addRole( new Role("greeter", new String [] {"greet", "is destination?"} ) {{
        addGoal( new Goal( "visit a planet", Sequence, new Goal [] {
            new Goal( "pilot", "fly to destination" ),
            new Goal( "greeter", "greet" )
        } ) );
    }} );
    addRole( new Role( "pilot", new String [] { "fly spacecraft" } ) {{
        addGoal( new Goal( "fly to destination", Parallel, new Goal [] {
            new Goal( "pilot", "fly spacecraft" ),
            new Goal( "arrive", Control, new Goal [] {
                new Goal( "crew", "look out" )
            } )
        } ) );
    }} );
    addRole( new Role( "crew", new String [] { "look for next planet" } ) {{
        addGoal( new Goal( "look out", Control, new Goal [] {
            new Goal( "look for destination", Loop, new Goal [] {
                new Goal( "crew", "look for next planet" ),
                new Goal( "end if destination", End, new Goal [] {
                    new Goal( "greeter", "is destination?" )
                } )
            } )
        } ) );
    }} );
}} );
```

For the sake of example, we have made an additional Control goal wrapping in the "crew" "look out" goal. This is done in order to cater for multiple "crew" fillers, where any one of them will make the "look out" goal to succeed. If there are multiple "crew", then the "look out" goal is instantiated for each "crew" filler in parallel, and unless there is a Control goal that force this parallel execution to succeed, it will be waiting for all the fillers to succeed before "look out" succeeds.

With that task team, the team's "visit a planet" goal would simply be to defer the goal to the "greeter" role.

The alternative design solutions provide very similar dynamic behaviour, except in light of multi-filled roles. If, for instance, there would be multiple fillers of the "greeter" role, then the second alternative would have a possibly unwanted effect of directing the "pilot" role to "fly to destination" many times in parallel.

3.2   Dynamic Data Context

Goals are performed with respect to both a *lexical belief context* and a *dynamic data context*, where the latter is a data structure created specifically for the individual goal execution. The dynamic data context is provided to support a business process modelling perspective, where in particular the task goals are seen to use and produce dynamic data. The lexical belief context supports the agent perspective of goal processing, allowing goals to use and update beliefs of more long-term persistence.

The dynamic data context is a collection of named data elements, where a data element carries a single value or multiple values. The data context is shared along an intention, but is split up to provide local data contexts for parallel intentions. When parallel intentions join, their local data contexts are joined into the parent context.

For example, consider the following goal hierarchy, which implements a contract net auction:

```
// In: RFQ, bidder*, Out: winner
addGoal( new Goal( "hold auction", Sequence, new Goal [] {
    // In: RFQ, bidder*, Out: bid*
    new Goal( "bidder", "request bid" ),
    // In: bid*, Out: winner
    new Goal( "select winner", BDI ),
    // In: bidder*, winner, Out:
    new Goal( "bidder", "tell winner" )
} ) );
```

The code snippet includes comments with details about the data used and produced by goals. These note that the incoming data context for the "hold action" goal has an "RFQ" data element with a value describing what is auctioned, and role "bidder" established with multiple fillers. The asterisk, "*", is used to indicate a multi-valued data item.

With multiple fillers for the "bidder" role, the first goal, "request bid", causes parallel intentions for each "bidder" to perform the "request bid" goal, each in their own way. A "bidder" eventually makes a response by means of defining a "bid" data element in the dynamic context. When all "bidder" intentions have completed, the parallel "bid" values are aggregated into a multi-valued "bid" data element, which is available to the next goal, "select winner". The "select winner" goal is a BDI goal for the team itself, and its outcome is a setting of the "winner" data element. This is followed by the third goal, "tell winner", which is directed to the "bidder" role and again gets repeated for each "bidder" role filler in parallel.

The dynamic data context prior to an intention split is shared between the parallel intentions, and the updates made on any one of the parallel branches only affects its own local data context. However, parallel intentions can interact by referring to, and update, values of the shared part.

3.3   Belief Structures and Context Predicates

Plans in GORITE have context predicates by which plan applicability is determined. In code, a context predicate is a data structure that represents the logical predicate as a relational query that provides a succession of bindings to the logical variables involved. This part of the framework includes a Ref class to represent logical variables, and a Query interface representing the abstract predicate. The Query interface is implemented by classes that represent expression forms, in particular the conjunctive and disjunctive forms, And and Or, and variable distinction, Distinct. Further, there is a Relation class that can be used for representing primitive terms, where a relation may include consistency rules in the form of "key constraints".

Conceptually a context predicate defines the required situation or situations in which a plan is applicable. Each way in which the predicate is true in terms of the bindings to the logical variables, defines a dynamic context variant for plan execution. The following code outline is an illustration:

```
Relation lamps = new Relation( "lamps", String.class, Boolean.class ).
    addConstraint( true, false );
...
addGoal( new Plan( "more light", Sequence, new Goal [] {
    // The Data for the sub goals will include a "lamp" data element
    new Goal( ..........
} ) {
    public Query context(Data d) {
        Ref<String> $lamp = new Ref<String>( "lamp" );
        return lamps.get( $lamp, false ); // Some lamp being off
    }
}
```

The first two code lines in the outline above defines a relation called "lamps", which would be a belief structure that holds the performer's beliefs about lamps being on or off. The relation is set up with a key constraint where the first column is a key field and the second a value field; i.e., the relation is designed to hold a single on/off state value for any lamp. Key constraints are applied when tuples are added to the relation, such that when the added tuple is in conflict with an old tuple by any key constraint, then the old tuple is removed.

The "more light" plan is supposed to achieve its goal by turning on a lamp that is off. To this end it includes a context predicate to recognise lamps being off, and consequently the plan has an instantiation variant for each such lamp. If all lamps are on already, then the plan is not applicable at all, and otherwise there is a variant for each lamp being off. The variants are all the same in terms of goal instantiation, but their executions differ in their dynamic context, where each variant has its own value for the "lamp" data element.

The diagram below is an expanded GORITE concept map, including the Plan concept of the process modelling perspective. As noted above, a GORITE Plan is a Goal augmented with a context predicate, which defines the plan's applicability with respect to the performer's situated beliefs. Technically a belief structure is a data structure of some kind; perhaps a <u>Relation</u> or perhaps some other Java structure. The context predicate is a <u>Query</u> that defines a predicate abstraction for accessing individual beliefs regardless of the underlying representation.

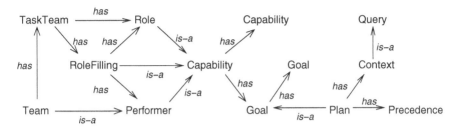

4 Conclusion

In this paper, we have presented the Goal Oriented Teams (GORITE) framework through an expanded example, and we have discussed its BDI style goal execution machinery in some detail. The framework is aimed at the Java programmer by providing a small set of programming elements, classes and interfaces, for implementing Goal Oriented Teams designs in Java, and it does not include and special design or development tool. The purpose behind that is to offer the Team Programming view and concepts dressed up in a standard Java solution, and thereby make the benefits of the paradigm accessible to a wider audience.

References

1. Rao, A., Georgeff, M.: Decision Procedures for BDI Logics. Journal of Logic and Computation 8(3), 293–342 (1998)
2. Kaminka, G., Yakir, A., Erusalichik, D., Cohen-Niv, N.: Towards Collaborative Task and Team Maintenance. In: AAMAS 2007 (2007)
3. Horling, B., Lesser, V., Vincent, R., Wagner, T.: The Soft Real-Time Agent Control Architecture. In: Autonomous Agents and Multi-Agent Systems, vol. 12(1), pp. 35–92. Springer, Heidelberg (2006)
4. JACK Intelligent Agents, http://www.agent-software.com
5. Landre, E., Olmheim, J., Waersland, G., Ronneberg, H.: Software Agents - An Emergent Software Technology That Enables Us To Build More Dynamic, Adaptable, and Robust Systems. In: ACTE 2006 (2006)
6. Kollingbaum, M., Norman, T., Mehandjiev, N., Brown, K.: Engineering Organisation-Oriented Software. In: WISER 2006, Proceedings of the 2nd International Workshop on Interdisciplinary Software Engineering Research, ICSE, Shanghai, China (May 2006)

Agents Do It for Money - Accounting Features in Agents

Jan Keiser, Benjamin Hirsch, and Sahin Albayrak

DAI-Labor, Technische Universität Berlin, Germany
{Jan.Keiser,Benjamin.Hirsch,Sahin.Albayrak}@dai-labor.de

Abstract. This paper presents a novel way of incorporating accounting features into agents. Network management techniques and methods are investigated and adopted to the agent case. We then use an example to show how sophisticated accounting technologies can be used. The example has been implemented using the JIAC platform.

1 Introduction

In [1], Jennings et al. famously coined the phrase *Objects do it for free, agents do it for money*. While the authors aimed to highlight that agents are autonomous and therefore can choose to refuse the provision of services, it can nowadays also be taken quite literally. In fact, according to the AgentLink Roadmap [2], agent based technology will become a mainstream technology in the next 10 – 15 years. This also includes the commercial use of agents. Currently, agents are used in commercial settings, but mainly within a closed system, where all the participating agents belong to the same owner. This however will almost necessarily change, as agents become more mainstream, and more and more pervasive network access does not pose roadblocks to using services over the internet. However, the commercial use of agents within an open architecture can be difficult because of the distributed nature of agents, as the provided service, the amount of work being done, as well as the necessary interaction is difficult to turn into an appropriate cost.

The aim of this work is to enable agents to function within commercial and open settings while still staying in the agent concepts. In our view, this requires agent systems to deal with (complex) management issues in general, and accounting in particular. While "standard" approaches concerning accounting and even communication (via e.g. webservices) are certainly an option, this would lead to the solutions living outside the agent oriented concepts.

In this paper, we present a method to incorporate accounting features into agents while staying within the agent paradigm, allowing us to not only measure usage of agents but also create complex tariff schemes. The accounting features are based on a general management layer within the agent framework that is adapted from network management technologies. In network management, proved and tested techniques are used to control and manage network nodes.

M. Dastani et al.(Eds.): ProMAS 2007, LNAI 4908, pp. 42–56, 2008.
© Springer-Verlag Berlin Heidelberg 2008

While we implemented the techniques in the agent framework JIAC (Java Intelligent Agent Componentware), the proposed management structure as well as the accounting features can be applied to other agent frameworks as well.

The rest of this paper is structured as follows. In the next section (Section 2), we give an overview of management technologies in general and accounting methods and technologies in particular. Section 3 describes a high-level model of how agents and management techniques can be combined. We then describe in detail our generic accounting infrastructure which is embedded in this model in Section 4. Before we go into implementation details, we give an overview over the agent framework which we used to implement the concepts described in this paper. We conclude and give an outlook in Section 5.

2   Enterprise Management

Most of today's technologies for management concern the network layer, and are based on OSI Management [3]. OSI stands for Open Systems Interconnection, and has been the basis of standardisation efforts for connecting open systems [4].

OSI Management

OSI management supports the user as well as the provider of communication services during planning, supervision, and control of system activity. This is achieved by providing technologies to coordinate, distribute, and assign resources within the communication network. We can distinguish between three areas of OSI management, which are systems management, n-layer management, and n-layer operations (also known as protocol management).

- Systems management includes vertical management activities that concerns all seven OSI layers, and happens on the application level.
- N-layer-management details functions, services, and protocols for a given layer N.
- N-layer-operations or protocol management concern techniques for monitoring connections with the given layer.

The ISO working group solely defines management standards for the first category, systems management. Here, different standardisation efforts exist, including the specification of procedures that offer specific management aspects.

There are also a number of actual implementations of management technologies. Here, we want to introduce two of them, the second of which is fairly known even outside enterprise network management.

TMN for telecommunication networks [5] is based on OSI management. It distinguishes three layers, namely an information architecture, a functional architecture, and a physical architecture. Each of the architectures is described using functional groups, functional components, reference points, and interfaces. TMN generally supposes a distinct network for the transmission of management relevant data, though it does allow to use the managed network to transmit data as well.

SNMP [6] is a well-known protocol for network management. While initially designed as an interim protocol, it has established itself and is currently available in its third incarnation. It is based on four elements: a management station, a management agent, a management information base, and a network management protocol. The first provides the user with management functionality, while the agent is a purely passive element located in the different managed devices. Manager and agent share a management information base which contains information about resource administration. SNMP provides three functions to interact, a namely *get*, *set*, and *trap*. The first two are for (manager initiated) reading and manipulation of variables defined in the management information base, while the last allows the managed entity to pro-actively send data to the managing component. Communication is done via UDP, and is generally routed over the managed network.

FCAPS

Management procedures are collected under the name FCAPS, which is an abbreviation for the five areas of management it covers.

Fault Management concerns all activities relating to the discovery, reaction, and solution of faults. This includes the definition of classes of failures, monitoring system behaviour, and the generation and transmission of failure-information.

Configuration Management details the identification, collection, control, provision, and execution of data which are important for the initialisation, execution, and adaptation of the system.

Accounting Management deals with the evaluation of services as well as the definition of rules governing accounting of (a combination of) those services. Furthermore, processes and data required to do actual accounting, like customer information and electronic bills are described. It should be noted that accounting is a necessary requirement for any billing system. It provides information and administration of communication, computing resources, storage space etc.

Performance Management or quality management concerns two areas. On the one hand, we have the monitoring of performance parameters such as the number of messages received or sent, the amount of data transmitted, and reaction times. Furthermore, it includes the possibility to configure monitored systems in order to improve performance.

Security Management includes security technologies such as authentication, authorisation, access control, and encryption, as well as the provision of security-relevant information.

Accounting Management

Most research and development activities of accounting management exist under the name AAA that is an abbreviation of authentication, authorisation and accounting. Accounting management contains the collection of resource consumption data for the purposes of capacity and trend analysis, cost allocation, auditing and billing [7]. This includes the measurement, rating and assignment of the consumption data as well as the communication of these data between appropriate parties.

Most of the proposals, specifications and solutions in the field of accounting management consider only the communication layer of applications (e.g. data transfer and network access) or do not cover further aspects of accounting such as charging. Simple accounting management architectures and protocols are specified by ITU-T [8], IETF [7], OMG [9] and M3I [10,11]. Examples for accounting attributes and record formats are ADIF [12] and IPDR [13].

3   Agents and Management

In the context of agents, accounting has to our knowledge not yet been implemented in a general and re-usable fashion. As argued in the introduction however it appears that, as agents move more towards open systems, metering and accounting gains importance.

Rather than focussing on accounting alone and developing an accounting solution from scratch, we base our work on the large body of work that has been done within the network management community as detailed in the previous section. In particular, we adopted the FCAPS management structure as a basis for our accounting implementation. We chose FCAPS for several reasons. It is a thoroughly tested and established approach which is used widely. Also, it allows us to extend our framework to provide not only accounting features but potentially any of the other FCAPS areas such as failure or performance management.

In the remainder of this section detail how we integrate management functionality in agents. While we have implemented it within a particular agent framework, we aimed at making the integration general enough to be applied to most agent frameworks.

Figure 1 shows three layers which occur in a managed agent system. We focus here on the functional aspects, and make no claim about the physical distribution of those functionalities. However, most basic mechanisms are generally located within the single agent. The layers describe on an abstract level the internal structure of the agents (with respect to manageability), the basic management techniques, and the abstract FCAPS management areas.

The lowest level details an agent architecture (e.g. a BDI architecture) which is to be managed. This can be described in terms of communication, knowledge management, execution, and events. Communication is of course an important element of a multi-agent system, but is also important from the view of a single agent. The low level technologies employed, as well as higher levels such as ACL's (e.g. FIPA ACL [14]) and protocols fall under that header. Knowledge management details the internal state of the agent. Actual computation, manipulation of knowledge, and the behaviour of the agent are based on an execution

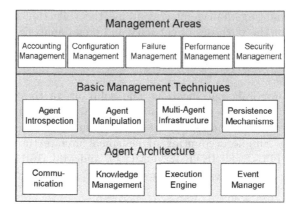

Fig. 1. Three layer management architecture

engine. Lastly, agents have to have means to communicate changes in their state, such as the sending and receiving of messages, invoked services, changes in the knowledge base, plans, and goals etc. The event manager provides an interface for management components to access those architecture specific events.

The next layer provides basic management mechanisms which build on the lower level. It works as a wrapper between the management interfaces of the used agent architecture and the higher-level management functions. Agent introspection provides standardised information about the state of the agent in terms of the four elements detailed above. Furthermore, the state of the agent should not only be monitored, but techniques for the manipulation of the internal state have to be provided. This includes changing the knowledge base, triggering events, adapting, adding or deleting goals, and changing the execution state of the agent. Also, abilities of the agent that refer to the infrastructure, such as migration, termination of the agent, and the (de-) registering of services (see FIPA Management [15]) have to be manageable. Lastly, any mechanisms pertaining to persistence of the agent need to be available.

Layer three uses the basic management mechanisms offered in layer two in order to provide value-added management functions such as fault, configuration, accounting, performance, and security management as independent from the actual agent framework as possible. In terms of agent based systems, this would provide

- detection of faulty or abnormally behaving agents, and providing means to evaluate and recover from errors occurring in the system;
- configuration mechanisms to adapt the system to new requirements, for example by including new features, or replacing old versions of agents with newer ones in an organised fashion by consideration of dependencies between modules;
- metering of resources and mapping to services offered by agents, allowing for a centralised account management and billing mechanisms [7];

– quality control, reliability, load balancing mechanisms (possibly based on information outside the actual agent system) and detection as well as elimination of bottlenecks;
– secure communication, public key infrastructures, access control for agent services, and trust relationships between agents and communities (see e.g. [16,17,18]).

There are two ways of realising above requirements and provide management technologies to agent frameworks. The first would be to extend the agent framework with one of the management technologies described above. For example, agents could be extended by adding an SNMP component which provides and manages data. This would also require the extension of management technologies to include agent relevant information. Alternatively, one can use the technology provided by agents themselves to manage the system instead of extending network management mechanisms. Here, existing techniques (such as FIPA communication) can be adapted to reflect management mechanisms.

We have chosen the latter approach, and base management extensions on FIPA standards.[1] This has the advantage of keeping a reasonably homogeneous system, where the available technologies are used as far as possible. Also, the nature of agents allows to for example provide management agents which monitor a set of agents, and which themselves can take advantage of agent technologies such as flexibility, robustness and intelligent behaviour. Last but not least the managed agents may keep their level of autonomy, e.g. by allowing them to refuse management requests which are in conflict to the own goals.

In order to really get a management framework which can be applied to different agent frameworks and which allows the interoperability between different implementations of this abstract model, several additional requirements should be met. Layer two mechanisms provide clearly defined services, use FIPA-ACL as communication language, and support most of the popular content languages (such as FIPA-SL, KIF[19], and RDF[20]). To this end, FIPA protocols are used. The Monitoring services use the FIPA Subscribe Interaction Protocol in order to provide information about events that occurred within the agent (push-strategy), and the FIPA Query Interaction Protocol to get the current state of (an element of) the specified agent (pull strategy). Agent control is provided using the FIPA Request Interaction Protocol, allowing to request specified actions from the agent.

In order to further detach the actual agent framework from the FCAPS management layer, ontologies describing the state, events, and agent elements should be standardised to allow inter-operability of different agents with the management framework. It should be noted that the nature of different systems precludes a set of events and actions that map to all possible events and actions. However, there is a common subset of events that *can* be specified. For example, the FIPA Abstract Architecture is used as basis for standardised events. Furthermore, many agent frameworks employ some sort of BDI-like architecture, which again should be abstracted to a set of events including the creation, modification, and

---

[1] The specifications mentioned in this paper can be found at http://www.fipa.org

deletion of beliefs, goals, and plans. Last but not least, events concerning the
life cycle of agents need to be provided. This includes the actual change of an
agent's life-cycle state, such as creation, deletion, and migration.

Having said that, it should also be noted that using agents to manage systems
can have serious implications on several levels. Most obviously perhaps, management mechanisms are also needed to control the system when the autonomy
of the agents leads to unpredictable and emergent behaviour that is in conflict
to the intrinsic intention. It seems counter-intuitive to employ agents (which can
behave unexpectedly) to control agents (though, by centralising and providing
means of control, this argument can be countered to a certain extend). Also,
management agents would be highly critical systems, and steps should be taken
to ensure that they can work as reliably and securely as possible.

4   Agents and Accounting

Now that we have detailed how agents and management technologies can be
combined, we describe how this theoretical approach can be applied in the context of accounting. We do this first by providing a scenario which incorporates
accounting features. Using this, we will then describe the accounting architecture
and show how we implemented it in the agent framework JIAC.

4.1   Scenario

In order to make the issue a bit more touchable, we present the following scenario:

A small company provides the online game "crazy eight". Several users may
play against each other on virtual tables. Each table is represented by a game
master agent and each player is represented by a human player agent, which also
provides the user interface for the game and the online charge control. To pay for
playing games every registered user has chosen one of the provided tariffs and
decided to get information about the current account. A linear tariff based on the
duration of the game (e.g. one cent per 10 seconds) and a flat-rate (e.g. 20 cents
for a game) are available. The first tariff uses a charging function parameterised
by rate and period and a tariff scheme based on time events.

Additionally to these tariffs the company now wants to provide a new tariff
based on the played cards of the user without changing the implementation of
the game. To do so also the definition of a new tariff scheme is needed that is
based on the associated events.

At this point, we want to take a step back. Firstly, we observe that agents need
to have some sort of introspection, i.e. the ability to know about internals such
as service provisioning, resources consumed, time, and more. This data has to be
made available to other agents, or managing entities. Also, the other direction of
information flow is needed, i.e. the ability of outside agents (or managing entities)
to directly influence the behaviour of the agent, for example the accounting agent
telling the service provisioning agent to cancel the (executing) service if the credit
limit of the user is reached.

4.2   Accounting Architecture

Figure 2 shows a generic accounting infrastructure while Figure 3 details the interaction sequence that occurs in the example of Section 4.1. The user agent (e.g. human player agent) requests application services (a card game service), which are provided by the managed application provider (the game master agent). The charging agents use the introspection services described in layer two of the management model to be informed about start and stop of application services. In this case, during the initialization or negotiation phase after a charging agent has received the information about the requested service, he uses a service of the user management to get the profile of the application service and user. The service profile contains a list of all supported tariffs or an empty list for non-commercial services. The user profile contains the valid tariff (as contracted between customer and provider) for the given service and user. Afterwards a service of the tariff management gives the description of the tariff, which is related to a charging function to calculate the price.

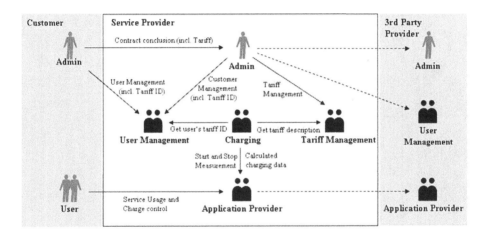

Fig. 2. Roles and interactions during accounting management

Accordingly, also by using the introspection services provided by the application provider the charging agent activates only the metering of events relevant to the charging function of the tariff (e.g. playing a card realised by sending a data speechact). If one of these events occurs during service provision (i.e. some state on which the function depends changes) the current price will be calculated again. As a result of a changed price the accounting rules of the charging agent may trigger actions, e.g. to stop the service or to inform the user about the current price by using the manipulation services of the application provider. If the application service stops, the metering will be deactivated and the final charge will be calculated. The service provider also plays the role of a customer if its application provider agents uses services of 3rd-party providers (see dashed lines of Figure 2).

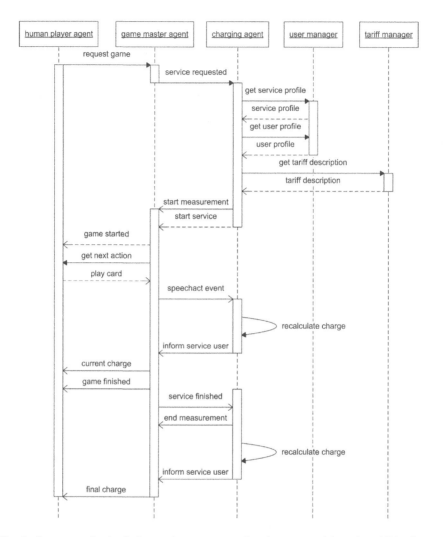

Fig. 3. Sequence chart of the card game scenario where a card-based tariff is chosen and one card was played

By using the introspection and manipulation mechanism introduced in Section 3, the provided services need not be re-implemented for accounting purposes. Furthermore, the possible tariffs are not restricted to just a few bits of information like service duration or number of access, which have to be decided upon before bringing the service online. Instead, all events measurable by the underlying agent framework may be used. Also the charging information about used subservices of 3rd-party provider may be considered by the tariffs. Some frameworks (including *JIAC*) allow even to add new (measurement) components to agents during run-time. It should be noted that in the case of service chaining with a revenue sharing model a proper prediction of final charges is very difficult if the number of involved services becomes large and the used tariff schemes are more complex.

4.3   Accounting in *JIAC*

We have implemented our accounting approach in and with the FIPA-compliant agent framework *JIAC* [21,22]. In the following we will describe the characteristics of this agent framework, before detailing the implementation of accounting. Note that the implemented management features are partially used in numerous projects [23,24].

JIAC consists of a run-time environment, a methodology, tools that support the creation of agents, as well as numerous extensions, such as web-service-connectivity, an owl-to-*Jadl* translator and more. An agent consists of a set of components.

JIAC's component model allows to exchange, add, and remove components during run-time. The components interact among each other by agent internal messages. Standard components (which themselves can be exchanged as well) include a fact-base component, execution-component, rule-component, and more [25]. These components provide individual messages to manage the appropriate actions, e.g. the *MonitorGoalMessage* executed by the *GoalBean* allows to subscribe for changes on the goal stack.

Agents are programmed using the language *Jadl* [26]. It is based on three-valued predicate logic [27], thereby providing an open world semantics, and implements an BDI approach. It comprises four main elements: *plans elements, goals, rules, ontologies*, and *services*.

Communication is based on services. A service invocation consists of several steps, and is based on a meta-protocol, an extension of the FIPA request protocol. First, the agent contacts the Directory Facilitator (DF) in order to receive a list of possible services that could fulfil the current goal. After selecting a service and informing the DF, the agent receives a list of agents providing that service. Now an optional negotiation protocol can be executed with which the actual service provider is chosen. Only then is the actual service protocol executed. The meta protocol handles service-independent elements like security, communication failures, and other management-related issues.

Now we describe the *JIAC*-based implementation of the accounting architecture as part of a comprehensive management framework. Firstly, for layer two of the management model (see Figure 1) we have implemented management components providing an consistent interface (within the agent) to the bottom layer components of the agent architecture described above. This agent internal interface allows to register or deregister for events matching a specified pattern. These matched events may be delivered immediately or at regular intervals. The ontology shown in Figure 4 describes the structure of the managed *JIAC*-specific events that need to be monitored for management functionality (e.g. accounting), such as speech acts, facts, goals, and intentions.

The introspection and manipulation services makes the internal interface available to other agents. We use priority mechanisms of *JIAC* to give the

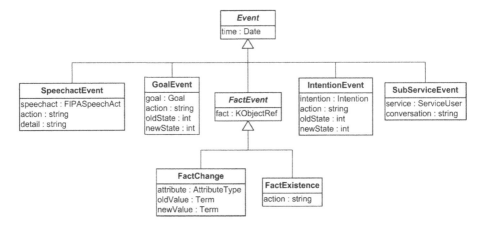

Fig. 4. Extensible ontology for the management of JIAC-based agents

management related actions and messages a higher importance than the application services. At the moment, we do not consider access controls, or levels of autonomy. The managed agents always provide all management capabilities if the managing agent is authorised. Restrictions of actions on specified agent elements and the ensuring of consistency of management actions with own goals are future work. Having said that, it should again be noted that the provision of those interfaces does not mean that agents necessarily loose all their autonomy. Instead, it is left to the programmer to decide which methods to employ, or how to react to management requests.

Up to now, standards for the introspection or manipulation of agents do not exist. But nevertheless to provide interoperability, we plan to implement the services using the referred FIPA protocols as alternative to the currently used *JIAC* meta-protocol. This includes conversion of the content between *Jadl* and the standardised languages SL, KIF or RDF, and translations between the different management ontologies (e.g. between the *JIAC*-management and a more

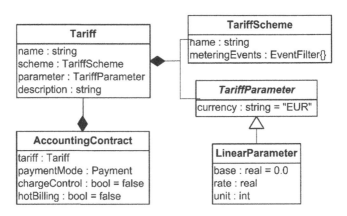

Fig. 5. Ontology for the description of tariffs

general BDI-management). As proof of concept, we have implemented services for multi-agent infrastructure of the abstract model using FIPA protocols, conversion of the content to *SL* and the ontology *fipa-agent-management*.

Based on these implementations we have realised parts of the management areas described by the abstract model, such as the accounting infrastructure introduced before. Also, applicable tools for the run-time administration of agents, user management, and the management of accounting information, including the creation of tariffs and tariff-schemata, were developed.

```
(act getSpeechactLinearPrice
    (var ?usageId:string ?account:ServiceAccount ?tariff:Tariff)
    ...
    (script
        (var ?meteredEvents:class:java.util.HashMap ?events:Event[]
            ?amount:real ?money:Money ?parameter:LinearParameter
            ?base:real ?rate:real ?unit:int ?currency:string)
        (seq
            // get tariff parameters
            (eval (att parameter ?tariff ?parameter))
            (eval (att currency ?parameter ?currency))
            (eval (att base ?parameter ?base))
            (eval (att rate ?parameter ?rate))
            (eval (att unit ?parameter ?unit))

            // get measured events
            (getEvents (var ?usageId ?meteredEvents))
            (bind ?events (fun getEntry ?meteredEvents "SpeechactFilter"))

            // calculate current charge based on number of events
            (bind ?amount (fun Real.add ?base (fun Real.mul ?rate
                    (fun int2real (fun Int.div (fun getLength ?events)
                    ?unit)))))

            // update current charge
            (bind ?money (obj Money (amount ?amount) (currency ?currency)))
            (update (att price ?account ?money))
        )
    )
)
```

Fig. 6. Code example for a charging function based on speechact events and linear parameter

In *JIAC* tariffs are described using the ontology shown in Figure 5. A tariff contains a tariff scheme and parameters. To get highest possible flexibility to define new tariffs, tariff schemes are described by a list of filters for metering events (see ontology in Figure 4), and the corresponding charging functions are implemented as plan elements (see example in Figure 6). Because expertise is needed for the flexible definition of tariff schemes, we have introduced tariff parameters which enables non-expert service providers to easily adapt the tariffs. In this example the attributes of the linear parameter are evaluated before reading out the list of metered events that match the speechact filter specified in the tariff scheme. Afterwards the charged amount is calculated based on the linear parameter and the length of the event list. Finally, the account will be updated with the new amount.

```
(obj ReceivedDataSpeechactFilter SpeechactFilter
    (EventFilter.name "SpeechactFilter")
    (EventFilter.role "de.dailab.management.accounting.role.ControlRole")
    (action "received")
    (detail "protocol")
    (speechacts (obj SpeechactPattern (performative "data"))))
)
```

Fig. 7. An example of a Speechact-Filter

An example of a filter is shown in Figure 7. Here, the speechacts are filtered based on the performative "data" and the fact that they are received within a service protocol.

5 Conclusion

In this paper we have described how advanced accounting mechanisms can be incorporated into agent frameworks. Based on management technologies known from networking, we have provided a general framework which allows agents to measure, meter, and bill for services they provide. This grounding allows us to for example extend the agent frameworks towards other FCAPS areas such as performance or configuration management.

We have implemented the underlying framework and the accounting infrastructure within JIAC, and shown how accounting features can be used in agent frameworks. As through the use of webservices and the internet in general open systems are bound to be more and more pervasive, it becomes necessary for agent frameworks to provide methods to deal with the commercial implications of providing services to outside entities (as opposed to having an agent framework that in essence is a distributed application).

Future work includes restrictions of actions on specified agent elements, as well as ensuring consistency of management actions with the goals of the managed agents. The extension of the framework to include more FCAPS areas (such as security and failure) is another direction of future work. It should be noted that in the end, the different areas cannot be viewed separately as they are often intertwined. For example, the issue of trust management and its implications on accounting needs to be investigated in the context of security. Also service level agreements and their enforcement are important issues that need to be addressed.

References

1. Jennings, N.R., Sycara, K., Wooldridge, M.: A roadmap of agent research and development. Autonomous Agents and Multi-Agent Systems, 1, 275–306 (1998)
2. Luck, M., McBurney, P., Shehory, O., Willmott, S.: Agent Technology Roadmap (2005)

3. ITU-T: Information technology – Open Systems Interconnection – Systems management overview. ITU-T Recommendation X.701, ISO/IEC 10040 (1998)
4. ITU-T: Information Technology – Open Systems Interconnection – Basic Reference Model: The Basic Model. ITU-T Recommendation X.200, ISO/IEC 7498-1 (1994)
5. ITU-T: Principles for a Telecommunications Management Network. ITU-T Recommendation M.3010 (2000)
6. Case, J., Fedor, M., Schoffstall, M., Davin, J.: A Simple Network Management Protocol (SNMP). In: RFC 1157, IETF (1990)
7. Aboba, B., Arkko, J., Harrington, D.: Introduction to Accounting Management. In: RFC 2975, IETF (2000)
8. ITU-T: Information technology – open systems interconnection – systems management:usage metering function for accounting purposes. Technical report, ITU Telecommunication Standardization Sector (1995)
9. OMG: Federated charging and rating facility. Technical report, Fraunhofer FOKUS (2002)
10. M3I-Consortium: Charging and accounting system (cas) design. Technical report, Market Managed Multi-service Internet Consortium, ETH Zürich (2000)
11. M3I-Consortium: Cas implementation. Technical report, Market Managed Multi-service Internet Consortium, ETH Zürich (2001)
12. Aboba, B., Lidyard, D.: The accounting data interchange format (adif). Technical report, IETF (2000)
13. IPDR: Network data management - usage: For ip-based service. Technical report, IPDR Organisation (2001)
14. FIPA: FIPA ACL Message Structure Specification. FIPA Specification SC00061G (2002)
15. FIPA: FIPA Agent Management Specification. FIPA Specification SC00023K (2004)
16. Schmidt, T.: ASITA: Advanced Security Infrastructure for Multi-Agent-Applications in the Telematic Area. PhD thesis, Technische Universität Berlin (2002)
17. Bsufka, K.: Public Key Infrastrukturen in Agentenarchitekturen zur Realisierung dienstbasierter Anwendungen. PhD thesis, Technische Universität Berlin (2006)
18. Bsufka, K., Holst, S., Schmidt, T.: Realization of an Agent-Based Certificate Authority and Key Distribution Center. In: Albayrak, Ş. (ed.) IATA 1999. LNCS (LNAI), vol. 1699, pp. 113–123. Springer, Heidelberg (1999)
19. Genesereth, M.R., Fikes, R.E.: Knowledge interchange format version 3.0 reference manual. Technical Report Logic-92-1, Stanford University, Computer Science Department (1992)
20. Lassila, O., Swick, R.: Resource description framework (rdf) model and syntax specification. Technical Report WD-rdf-syntax-971002, W3C (1999)
21. Fricke, S., Bsufka, K., Keiser, J., Schmidt, T., Sesseler, R., Albayrak, S.: Agent-based Telematic Services and Telecom Applications. Communications of the ACM 44(4), 43–48 (2001)
22. Sesseler, R., Albayrak, S.: Service-ware framework for developing 3g mobile services. In: The Sixteenth International Symposium on Computer and Information Sciences (2001)
23. Albayrak, S., Milosevic, D.: Generic intelligent personal information agent. In: International Conference on Advances in Internet, Processing, Systems, and Interdisciplinary Research (2004)

24. Wohltorf, J., Cissée, R., Rieger, A.: BerlinTainment: An agent-based context-aware entertainment planning system. IEEE Communications Magazine 43(6), 102–109 (2005)
25. Sesseler, R.: Eine modulare Architektur für dienstbasierte Interaktion zwischen Agenten. PhD thesis, Technische Universität Berlin (2002)
26. Konnerth, T., Hirsch, B., Albayrak, S.: JADL – An Agent Description Language for Smart Agents. In: Baldoni, M., Endriss, U. (eds.) DALT 2006. LNCS (LNAI), vol. 4327, pp. 141–155. Springer, Heidelberg (2006)
27. Kleene, S.C.: Introduction to Metamathematics. Wolters-Noordhoff Publishing and North-Holland Publishing Company (1971) (Written in 1953)

From Norms to Interaction Patterns: Deriving Protocols for Agent Institutions

Huib Aldewereld, Frank Dignum, and John-Jules Ch. Meyer

Institute of Information and Computing Sciences
Utrecht University, The Netherlands
{huib,dignum,jj}@cs.uu.nl

Abstract. We show how protocols (or interaction patterns) can be derived from norms using landmarks. The resulting protocols can be used by agents to perform their interactions while being certain to stay within the norms governing an e-institution without having to have a capability for normative reasoning. It can also be used by normative agents as a default protocol to be used, but from which they can deviate in specific circumstances.

1 Introduction

Agent-mediated institutions (or e-institutions), introduced in [13,14], are *open* agent systems that allow heterogeneous agents to enter and perform tasks. The e-institutions specify the admissible behaviour of the agents by means of norms, which are declarative and abstract by nature. On the one hand this allows for a stable specification suitable for almost any conceivable situation that arises in the institution, but in the other hand the norms hardly give any indication which interaction patterns would guarantee satisfaction of the norms.

One could aim for the use of normative agents in e-institutions as propagated in [12]. In this perspective the agents are capable of reasoning about the norms and planning their actions accordingly. However, it seems not very realistic that all agents will have this capacity. Most agents will be standard agents that are only capable to reason about standard protocols as part of their interactions with other agents. Therefore, in this paper, we aim to provide ways to generate protocols (on the basis of the normative descriptions) that are guaranteed to fulfil all norms of the e-institution. Given these protocols agents entering the e-institution can just follow these protocols and be sure they will always stay within the "law". Note that we do not necessarily require the agents to follow these protocols. They can be seen as available templates for use by the agents. Agents can still perform normative reasoning if they are capable, but, with the help of these protocols, they do not need to do that in order to participate in the e-institution.

Our approach is inspired by how the gap between the normative and procedural dimensions is bridged in human institutions. Human laws express in a very abstract way wanted (legal) and unwanted (illegal) states of affairs. Although

M. Dastani et al.(Eds.): ProMAS 2007, LNAI 4908, pp. 57–72, 2008.
© Springer-Verlag Berlin Heidelberg 2008

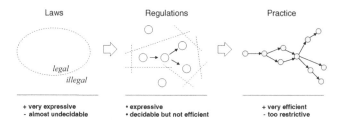

Fig. 1. Comparison between Laws, Regulations and Practice

laws are very expressive, they do not express how to achieve a given state of affairs, and therefore they are very hard to use in practice to, e.g., guide each decision in a process. In practice more efficient representations are needed, such as protocols or guidelines. In rule-based legal systems (those based in Roman-Germanic law), *regulations* add an intermediate level between laws and practice, by giving some high-level specifications on some constraints about how things can or cannot be done. These high-level descriptions are therefore interpretations of the law that add some operational constraints to be met by practice (see figure 1). Using this idea, we introduce an intermediate level between institutional norm specifications and institutional protocols based on *landmarks* in a similar way as done in [9,3]. The landmarks are further discussed in section 2.

From the norms we will automatically generate finite state automata, using a technique introduced by Wolper in [17]. This is a general technique to convert temporal logic formulas in LTL into so-called Büchi automata. The landmark patterns can be obtained from these automata by looking at their corresponding recognised languages. This technique is described in section 3. In section 4 we show how we can compose protocols by strengthening the landmark patterns, through adding additional information concerning the (presumed) capabilities of the agents. In section 5 an example of the whole process of generating a protocol from norms is given. The paper concludes with some observations and future in research in section 6.

2   Norms and Landmarks

The relevance of landmarks in protocol specification is dictated by the simple observation that several different actions can bring about the same outcome. Once the outcomes of actions are organised in a structured description (i.e. a landmark pattern), it becomes possible to represent families of protocols abstracting from the actual transitions by which each protocol is constituted. This makes landmarks an ideal solution for bridging the gap between the abstract normative level and the procedural level of protocols. The landmark pattern fully captures the order in which states should occur, representing the important steps that any protocol should contain, while still abstracting from the actual procedural information on how the transition from one state to another should be achieved. In essence, a landmark pattern represents "those steps that should be taken and in which order".

Given that landmarks are considered as state descriptions [3], a landmark pattern is defined as follows.

Definition 1 (Landmark Pattern)
A landmark pattern is a structure $\mathfrak{L} = \langle L^+, \leq \rangle$ where L^+ is a finite set of landmarks (state descriptions) and $\leq$ is a partial order on L^+.

Similar to the relation between norms, regulations and practice, where regulations add operational information to the restrictions given by the norms, a landmark pattern should add additional information to the normative goals in order to bridge the gap between the norms and the practice. The norms only give a (temporal) ordering of the states that should be reached. The normative landmark pattern extracted from these norms will thus leave many blanks, situations where the order of events/actions is undetermined by the norms or only minimally described. The choices in ordering that are not specified in the pattern, however, will in most cases influence the efficiency or even the feasibility of the pattern. For example, norms concerning organ transplantation describe that permission for organ removal (π) must be obtained before the organs are removed (ρ), as well as that doctors should check whether a patient is brain death (δ) before starting the operation for removing organs of the patient. These two norms only describe that two states, π and δ, should be reached before another state, ρ, happens. No information is given about the ordering of states π and δ, but obviously making sure that δ happens before π is more practical then having π occur before δ. This would mean that we add the ordering $\delta \leq \pi$ to our landmark pattern, to obtain $\langle \{\pi, \delta, \rho\}, \{\pi \leq \rho, \delta \leq \rho, \delta \leq \pi\} \rangle$.

In this case we added an extra ordering between existing landmarks to exclude the possibility of inefficient situations arising, but additional landmarks can be added to the existing pattern to express information concerning efficiency and feasibility. Consider again our organ transplant example, where we now include the additional step of assigning the organ (α). According to the law, the assignment procedure can only start after the organ has been removed ($\rho \leq \alpha$). The procedure of assigning organs, however, needs certain information about the organ to make sure that the assigned receiver is a compatible recipient. In the current landmark pattern, this information will need to be gathered at the moment the assignment is taking place. Some of the information needed for the assignment process (for instance, the blood type of the deceased (β)) can be checked in the very beginning of the protocol, and doing so can greatly improve the speed at which an organ is assigned (thus increasing the efficiency of the process, as well as the feasibility, due to degradation of organs after removal). The resulting pattern would then be $\langle \{\pi, \delta, \rho, \alpha, \beta\}, \{\pi \leq \rho, \delta \leq \rho, \delta \leq \pi, \rho \leq \alpha, \delta \leq \beta, \beta \leq \pi\} \rangle$.

Even though all kinds of information concerning efficiency and feasibility can be added to the landmark pattern, some limitations still exist that should not be overlooked. The pattern will have to satisfy certain principles to be useful. Firstly, the pattern needs to be norm-compliant. No landmarks should be added that are in conflict with the requirements specified by the norms. Secondly, the pattern needs to contain only reachable landmarks; the pattern should not contain landmarks that are unachievable by definition (e.g. a state satisfying

$a \wedge \neg a$), or express an ordering that is impossible to fulfil. Lastly, a landmark pattern should only express goals that are within the capabilities of the agents.

3   From Norms to Landmarks

Creating a protocol for a normative domain is done by using an intermediate level of landmarks that we presented above. This process of generating a (proto-typical) protocol for a normative domain is the following. First a set of landmarks is extracted from the norms governing the domain. To extract this (normative) landmark pattern from the norms we use a technique presented in [17], which was originally developed with model-checking in mind (some model-checkers, like SPIN, [11], are built around principles very similar to those of this technique). The idea is that we create a generic, canonical-like model representing *all* LTL models that satisfy the norms of the system. This canonical model is, in fact, a finite state machine as we show later. From this finite state machine we generate a *regular expression* expressing the characteristic features of all models satisfying the norms. We will show that this expression is, in fact, a basic landmark pattern, exactly containing all the important states (landmarks) expressed in the norms, as well as the order in which these states must occur (thus making it a landmark pattern). This normative pattern will then be expanded with extra landmarks to strengthen it to a full landmark pattern (as described above). The landmark pattern, now including all important states, both normative-wise and efficiency-wise, will then be translated into a protocol for the normative domain.

Norms are expressed in linear-time temporal logic (similar to [8]). The temporal logic that we are going to use is the following (note that any LTL logic can be used for this, as long as the formulas are in negated normal form). The formulas of linear-time temporal logic built from a set of atomic propositions P are the following:

- **true**, **false**, $p, \neg p$ for all $p \in P$;
- $\varphi_1 \wedge \varphi_2$ and $\varphi_1 \vee \varphi_2$, where φ_1 and φ_2 are LTL formulas;
- $\bigcirc \varphi_1, \varphi_1$ **until** φ_2, and φ_1 **releases** φ_2, where φ_1 and φ_2 are LTL formulas.

The operator $\bigcirc$ is a next-state operator, denoting that φ_1 must hold in the state following the present one. The **until** operator is a strong until, denoting that φ_1 must hold in all states up to a state where φ_2 holds (which should appear). The **release** operator is the dual of **until** and requires that φ_2 is always true, a requirement that is released as soon as φ_1 holds. The *sometime* ($\Diamond \varphi_1$) and *always* ($\Box \varphi_1$) operators, denoting that φ_1 holds somewhere in the future or in every state from now on, respectively, are introduced as the following abbreviations: $\Diamond \varphi_1 \equiv$ **true until** φ_1 and $\Box \varphi_1 \equiv$ **false releases** φ_1.

The semantics of this logics, with respect to sequences $\sigma : \mathbb{N} \to 2^P$, where we write $\sigma(i)$ to denote the ith state of σ and σ^j to denote the suffix of σ obtained through removing the first j states of σ (i.e. $\sigma^j(i) = \sigma(j + i)$), is given by the following rules:

- For all σ, we have $\sigma \vDash$ **true** and $\sigma \nvDash$ **false**;
- $\sigma \vDash p$ for $p \in P$ iff $p \in \sigma(0)$;

- $\sigma \vDash \neg p$ for $p \in P$ iff $p \notin \sigma(0)$;
- $\sigma \vDash \varphi_1 \wedge \varphi_2$ iff $\sigma \vDash \varphi_1$ and $\sigma \vDash \varphi_2$;
- $\sigma \vDash \varphi_1 \vee \varphi_2$ iff $\sigma \vDash \varphi_1$ or $\sigma \vDash \varphi_2$;
- $\sigma \vDash \bigcirc\varphi_1$ iff $\sigma^1 \vDash \varphi_1$;
- $\sigma \vDash \varphi_1$ **until** φ_2 iff there exists $i \geq 0$ such that $\sigma^i \vDash \varphi_2$ and for all $0 \leq j < i$, we have $\sigma^j \vDash \varphi_1$;
- $\sigma \vDash \varphi_1$ **releases** φ_2 iff for all $i \geq 0$ such that $\sigma^i \nvDash \varphi_2$, there exists $0 \leq j < i$ such that $\sigma^j \vDash \varphi_1$.

Using this logic we can, as done in [8], give a representation of the normative operators that we are going to use to represent the norms. The norms are introduced as an Anderson's reduction [4], by the introduction of a special proposition $v(\rho, \delta)$ to denote that a violation concerning ρ and δ has occurred. We limit ourselves to obligations, which can be expressed in the logic presented above as:

$$O(\rho < \delta) \Leftrightarrow \Diamond \delta \wedge \Big[(\neg\delta \wedge \neg\rho \wedge \neg v(\rho,\delta)) \textbf{ until}$$
$$((\rho \wedge \neg\delta \wedge \Box\neg v(\rho,\delta)) \vee (\neg\rho \wedge \delta \wedge \bigcirc v(\rho,\delta))) \Big]$$

Although prohibitions also play an important role in normative specifications we do not treat them separately here as they can be expressed in terms of obligations; i.e. $F(\rho) \Leftrightarrow \Box O(\neg\rho < \textbf{true})$.

As mentioned before, the landmarks will be extracted from an automaton that is generated on basis of the LTL specification of the norms.

Automata on Infinite Sequences. The automata that we consider are Büchi automata on infinite words. Infinite words are sequences of symbols isomorphic to the natural numbers, i.e. a mapping from the infinite sequence to symbols of the alphabet Σ; $w : \mathbb{N} \to \Sigma$. Büchi automata have exactly the same structure as traditional finite word automata, with the exception that their semantics are defined over infinite words. A Büchi automaton is defined as a tuple $A = (\Sigma, S, \Delta, S_0, \mathscr{F})$ where

- Σ is an alphabet,
- S is a set of states,
- $\Delta : S \times \Sigma \to S$ (deterministic) or $\Delta : S \times \Sigma \to 2^S$ (nondeterministic) is a transition function,
- $S_0 \subseteq S$ is a set of initial states (a singleton for deterministic automata), and
- $\mathscr{F} = \{F_1, \ldots, F_k\}$, a set of sets of accepting states where $F_i \subseteq S$ for every $F_i \in \mathscr{F}$

A word w is accepted (or recognised) by A if there exists a sequence $\lambda : \mathbb{N} \to S$ of states such that

- $\lambda(0) \in S_0$ (the initial state of λ is an initial state of A),
- $\forall 0 \leq i, \lambda(i + 1) \in \Delta(\lambda(i), w(i))$ (the sequence of states is compatible with the transition relation of A),

– For each $F_i \in \mathcal{F}$, $\inf(\lambda) \cap F_i \neq \varnothing$ where $\inf(\lambda)$ is the set of states that appear infinitely often in λ (the set of repeating states of λ intersects the accepting set F).

Given these definitions of LTL and Büchi automata we can now present the relation between the logic and the automata and the procedure to create a automaton that accepts exactly those sequences that satisfy a formula φ. The translation from LTL formulas to Büchi automata is taken from work presented in [17]. The idea is that the sequences accepted by an automaton correspond exactly to those LTL sequences satisfying the formula.

A state s in the sequence σ is an LTL state characterised in the propositional elements that hold in that LTL state. These LTL state descriptions will ultimately form the symbols of the language accepted by the automaton, the sequence of these state descriptions being the words accepted by the automaton. A closure labelling τ is defined to denote the temporal formulas that must *at least* hold at the different stages of an automaton run, they will ultimately be used as the labellings of the automaton states. This labelling τ of a sequence σ indicates which (temporal) subformulas of φ hold at each state of σ, i.e. a subformula φ_1 of φ labels a position i (written as $\varphi_1 \in \tau(i)$), if and only if $\sigma_i \vDash \varphi_1$. We define the set of subformulas of a formula φ, called the *closure* of φ ($cl(\varphi)$), as follows:

– $\varphi \in cl(\varphi)$;
– $\varphi_1 \wedge \varphi_2 \in cl(\varphi) \Rightarrow \varphi_1, \varphi_2 \in cl(\varphi)$;
– $\varphi_1 \vee \varphi_2 \in cl(\varphi) \Rightarrow \varphi_1, \varphi_2 \in cl(\varphi)$;
– $\bigcirc \varphi_1 \in cl(\varphi) \Rightarrow \varphi_1 \in cl(\varphi)$;
– φ_1 **until** $\varphi_2 \in cl(\varphi) \Rightarrow \varphi_1, \varphi_2 \in cl(\varphi)$;
– φ_1 **releases** $\varphi_2 \in cl(\varphi) \Rightarrow \varphi_1, \varphi_2 \in cl(\varphi)$.

The closure labelling τ of a sequence σ, denoting the formulas of the closure of φ that hold at a given position, is then defined in such a way that it guarantees the correspondence between the positions in τ with positions in σ; i.e. the closure labelling is defined by means of a set of rules that mirror LTL semantics. The closure labelling $\tau : \mathbb{N} \to 2^{cl(\varphi)}$ of a sequence $\sigma : \mathbb{N} \to 2^P$ for a formula φ over a set of atomic propositions P is valid when it satisfies the following rules for every $i \geq 0$:

1. **falsum** $\notin \tau(i)$;
2. for $p \in P$, if $p \in \tau(i)$ then $p \in \sigma(i)$, and if $\neg p \in \tau(i)$ then $p \notin \sigma(i)$;
3. if $\varphi_1 \wedge \varphi_2 \in \tau(i)$ then $\varphi_1 \in \tau(i)$ and $\varphi_2 \in \tau(i)$;
4. if $\varphi_1 \vee \varphi_2 \in \tau(i)$ then $\varphi_1 \in \tau(i)$ or $\varphi_2 \in \tau(i)$;

These rules ensure that the propositional part of LTL is satisfied by the closure labelling. Note that because the rules are specified as "if" rules and not as "if and only if" rules, the closure labelling is not required to be *maximal*, i.e. the rules give the requirements that *must* be satisfied by the closure labelling, but do not require that all formulas of the closure that hold at a given position are included in the label of that position.

For the temporal operators, the following rules are given.

5. if $\bigcirc\varphi_1 \in \tau(i)$ then $\varphi_1 \in \tau(i+1)$;
6. if φ_1 **until** $\varphi_2 \in \tau(i)$ then either $\varphi_2 \in \tau(i)$, or $\varphi_1 \in \tau(i)$ and
   φ_1 **until** $\varphi_2 \in \tau(i+1)$;
7. if φ_1 **releases** $\varphi_2 \in \tau(i)$ then $\varphi_2 \in \tau(i)$, and either $\varphi_1 \in \tau(i)$ or
   φ_1 **releases** $\varphi_2 \in \tau(i)$.

Rule 5 for the $\bigcirc$ operator follows directly from the LTL semantics of the operator. For the **until** and **releases** operators, however, the equivalences φ_1 **until** $\varphi_2 \equiv$ $(\varphi_2 \vee (\varphi_1 \wedge \bigcirc(\varphi_1$ **until** $\varphi_2)))$ and φ_1 **releases** $\varphi_2 \equiv (\varphi_2 \wedge (\varphi_1 \vee \bigcirc(\varphi_1$ **releases** $\varphi_2)))$ are used for the definition of rules 6 and 7 instead, since they avoid the reference to a possibly infinite set of points in the sequence (it can be easily shown that these equivalences follow from the semantics of these operators).

Unfortunately, an extra rule is required to guarantee that the labelling satisfies subformulas with an **until**. Since rule 6 does not force the existence of a point at which φ_2 appears, this can be postponed forever (which is inconsistent to the LTL semantics of the **until** operator). An extra rule to guarantee the existence of this point satisfying the *eventuality* (formulas of the form φ_1 **until** φ_2 are called eventualities, because φ_2 must eventually hold) has to be added:

8. if φ_1 **until** $\varphi_2 \in \tau(i)$ then there is a $j \geq i$ such that $\varphi_2 \in \tau(j)$.

Given these restrictions, a formalisation of the relation between the closure labelling and the LTL sequence is given in [17]:

Theorem 1. *Consider a formula φ defined over a set of propositions P and a sequence $\sigma : \mathbb{N} \to 2^P$. One then has that $\sigma \vDash \varphi$ iff there is a closure labelling $\tau : \mathbb{N} \to 2^{cl(\varphi)}$ of σ satisfying rules 1-8 and such that $\varphi \in \tau(0)$.*

Given this theorem, the relation between an automaton A accepting all sequences satisfying φ and the LTL models is rather obvious. Recall that automata accept infinite sequences (words) when this sequence can be labelled by states of the automaton, while satisfying the conditions that the first state of the sequence is a start state of A, the transition relation of A is respected and the acceptance condition of A is met. It then becomes obvious to use $2^{cl(\varphi)}$ as state set (and possible state labels), and create an automaton over the alphabet 2^P that satisfies the necessary properties expressed in the labelling rules expressed above. [1]

Definition 2
A Büchi automaton for a formula φ is a tuple $A_\varphi = (\Sigma, S, \Delta, S_0, \mathcal{F})$, where

- $\Sigma = 2^P$
- S *is the set of states* $s \subseteq 2^{cl(\varphi)}$ *that satisfy*

---

[1] The alphabet of an automaton A for a formula φ consists of all possible LTL-worlds, being that an LTL-world is described as the collection of the propositions that hold in that world. For instance, if we only consider the propositions ρ, δ and γ, the LTL-world that satisfies only ρ and δ will be denoted by $\{\rho, \delta\}$ (we also use $\rho\delta$ or $\delta\rho$ to denote this world). Conversely, the label γ denotes the LTL world in which γ holds, but ρ and δ are false.

- **falsum** $\notin$ **s**;
- *if* $\varphi_1 \wedge \varphi_2 \in$ **s** *then* $\varphi_1 \in$ **s** *and* $\varphi_2 \in$ **s**;
- *if* $\varphi_1 \vee \varphi_2 \in$ **s** *then* $\varphi_1 \in$ **s** *or* $\varphi_2 \in$ **s**.
- *The transition function* Δ *is defined as* **t** $\in \Delta(\mathbf{s}, \mathbf{a})$ *iff*
  - *For all* $p \in P$, *if* $p \in$ **s** *then* $p \in$ **a**.
  - *For all* $p \in P$, *if* $\neg p \in$ **s** *then* $p \notin$ **a**.
  - *If* $\bigcirc \varphi_1 \in$ **s** *then* $\varphi_1 \in$ **t**.
  - *If* φ_1 **until** $\varphi_2 \in$ **s** *then either* $\varphi_2 \in$ **s**, *or* $\varphi_1 \in$ **s** *and* φ_1 **until** $\varphi_2 \in$ **t**.
  - *If* φ_1 **unless** $\varphi_2 \in$ **s** *then* $\varphi_2 \in$ **s** *and either* $\varphi_1 \in$ **s**, *or* φ_1 **unless** $\varphi_2 \in$ **t**.
- $S_0 = \{\mathbf{s} \in S \mid \varphi \in \mathbf{s}\}$.

Proposition 1. *The Büchi automaton* A_φ *from definition 2 accepts all and only the sequences* $\sigma : \mathbb{N} \to 2^P$ *that satisfy the formula* φ.

The restriction on the states S of A_φ ensures that the states (and thus the closure labels) satisfy rule 1 as well as rules 3 and 4 specified above. Rule 2 and rules 5-7 are enforced in the transition function Δ of A_φ. This ensures that the automaton A_φ complies to the rules 1-7 of the closure labelling specified above. The restriction on the start states S_0 of A_φ ensures that φ appears in the label of the first position of the sequence (thus limiting the labellings of A_φ to those where $\varphi \in \tau(0)$, as required by theorem 1). To ensure rule 8, the acceptance condition of the automaton is used. Rule 8 specifies that every state that contains an eventuality $e(\varphi')$ (where φ_1 **until** $\varphi' \in cl(\varphi) \Rightarrow e(\varphi') \in cl(\varphi)$) is followed at some point by a state that contains φ'. This means that labellings where $e(\varphi')$ appears indefinitely without φ' ever appearing must be avoided. These labellings can be avoided by requiring that the automaton goes infinitely often through a state in which both $e(\varphi')$ and φ' appear or in which $e(\varphi')$ does not hold. To achieve this, the acceptance condition of A_φ is specified as the following generalised Büchi condition:

- Given eventualities $e_1(\varphi_1), \ldots, e_m(\varphi_m)$ in $cl(\varphi)$, we have $\mathcal{F} = \{F_1, \ldots, F_m\}$ where $F_i = \{\mathbf{s} \in S \mid e_i, \varphi_i \in \mathbf{s} \vee e_i \notin \mathbf{s}\}$.

In accordance to this definition of an automaton accepting the sequences that satisfy φ, [17] states a procedure to generate a minimal Büchi automaton satisfying the constraints mentioned.

Extracting the Landmarks. Using the relation between LTL and automata presented above we can now create an automaton that models all LTL sequences that satisfy the norms of a given domain. The norms, expressed as LTL formulas as presented earlier in this section, form the basis of the formula φ of which the automaton is built. Lets consider, for illustrative purposes, a domain governed by a single deadline $O(\rho < \delta)$ (ρ needs to happen in one or more states before δ appears). If a protocol needs to be created for this domain, we need to extract the landmarks specified by the norms governing the domain. These landmarks, as explained earlier, are the characteristic features of the norms that define the basic structure of protocols that comply to that norms. The landmarks are extracted

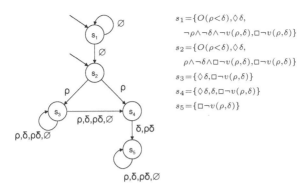

$$s_1 = \{O(\rho < \delta), \Diamond \delta,$$
$$\neg \rho \wedge \neg \delta \wedge \neg v(\rho, \delta), \Box \neg v(\rho, \delta)\}$$
$$s_2 = \{O(\rho < \delta), \Diamond \delta,$$
$$\rho \wedge \neg \delta \wedge \Box \neg v(\rho, \delta), \Box \neg v(\rho, \delta)\}$$
$$s_3 = \{\Diamond \delta, \Box \neg v(\rho, \delta)\}$$
$$s_4 = \{\Diamond \delta, \delta, \Box \neg v(\rho, \delta)\}$$
$$s_5 = \{\Box \neg v(\rho, \delta)\}$$

Fig. 2. A Büchi automaton for $O(\rho < \delta)$

from the norms by creating an automaton (which, in fact, is a general, canonical-like model of the norms, since it represents all LTL sequences satisfying that set of norms) by means of the procedure described above. However, building an automaton on basis of the logical representation of the norms gives a model of the norms that also includes the LTL sequences where (one of the) norms have been violated, since the violation of a norm is just as much a part of the logical representation because of its prescriptive nature (norms express what should be, not what is). Instead, we are more interested in only those LTL sequences where the norms hold but are not violated, since these sequences characterise the patterns that we want to capture in the protocol that we are creating. In case of our example, this means we need to build an automaton for the formula $O(\rho < \delta) \wedge \Box \neg v(\rho, \delta)$. The resulting automaton A_φ, generated by the procedure described above, is shown in figure 2. The alphabet of the automaton is taken as $\Sigma_\varphi = 2^{\{\rho, \delta, v(\rho, \delta)\}}$, the states $s_1, \ldots, s_5 \subseteq 2^{cl(\varphi)}$ (parts of the state labels are given in figure 2), the starting states of the automaton are s_1 and s_2, and the acceptance set is defined as $\mathcal{F}_\varphi = \{\{s_4, s_5\}, \{s_2, s_4, s_5\}\}$.

As can be seen, this automaton exactly represents our intuition of a deadline (as expressed in LTL logics). All LTL sequences satisfying a deadline, should have a number of states (possibly zero) in which nothing interesting happens (this is represented in state s_1). Then a state occurs where ρ holds (state s_2), after which, one or more states later, δ holds (the intermediate states are represented in state s_3, the state where δ occurs is represented in state s_4). After the obligation has been fulfilled (δ has happened, while ρ happened one or more states before δ), an infinite sequence of states occurs where anything can happen as long as $v(\rho, \delta)$ does not happen; this is represented in state s_5 (since no more restrictions are posed on ρ and δ, they can hold in any order at any state after the deadline has been fulfilled). Note that, as required, none of the states satisfy $v(\rho, \delta)$. To fulfil the Büchi acceptance condition the sequences before ρ has happened (i.e. the transition from s_1 to s_1), and the sequence before δ happens (i.e. the transition from s_3 to s_3), can only be of finite length, the only infinite recursion in this automaton is the transition from s_5 to itself.

After translating the norms to a Büchi automaton we can extract a regular expression characterising the language expressed by the automaton. The idea is that the main characteristics, the basic landmark structure, obtained from the norms that are represented in the Büchi automaton, can be easily extracted through this regular expression.

Büchi automata accept a specific type of regular languages, namely ω-regular languages (or ω-languages, see [16,15]) The major difference between these ω-languages and regular languages is, like the difference between Büchi automata and normal finite automata, that ω-languages are composed of infinite sequences (ω-words), where regular languages only contain finite words (the sequences are of finite length). The following property of Büchi automata, taken from [6] then expresses the language recognised by a Büchi automaton A.

Theorem 2. *An ω-language $L_\omega \subseteq \Sigma^\omega$ is Büchi recognisable iff L is a finite union of sets $U.V^\omega$ where $U, V \subseteq \Sigma^*$ are regular sets of finite words.*

The representation of the ω-languages by $L_\omega = \bigcup_{i=1}^n U_i.V_i^\omega$, where U_i, V_i are given by regular expressions, is called an ω-regular expression.

For the automaton presented in figure 2, we can express the accepted language by the following ω-regular expression (we use *all* to denote $(\varnothing + \rho + \delta + \rho\delta)$)

$$L_\omega(A_\varphi) = \varnothing^*.\rho.all^*.(\delta + \rho\delta).all^\omega.$$

As can be easily seen from this ω-regular expression, the points of interest of every LTL sequence satisfying φ are the state where ρ holds and the state where either δ or $\rho\delta$ holds (the former being the state where $\delta \wedge \neg\rho \wedge \neg v(\rho, \delta)$ holds, the latter where $\delta \wedge \rho \wedge \neg v(\rho, \delta)$ holds). As seen in the expression, confirming the intuition about deadlines, all LTL sequences satisfying $O(\rho < \delta)$ have a state where ρ holds (possibly preceded by a number of states where neither ρ nor δ hold), which always happens before a state occurs where δ holds (the ω-regular expression allows a number of states, possibly zero, between the occurrence of ρ and δ, in which ρ may occur as well). The fact that the state where δ should hold is denoted in the expression as $\delta + \rho\delta$ is mainly because, since the restriction of ρ at least happening before δ has already been met, at this point it does not really matter whether ρ holds or not (basically, the transition label $\delta + \rho\delta$ expresses no information concerning ρ or $\neg\rho$, but expresses that *at least* δ holds).

Given that we can deduce from the label $\delta + \rho\delta$ that at least δ holds, we can simplify the regular expression to the following landmark pattern

$$\mathfrak{L}_\varphi = \langle \{\rho, \delta\}, \{\rho \leq \delta\} \rangle$$

This is the normative landmark pattern extracted from the norms of the domain (just $O(\rho < \delta)$ in this case). This landmark pattern is the basis of the landmark pattern that we construct to create protocols. The landmark pattern will now be extended with additional landmarks to denote domain-specific information and information to increase the efficiency and feasibility of the pattern.

4   Strengthening the Pattern

Earlier we mentioned that the landmarks, used as an intermediate level between the norms and the practice, add extra information to the norms to bridge the gap between the norms and the protocols. Using the "skeleton" landmark pattern extracted from the norms, as presented above, we extend this normative landmark pattern with additional landmarks (and orderings) to create a landmark pattern that expresses both normative and efficiency restrictions that the protocol must satisfy.

This would mean that the landmark pattern for our example domain, $\mathfrak{L}_\varphi$, is extended with additional landmarks and orderings. The additional landmarks are, in fact, filling in the "gaps" between the normative landmarks in the ω-regular expression of this normative domain, $L_\omega(A) = \varnothing^*.\rho.all^*.(\delta + \rho\delta).all^\omega$. We will show that adding these additional landmarks creates a new ω-regular expression that represents a language L'_ω that is accepted by A_φ if the alphabet of A_φ is extended accordingly. Note, though, that this does not count as a one-one relation, as the adapted automaton accepts more words than just those expressed in L'_ω (though still satisfying only the LTL sequences that satisfy φ). Meaning, the automaton A'_φ, which is the adaptation of A_φ, accepts words that are not included in L'_ω. We do not intent to built a new automaton that exactly matches the restrictions in the extended landmark pattern, but just to show that the new landmark pattern is an instantiation of the normative landmark pattern (i.e. the extended landmark pattern is a special case of the normative landmark pattern).

Let us assume that a landmark γ can be added to the normative landmark pattern, between ρ and δ, to increase efficiency. The landmark pattern resulting from this addition would be

$$\mathfrak{L}'_\varphi = \langle \{\rho, \delta, \gamma\}, \{\rho \leq \gamma, \gamma \leq \delta, \rho \leq \delta\} \rangle.$$

By extending the ω-regular expression from the normative landmark pattern in a similar way, we can show that the (slightly changed) automaton A'_φ accepts the words represented by this pattern, thus reinforcing that the extended landmark pattern is still compliant to the norms. This extended ω-regular expression is the following

$$L'_\omega(A'_\varphi) = \varnothing^*.\rho.(\varnothing + \rho + \gamma + \rho\gamma)^*.(\gamma + \rho\gamma).all^*.(\delta + \rho\delta).all^\omega.{}^2$$

The change to the automaton A_φ to create A'_φ that accepts words from this language, is merely the addition of γ to the alphabet (if the alphabet of the automaton does not contain γ it can never accept words that include γ). This change also means that the labels of the transitions of the automaton are changed. Basically, we re-run the procedure presented above to create an automaton for φ

---

[2] Note that the first intuition of this ω-regular expression, being $\varnothing^*.\rho.all^*.\gamma.all^*.(\delta + \rho\delta).all^\omega$, is not correct, due to the fact that it allows δ to appear before γ appears (remember that $all = (\varnothing + \rho + \delta + \rho\delta)$).

over an alphabet $\Sigma'_\varphi = 2^{\{\rho,\delta,\gamma,v(\rho,\delta)\}}$, however, since we did not add any information to the formula φ that has to be satisfied by the sequences of A'_φ, nothing changes in the structure of A'_φ (no new states or transitions are added), we only added a proposition of which no restrictions are given (i.e. γ can be true or false in any state of the LTL sequences, or, no information about the truthvalue of γ is given in any of the states of the automaton).

The relations that the additional landmarks express are not incorporated in the automaton A'_φ and if one would want these restrictions to be expressed in A'_φ, the procedure presented above can be run on an adapted formula φ' that expresses, next to the norms, these restrictions. However, for the purpose that we expressed in section 2, it is enough to proceed as presented above, i.e. only check whether the extended landmark pattern is still compliant to the norms.

4.1   Landmarks to Protocols

Given that the landmark pattern expresses states that should be achieved, it can be viewed as a collection of goals and the order in which these goals must be achieved. A translation from a landmark pattern to a basic, prototypical protocol is then achieved by means of use of *seeing to it that* operators (*stit*) [5]. While the *stit* operator ignores the means by which an agent will bring about a state of affairs, it does provide the link to make states (the landmarks) into procedural goals. It is then possible to create a protocol given this specification of goals (while retaining the order in which they should be achieved) by linking these goals to the capabilities of agents via a planning algorithm, e.g. like STRIPS [10].

Let us illustrate this by means of our example, where it means that the landmark pattern $\mathcal{L}'_\varphi = \langle \{\rho, \delta, \gamma\}, \{\rho \leq \gamma, \gamma \leq \delta, \rho \leq \delta\} \rangle$ is translated to an ordering of goals, represented as a sequence of (still abstract) actions: $(stit\,\rho)$; $(stit\,\gamma)$; $(stit\,\delta)$, thus expressing that it should be the case that ρ is achieved first, then γ and finally δ. The capabilities of the agents in the domain can then be used to expand this action sequence composed of abstract actions (which abstracts from the means necessary to achieve the expressed goals) to a full protocol (again, expressed as a sequence of actions). For this example, let us assume that the agents have the following capabilities (we use a "STRIPS-like" representation of the agents capabilities, by expressing the necessary pre-conditions and post-conditions of the actions, such a definition of an agent's capabilities is found in, for example, the 3APL agent programming language, [7]):

$$Op(\text{Action} : action_1, \text{ Effect} : \rho)$$
$$Op(\text{Action} : action_2, \text{ Precond} : \rho, \text{ Effect} : \eta)$$
$$Op(\text{Action} : action_3, \text{ Precond} : \eta, \text{ Effect} : \gamma)$$
$$Op(\text{Action} : action_4, \text{ Precond} : \gamma, \text{ Effect} : \delta)$$

Using these capabilities, we can use the planning algorithm to expand the abstract protocol $(stit\,\rho)$; $(stit\,\gamma)$; $(stit\,\delta)$ to the following full protocol.

$$action_1 \,;\, action_2 \,;\, action_3 \,;\, action_4$$

It might be possible that a landmark expresses a state that is not reachable by a single agent alone; a cooperation of agents might be needed to achieve (parts of) the landmark pattern. In this case, methods for designing interaction patterns between agents, such as the ones in OPERA, [9], can be applied to create the necessary interaction protocols for reaching those complex goals.

5 Example

Let us look at an example to show the entire process described in the previous sections. For simplicity reasons and due to space limitations we only show how the technique presented above works with a single norm. For a more in depth view of using multiple norms, or the creation of protocols involving multiple agents, we refer to [2].

The example we use here is based on the domain of organ transplantation. The task at hand, that should be achieved by the protocol, is to assign organs that have just become available (a suitable donor has been found, i.e. a patient who made a statement to permit post-mortem liver transplantation has died). This task, *assign_organ*, is the goal of the protocol that has to be achieved while keeping in mind the restrictions given by the norms of the domain. We assume that there exist one norm for this task (from the Dutch law on organ transplantations):

> Before an organ is removed, death is certified by a professional doctor in accordance with the latest medically valid methods and criteria for determining brain death.

We represent this norm as the following (LTL) formula:

$$O(certify\_death < remove\_organ)$$

Naturally, there exist a precedence ordering between the *remove_organ* state and the *assign_organ* state (one cannot assign organs before extraction). Since we use *assign_organ* as the ultimate goal state, we need to model this ordering as well:

$$\neg assign\_organ \textbf{ until } remove\_organ \land \Diamond assign\_organ$$

This formula expresses that $\neg assign\_organ$ necessarily holds up to the point at which *remove_organ* holds, after which, at some moment, *assign_organ* will hold. Combined with the norm specified above, this gives us the LTL formula ψ that restricts the domain, and needs to be converted to a landmark pattern:

$$\psi \equiv O(certify\_death < remove\_organ) \land$$
$$\neg assign\_organ \textbf{ until } remove\_organ \land \Diamond assign\_organ$$

The Büchi automaton A_ψ resulting from the translation of this set of norms is shown in figure 3 below (we abbreviate *remove_organ* to ρ, *assign_organ* to α and *certify_death* to γ). The acceptance condition of A_ψ is given as the set $\mathscr{F}_\psi = \{\{s_6, s_7\}, \{s_4, s_5, s_6, s_7\}, \{s_2, s_4, s_5, s_6, s_7\}\}$.

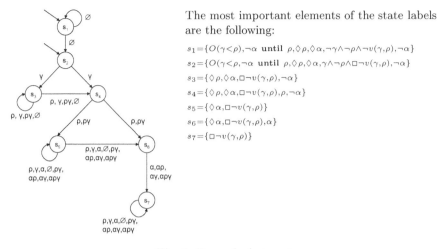

The most important elements of the state labels are the following:

$s_1 = \{O(\gamma < \rho), \neg \alpha$ **until** $\rho, \Diamond \rho, \Diamond \alpha, \neg \gamma \wedge \neg \rho \wedge \neg v(\gamma, \rho), \neg \alpha\}$

$s_2 = \{O(\gamma < \rho, \neg \alpha$ **until** $\rho, \Diamond \rho, \Diamond \alpha, \gamma \wedge \neg \rho \wedge \Box \neg v(\gamma, \rho), \neg \alpha\}$

$s_3 = \{\Diamond \rho, \Diamond \alpha, \Box \neg v(\gamma, \rho), \neg \alpha\}$

$s_4 = \{\Diamond \rho, \Diamond \alpha, \Box \neg v(\gamma, \rho), \rho, \neg \alpha\}$

$s_5 = \{\Diamond \alpha, \Box \neg v(\gamma, \rho)\}$

$s_6 = \{\Diamond \alpha, \Box \neg v(\gamma, \rho), \alpha\}$

$s_7 = \{\Box \neg v(\gamma, \rho)\}$

Fig. 3. Example Automaton

Using the automaton of figure 3 we create an ω-regular expression to describe the language accepted by the automaton. This ω-regular expression captures all the important features of the LTL structures of ψ that are represented in A_ψ. We abbreviate $(\rho + \gamma + \alpha + \varnothing + \rho\gamma + \alpha\rho + \alpha\gamma + \alpha\rho\gamma)$ to *all* (it denotes that everything but $v(\gamma, \rho)$ can hold at that moment). Note that the expression allows for multiple occurrences of γ, ρ and α (although they need to occur in a particular order), i.e. words like $\rho.\gamma\rho.\alpha\rho.\alpha^\omega$ are accepted by the automaton, while, in practice, only one occurrence of each of these states is more likely; e.g. after the death of the patient has been certified, it will not have to be done again (for that same patient). Basically, the practice that we are trying to model is best described by the ω-expression: $\varnothing^*.\gamma.\varnothing^*.\rho.\varnothing^*.\alpha.\varnothing^\omega$. This, however, is not a weakness of the technique we are describing here, but merely a weakness of the LTL representation that we used. Since we have not specified in our LTL representation that the states will only happen once, they *can* happen multiple times. The LTL representation only models the restrictions on the ordering of the state occurrences.

$$\varnothing^*.\gamma.(\rho + \gamma + \rho\gamma + \varnothing)^*.(\rho + \rho\gamma).all^*.(\alpha + \alpha\rho + \alpha\gamma + \alpha\gamma\rho).all^\omega$$

From this ω-regular expression we can derive the following (normative) landmark pattern (remember that $\rho + \gamma\rho$ denotes that *at least* ρ should hold, and that $\alpha + \alpha\rho + \alpha\gamma + \alpha\gamma\rho$ denotes that *at least* α holds):

$$\mathfrak{L}'_\psi = \langle \{\gamma, \rho, \alpha\}, \{\gamma \leq \rho, \rho \leq \alpha\}\rangle$$

Using knowledge from the domain we strengthen the landmark pattern with additional landmarks. In this case, we use the knowledge that before the assignment the compatibility between the organ and the donor must be checked, e.g. to see if the blood type of the donor and the recipient match. To increase the efficiency of the assigning, we can check the blood of the donor when the death has been certified (*check_bloodtype*, shortened as β), giving us the following landmark pattern:

$$\mathfrak{L}_\psi = \langle \{\gamma, \rho, \alpha, \beta\}, \{\gamma \leq \rho, \rho \leq \alpha, \gamma \leq \beta, \beta \leq \rho\} \rangle$$

The last step of the process is converting the landmark pattern to a basic, prototypical protocol, using *stit* operators: $stit(\gamma); stit(\beta); stit(\rho); stit(\alpha)$, which is then translated, by using the capabilities of the agents, to a protocol:

> *execute_brain_death_protocol* ; *take_blood_sample* ;
> *test_blood(bloodtype)* ; *start_operation* ; *remove_organ* ;
> *assign_organ(patient, bloodtype)* ; *operate(patient)*

This protocol can be used as a basic pattern for agents that have to fulfil the norm that we started out with. Of course it can still be extended with extra actions to provide for specific situations.

6 Conclusion

In this paper we have described a procedure to derive a basic protocol from norms described as obligations with deadlines. This procedure can be used to provide protocols for e-institutions governed by norms such that agents that follow these protocols will always fulfil all the norms of the e-institution.

We have not shown in this paper how the process can be conducted using multiple norms. Basically, this process is a very simple extension of the above described procedure. The different norms are all described in LTL. We can combine the norms in LTL by just taking the conjunction of them. If more knowledge is available on the relation between the norms that is not explicit in the norms themselves this can also be added in the LTL description. Often this amounts to temporal orderings between deadlines of the norms that derive from common-sense knowledge. E.g. asking consent for organ donation from family of a donor should be done after the donor has died (not before). The resulting formula can then be processed as before again.

Another point that we could not expose in depth due to space limitations is the construction of a protocol involving multiple parties. Mainly what comes out of the procedure above is a set of states that should be reached by the agents. If a state can only be reached by a coordinated action of several agents we can use techniques from MAS planning to create an interaction pattern to reach that state. Although not at all trivial we assume that existing techniques suffice to bridge this gap.

Finally, we have not formally shown that the resulting protocols indeed satisfy the norms. This can be done by verifying that the protocol will never lead to a violation state. In [1] it has been shown that it is indeed possible to perform this exercise, therewith ensuring the correctness of the complete procedure.

References

1. Aldewereld, H., Dignum, F., Meyer, J.-J.C., Vázquez-Salceda, J.: Proving norm compliancy of protocols in electronic institutions. Technical Report UU-CS-2005-010, Utrecht University (2005)
2. Aldewereld, H.: Autonomy vs. Conformity: An Institutional Perspective on Norms and Protocols. PhD thesis, Universiteit Utrecht (2007)
3. Aldewereld, H., Grossi, D., Vázquez-Salceda, J., Dignum, F.: Designing normative behaviour via landmarks. In: Bossier, O., et al. (eds.) Coordination, Organisation, Institutions and Norms in Agent Systems I, pp. 150–162. Springer, Heidelberg (2006)
4. Anderson, A.R.: A reduction of deontic logic to alethic modal logic. Mind 67, 100–103 (1958)
5. Belnap, N., Perloff, M.: Seeing to it that: A canonical form for agentives. Theoria 54, 175–199 (1988)
6. Büchi, J.R.: On a decision method in restricted second order arithmetic. In: Proceedings of the 1960 International Conference on Logic, Methodology and Philosophy of Science, pp. 1–11. Stanford University Press, Stanford (1962)
7. Dastani, M., van Riemsdijk, B., Meyer, J.-J.C.: Programming multi-agent systems in 3apl. In: Bordini, R.H., et al. (eds.) Multi-Agent Programming: Languages, Platforms and Applications, Springer, Berlin (2005)
8. Dignum, F., Broersen, J., Dignum, V., Meyer, J.-J.C.: Meeting the deadline: Why, when and how. In: 3rd Goddard Workshop on Formal Approaches to Agent-Based Systems (FAABS), Maryland (April 2004)
9. Dignum, V.: A Model for Organizational Interaction: Based on Agents, Founded in Logic. PhD thesis, Universiteit Utrecht, The Netherlands (2004)
10. Fikes, R., Nilsson, N.J.: Strips: A new approach to the application of theorem proving to problem solving. Artificial Intelligence 2(3/4), 189–208 (1971)
11. Holzmann, G.J.: The model checker spin. IEEE Transactions On Software Engineering 23(5), 279 (1997)
12. López y López, F., Luck, M.: Towards a model of the dynamics of normative multi-agent systems. In: Lindemann, G., Moldt, D., Paolucci, M. (eds.) RASTA 2002. LNCS (LNAI), vol. 2934, pp. 175–194. Springer, Heidelberg (2004)
13. P. Noriega. Agent-Mediated Auctions: The Fishmarket Metaphor. PhD thesis, Inst. d'Investigació en Intel.ligència Artificial (1997)
14. Rodriguez, J.A.: On the Design and Construction of Agent-mediated Electronic Institutions. PhD thesis, Inst. d'Investigació en Intel.ligència Artificial (2001)
15. Staiger, L.: ω-languages. In: Rozenberg, G., Salomaa, A. (eds.) Handbook of Formal Languages, vol. 3, pp. 339–387. Springer-Verlag, Berlin (1997)
16. Thomas, W.: Automata on infinite objects. In: van Leeuwen, J. (ed.) Handbook of Theoretical Computer Science, ch. 4, vol. B, Elsevier Science Publishers, Amsterdam (1990)
17. Wolper, P.: Constructing Automata from Temporal Logic Formulas: A Tutorial. In: Brinksma, E., Hermanns, H., Katoen, J.-P. (eds.) EEF School 2000 and FMPA 2000. LNCS, vol. 2090, pp. 261–277. Springer, Heidelberg (2001)

Interoperability for Bayesian Agents in the Semantic Web

Elder Rizzon Santos, Moser Silva Fagundes, and Rosa Maria Vicari

Instituto de Informática - Universidade Federal do Rio Grande do Sul (UFRGS)
Po. B 15.064 - 91.501-970 - Porto Alegre - RS - Brazil
Tel.:/Fax:+55 51 33166161
{ersantos,msfagundes,rosa}@inf.ufrgs.br

Abstract. This paper presents an ontology-based approach to promote the interoperability among agents that represent their knowledge through Bayesian networks. This research relies on Semantic Web foundations to achieve knowledge interoperability in the context of multiagent systems. Our first step was the specification of an ontology that formalizes the structures of the Bayesian network representation. It was developed using OWL, which is a W3C recommendation for ontology language. Once handled the issue of the knowledge representation, we specify how a Bayesian agent operates such representation. Thus, we define a model of internal architecture to support Bayesian agents in the knowledge sharing and maintenance tasks. The utilization of the architecture is exemplified through a case study developed in the context of a multiagent educational portal (PortEdu). The case study demonstrates the interoperability resulted from the architecture integration with Bayesian agents hosted in PortEdu.

Keywords: Semantic Web, Ontology, Interoperability, Bayesian Networks, Agent Architecture.

1 Introduction

Studies on interoperability on the context of Artificial Intelligence have been done mostly for the communication among intelligent agents [1,2]. Today, such researches can be applied for the development of the Semantic Web [3], which is the mainstream on Internet technology. The purpose of the Semantic Web is to aggregate meaning to web pages, in a way that not only humans, but also computer software may interpret its content. Considering the Semantic Web as an open system, populated by autonomous agents carrying out activities in behalf of its owners, interoperability issues (i.e. how these agents from different domains and with different goals will share their knowledge, co-operate and maximize the utility of the whole system) arise.

This paper presents an agent architecture that allows the interoperability of knowledge among Bayesian agents. We consider Bayesian agents those that have their knowledge expressed through Bayesian networks. The fact that the

M. Dastani et al.(Eds.): ProMAS 2007, LNAI 4908, pp. 73–88, 2008.
© Springer-Verlag Berlin Heidelberg 2008

agents use the same knowledge representation (i.e. Bayesian networks) does not guarantee that it is implemented in an interoperable way.

Our case study is contextualized in a multiagent system (MAS) that supports agent-based educational systems. This MAS, called PortEdu [4], is a FIPA (Foundation for Intelligent Physical Agents) [2] compliant agent platform that provides infrastructure and services for the systems in the portal. One of these services is provided by the Social Agent [5], responsible for organizing the users in groups considering cognitive and emotional aspects. Such social aspects are represented by the agent as Bayesian networks. The case study consists in applying the proposed architecture in the Social Agent.

The interoperability core relies on the specified ontology for Bayesian networks. Ontologies are used to provide means to formalize concepts and the relationships among them, allowing agents to interpret their meaning flexibly and unambiguously [6]. In open systems, such as the Semantic Web, it is necessary to have a standard way to communicate the knowledge. The W3C (World Wide Web Consortium) is developing a set of recommendations to deal with this issue. One of them is OWL (Web Ontology Language) [7,8]. It is designed specifically for the purpose of knowledge communication in the Semantic Web. Currently, it is considered the standard for content languages to be adopted in the Semantic Web. Relying on a standard for communication solves an important interoperability issue, the agreement on a well defined and common language.

The remaining of this paper is organized as follows: section 2 presents the related researches; section 3 specifies the Bayesian network ontology; in section 4 we describe the Bayesian agent internal architecture to interoperability; section 5 presents the application of the architecture on the social agent; and in section 6 it is presented our conclusions and future work.

2   Related Research

BayesOWL [9] was developed to handle the issue of automatic ontology mapping. This approach defines additional markups that can add probabilities to concepts, individuals, properties and its relationships. It also defines a set of translation rules to convert the probabilistic annotated ontology into a Bayesian network. The focus on ontology mapping limits the BayesOWL markups since it was not necessary to represent variables with states different than true or false. The reason for this is that the probabilistic knowledge associated with each ontology concept was used only for

Another approach that represents probabilistic knowledge through OWL is PR-OWL [10]. Its goal is to provide a framework for probabilistic ontologies. It constitutes an extension of OWL to express probabilistic knowledge. The PR-OWL language adds new definitions to OWL allowing the expression of uncertainty. The need for standardization represents a drawback for short-term solutions but also points to a very interesting medium to long term solution, as it fits well (providing the formal foundation of a first-order logic) in the W3C model of standards.

The objective of [11] is to provide the necessary structure to share Petri nets on the Semantic Web context. This work reviews previous efforts done in Petri net sharing and Petri net formalizations. Then, it specifies a Petri net ontology using OWL language. Another work concerning Petri net representation is [12]. Its main goal is the understanding of the model executability. In order to achieve this goal, it discusses Petri net related concepts, classifying them in static or dynamic. The final result is a three level Petri net metamodel. The first level is the definition metamodel that specifies the static part of the nets. The second level defines a particular situation of a Petri net. The third level is an execution metamodel that defines a sequence of situations.

Agent communication issues regarding probabilities are addressed in [13], where is presented PACL (Probabilistic Agent Communication Language). It is an extension of the FIPA-ACL designed to deal with the communication of probabilistic knowledge. PACL specifies new communication axioms that are necessary to model the probabilistic communication. Besides the axioms, the language also designs assertive and directive probabilistic speech acts, which extends FIPA-ACL. The PACL language provides a way to communicate probabilistic knowledge extending FIPA-ACL and allowing more expressiveness to this language. It does not deals with the communication of uncertainty at the message content level, concerning how different Bayesian agents might exchange knowledge regarding their networks and evidences.

In [14] it is described an approach to promote interoperability providing a conversion engine based on OWL. The work defines an ontology that covers elementary aspects necessary to construct Bayesian networks individuals, but it does not formalizes the Bayesian network knowledge representation. The conversion engine uses the ontology to automatically generate individuals from a Bayesian network implementation following a standard format. The resulting knowledge base is part of an architecture to promote interoperability for a specific agent.

3 Bayesian Network Ontology

One of the contributions of this research is the specification of an ontology to formalize the Bayesian network knowledge representation. Our ontology specification extends the concepts defined in [14], allowing a broader utilization of the ontology. In our case, the ontology is used to allow heterogeneous agents to communicate their Bayesian network knowledge (note that even if the representations of the agents are Bayesian networks, it still does not guarantee that they can communicate it). One way to deal with this issue complying with current standards is to use an OWL ontology. Sections 4 and 5 describe how the ontology presented here is used to deal with interoperability issues.

In the following sub-sections we provide a detailed description of the developed ontology to represent Bayesian knowledge. First, we present the common concepts among different probabilistic networks and a specialization of this knowledge presenting the discrete Bayesian network definitions. Then, we detail the evidence-related concepts and their relation to the evolution of the Bayesian network individuals.

The figures in this section illustrates concept maps of the classes specified in the ontology. This graphical representation provides a way to visualize the classes (depicted as rectangles) and the relationship among them (illustrated as arrows).

3.1   Probabilistic Network Concepts

Probabilistic networks are graphical models of causal interactions among a set of variables, where the variables are represented as nodes of a graph and the interactions as directed arcs between nodes [15].

A graph is the basic structure shared between probabilistic network models. It is formalized in the ontology by the *Graph* class (Figure 1a). The *Probabilistic-Network* class (Figure 1b) represents a probabilistic network and it is a subclass of *Graph*. The *ProbabilisticNetwork* class models common aspects among variations in this kind of knowledge representation (i.e. Bayesian networks, influence diagrams and object-oriented probabilistic networks). Those common elements are the directed arcs and the nodes, respectively referenced by the inherited properties *hasArc* and *hasNode*. The *hasArc* property is semantically restricted to reference only *DirectedArc* class individuals.

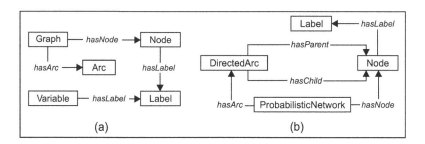

Fig. 1. (a) Graph and (b) Probabilistic Network representations

To specify the direct link between a parent and a child node we define the *DirectedArc* class, a specialization of the *Arc* class. Such link is represented through the properties *hasChild* and *hasParent* of the arc class. The value of these properties is an individual of the *Node* class.

Another general concept concerning probabilistic networks is defined by the *Variable* class. It represents a set of mutually exclusive states. The states, also called events or choices, correspond to the domain of the variable, which can be discrete or continuous. In this work we consider only discrete variables (finite sets). A probabilistic network has two categories of variable: chance variables, representing random states, and decision variables, representing choices controlled by some agent.

3.2   Discrete Bayesian Network Concepts

A discrete Bayesian network consists of a DAG (Directed Acyclic Graph) and a set of conditional probability distributions [16]. Each node in the network, called chance node, corresponds to exactly one discrete random variable which has a finite set of mutually exclusive states. The directed arcs specify the causal relation between the random variables. Each random variable associated with a chance node has a conditional probability distribution.

The *BayesianNetwork* class (Figure 2) is the core of our Bayesian network definition. It is a subclass of *ProbabilisticNetwork*. The differences among the classes are the semantic constraints imposed to the properties to specify the correct type of nodes and arcs allowed in a Bayesian network. Such kinds of nodes and arcs are represented by the *ChanceNode* and *BayesianArc* classes respectively.

A *BayesianArc* individual defines a link between two chance nodes. It imposes constraints to formalize that only individuals of the *ChanceNode* class can be assigned to these properties. A *ChanceNode* individual has a chance variable associated to its definition. This property allows only individuals of the classes *PriorChanceVariable* and *ConditionalChanceVariable*. Such constraint is necessary in order to differentiate prior nodes variables from non-prior nodes.

Before defining a chance variable it is necessary to define a state and its related concepts (Figure 3). A state is represented by the *State* class, which has only the *hasLabel* property responsible for the node identification. The *State* class has two direct subclasses. The first denotes a chance associated with a state and it is called *StateProbability*. The second specialization is named *ConditionalState* and it specifies the multiple conditional chances associated with a state. A set of *ConditionalState* individuals constitutes a Conditional Probability Table (CPT).

The *ConditionProbability* class represents the conditional chances associated with a state. This class is defined by the *probability* and the *hasCondition* properties. The former is a float data type property that represents the numerical *probability* of a variable's state under the conditions specified in the *hasCondition* property. This property references multiple individuals of the *Condition* class, and it denotes the conditions imposed in the probability of a state. The *Condition* class is constituted by a conditioning node and a state of this node, respectively referenced by the properties *hasNode* and *hasState*. The individual referenced by the *hasNode* property must be a *ChanceNode* since only chance

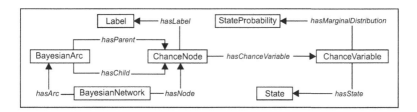

Fig. 2. Bayesian Network representation

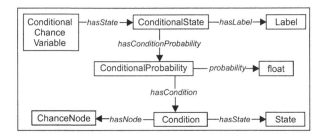

Fig. 3. Conditional Probability Table representation

nodes have random variables. The *hasState* property references an individual of the *State* class that indicates the specific state of the conditioning chance variable.

The *ChanceVariable* class is a specialization of *Variable* and it represents a chance variable. Additionally to the inherited properties from the *Variable* class, it specifies the *hasState* and *hasMarginalDistribution* properties. The first specifies the necessity of at least one state (represented by *State* individuals) associated with a variable (i.e. true or false in the context of a boolean variable). The second property represents the computed marginal distribution for the chance variable, and it references multiple *StateProbability* individuals. Each individual represents a state and its computed chance of occurrence.

It was necessary to differentiate prior node variables from non-prior ones, since a non-prior node has a CPT, and a prior node has only states and probabilities without conditioning variables. Thus, the classes *PriorChanceVariable* and *ConditionalChanceVariable* were created as subclasses of *ChanceVariable*. The difference between these two subclasses lies in the *hasState* property constraint. In the *PriorChanceVariable* class the *hasState* property has been restricted and it can reference only *StateProbability* individuals. As stated earlier, a state probability represents a state and its chance of occurrence. The set of *StateProbability* individuals referenced by the *hasState* property denotes all possible states associated with a prior chance variable. The *hasState* property of *ConditionalChance-Variable* class has also been constrained and only *ConditionalState* individuals can be assigned to it. The *ConditionalState* individuals represent a Conditional Probability Table of a variable associated with a non-prior node.

The *hasLabel*, a common property among *Node*, *Variable* and *State* concepts, has as default value a *Label* class individual. The *Label* class is composed just by a string indicating the label name. However, the *hasLabel* property is also able to indicate individuals of other classes, which enables the developers to add semantics to those concepts.

3.3   Situation Concepts

In our definition, a situation is a particular configuration that a probabilistic network assumes given a set (possibly empty) of evidences of events occurrence.

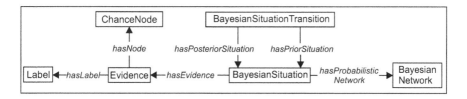

Fig. 4. Situation representation

When the evidences of events are reflected in the network, a new situation arises. Such situations are useful to keep the history of modifications of a Bayesian network. The Figure 4 depicts the situation related concepts.

An evidence, represented by the *Evidence* class, corresponds to any information regarding the state of a variable from a probabilistic network. The *Evidence* class is composed by a node, a label and a chance, represented by properties *hasNode*, *hasLabel* and *probability*, respectively. The *hasNode* property can reference only individuals of the *ChanceNode* class, since chance nodes are the only kind of node that represent random events. In order to specify a hard evidence (an observation of an event), we specialize the *Evidence* class creating the *HardEvidence* class. This class specifies a constraint defining that the *probability* property must assume the numeric value one.

A situation, represented by the *Situation* class, has two properties. The first is the *hasProbabilisticNetwork* property used to reference the network individual whose configuration corresponds to the given situation. The second property is the *hasEvidence* that corresponds to the set of evidences that originates the situation. A particular kind of situation is represented by the *BayesianSituation* class. Its inherited *hasProbabilisticNetwork* property can reference only Bayesian networks.

In order to establish a link between two sequential situations we created a class named *SituationTransition*. This class is described by *hasPriorSituation* property and *hasPosteriorSituation* property, which represents a prior and a posterior situation, respectively. A situation transition between Bayesian networks is represented in the class *BayesianSituationTransition*. This class inherits the properties from *SituationTransition* and restricts them specifying that they can only reference *BayesianSituation* individuals.

4   Bayesian Agent Internal Architecture

The main goal of our agent architecture is to enhance the interoperability of Bayesian network knowledge among agents. The interoperability is achieved by an ontology-based approach to represent the uncertain knowledge of the agent. There are several levels of interoperability to be achieved, especially in agent communication. Adopting the current agent development standard, FIPA, communication issues such as agent language and protocols are solved. To allow a broader use of the standard the content language was not standardized. They do provide a content language, FIPA-SL, but its utilization is not mandatory.

Our approach uses OWL, which could be considered a knowledge representation standard, developed in the semantic web context. By adopting OWL as a content language we aim to provide interoperability at the semantic level (in our context, this means allowing heterogeneous agents to exchange their knowledge, expressed through Bayesian networks). The architecture presented in this section shows a possible way to integrate an ontology-based knowledge base into an agent, aiming to improve its interoperability. Following, we detail the agents' internal architecture, depicted in the Figure 5.

It is necessary to differentiate the architecture components from the agent implementation specific ones. The architecture components are represented in the figure by the gray elements. The *Agent Implementation Specific Components* are represented in the figure by the white element. They are not specified by this architecture since they relate to the particular purpose of each agent design. However, we specify the way they interact with the architecture components. Usually, the *Agent Implementation Specific Components* define the manner that the agent reasons about its goals and how it achieves them (i.e. planning and goal deliberation).

4.1 Architecture Components

The first component of the architecture is the *Perception Handler*, which receives and forwards the perceptions to the respective components capable of interpreting them. The characteristics of a perception (metadata) are taken into account to decide which component will receive it. Since in the context of this work we are dealing with interoperability among Bayesian agents, we focus on two particular categories of perception: *Bayesian Network Knowledge* and *Query*. The first corresponds to individuals of the ontology presented in the Section 3. The perceptions of this category are forwarded to the *Knowledge Base (KB) Update* component. The second corresponds to queries about the agent's knowledge that are forwarded to the *KB Query* component.

The second component of the architecture is the *KB Update*. Its purpose is to evaluate the incoming OWL *Bayesian Network Knowledge*, and insert the selected ones in the knowledge base as individuals of the Bayesian network ontology. The information to be inserted is selected following the criteria defined by the designer. A simple implementation of this component performs insertions in the KB without restrictions. A more sophisticated implementation interacts with the *KB Query* component to retrieve already inserted Bayesian information to constrain the information to be inserted.

Our knowledge base is constituted by the Bayesian network ontology, detailed in the Section 3, and its individuals. It stores the Bayesian networks situations, the transitions between situations and the evidences. The base can contain multiple different Bayesian networks. Any modification in a Bayesian network characterizes a new situation, and the sequence of situations represents a history of a network. The history may be useful for an agent planning, in example.

In order to perform probabilistic reasoning in the Bayesian networks stored in the knowledge base, we specify the *Bayesian Inference* component. Its inputs

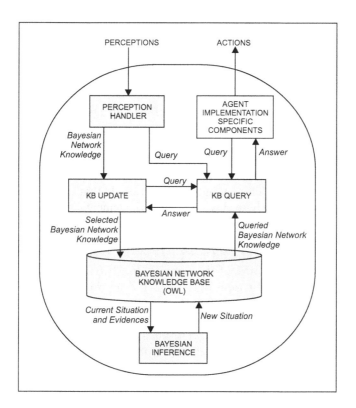

Fig. 5. Bayesian Agent Internal Architecture

are the *Current Situation* of a Bayesian network and a set of *Evidences*. The *Bayesian Inference* output is the *New Situation* with its probabilities recalculated considering the *Evidences*. It is worth to point out that both situations are individuals of the *BayesianNetwork* class and that the *Evidences* are *Evidence* class individuals. The *New Situation* resulting from the inference process constitutes the most up-to-date knowledge that the agent has about its domain. The presence of this component is indispensable since updated knowledge is necessary to support the agent decisions and actions.

The *KB Query* component receives queries from *Agent Implementation Specific Components*, *Perception Handler* and *KB Update*. These queries can return events (states) and their occurrence probabilities, causal relations between variables and other information that can be inferred from the Bayesian networks knowledge base. Queries from the agent specific components usually are performed to aid the agent in its decision making process. The queries forwarded by *Perception Handler* are related to knowledge that external agents need to be informed about. Finally, the queries from the *KB Update* component are executed with the purpose of selecting which information will be inserted on the KB.

The core of the interoperability relies on the Bayesian network ontology. It provides the fundamental domain concepts among the Bayesian agents making possible their knowledge exchange. The architecture supports the knowledge representation in a broader way, not only in the interaction with other Bayesian agents. The architecture also provides the means for the knowledge maintenance.

4.2   Interoperability Example

An example of interoperability between two Bayesian agents, *Agent X* and *Agent Y*, is illustrated in the Figure 6. Both agents have one Bayesian network in its knowledge base. Their Bayesian networks are different, but they have one node, labeled *A*, which represents the same information in both networks. In our approach, the *ChanceNode*, *ChanceVariable* and *State* classes have a property named *hasLabel*, which may indicate individuals that add semantics to the concepts represented by those Bayesian network elements.

The Bayesian network of *Agent X* has three nodes, labeled *A*, *B* and *C*. It is depicted only the current situation *Sm* of the network of the *Agent X*. In the situation *Sm*, the node *A* has an evidence that indicates the occurrence of the state *TRUE*. The Bayesian network of the *Agent Y* has two nodes, labeled *A* and *D*. It is shown the last two situations of the *Agent Y* network. The first, named *Sn*, represents the current situation before the execution of the inference process that considered the received evidence in the node *A*. The second is the actual situation, called *Sn+1*, resulting from the inference process. The inference is illustrated in the figure by a gray arrow from the situation *Sn* to the situation *Sn+1*.

A message exchanged among *Agent X* and *Agent Y* is represented by the gray arrow between them. The message, written in OWL language, contains the evidence associated with the node *A*. In the bottom we present a snippet of the OWL source code corresponding to the message content.

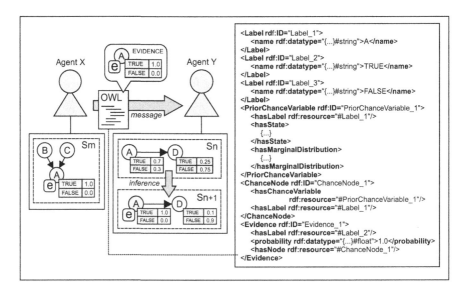

Fig. 6. Bayesian Agents Interoperability Example

Following the flow of information, *Agent X* sends to *Agent Y* a message containing the evidence associated with the node *A*. Upon receiving the OWL message, the *Agent Y* updates its knowledge base by inserting the content of the message in it. Since the state of *A* is known, it is necessary to perform the inference to recalculate the probabilities associated with the node *D*. The inference generates a new situation *Sn+1* from the situation *Sn*, considering the evidence in the node *A*.

5 Case Study

The goal of this case study is to demonstrate a Bayesian knowledge exchange among the Social Agent and the Student Model Agent. They are Bayesian agents that belongs to PortEdu and AMPLIA [17] respectively. The idea is present a way to apply our agent architecture, allowing the Student Model Agent to send Bayesian information to the Social Agent [5].

PortEdu, a multiagent portal that hosts educational systems like Intelligent Tutoring Systems (ITS), provides infrastructure and services for the systems through an agent society. One of these agents is the Social Agent, responsible for organizing the users in groups considering cognitive and emotional aspects. The AMPLIA, one of the educational systems hosted in PortEdu, is an intelligent multiagent learning environment that focuses on the medical area. The functionalities of the AMPLIA are also provided by an agent society. The Student Model Agent, part of the AMPLIA multiagent system, represents the student beliefs in a specific domain and the confidence degree this learner has on the built network model.

Figure 7 illustrates a view of PortEdu in relation to its supporting platform. The agents of PortEdu, inside the doted circle, the AMPLIA agents and also agents from other ITS are part of the same FIPA platform, allowing direct interaction among the agents of the society.

The main objective of the Social Agent is to improve student's learning stimulating his interaction with other students, tutors and professors. The interaction is stimulated by recommending the students to join workgroups in order to provide and receive help from other students. The Social Agent's knowledge is implemented with Bayesian networks. In these networks it is represented student features such as social profile, acceptance degree, sociability degree, mood state, interest, commitment degree, leadership and performance. Figure 8 depicts the Bayesian network related to the student features. However, to communicate with PortEdu and AMPLIA agents, it is necessary to express such probabilistic knowledge in a way that these agents may process it. Such requirement is addressed using our agent architecture.

We begin the description of the architecture integration in the Social Agent specifying how the *Knowledge Base* component is implemented. The knowledge base is composed by the Bayesian network ontology specification (Section 3) and the ontology individuals (i.e. Bayesian networks, evidences, situation transitions). The network illustrated in the Figure 8, in example, is stored in the knowledge base of the Social Agent as a *BayesianNetwork* class individual. The

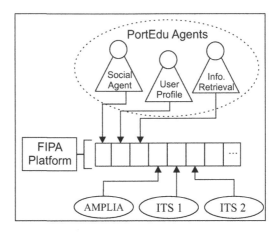

Fig. 7. PortEdu platform

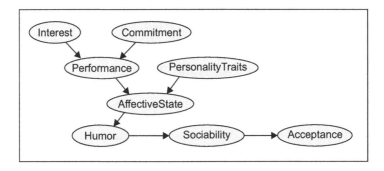

Fig. 8. Bayesian network representing student features

ontology specification and initial population of the knowledge base were created in OWL using the Protégé tool [18].

The interaction of the Social Agent with other agents is done following the FIPA specifications, which are considered the current standard for interoperability among heterogeneous agents and, since 2005, are sponsored by IEEE. Considering the relevance of the FIPA standards, PortEdu adopts them for the platform specification and agent communication. The Social Agent was developed using the JADE [19] framework, which provides a FIPA-compliant middleware for multiagent system development. Developing an agent with this kind of abstraction allows more reutilization and directs the programming towards the agent-oriented paradigm.

We implemented the *Perception Handler, KB Update, KB Query* and *Bayesian Inference* as JADE Behaviors (implementations of agent's tasks) of the Social Agent. The *Perception Handler* manages interactions in compliance with FIPA protocols specifications, using JADE communication resources. In order to allow direct access to the *Knowledge Base* for the *KB Update* component we used the Jena [20] toolkit, which provides support for applications using OWL. Specifically, the current implementation of the *KB Update* component uses the Jena API to create and insert new individuals on the KB. The *KB Query* component also relies on Jena to execute the queries on the base. The *Bayesian Inference* component adopts the same algorithm used in the AMPLIA system. The inference is performed every time a new evidence is provided.

The *Agent Implementation Specific Components* of the Social Agent were implemented using a BDI approach, where beliefs are represented through Bayesian networks (*Knowledge Base component*). In this approach, our agent believes that a state of a chance variable has a probability of occurrence given a set of conditions imposed by the parent variables. Assuming that desires correspond to states of affairs that an agent wishes to bring about, this approach represents this mental states through states of chance variables that the agent desires to observe. Intentions are also represented in this way, since they are desires that an agent has committed to achieve. The beliefs provide support to the deliberative process, responsible for deciding which states of affairs the agent will intend to achieve. The BDI deliberative process interacts with the *Knowledge Base component* (beliefs) through the *KB Query* component. The actions are associated with the intentions selected by the agent. Since our focus in this paper is on the proposed architecture components and its contributions to interoperability of Bayesian agents, we do not detail the deliberative process and action execution.

Since the architecture is implemented in the Social Agent, it is possible to perform an interaction aiming Bayesian knowledge exchange. The particular interaction defined in this section describes the interoperation of Bayesian evidence from Student Model Agent to Social Agent. The Figure 9 illustrates the Student Model Agent sending a FIPA-ACL message to Social Agent. The message performative is an inform, the content language is OWL and the agreed ontology specifies the Bayesian network domain.

In the message content is the OWL code of an *Evidence* individual that indicates the observation of the state *Good* in the node *Humor*. The reception of this evidence by the Social Agent will trigger the Bayesian inference process, generating a new situation in the Bayesian network illustrated in the Figure 8.

6   Conclusion and Future Work

In this paper, we present a way to interoperate Bayesian network knowledge among agents. In order to achieve it, we defined a Bayesian agent internal architecture (Section 4), an ontology to model the Bayesian network domain (Section 3), and developed a case study (Section 5) to demonstrate the integration of the architecture with the Social Agent, dealing with interoperability issues in the PortEdu environment.

Our approach to represent uncertain knowledge, differently from PR-OWL and PACL, does not propose any modification in standards like OWL or FIPA. We apply the current standards to provide a Bayesian knowledge representation

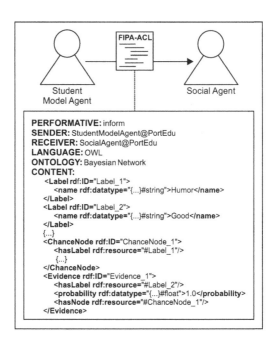

Fig. 9. Interoperability among Social Agent and Student Model Agent

through OWL. This approach allows our Bayesian agents to interoperate their knowledge and also contributes to researches on the expression of uncertain knowledge on the Semantic Web.

We define an internal architecture that provides support for knowledge intense agents to interoperate their knowledge. In this case, the interoperation is in the scope of Bayesian knowledge regarding an adequate way to express it. Besides that, the architecture provides resources for maintaining such Bayesian knowledge. Maintenance features allow the execution of updates, queries and an inference process to propagate evidences to the corresponding networks present in the knowledge base. The interoperability provided by this architecture aids agent specific decision making since it facilitates the discovery of new knowledge, allowing the agent to consider evidences that were not part of its original KB.

In our case study we concluded that our proposal can be integrated with the FIPA standards, more specifically with the FIPA-ACL. The adoption of OWL as a content language for ACL messages handles the issue of a common knowledge language. Our OWL ontology aggregates meaning to the message content. It is necessary to add a high-level architecture component (at FIPA level) to ensure content language compliance. Such component would be similar to the one used to guarantee language and protocol compliance. Currently, the content language is specified through a field in the message envelope, which needs to be integrated with a specific component to verify OWL language. The utilization of OWL and the specification of the ontology to contextualize the content, allow the expression of knowledge in an open and explicit way.

Future works are fourfold. The first is concerned with the executability aspects of the Bayesian networks. Its goal is to represent, in the ontology, concepts involved in the inference, expliciting this operational knowledge. This kind of knowledge allows an agent to share the way that the inference process is performed. The second corresponds to an extension of the ontology to describe also influence diagrams. In order to represent this kind of probabilistic network, decision and utility nodes must be incorporated in the ontology. The third is related to the communication of BDI mental states abstracted through Bayesian networks. Cooperative agent systems can be developed with that framework by communicating desires and intention to be achieved collectively. The last consists of aggregating meaning to the chance variables and states in the Social Agent case study. It can be done by developing an ontology to specify the concepts used in the Social Agents Knowledge Base. Once developed the ontology, to explore this domain specific knowledge to improve the agents cognitive processes.

References

1. Finin, T., Fritzson, R., McKay, D., McEntire, R.: KQML as an agent communication language. In: Proceedings of the 3rd International Conference on Information and Knowledge Management, Gaithersburg, MD, USA, pp. 456–463. ACM Press, New York (1994)
2. The Foundation for Intelligent Physical Agents: Specifications (2006), http://www.fipa.org
3. Berners-Lee, T., Hendler, J., Lassila, O.: The semantic web. Scientific American 284(5), 34–43 (2001)
4. Nakayama, L., Vicari, R.M., Coelho, H.: An information retrieving service for distance learning. Transactions on Internet Research 1(1), 49–56 (2005)
5. Boff, E., Santos, E.R., Vicari, R.M.: Social agents to improve collaboration on an educational portal. In: IEEE International Conference on Advanced Learning Technologies, pp. 896–900. IEEE Computer Society, Los Alamitos (2006)
6. Horrocks, I., Patel-Schneider, P., van Harmelen, F.: From SHIQ and RDF to OWL: The making of a web ontology language. Journal of Web Semantics 1(1), 7–26 (2003)
7. Dean, M., Schreiber, G.: OWL Web Ontology Language Reference. Technical report, W3C (February 2004)
8. Ding, L., Kolari, P., Ding, Z., Avancha, S., Finin, T., Joshi, A.: Using Ontologies in the Semantic Web: A Survey. Technical report, UMBC (July 2005)
9. Ding, Z., Peng, Y.: A probabilistic extension to ontology language OWL. In: Hawaii International Conference On System Sciences (2004)
10. da Costa, P.C.G., Laskey, K.B., Laskey, K.J.: PR-OWL: A bayesian ontology language for the semantic web. In: Workshop on Uncertainty Reasoning for the Semantic Web, International Semantic Web Conference, pp. 23–33 (2005)
11. Gasevic, D., Devedzic, V.: Petri net ontology. Knowledge Based Systems 19(4), 220–234 (2006)
12. Breton, E., Bézivin, J.: Towards an understanding of model executability. In: International Conference on Formal Ontology in Information Systems, pp. 70–80 (2001)

13. Gluz, J.C., Flores, C.D., Seixas, L., Vicari, R.M.: Formal analysis of a probabilistic knowledge communication framework. In: IBERAMIA/SBIA Joint Conference (2006)
14. Santos, E.R., Boff, E., Vicari, R.M.: Semantic Web Technologies Applied to Interoperability on an Educational Portal. In: Ikeda, M., Ashley, K.D., Chan, T.-W. (eds.) ITS 2006. LNCS, vol. 4053, pp. 308–317. Springer, Heidelberg (2006)
15. Cowell, R.G., Dawid, A.P., Lauritzen, S.L., Spiegelhalter, D.J.: Probabilistic Networks and Expert Systems. Springer, Heidelberg (1999)
16. Pearl, J.: Belief networks revisited. Artificial Intelligence 59(1-2), 49–56 (1993)
17. Vicari, R.M., Flores, C.D., Silvestre, A.M., Seixas, L.J., Ladeira, M., Coelho, H.: A multi-agent intelligent environment for medical knowledge. Artificial Intelligence in Medicine 27(3), 335–366 (2003)
18. Stanford University: The Protégé Ontology Editor and Knowledge Acquisition System, http://protege.stanford.edu
19. Bellifemine, F., Poggi, A., Rimassa, G.: JADE – A FIPA-compliant agent framework. In: Proceedings of the 4th International Conference and Exhibition on The Practical Application of Intelligent Agents and Multi-Agent Technology, pp. 97–108 (1999)
20. Carroll, J.J., Dickinson, I., Dollin, C., Reynolds, D., Seaborne, A., Wilkinson, K.: Jena: Implementing the semantic web recommendations. Technical report, Hewlett Packard Laboratories (December 2003)

The **A&A** Programming Model and Technology for Developing Agent Environments in MAS

Alessandro Ricci, Mirko Viroli, and Andrea Omicini

DEIS, Alma Mater Studiorum – Università di Bologna
via Venezia 52, 47023 Cesena, Italy
{a.ricci,mirko.viroli,andrea.omicini}@unibo.it

Abstract. In human society, almost any cooperative working context accounts for different kinds of object, tool, artifact in general, that humans adopt, share and intelligently exploit so as to support their working activities, in particular social ones. According to theories in human sciences, such entities have a key role in determining the success or failure of the activities, playing an essential function in simplifying complex tasks and—more generally—in designing solutions that scale with activity complexity. Analogously to the human case, we claim that also (cognitive) multi-agent systems (MAS) could greatly benefit from the definition and systematic exploitation of a suitable notion of *working environment*, composed by different sorts of artifacts, dynamically constructed, shared and used by agents to support their working activities. Along this line, in this paper we introduce and discuss a programming model called A&A (Agents and Artifacts), which aims at directly modelling and engineering such aspects in the context of cognitive MAS. Besides the conceptual framework, we present the current state of prototyping technologies implementing A&A principles—CARTAGO platform in particular—, and show how they can be integrated with existing cognitive MAS programming frameworks, adopting the *Jason* programming platform as the reference case.

1 Introduction

"Artifacts play a critical role in almost all human activity [...]. Indeed [...] the development of artifacts, their use, and then the propagation of knowledge and skills of the artifacts to subsequent generations of humans are among the distinctive characteristics of human beings as a specie", Donald Norman, [8]

"The use of tools is a hallmark of intelligent behaviour. It would be hard to describe modern human life without mentioning tools of one sort or another", Robert Amant, [2]

In their articles, Norman [8] and Amant [2] remark—in different contexts—the fundamental role that *tools* and, more generally, *artifacts* play in human society. Artifacts and tools here could be understood as whatever kinds of device

M. Dastani et al.(Eds.): ProMAS 2007, LNAI 4908, pp. 89–106, 2008.
© Springer-Verlag Berlin Heidelberg 2008

explicitly designed and used by humans so as to mediate and support their activities, especially social. Analogous observations are found in the work of Agre and Horswill in their *Lifeworld analysis* [1], as well as in the work of Kirsch [5,6]. Actually, such a perspective is central in theories developed in the context of human sciences, such as Activity Theory and Distributed Cognition, and currently taken as a reference by computer science related disciplines such as CSCW (Computer Supported Cooperative Work) and HCI (Human-Computer Interaction) [7]. There, a fundamental point is devising out the best kind of artifacts to populate humans' *fields of works*, and to organise them so as to improve as much as possible the performance of their activities, in particular coordinative ones [13,6].

Analogously to human society, we think that such a perspective is and will be fundamental also in the context of agent societies, and in particular for designing and programming complex software systems based on cognitive MAS. Quite provocatively, analogously to the human case, we think that the next evolution step in the development of cognitive MAS will *mandatorily* require the definition of MAS models and architectures with agents situated in suitable *working environments*. There, agents autonomously—besides speaking to each others—construct, share, and co-operatively use different kinds of artifact, designed either by MAS designers or by the agent themselves, to perform MAS activities. Indeed, this notion of environment is quite different with respect to the one traditionally adopted in mainstream cognitive agent theory: there, the environment is typically conceived as something "out of the MAS", then not a subject of design. On the contrary, the notion of "working environment" promotes MAS environment as an essential part of the MAS to be explicitly designed and fruitfully exploited by agents in their working activities.

Along this line, in this paper we introduce and discuss a first programming model called A&A (Agents and Artifacts) which aims at directly modelling and engineering working environments in the context of cognitive multi-agent systems. Such a perspective is strenghtened by recent efforts in AOSE (Agent-Oriented Software Engineering) that remark the fundamental role of the environment for the engineering of MAS [14]. The A&A approach can be considered an instance of such approaches, with some specific peculiarity: *(i) abstractions and generality*—the aim is to find a basic set of conceptual abstractions and related theory which, analogously to the agent abstraction, could be general enough to be the basis to define concrete architectures and programming environments, but specific enough to capture the essential properties of systems; *(ii) cognitive*—analogous to designed environment in human society, the properties of such environment abstractions should be conceived to be suitably and effectively exploited by cognitive agents, as intelligent constructors / users / manipulators of the environment.

Besides the abstract programming model, in this paper we describe also the concrete technologies developed to experiment the model: in particular we discuss **CARTAGO** technology, a platform for programming and supporting the execution of artifact-based working environments, developed on top of the Java platform, and its integration with the Jason agent programming environment.

The basic notion of artifact has been already introduced and published elsewhere [11,9,10], and the same applies for the first version of CARTAGO technology [12]. On the one side, besided purely conceptual papers such as [9], papers such as [11,10] can be considered first steps introducing the concept of artifact for programming MAS, without having a reference programming model defined here—called A&A—and related functioning technologies, i.e. CARTAGO, that can be integrated to existing platform. On the other side, the artifact programming model and its implementation in CARTAGO technologies has been substantially evolved with respect to the most recent one, described in [12]. In particular, the basic model of usage-interface and operation presented in [12] is quite simple and is not able to properly take into account the possibility to have the concurrent execution of operations on an artifact (the interested reader is forwarded to the paper for the details). Such a model has been completely revised, and this new version—which substantially change the way a MAS programmers can adopt to program artifact operations and behaviour—is described in detail in this work. Besides this, the work published in [12] is more oriented on the environment / infrastructure level: in this paper instead, besides describing in detail CARTAGO, we focus more on the A&A programming model and CARTAGO is described as an existing functioning technology supporting such a model.

The remainder of the paper is organised as follows. First, we provide a description of the basic concepts and principles of A&A (Section 2), by introducing an abstract model embedding such principles (Section 2.3). Then, we briefly present the current models and technologies that have been developed for concretely prototyping MAS applications in the A&A perspective (Section 3)—among which the one called CARTAGO—and discuss the issue of integration of such technologies with existing cognitive MAS programming platform, adopting *Jason* as our reference case study. Finally, we conclude the paper with some final remarks, and sketch some future line of work (Section 4).

2   Programming Model Building Blocks

2.1   Artifacts and Workspaces

A *working environment* in A&A is defined as the part of the MAS that is designed and dynamically constructed and used by agents to support their working activities. MAS programmers design and define the types of artifacts that agents will dynamically instantiate and cooperatively use.

A working environment is conceived as a dynamic set of *artifacts*, organised in *workspaces*. Workspaces are the logical containers of artifacts, useful to define the topology of the working environment. A workspace provides a notion of locality for agents: an agent can work only with artifacts belonging to the workspace where it is playing, but can be conceptually situated in multiple workspaces at the same time, possibly distributed on different Internet nodes. This concept can be used to define the distribution model of an application at an abstract level: a working environment—which corresponds to a possibly distributed application

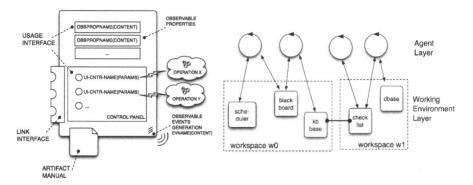

Fig. 1. *(Left)* Abstract representation of an artifact. *(Right)* Abstract representation of a working environment with two workspaces, with some artifacts of different kinds inside.

or MAS—can account for one or multiple workspaces, possibly spread among multiple network (Internet) nodes.

Current model does not explicitly take into the account security and organisation issues: for examples roles that can be defined in a workspace and the possible permits related to roles. These aspects are part of future work: we plan to adopt RBAC-like approach as a basic organisation and security model, as we did for the TuCSoN coordination model [15].

The notion of artifact is the core abstraction of the programming model: it is meant to represent any entity belonging to the working environment— hence existing outside the agent mind—that is created, shared & used (and eventually disposed) by agents to carry on their activities, in particular social ones. So, an artifact (type) is typically meant to be explicitly designed by MAS engineers so as to encapsulate some kind of *function*, here synonym of "intended purpose". An abstract representation of an artifact is shown in Fig. 1 and it is very similar to artifacts as found in human society. The functionality of an artifact is structured in terms of *operations*, whose execution can be triggered by agents through artifact *usage interface*. Analogously to usage interface of artifacts in our world (think, for example, of a coffee machine), an artifact usage interface in A&A is composed of a set of commands or *controls* that agents can use to trigger and control operation execution (such as the control panel of a coffee machine), each one identified by a label (typically equals to the operation name to be triggered) and a list of input parameters. The usage interface can change dynamically, according to state of the artifact; in other words, it is possible to design artifacts that expose a different usage interface according to their functioning stage. Besides the control to act, the usage interface might contain also a set of *observable properties* (think of the coffee machine display); that is, properties whose dynamic values can be observed by agents without necessarily interacting with (or operating upon) the artifact.

The execution of an operation upon an artifact can result both in changing the artifact's inner (i.e., non-observable) state, and in the generation of a stream of *observable events* that can be perceived by agents that are using or simply observing the artifact. Such a model strictly mimics the way in which humans use their artifacts: a simple example is the coffee machine, whose usage interface includes suitable controls—such as the buttons—and means to make (part of) the machine behaviour observable—such as displays—and to collect the results produced by the machine—such as the coffee can. It's worth remarking here the differences between observable properties and observable events. The former are dynamic and persistent attributes that belong to an artifact and that can be observed by agents without interacting with it (i.e. without using the ui-controls). Like the display of a coffee machine. The latter are non-persistent information, as signals carrying also an information content. Like the sound emitted by a coffee machine when the coffee is ready.

Artifacts can embed complex functionalities: accordingly, operations executed can be complex and an articulated operation model is provided for this purpose. Generally speaking, operation execution can be conceived as a process (from a conceptual point of view) combining the execution of possibly multiple *atomic guarded* operation *steps*. Multiple operations can be in execution upon an artifact by interleaving the execution of the operation steps. In order to avoid interferences, during the execution of a single operation step, the usage interface is disabled. This approach, in the overall, makes it possible to support the execution of multiple operations concurrently on the artifact, keeping mutual exclusion in artifact state access.

Analogously to artifacts in the human case, in A&A each artifact is meant to be equipped with a *manual* describing the artifact's function (i.e., its intended purpose), the artifact's usage interface (i.e., the observable "shape" of the artifact), and artifact's *operating instructions* (i.e., usage protocols or simply how to correctly use the artifact so as to take advantage of all its functionalities). A manual is meant to be inspected and used at runtime by agents, in particular intelligent agents, for reasoning about how to select and use artifacts so as to best achieve their goals. Accordingly, suitable formal languages and ontologies could be defined for manual description. Currently, no specific commitments towards specific technologies have as yet been made, as this is part of ongoing work.

Finally, as a principle of composition, artifacts can be linked together, in order to enable artifact–artifact interaction. This is realised through *link interfaces*, which are analogous to interfaces of artifacts in the human case (e.g. linking/connecting/plugging the earphones into an MP3 player, or using the remote control with a TV). In the overall link interfaces serve two purposes: on the one side, to explicitly define a principle of composability for artifacts, enabling the ruled construction of articulated and complex artifacts by means of simpler ones; on the other side, to realise distributed (composed) artifacts, by linking artifacts belonging to different workspaces.

2.2   Agent Bodies

In this overall picture, nothing is said about the specific cognitive model of the agent: actually A&A is meant to be orthogonal to this aspect: agents are simply conceived as autonomous entities executing some kind of working activities, either individually or collectively—typically in order to achieve some individual or social goal, or to fulfill some individual or social task. Such activities—from an abstract point of view—are seen as the execution of sequences of actions, which according to the A&A model can be roughly classified as: *(i)* internal actions, *(ii)* communicative actions, involving direct communications with one or more agents through some kind of ACL, and *(iii)* pragmatical actions, as interactions within working environments that concern construction, sharing, and use of artifacts.

Despite their specific cognitive model / architecture, in order to execute actions over the artifact and perceive observable events, agents must be *situated* in a working environment: for this purpose, the notion of *agent body* is introduced. The agent body functions as the medium through which the agent *mind*—i.e. those parts that are designed and programmed according to a certain kind of cognitive model / architecture—can sense and affect a working environment. Such a notion is essential to decouple—for engineering purposes—the agent mind from the working environment in which the agent is situated, so as to be able to use A&A with different kinds of programming models for agent mind.

Agent bodies contain *effectors* to perform actions upon the working environment, and a dynamic set of *sensors* to collect stimuli from the working environment. Sensors in particular play here a fundamental role, that of *perceptual memory*, whose functionality accounts for keeping track of stimuli arrived from the environment, possibly applying filters and specific kinds of "buffering" policy. According to the specific interaction modality adopted for using and observing artifacts, as described later in this section, it might be useful to provide agents with basic internal actions for managing and inspecting sensors, as a kind of private memory. In particular, it could be useful for an agent to organise in a flexible way the perception of observable events, possibly generated by multiple different artifacts that an agent can be using for different, even concurrent, activities.

2.3   The Agent Programming Interface

In this subsection we provide an abstract description of the basic interface available to agent minds to play inside a working environment. Such an interface accounts for three basic groups of actions: *(i)* join and leave workspaces; *(ii)* use an artifact by acting on its usage interface and perceive observable events generated by artifacts; *(iii)* observe an artifact. Table 1 provides a synthetic view of the set of actions, grouped into the three main groups; as for the syntax, a pseudo-code first-order logic-like syntax is adopted, while semantics is described informally. Atoms `AName`, `WName` and `SName` are used to represent a unique name (identifier) for respectively artifact instances, workspaces and sensors. Following the semantics adopted in the cognitive agent-oriented programming approaches considered here, an action consists in the atomic execution of a statement which can result in changing the agent's state and/or interacting with the agent's environment, and can succeed or fail.

The first group of actions (labelled 1–2) are useful for managing a working session inside a workspace. Intuitively, `join` makes it possible to "enter" a

Table 1. Basic set of actions to interact with A&A work environments. + is used for optional parameters, ? for input parameters.

---

(1) `joinWorkspace(WName,+Node)`
(2) `quitWorkspace`

---

(3) `use(AName,UIControlName(Params),+SName,+Timeout,+Filter)`
(4) `sense(SName,?Perception,+Filter,+Timeout)`

---

(5) `focus(AName,SName,+Filter)`
(6) `stopFocussing(AName)`
(7) `observeProperty(AName,PropertyName,?Property)`

---

workspace, whose name is specified as a parameter and `quit` to leave the current workspace. Since workspaces are meant to be distributed over a network, optionally the node where the workspace resides can be specified.

The second group of actions (labelled 3–4) concerns the *use* of artifacts. In particular **use** action accounts for using the artifact identified by `AName`, by acting on the `UIControl` usage-interface control, specifying some `Params` parameters, and optionally specifying a sensor `SName` to be used to collect the events generated by the artifact, a filter `Filter` and a timeout `Timeout`. The action succeeds if the specified artifact exists and its usage interface actually has the specified control, and as a result the related operation is triggered for execution. Then, if a sensor has been specified, every observable event subsequently generated by the artifact, as effect of the operation execution, is made observable to the agent as a stimulus `artifact_event(AName,Event)` collected in the sensor. The filter can be used to specify which kinds of events the agent is interested in perceiving. If the usage interface of the artifact is disabled when executing the action, for instance because the artifact is executing an operation (step), then the agent action is suspended until the usage interface is enabled again; the timeout specifies how long the agent can wait before considering the action as failed. Then, a **sense** action is provided to inspect the content of a sensor (i.e. the perceptual memory), so that the agent can become aware of any new percepts. In particular, the action succeeds if within `Timeout` time an event (stimulous) matching the specified filter `Filter` is found in the specified sensor `SName`. In that case, `Perception` is bound with such event. Both the timeout and the filter can be omitted. The same sensor can be used for collecting events of different usage interactions, possibly with different artifacts. It's worth remarking that the execution (and completion) of the use action is *completely asynchronous* with respect to the execution of the operation by the artifact and to the possible consequent generation of events. It is synchronous however with respect to the presence of the specified ui-control in the usage interface: if the action succeeds, then it means that such ui-control was part of the usage interface, that it has been "pressed" and that the related operation has been triggered for being executed (as soon as its guard is satisfied).

The third group of actions (labelled 5–7) concerns artifact observation, i.e. the capability of perceiving artifacts observable events and properties without directly interacting with them. The focus action can be used to start a continuous observation of an artifact (intuitively, to focus one's attention on that artifact so as to observe any changes that occur in it over time). The action succeeds if the AName artifact exists, and as an effect every observable event generated by the artifact (despite the specific operation that caused it, possibly executed by any other agent) is made observable to the agent as a stimulus artifact_event(AName,Event) collected in the specified sensor. Also for focus, a filter can be specified in order to select which kinds of event to actually observe. stopFocussing is used to stop observing the artifact. It's worth remarking here the differences between focus and sense actions: sense is an internal action, since it inspects a sensor (which is considered part of the agent); focus, instead, is external, enabling continuos observation of events that directly cause belief base update in the first modality, and sensor content update in the second modality. Finally observeProperty can be used to inspect the observable properties of the specified AName artifact, specifying the name PropertyName of the property to be observed. The action succeeds if the AName artifact exists and has a property with the specified name, and as result the current value of the property is bound to Property.

This abstract model is meant to be as much as possible orthogonal to the model(s) adopted for defining agent mind at the agent level. This should make it easier to integrate A&A concrete models and technologies with existing agent technologies—as described in Section 3.2.

2.4   The Artifact Programming Interface

Besides the API to use artifacts, a programming model for defining artifact types is given: Table 2 shows an abstract description of the main primitives used to define artifacts behaviour.

An artifact type or template defines the structure and behaviour of artifacts instances of such a type. For some extent, an artifact type is quite similar to the notion of class in Object-Oriented Programming, with artifacts analogous to objects, and to the notion of monitor, as defined in concurrent programming. As in the case of objects, the structure defines the artifact inner state and working machinery hidden to agent users. The behaviour is structured in a set of *operations*, which define in the overall artifact function. An operation encapsulates the computational and interaction behaviour—such as the update of the internal state and the generation of observable events—so as to provide some kinds of functionality. Operations execution is triggered and controlled by acting on the controls which are part of the artifact usage interface. During the execution of an operation, observable events (signals) can be generated by using a specific primitive, signal (label 1 in Table 2), specifying the event content as a labelled tuple.

Table 2. Basic API available for programming an artifact + is used for optional parameters, ? for input / output parameters.

---

(1) `signal(Event)`

---

(2) `nextStep(OpStep(Params),+Guard(Params))`
(3) `switchToObsState(StateName)`

---

(4) `updateObsProperty(Property)`
(5) `readObsProperty(?Property)`

In order to enforce mutual exclusion in updating artifact state on the one side and allow for concurrent operations execution on the other side, artifact operations can be composed by one or multiple *operation steps*, which are meant to be executed atomically. At a given time only one operation (step) can be in execution: multiple operations can be executed concurrently by interleaving their steps. For each step *a guard* can be defined, which specifies when the step—once it has been striggered in the context of an operation—can actually be executed. Guards represent the condition that must be satisfied, as a predicate over the artifact state, to execute a step. So, an operation (step) is first triggered by agent user, the executed when the guard is satisfied. A step can trigger other steps, by means of the `nextStep` primitive (label 2 in Table 2), specifying the operation step to be executed and possibly the guard. An operation is considered completed when no more steps have been triggered. In the overall, this model makes it possible to design a complex articulated operation, that—for instance— can be controlled by using different controls in different times in the user interface before being completed, or—as another example—would need the execution of other operations to complete.

Besides the analogies with classes and monitors in object-oriented and concurrent programming, it's worth remarking here the deep difference with respect to those concepts, in particular for what concerns the interaction model: by virtue of agent autonomy, artifact operation (step) execution does not involve any control flow from the invoker agent to the invoked artifact, i.e. is not a method or function call.

The usage interface of an artifact can change according to artifact *observable state*, exposing different sets of operations and *observable properties* according to the specific functioning state of the artifact. The notion of observable state is adopted to structure the behaviour of an artifact in a set of labelled states, that can be recognised (observed) by the artifact users. For each artifact type a finite set of labelled observable states can be defined. Each artifact instance has a *current observable state*, that can be changed dynamically during artifact functioning by means of the `switchToObsState` primitive (label 3 in Table 2, specifying the label of the target observable state. For each observable state a different usage interface can be defined: this feature makes it possible to set the appropriate usage interface according to the functioning stage of the artifact. Dynamically, an agent can trigger the execution of an operation on an artifact if and only the operation is (in that moment) part of the usage interface; if the operation is not part the usage interface, the agent action fails. Observable properties can be defined as labelled tuple of information that can be observed by agents without directly using the artifacts. Basic primitives are available as part of artifact API for updating (`updateObsProperty`, label 4) and reading (`readObsProperty`, label 5) the value of an observable property: also properties are represented by labelled tuples and their access is meant to be associative.

3   Prototyping Technologies

Starting from the A&A abstract model, we developed some first concrete technologies, with the objective to have concrete frameworks for prototyping MAS-based applications engineered upon A&A basic abstractions, and for being integrated with existing agent technologies extended with the A&A support.

A primary technology is called CARTAGO (Common ARtifact Infrastructure for AGent Open environment), which is a framework providing essentially the capability to define new artifacts type, suitable API for agents to work with artifacts and workspaces, and a runtime supporting the existence and dynamic management of working environments. Another technology is called simpA (simple A&A programming environment), a framework extending CARTAGO with a support for defining and running agents (MAS) besides the working environments. While CARTAGO is meant to be integrated with existing (cognitive) agent models and technologies as a seamless support to define and create artifact-based working environments, simpA can be exploited alone to develop full-fledged applications engineered in terms of agents, artifacts and workspace. For lack of space, in this paper simpA is not described: the interested reader can refer to simpA web site[1]. Both technologies are based on Java and are available as open-source projects freely downloadable from the project web sites[2].

3.1   CARTAGO Overview

The CARTAGO architecture implements quite faithfully the abstract model described in Section 2.3. Pragmatically, we chose Java as the programming language to implement and map the programming model elements, adopting choices that would favour rapid prototyping, reusing as much as possible the support given by the Java Object-Oriented framework. In the following we briefly describe the three main parts of CARTAGO:

– *API for creating and interacting with artifact-based working environments* —
   These API are meant to extend the existing basic set of agent actions with

---

[1] http://www.alice.unibo.it/simpa
[2] http://www.alice.unibo.it/cartago

new ones, abstractly described in Section 2.3, essentially for creating and disposing artifacts, interacting with them through their usage interface—by executing operation and perceiving artifact observable states and events—reading artifact function description and operating instructions, managing sensors, and so on.

- *API for defining artifact types* — These API allow MAS programmers to develop new types of artifacts. An artifact type can be defined by extending the basic `Artifact` class provided in the API: at runtime, artifacts instances are instances of this class. Artifact structure (internal state) is defined in terms of instance fields of the class. Operations and operations steps body is defined by methods tagged by `@OPERATION` and `@OPSTEP`, where the operation (step) name and parameters are mapped onto the name and the parameter of the methods[3]. Guards are represented by boolean method annotated with the `@GUARD` annotation. Methods representing operations / operation steps have no return argument—a return argument would be meaningless in the A&A model. Observable events—which are the means to make agents perceive operation results—can be generated in the body of an operation by primitives of the kind `signal`, available as protected methods of the artifact. Events are collected by agent body sensors as stimuli, and then perceived by agents through `sense` action. Artifact function description and operating instructions, as well as the list of the observable states, can be explicitly declared through the `@ARTIFACT_MANUAL` annotation preceding the artifact class declaration.

  A simple example of artifact definition is shown in Fig. 2: a simple type `MyArtifact` is defined, with an internal variable `m` and two operations, `op1` and `op2`, the former composed by two steps, the first one coinciding the first of the operation and the second one, `opStepA` with guard `canExecA` triggered by the first step by means of the `nextStep` CARTAGO primitive. The operation `op1` initialized the variable to 1 and then completes only when the variable value reaches the value 3, a condition that triggers the execution of the second step which generates the observable event `maxReached`. Each time the operation `op2` is executed, the variable is incremented and an observable event `newValue` generated. More complex and useful examples can be found in CARTAGO distribution.

- *Runtime environment and related tools* — This is the part actually responsible of the life-cycle management of working environments at runtime. Conceptually, it is the *virtual machine* where artifacts and agent bodies are instantiated and managed that is responsible of executing operations on artifacts and collecting and routing observable events generated by artifacts (see Fig. 3 for an abstract representation of a MAS application running on top of CARTAGO). Some tools are also made available in CARTAGO for on-line inspection of working environment state, in particular artifact state, and above the observation of artifact behaviour, in terms operation executed and events generated.

---

[3] Annotations have been introduced with the 5.0 version of Java.

```
import alice.cartago.*;

class MyArtifact extends Artifact {          ...
  private int m;                             ArtifactId id =
                                               createArtifact("myArtifact", MyArtifact.class);
  @OPERATION void op1(){                     SensorId sid =
    m=1;                                       linkSensor(new DefaultSensor());
    nextStep("opStepA", "canExecA");
  }                                          use(id, new Op("op1"));
  @OPERATION void op2(){
    m++;                                     while (true){
    signal("newValue",m);                      use(id, new Op("op2"),sid);
  }                                            Perception p = sense(sid);
  @GUARD boolean canExecA(){                   if (p.getLabel().equals("maxReached")){
    return m == 3;                               break;
  }                                            }
  @OPSTEP void opStepA(){                    }
    signal("maxReached");                    ...
    m = 1;
  }
}
```

Fig. 2. *(Left)* A simple type of artifact, with two operations, **op1** and **op2**, the former composed by two steps, the first one coinciding the beginning of the operation and the second one, **opStepA** with guard **canExecA** triggered by the first step. *(Right)* A Java fragment using CARTAGO API to create an artifact, link a sensor, execute the **op1** operation and then repeatedly execute the **op2** operation until a **maxReached** event is observed. **createArtifact** and **linkSensor** are auxiliary actions part of the Java CARTAGO implementation.

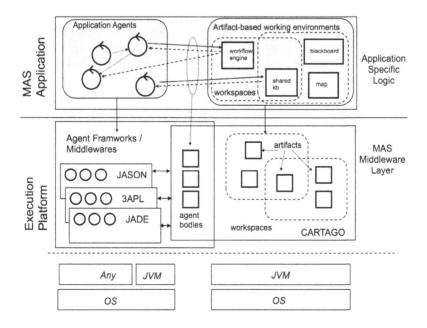

Fig. 3. Abstract representation of a MAS application exploiting CARTAGO

Further details about CARTAGO API and architecture, along with complete examples, can be found on the web site.

3.2   Integration with Existing MAS Programming Environments

As mentioned previously, an important aspect of A&A and of technologies such as CARTAGO is the possibility of integration with existing cognitive MAS architectures and models / languages / platforms, so as to extend them to create and work with artifact-based environments.

Actually, most available agent programming models and platforms for developing general-purpose applications—such as *Jason*, 3APL, Jadex, JACK, and others surveied in [3]—lack a true notion of environment, and when such a notion is accounted for, it is typically modelled and implemented in terms of low-level interfaces to the hosting VM or OS environment, or by considering a general monolithic abstraction of "Environment" and of "Event". This is perfectly reasonable according to the notion of environment as traditionally dealt with in agent theories. By integrating these platforms with A&A, the environment notion is seamlessly extended with the capability for cognitive agents written in existing programming environments to create, share and use artifacts according to the specific needs, with MAS designers directly programming artifacts so as to create the best working environments for supporting agent activities. Also, existing types of artifact can be reused, especially those providing general purpose functionalities such as the coordination artifacts. Furthermore, from a conceptual point of view it would be possible and interesting to build MAS applications composed by heterogeneous agent societies, made of cognitive agents programmed with different agent languages or architectures, working together in the same working environments, and interacting through the same mediating artifacts—besides communicating by means of the same ACL as usual.

In the following subsection we sketch the first results obtained with a concrete case, concerning the integration of CARTAGO with the *Jason* agent-oriented programming platform.

3.3   A Case Study: *Jason* Using CARTAGO

Jason is an interpreter written in Java for an extended version of AgentSpeak [4], a logic-based agent-oriented programming language that is suitable for the implementation of reactive planning systems according to the BDI architecture. *Jason* is taken here is as reference case: analogous considerations can be done using other platforms such as 3APL or Jadex.

By the integration then, it is possible to create a MAS application composed by a set of *Jason* agents working inside the same CARTAGO environment. By default, each *Jason* agent has an agent body inside the CARTAGO environment, and his basic set of external actions is extended to include the basic ones abstractly described in Section 2.3. In particular, a *Jason* agent can use an artifact by means of `use` and perceive artifact events collected by its sensors through `sense` action, and so on. In current simple integration model, percepts that are fetched by `sense` action are mapped to beliefs

```
/* TABLE ARTIFACT */

import alice.cartago.*;

public class Table extends Artifact {
 private boolean[] chops;

  public Table(int nchops){
    chops = new boolean[nchops];
    for (int i = 0; i<chops.length; i++){
      chops[i]=true;
    }
  }
  @OPERATION(
    guard = "chopsAvailable"
  ) void getChops(int lc, int rc){
    chops[lc] = chops[rc] = false;
    signal("chops_acquired");
  }
  @GUARD boolean chopsAvailable(int lc,int rc){
    return chops[lc] && chops[rc];
  }
  @OPERATION void releaseChops(int lc, int rc){
    chops[lc] = chops[rc] = true;
    signal("chops_released");
  }
}
```

```
MAS cartagoTest {

  infrastructure: Centralised

  environment: CartagoEnvironment

  agents:
    rosa philo.asl;
    beppo philo.asl;
    pippo philo.asl;
    maria philo.asl;
    giulia philo.asl;
    alfredo waiter.asl;
}
```

Fig. 4. *(Left)* Definition of a Jason MAS called `cartagoTest`, composed by five philosopher agents (`rosa`, `beppo`, `pippo`, `maria`, `giulia`) and a waiter agent (`alfredo`), sharing a CARTAGO environment. *(Right)* Definition of the `Table` artifact type

of the type `artifact_event(Type,SensorId,ArtifactId,EventTime)`, while exceptions regarding timeouts elapsed during sense actions to beliefs of the kind `sensing_timeout(SensorID)`.

Hello Philosophers! As a simple integration example, we consider the case "Hello philosophers" used here with analogous function of the "Hello world" example for traditional programming languages.

The example refers to the well-known problem introduced by Dijkstra in the context of concurrent programming to check the expressiveness of mechanisms and abstractions introduced to coordinate set of cooperating / competing computing agents. Briefly, the problem is about a set of N philosophers (typically 5) sharing N chopsticks for eating spaghetti, sitting at a round table (so each philosopher share her left and right chopsticks with a friend philosopher on the left and one on the right). The goal of each philosopher is to live a joyful life, interleaving thinking activity, for which they actually do not need any resources, to eating activity, for which they need to take and use both the chopsticks. The goal of the overall philosophers society is to share the chopsticks fruitfully, and coordinate the access to shared resources so as to avoid forms of deadlock or starvation of individual philosophers—e.g. when all philosophers have one chopstick each. The social constraint of the society is that a chopstick cannot be used simultaneously by more than one philosopher.

The problem can be solved indeed in many different ways. By adopting the A&A perspective, it is natural to model the philosophers as cooperative agents

```
/* PHILOSOPHER AGENT */

!live.
+!live : true
   <- .print("Hello world! Waiting to know my chopsticks...").

+chops_assigned(Table,C0,C1) : true
   <- .print("I know my chopsticks, I can start my activity.");
      +my_chopsticks(Table,C0,C1) ;
      +wants_to_live_for_another_round.

+wants_to_live_for_another_round : true   <- !think.

+!think : not(hungry)
   <- .print("Thinking.");
      -wants_to_live_for_another_round; +hungry.

+hungry :  my_chopsticks(Table,C1,C2) &
           not(got_chopsticks(C1,C2)) &
           not(chopsticks_requested(C1,C2))
   <- .print("Got hungry, try to eat") ;
      use(Table,getChops(C1,C2),mySensor);
      +chopsticks_requested(C1,C2);
      sense(mySensor,8000).

+artifact_event(chops_acquired,mySensor,Table,EventTime) :
           chopsticks_requested(C1,C2)
   <- .print("Got chopsticks, can eat.");
      -chopsticks_requested(C1,C2);
      +got_chopsticks(C1,C2); -hungry;
      use(Table,releaseChops(C1,C2),mySensor);
      sense(mySensor).
+sensing_timeout(mySensor) : chopsticks_requested(C1,C2)
   <- .print("Starved, good bye world.");
      .myName(Me); .killAgent(Me).

+artifact_event(chops_released,mySensor,Table,_) :
           got_chopsticks(C1,C2)
   <- .print("Chopsticks released.");
      -got_chopsticks(C1,C2);
      +wants_to_live_for_another_round.
```

```
/* WAITER AGENT */

!live.
+!live : true
<- .print("Hello world!") ;
   .print("Preparing the table...") ;
   createArtifact(myTable,"Table",[5]);
   .print("The table is ready.") ;
   .print("Assigning the chopsticks");
   .send("rosa",tell,
       chops_assigned(myTable,0,1));
   .send("beppo",tell,
       chops_assigned(myTable,1,2));
   .send("pippo",tell,
       chops_assigned(myTable,2,3));
   .send("maria",tell,
       chops_assigned(myTable,3,4));
   .send("giulia",tell,
       chops_assigned(myTable,4,0));
   .print("Good luck.").
```

Fig. 5. *Jason* implementation of waiter agents *(left)* and dining philosopher agents *(right)*

and *the table*—managing the set of chopsticks—as the coordination artifact that agents share and use to perform their (eating) activities. It is easy to encapsulate in the table artifact the enactment of the social policy that makes it possible to satisfy both mutual exclusion for the access on the individual chopsticks, and avoid deadlock situations. Fig. 5 shows the full executable implementation of the *Jason* project (available at CARTAGO web site). It accounts for a MAS file describing the multi-agent system initially composed by a waiter agent called alfredo, five philo agents called rosa,beppo,pippo,maria,giulia, working inside a common CARTAGO working environment. An artifact of type Table is dynamically created and exploited by the agents.

A brief description of the components follows. The waiter agent is responsible for creating a table identified by myTable with 5 chopsticks, and informing all the other agents which chopsticks should they use. The usage interface of the table artifact is composed by only two operations, getChops and releaseChops, which can be used respectively to get two chopsticks from the table and to give them back. The inner machinery of the table artifact ensures mutual exclusion on the access on chopsticks (an artifact executes one operation at a time, analogously to monitors) and deadlock avoidance (by releasing the chopsticks only if both are available, enqueueing the pending requests). The source code of the philosopher in is quite intuitive: after receiving the information about the chopsticks to use, the philosopher starts a life-cycle interleaving thinking and eating. By thinking, a philosopher gets hungry. The belief to be hungry triggers the plan to eat: first, if it does not believe to own the chopsticks, then it suitably interacts with table to get them, by triggering the `getChops` operation and start observing the table. Note that the `use` action is not blocking: instead `sense` action can (optionally) block the agent control flow for a certain amount of time, waiting to get some stimuli on the specified sensor. If no perception is sensed in this amount of time, an sensing timeout belief is generated, and the philosopher sadly decides to die for starvation. When a philosopher perceives that the chopsticks have been acquired, then it can eat. After completing the eating activity, being no longer hungry, the philosopher releases the chopsticks by executing the `releaseChops` operation and starts thinking again.

3.4   Some Remarks

Some considerations are worth remarking. First the example is not meant to be as complex as real-world MAS working environments, and in particular it is not robust to possible failures as it should be—in particular to agent failures in giving back the chopsticks. Despite its simplicity, the example is useful to give an idea of the basic A&A philosophy in designing systems balancing the responsibilities among agents and artifacts. Simple alternative solutions to this one would account for having either an agent playing the role of the table, or avoiding a table and let agents coordinate through suitable conversation protocols.

With respect to the former one, the A&A approach makes it possible to avoid the need to design and implement parts of the system with "wrapper" agents though they are clearly not autonomous neither proactive. We think that this is very important both from a conceptual point of view—avoiding semantic gap between analysis and then design and implementation—but also a pragmatical point of view: it is intuitive that artifacts in general, despite specific cases, are entities largely more lightweight than agents: on the one side, artifacts are typically passive, with simple mechanisms to trigger and execute operations, and possibly changing the observable state and generating events; on the other side, agents typically encapsulate one or multiple control flows, and have complex machinery for managing knowledge, selecting pro-actively actions to do, and so on. So, adopting artifacts and not agents to represent automatised resources and tools can be effective from the point of view of maintenaince and performance—in using time and memory resources— in particular to scale with system complexity in terms of number of agents and artifacts involved.

With respect to the latter case, we think that the situation is pretty analogous to human working environments: not always the language and direct communication is the best way to coordinate the independent activities of individual. There are cases where well-designed coordination artifacts could be largely more effective, for instance enabling communication and coordination without requiring a strong temporal and spatial coupling between agents. Conversely, we think that the point is to find a way (models and theories) in MAS to use language—i.e.

direct communication—and artifacts in synergy, as happen in human contexts. Indeed, we consider this as one of the crucial points that would be worth investigating in future research on artifacts in MAS.

4   Conclusions and Future Works

The fact that the environment can play an important role in designing and programming MAS is now a well-known and accepted fact [16]: the point is now which kind of reference model we should adopt and systematically use to conceive and design a "good" environment for agent activities, so as to create cognitive MAS that suitably exploit such an environment to perform their individual and social activities. An important point here is *abstraction*: it is opinion of the authors that reference models should aim not merely at identifying mechanisms and/or architectures, but first of all at framing the issue of MAS environment in terms of new abstractions introduced with respect to the basic agent and MAS meta-model—and the related theoretical foundation.

By drawing inspiration from human cooperative working environments, in this paper we propose a general conceptual framework called A&A, which makes it possible to entail such design in terms of set of suitably designed artifacts, populating workspaces and constituting in the overall the MAS working environment. Then we discuss current technologies—among which the prominent one is called CARTAGO—that make it possible to prototype MAS applications exploiting artifact-based working environments. Finally, we consider the issue of integration of such technologies with existing MAS cognitive environments, by adopting as a reference case the *Jason* programming platform, towards scenarios in which MAS composed by intelligent agents—possibly developed with different agent programming languages or architectures—suitably share and exploit artifact-based working environments to interact and cooperate.

Indeed, in this paper we introduced and described just the basic—and somewhat simplest—points concerning A&A and the notion of artifacts in MAS: several other important points have not being considered either for lack of space or because they are still part of the future work. Among the many others, two main ones are worth to be pointed out here: *artifact composition* (linkability) and *intelligent use of artifacts*. Concerning this second point in particular, theoretical work on models and theories for the cognitive use of artifacts is still in its infancy. The objective here is to find on the one side suitable languages and theoretical frameworks to formally describe—in particular— the function of artifacts, their operating instructions and more generally artifact observable state, so as to make them useful and effective in agent reasoning; on the other side, revisiting agent reasoning model and techniques so as to exploit as much as possible the availability of working environments suitably designed to help their activities. Existing work on MAS in semantic web and the research work investigating human and autonomous agents reasoning on (real-world) tools [2] indeed could provide useful insights to face the problem.

References

1. Agre, P., Horswill, I.: Lifeworld analysis. Journal of Artificial Intelligence Reserach 6, 111–145 (1997)
2. Amant, R.S., Wood, A.B.: Tool use for autonomous agents. In: Veloso, M.M., Kambhampati, S. (eds.) AAAI/IAAI 2005 Conference, Pittsburgh, PA, USA, July 9–13, 2005, pp. 184–189. AAAI Press / The MIT Press (2005)
3. Bordini, R., Braubach, L., Dastani, M., Seghrouchni, A.E.F., Gomez-Sanz, J., Leite, J., O'Hare, G., Pokahr, A., Ricci, A.: A survey of programming languages and platforms for multi-agent systems. Informatica 30, 33–44 (2006)
4. Bordini, R.H., Hübner, J.F.: BDI agent programming in AgentSpeak using Jason. In: Toni, F., Torroni, P. (eds.) CLIMA 2005. LNCS (LNAI), vol. 3900, pp. 143–164. Springer, Heidelberg (2006)
5. Kirsh, D.: The intelligent use of space. Artif. Intell. 73(1-2), 31–68 (1995)
6. Kirsh, D.: Distributed cognition, coordination and environment design. In: European conference on Cognitive Science, pp. 1–11 (1999)
7. Nardi, B.A.: Context and Consciousness: Activity Theory and Human-Computer Interaction. MIT Press, Cambridge (1996)
8. Norman, D.: Cognitive artifacts. In: Carroll, J. (ed.) Designing interaction: Psychology at the human–computer interface, pp. 17–38. Cambridge University Press, New York (1991)
9. Omicini, A., Ricci, A., Viroli, M.: Agens Faber: Toward a theory of artefacts for MAS. Electronic Notes in Theoretical Computer Sciences 150(3), 21–36 (May 29, 2006), In: Proceedings of 1st International Workshop Coordination and Organization (CoOrg 2005), COORDINATION 2005, Namur, Belgium, (April 22, 2005)
10. Omicini, A., Ricci, A., Viroli, M., Castelfranchi, C., Tummolini, L.: Coordination artifacts: Environment-based coordination for intelligent agents. In: AAMAS 2004, vol. 1, pp. 286–293. ACM, New York (2004)
11. Ricci, A., Viroli, M., Omicini, A.: Programming MAS with Artifacts. In: Bordini, R.H., Dastani, M., Dix, J., Seghrouchni, A.E.F. (eds.) PROMAS 2005. LNCS (LNAI), vol. 3862, pp. 206–221. Springer, Heidelberg (2006)
12. Ricci, A., Viroli, M., Omicini, A.: CArtAgO: A framework for prototyping artifact-based environments in MAS. In: Weyns, D., Van Dyke Parunak, H., Michel, F. (eds.) E4MAS 2006. LNCS (LNAI), vol. 4389, pp. 67–86. Springer, Heidelberg (2007)
13. Schmidt, K., Simone, C.: Coordination mechanisms: Towards a conceptual foundation of CSCW systems design. Computer Supported Cooperative Work 5(2/3), 155–200 (1996)
14. Viroli, M., Holvoet, T., Ricci, A., Schelfthout, K., Zambonelli, F.: Infrastructures for the environment of multiagent systems. Autonomous Agents and Multi-Agent Systems 14(1), 49–60 (2007)
15. Viroli, M., Omicini, A., Ricci, A.: Infrastructure for RBAC-MAS: An approach based on Agent Coordination Contexts. Applied Artificial Intelligence 21(4–5), 443–467 (April 2007) Special Issue: State of Applications in AI Research from AI*IA 2005
16. Weyns, D., Parunak, H.V.D. (eds.): Journal of Autonomous Agents and Multi-Agent Systems. Special Issue: Environment for Multi-Agent Systems 14(1) (2007)

A Practical Agent Programming Language

Mehdi Dastani and John-Jules Ch. Meyer

Utrecht University
The Netherlands
{mehdi,jj}@cs.uu.nl

Abstract. This paper discusses the need for an effective and practical BDI-based agent-oriented programming language with formal semantics. It proposes an alternative by presenting the syntax and semantics of a programming language, called 2APL (A Practical Agent Programming Language). This programming language facilitates the implementation of multi-agent systems consisting of individual cognitive agents. 2APL distinguishes itself from other BDI-based agent-oriented programming languages by having formal semantics while realising an effective integration of declarative and imperative style programming. This is done by introducing a set of practical programming constructs, including both declarative goals and events (which are used interchangeably in other programming languages), and specifying their operational semantics.

1 Introduction

Existing BDI-based agent-oriented programming languages such as Jason[2], Jack[8], Jadex[7], and 3APL[3,5] provide programming constructs and mechanisms that allow direct implementation of software agents in terms of BDI concepts. These programming languages differ from each other as they facilitate the implementation of different but overlapping sets of agent concepts. For example, they all share programming constructs to support the implementation of an agent's beliefs and plans. However, 3APL differs from other programming languages as it supports the implementation of declarative goals as well as plan revision mechanism, but lacks programming constructs to support the implementation of events and event handling mechanism. Although, a comparison between these BDI-based programming languages is outside the scope of this paper, we would like to emphasize that some of the concepts that are shared by these languages have different semantics or even are not comparable at all. For example, the beliefs and goals in 3APL (and the beliefs in Jason) are propositions having declarative semantics while the beliefs in Jack and Jadex can be represented by conventional data structures lacking a formal semantics. The situation gets even worse because different languages use different concepts with the same name or they use the same concept with different names. For example, although both Jason and 3APL use the concept of goal, a goal in Jason is an event that triggers a plan while a goal in 3APL is a proposition that can be reasoned with [3,4]. The declarative nature of goals in 3APL allows the implementation of generic planning rules that assign plans to *subgoals*, i.e., goals that are derivable from the goal base.

M. Dastani et al.(Eds.): ProMAS 2007, LNAI 4908, pp. 107–123, 2008.
© Springer-Verlag Berlin Heidelberg 2008

Our experience with using these agent-oriented programming languages in various academic courses and research projects have shown that some of the existing programming constructs, tools, and mechanisms are indeed useful, expressive and effective in programming software agents. It also made it clear that new programming constructs, mechanisms and tools are needed to make the BDI-based programming languages more expressive and *practical*. We have also learned that the use and a deep understanding of these programming languages are significantly improved by the availability of their formal semantics. In our opinion, a challenge of a practical BDI-based agent-oriented programming language is 1) to realise an effective integration of declarative and imperative style programming, and 2) to have formal semantics. The declarative style programming should facilitate the implementation of the mental state of agents allowing agents to reason about their mental states and update them accordingly. The imperative style programming should facilitate the implementation of processes, the flow of control, and mechanisms such as procedure call, recursion, and interface to existing imperative programming languages.

In this paper, we present a BDI-based agent-oriented programming language called 2APL (A *Practical* Agent Programming Language). The main motivation to design and develop 2APL is an *effective integration* of programming constructs that support the implementation of declarative concepts such as belief and goals with imperative style programming such as events and plans. Like most BDI-based programming languages, different types of actions such as belief and goal update actions, test actions, external actions, and communication actions are distinguished. These actions are composed by conditional choice operator, iteration operator, and sequence operator. The composed actions constitute the plans of the agents. Like the existing agent programming languages, 2APL provides rules to indicate that a certain goal can be achieved by a certain pre-compiled plan. Agents may select and apply such rules to generate plans to achieve their goals.

As agents may operate in dynamic environments, they have to observe their environmental changes. In 2APL environmental changes will be notified to the agents by means of *events*. It should be noted that in some agent programming languages events are used for various purposes. For example, a goal in Jason is an event, while in Jadex events are generated to notify an agent's internal changes as well. In our view, although both goals and events cause an agent to execute actions, there are fundamental differences between them. For example, an agent's goal denotes a desirable state for which the agent performs actions to achieve it, while an event carries information about (environmental) changes which may cause an agent to react and execute certain actions. After the execution of actions, an agent's goal may be dropped if the state denoted by it is achieved, while an event can be dropped just before (or immediately after) executing the actions that are triggered by it. Moreover, because of the declarative nature of goals, an agent can reason about its goals while an event only carries information which is not necessarily the subject of reasoning.

Some characterizing 2APL features are related to the constructs designed with respect to an agent's plans. The first construct is a part of an exception handling mechanism allowing a programmer to specify how an agent should repair its plans when their executions fail. This construct has the form of a rule which indicates how a plan should be repaired. It is similar to the plan revision rules introduced in 3APL, but it differs from it as 2APL rules can only be applied to repair *failed* plans. In contrast, the plan revision rules of 3APL is applied to all plans continuously. In our view, it does not make sense to modify a plan if the plan is correct and executable. The second 2APL programming construct with respect to plans is related to the so-called atomic plans. In most agent-oriented programming languages, an agent can have various plans whose executions can be interleaved. The arbitrary interleaving of plans may be problematic in some cases such that a programmer may want to indicate that a certain part of a plan should be executed atomically at once without being interleaved with the actions of other plans. Similar construct is also introduced in Jadex[7].

In the following sections, we first present the complete syntax of 2APL and discuss the intuitive meaning of its ingredients. Then, because of space limitation, the formal semantics of only some characterizing programming constructs of 2APL is presented. We conclude the paper by discussing the implementation of 2APL interpreter and its corresponding platform.

2   2APL: Syntax

This section presents the complete syntax of 2APL, which is specified using the EBNF notation. In this specification, illustrated in Figure 1, we use ⟨*atom*⟩ to denote a Prolog like atomic formula starting with lowercase letter, ⟨*Atom*⟩ to denote a Prolog like atomic formula starting with a capital latter (parentheses are required for such formula with zero argument), ⟨*ident*⟩ to denote a string and ⟨*Var*⟩ to denote a string starting with a capital letter. We use ⟨*ground_atom*⟩ to denote a ground atomic formula. An individual 2APL agent may be composed of various ingredients that specify different aspects of the agency. A 2APL agent can be programmed by implementing the initial state of those ingredients. In the following, we discuss each ingredients and give examples to illustrate them.

2.1   Beliefs and Goals

A 2APL agent may have beliefs and goals which change during the agent's execution. The *beliefs* of the agents are implemented by the belief base, which contains information the agent believes about its surrounding world including other agents. The implementation of the initial belief base starts with the keyword 'Beliefs:' followed by one or more belief expressions of the form ⟨*belief*⟩.

```
Beliefs:
  pos(1,1).
  hasGold(0).
  trash(2,5).
  trash(6,8).
  clean(blockWorld) :- not trash(_,_).
```

Note that a ⟨*belief*⟩ expression is a Prolog fact or rule such that the belief base of a 2APL agent becomes a Prolog program. All facts are assumed to be ground. The example above illustrates the implementation of the initial belief base of a 2APL agent. This

⟨2APL_Prog⟩   ::= ("Include:" ⟨ident⟩
                   | "BeliefUpdates:" ⟨BelUpSpec⟩
                   | "Beliefs:" ⟨belief⟩
                   | "Goals:" ⟨goals⟩
                   | "Plans:" ⟨plans⟩
                   | "PG-rules:" ⟨pgrules⟩
                   | "PC-rules:" ⟨pcrules⟩
                   | "PR-rules:" ⟨prrules⟩)*
⟨BelUpSpec⟩   ::= ("{" ⟨belquery⟩ "}" ⟨beliefupdate⟩ "{" ⟨literals⟩ "}")+
⟨belief⟩   ::= (⟨ground_atom⟩ "." | ⟨atom⟩ ": −" ⟨literals⟩ ".")+
⟨goals⟩   ::= ⟨goal⟩ ("," ⟨goal⟩)*
⟨goal⟩   ::= ⟨ground_atom⟩ ("and" ⟨ground_atom⟩)*
⟨baction⟩   ::= "skip" | ⟨beliefupdate⟩ | ⟨sendaction⟩ | ⟨externalaction⟩
                   | ⟨abstractaction⟩ | ⟨test⟩ | ⟨adoptgoal⟩ | ⟨dropgoal⟩
⟨plans⟩   ::= ⟨plan⟩ ("," ⟨plan⟩)*
⟨plan⟩   ::= ⟨baction⟩ | ⟨sequenceplan⟩ | ⟨ifplan⟩ | ⟨whileplan⟩ | ⟨atomicplan⟩
⟨beliefupdate⟩   ::= ⟨Atom⟩
⟨sendaction⟩   ::= "send(" ⟨iv⟩ "," ⟨iv⟩ "," ⟨atom⟩ ")"
                   | "send(" ⟨iv⟩ "," ⟨iv⟩ "," ⟨iv⟩ "," ⟨iv⟩ "," ⟨atom⟩ ")"
⟨externalaction⟩   ::= "@" ⟨iv⟩"("⟨atom⟩ "," ⟨Var⟩ ")"
⟨abstractaction⟩   ::= ⟨atom⟩
⟨test⟩   ::= "B(" ⟨belquery⟩ ")" | "G(" ⟨goalquery⟩ ")" | ⟨test⟩ "&" ⟨test⟩
⟨adoptgoal⟩   ::= "adopta(" ⟨goalvar⟩ ")" | "adoptz(" ⟨goalvar⟩ ")"
⟨dropgoal⟩   ::= "dropGoal(" ⟨goalvar⟩ ")" | "dropSubgoal(" ⟨goalvar⟩ ")"
                   | "dropExactgoal(" ⟨goalvar⟩ ")"
⟨sequenceplan⟩   ::= ⟨plan⟩ ";" ⟨plan⟩
⟨ifplan⟩   ::= "if" ⟨test⟩ "then" ⟨scopeplan⟩ ("else" ⟨scopeplan⟩)?
⟨whileplan⟩   ::= "while" ⟨test⟩ "do" ⟨scopeplan⟩
⟨atomicplan⟩   ::= "[" ⟨plan⟩ "]"
⟨scopeplan⟩   ::= "{" ⟨plan⟩ "}"
⟨pgrules⟩   ::= ⟨pgrule⟩+
⟨pgrule⟩   ::= ⟨goalquery⟩? "< −" ⟨belquery⟩ "|" ⟨plan⟩
⟨pcrules⟩   ::= ⟨pcrule⟩+
⟨pcrule⟩   ::= ⟨atom⟩ "< −" ⟨belquery⟩ "|" ⟨plan⟩
⟨prrules⟩   ::= ⟨prrule⟩+
⟨prrule⟩   ::= ⟨planvar⟩ "< −" ⟨belquery⟩ "|" ⟨planvar⟩
⟨goalvar⟩   ::= ⟨atom⟩("and"⟨atom⟩)*
⟨planvar⟩   ::= ⟨plan⟩ | ⟨Var⟩ | "if" ⟨test⟩ "then" ⟨scopeplanvar⟩ ("else" ⟨scopeplanvar⟩)?
                   | "while" ⟨test⟩ "do" ⟨scopeplanvar⟩ | ⟨planvar⟩ ";" ⟨planvar⟩
⟨scopeplanvar⟩   ::= "{" ⟨planvar⟩ "}"
⟨literals⟩   ::= ⟨literal⟩ ("," ⟨literal⟩)*
⟨literal⟩   ::= ⟨atom⟩ | "not" ⟨atom⟩
⟨ground_literal⟩   ::= ⟨ground_atom⟩ | "not" ⟨ground_atom⟩
⟨belquery⟩   ::= "true" | ⟨belquery⟩ "and" ⟨belquery⟩ | ⟨belquery⟩ "or" ⟨belquery⟩
                   | "(" ⟨belquery⟩ ")" | ⟨literal⟩
⟨goalquery⟩   ::= "true" | ⟨goalquery⟩ "and" ⟨goalquery⟩ | ⟨goalquery⟩ "or" ⟨goalquery⟩
                   | "(" ⟨goalquery⟩ ")" | ⟨atom⟩
⟨iv⟩   ::= ⟨ident⟩ | ⟨Var⟩

Fig. 1. The EBNF syntax of 2APL

belief base represents the information of an agent about its blockworld environment. In particular, the agent believes that its position in this environment is (1,1), it has no gold item in possession, there are trash at positions (2,5) and (6,8), and that the blockworld environment is clean if there are no trash anymore.

The *goals* of a 2APL agent are implemented by its goal base, which is a list of formulas each of which denotes a situation the agent wants to realize (not necessary all at once). The implementation of the initial goal base starts with the keyword 'Goals:' followed by a list of goal expressions of the form ⟨*goal*⟩. Each goal expression is a conjunction of ground atoms. Note that a ground atom is treated as a Prolog fact. The following example is the implementation of the initial goal base of a 2APL agent. This goal base indicates that the agent wants to achieve a desirable situation in which it has five gold items and the blockworld is clean. Note that this single conjunctive goal is different than having two separate goals 'hasGold(5)' and 'clean(blockworld)'. In the latter case, the agent wants to achieve two desirable situations independently of each other, i.e., one in which the agent has a clean blockworld, not necessarily with a gold item, and one in which it has five gold items and perhaps a blockworld which is not clean. Note that different goals in the goal base are separated by a comma.

```
Goals:
  hasGold(5) and clean(blockworld)
```

The beliefs and goals of agents are related to each other. In fact, if an agent believes a certain fact, then the agent does not pursue that fact as a goal. This means that if an agent modifies its belief base, then its goal base may be modified as well.

2.2   Basic Actions

Basic actions specify the capabilities that an agent can perform to achieve its desirable situation. The basic actions will constitute an agent's plan, as we will see in the next subsection. In 2APL, six types of basic actions are distinguished: actions to update the belief base, communication actions, external actions to be performed in an agent's environment, abstract actions, actions to test the belief and goal bases, and actions to manage the dynamics of goals.

Belief Update Action. A *belief update action* updates the belief base of an agent when executed. A belief update action ⟨*beliefupdate*⟩ is an expression of the form ⟨*Atom*⟩ (i.e., a first-order atom in which the predicate starts with a capital letter). Such an action is specified in terms of pre- and post-conditions. An agent can execute a belief update action if the pre-condition of the action is derivable from its belief base. The pre-condition is a formula consisting of literals composed by disjunction and conjunction operators. The execution of a belief update action modifies the belief base in such a way that after the execution the post-condition of the action is derivable from the belief base. The post-condition of a belief update action is a list of literals. The update of the belief base by such an action removes the atom of the negative literals from the belief base and adds the positive literals to the belief base. The specification of the belief update actions starts with the keyword 'BeliefUpdates:' followed by the specifications of a set of belief update actions ⟨*BelUpSpec*⟩.

```
BeliefUpdates:
  {not carry(gold)}        PickUp()        {carry(gold)}
  {trash(X,Y) and pos(X,Y)} RemoveTrash() {not trash(X,Y)}
  {hasGold(X)}             AddGold()       {not hasGold(X),
                                            not carry(gold),
                                            hasGold(X+1)}
  {pos(X,Y)}               ChgPos(X1,Y1)  {not pos(X,Y),
                                            pos(X1,Y1)}
```

Above is an example of the specification of the belief update actions. In this example, the specification of the PickUp() indicates that this belief update action can be performed if the agent does not already carry gold items and that after performing this action the agent will carry one gold item. The agent is assumed to be able to carry only one gold item. Note that the agent cannot perform two PickUp() action consecutively. Note also the use of variables in the specification of ChgPos(X1,Y1). It requires that an agent can change its current position to (X1,Y1) if its current position is (X,Y). After the execution of this belief update action, the agent believes that its position is (X1,Y1) and not (X,Y). Note also that variables in the post-conditions are bounded since otherwise the facts in the belief base will not be ground.

Communication Action. A *communication action* passes a message to another agent. A communication action ⟨*sendaction*⟩ can have either three or five parameters. In the first case, the communication action is the expression send(Receiver, Performative, Language, Ontology, Content) where Receiver is a name referring to the receiving agent, Performative is a speech act name (e.g. inform, request, etc.), Language is the name of the language used to express the content of the message, ontology is the name of the ontology used to give a meaning to the symbols in the content expression, and Content is an expression representing the content of the message. It is often the case that agents assume a certain language and ontology such that it is not necessary to pass them as parameters of their communication actions. The second version of the communication action is therefore the expression send(Receiver, Performative, Content). It should be noted that 2APL interpreter is built on the FIPA compliant JADE platform. For this reason, the name of the receiving agent can be a local name or a full JADE name. A full jade name has the form localname@host:port/JADE where localname is the name as used by 2APL, host is the name of the host running the agent's container and port is the port number where the agent's container, should listen to (see [1] for more information on JADE standards).

External Action. An *external action* is supposed to change the external environment in which agents operate. The effects of external actions are assumed to be determined by the environment and might not be known to the agents beforehand. An agent thus decides to perform an external action and the external environment determines the effect of the action. The agent can know the effects of an external action by performing a sense action (also defined as an external action), by means of events generated by the environment, or by means of a return parameter. An external action ⟨*externalaction*⟩ is an expression of the form @Env(ActionName,Return). The parameter Env is the name of the agent's environment, implemented as a Java class. The parameter `ActionName` is a method call (of the Java class) that specifies the effect of the external action in the environment. The environment is assumed to have a state represented by the instance variables of the class. The execution of an action in an environment is then a read/write operation on the state of the environment. The parameter `Return` is a list of values, possibly an empty list, returned by the corresponding method. An example of the implementation of an external action is `@blockworld(east(),L)` (go one step east in the blockworld environment). The effect of this action is that the position of the agent in the blockworld environment is shifted one slot to the right. The list L is expected as the return value.

Abstract Action. The general idea of an abstract action is similar to a procedure call in imperative programming languages. The procedures should be defined in 2APL by means of the co-called PC-rules, which stands for procedure call rules (see subsection 2.4 for a description of PC-rules). As we will see in subsection 2.4, a PC-rule can be used to associate a plan to an abstract action. The execution of an abstract action in a plan removes the abstract action from the plan and replaces it with an instantiation of the plan that is associated to the abstract action by a PC-rule. Like a procedure call in imperative programming languages, an abstract action $\langle abstractaction \rangle$ is an expression of the form $\langle atom \rangle$ (i.e. a first order expression in which the predicate starts with a lowercase letter). An abstract action can be used to pass parameters from one plan to another plan. In particular, the execution of an abstract action passes parameters from the plan in which it occurs to another plan that is associated to it by a PC-rule.

Test Actions. A *test action* is to check whether the agent has certain beliefs and goals. A test action is an expression of the form $\langle test \rangle$ consisting of belief and goal query expressions. A belief query expression has the form $B(\phi)$, where ϕ consists of *literals* composed by conjunction and disjunction operators. A goal query expression has the form $G(\phi)$, where ϕ consists of *atoms* composed by conjunction and disjunction operators.

A belief query expression, which constitutes a test action, is basically a (Prolog) query to the belief base and generates a substitution for the variables that are used in the belief query expression. A goal query expression, which also constitutes a test action, is a query to an individual goal in the goal base, i.e., it is to check if there is a goal in the goal base that satisfies the query. Such a query may also generate a substitution for the involved variables.

A test action can be used in a plan to 1) instantiate variables in the subsequent actions of the plan (if the test succeeds), or 2) block the execution of the plan (if the test fails). The instantiation of variables in a test action is determined through belief and goal queries performed from left to the right. For example, let an agent believes `p(a)` and has the goal `q(b)`, then the test action `B(p(X)) & G(q(X))` fails, while the test action `B(p(X)) & G(q(Y) or r(X))` succeeds with {X/a , Y/b} as the resulting substitution.

Goal Dynamics Actions. The *adopt goal* and *drop goal* actions are used to adopt and drop a goal to and from an agent's goal base, respectively. The adopt goal action $\langle adoptgoal \rangle$ can have two different forms: `adopta(`ϕ`)` and `adoptz(`ϕ`)`. These two actions can be used to add the goal ϕ (a conjunction of atoms) to the begin and to the end of an agent's goal base, respectively. Note that the programmer has to ensure that the variables in ϕ are instantiated before these actions are executed since the goal base should contain only ground formula. Finally, the drop goal action $\langle dropgoal \rangle$ can have three different forms: dropGoal(ϕ), dropSubGoal(ϕ), and dropExactGoal(ϕ). These actions can be used to drop from an agent's goal base, respectively, all goals that are a logical subgoal of ϕ, all goals that have ϕ as a logical subgoal, and exactly the goal ϕ, respectively. Similar actions are proposed in [6].

2.3 Plans

In order to reach its goals, a 2APL agent adopts *plans*. A plan consists of basic actions composed by some process composition operators. In particular, basic actions can be composed by means of the sequence operator, conditional choice operators, conditional iteration operator, and an unary operator to identify atomic plans.

The sequence operator ; is a binary operator that takes two plans and generates one $\langle sequence plan \rangle$ plan. The sequence operator indicates that the first plan should be performed before the second plan. The conditional choice operator generates $\langle if plan \rangle$ plans of the form if ϕ then π_1 else π_2, where π_1 and π_1 are arbitrary plans. The condition part of this expression (i.e., ϕ) is a test that should be evaluated with respect to an agent's belief and goal bases. Such a plan can be interpreted as to perform the if-part of the plan (i.e., π_1) when the test ϕ succeeds, otherwise perform the else-part of the plan (i.e., π_2). The conditional iteration operator generates $\langle while plan \rangle$ plans of the form while ϕ do π, where π is an arbitrary plan. The condition ϕ is also a test that should be evaluated with respect to an agent's belief and goal bases. The iteration expression is then interpreted as to perform the plan π as long as the test ϕ succeeds.

The last unary operator generates $\langle atomic plan \rangle$ plans, which are expressions of the form $[\pi]$, where π is an arbitrary plan. This plan is interpreted as an atomic plan π, which should be executed at once ensuring that the execution of π is not interleaved with the actions of other plans. Note that an agent can have different plans at the same time and that plans cannot be composed by an explicit parallel operator. As there is no explicit parallel composition operator, the nested application of the unary operator has no effect, i.e., the executions of plans $[\pi_1; \pi_2]$ and $[\pi; [\pi_2]]$ result identical behaviors.

The plans of a 2APL agent are implemented by its plan base. The implementation of the initial plan base starts with the keyword 'Plans:' followed by a list of plans. The following example illustrates the 2APL implementation of the initial plan base of an agent. The first plan is an atomic plan ensuring that the agent updates its belief base with its initial position $(5,5)$ immediately after performing the external action enter in the blockworld environment. The second plan is a single action by which the agent requests the administrator to register him.

```
Plans:
  [@blockworld(enter(5,5,red),L);ChgPos(5,5)],
  Send(admin,request,register(me))
```

2.4 Reasoning Rules

The 2APL programming language provides constructs to implement practical reasoning rules that can be used to implement the generation of plans. In particular, three types of practical reasoning rules are proposed: planning goal rules, procedure call rules, and plan repair rules. In the following subsections, we explain these three types of rules.

Planning Goal Rules (PG-rules). A planning goal rule can be used to implement an agent that generates a plan if it has certain goals and beliefs. The specification of a planning goal rule ⟨*pgrule*⟩ consists of three entries: the head of the rule, the condition of the rule, and the body of the rule. The head and the condition of a planning goal rule are query expressions used to check if the agent has a certain goal and belief, respectively. The body of the rule consists of a plan in which variables may occur. These variables should be bound by the goal and belief expressions. A planning goal rule of an agent can be applied when the goal and belief expressions (in the head and the condition of the rule) are derivable from the agent's goal and belief bases, respectively. The application of a planning goal rule generates a substitution for variables that occur in the head and condition of the rule as they are queried from the goal and belief bases. The resulted substitution will be applied to the generated plan to instantiate it. A planning goal rule is of the form: ⟨*goalquery*⟩? "< −" ⟨*belquery*⟩ "|" ⟨*plan*⟩.

Note that the head of the rule is optional which means that the agent can generate a plan only based on its belief condition. The following is an example of a planning goal rule indicating that a plan to go to a position (X2,Y2), departing from a position (X1,Y1), to remove trash can be generated if the agent has the goal clean(blockworld) and it believes its current position is pos(X1,Y1) and there is trash at position (X2,Y2).

```
PG-rules:
    clean(blockworld) <- pos(X1,Y1) and trash(X2,Y2) |
                         {goTo(X1,Y1,X2,Y2);RemoveTrash()}
```

The action goTo(X1,Y1,X2,Y2) in the above PG-rule is an abstract action (see subsection 2.4 for how to execute an abstract action). Note that this rule can be applied if (beside the satisfaction of the belief condition) the agent has a conjunctive goal hadGold(5) and clean(blockworld) since the head of the rule is derivable from this goal.

Procedure Call Rules (PC-rules). The procedure call rules is introduced for various reasons and purposes. Besides their use as procedure definition (used for executing abstract actions), they can also be used to respond to messages and handle external events. In fact, a procedure call rule can be used to generate plans as a response to the reception of messages send by other agents, events generated by the external environment, and the execution of abstract actions. Like planning goal rules, the specification of procedure call rules consist of three entries. The only difference is that the head of the procedure call rules is an atom ⟨*atom*⟩, rather than a goal query expression ⟨*goalquery*⟩. The head of a PC-rule can be a message, an event, or an abstract action. A message and an event are represented by atoms with the special predicates message/3 (message/5) and event/2, respectively. An abstract action is represented by any predicate name starting with a lowercase letter. Note that like planning goal rules, a procedure call rule has a belief condition indicating when a message (or event or abstract action) should generate a plan. Thus, a procedure call rule can be applied if the agent has received a message (or an event or executes an abstract action) and the belief query of the rule is derivable from its belief base. The resulted substitution for variables are applied in order to instantiate the generated plan. A procedure call rule ⟨*pcrule*⟩ is of the form: ⟨*atom*⟩ "< −" ⟨*belquery*⟩ "|" ⟨*plan*⟩. The following are examples of procedure call rules.

```
PC-rules:
  message(A,inform,La,On,goldAt(X2,Y2)) <-  not carry(gold) |
        {[  pos(X1,Y1)?; goTo(X1,Y1,X2,Y2);
            @blockworld(pickup(),_); PickUp();
            goTo(X2,Y2,3,3);
            @blockworld(drop(),_); AddGold()]
        }

  event(gold(X2,Y2),blockworld) <-  not carry(gold) |
        {[  pos(X1,Y1)?;goTo(X1,Y1,X2,Y2);
            @blockworld(pichup(),_);PickUp();
            goTo(X2,Y2,3,3);
            @blockworld(drop(),_);AddGold()]
        }

  goTo(X1,Y1,X2,Y2) <- X1 < X2 |
        {[  @blockworld(east(),_);ChgPos(X1+1,Y1);
          goTo(X1+1,Y1,X2,Y2)]
        }
```

The first rule indicates that if an agent A informs that there is some gold at position (X2,Y2) and the agent believes it does not carry any gold, then the agent has to go from its current position to the gold position, pick up the gold, go to the depot position (i.e. position (3,3)), and drop the gold in the depot. The PickUp() and AddGold() are belief update actions to administrate the facts that the agent is carrying gold and has certain amount of gold, respectively. The second rule indicates that if the environment blockworld notifies the agent that there is some gold at position (X2,Y2) and the agent believes it does not carry gold, then the abovementioned sequence of actions should take place. The generation of plans without a belief condition enables a programmer to implement reactive agent behavior, i.e., plans are generated if the agent is notified about an environmental change. Finally, the last rule indicates that the abstract action goTo should be performed as a certain sequence of actions. Note that all plans are implemented as atomic plans. The reason is that in these plans external actions and belief update actions are executed consecutively such that an unfortunate interleaving of actions can have undesirable effects. Note the use of recursion in this PC-rule.

Plan Repair Rules (PR-rules). Like other practical reasoning rules, a plan repair rule consists of three entries: two abstract plan expressions and one belief query expression. We have used the term abstract plan expression since such plan expressions include variables that can be substituted with a plan. A plan repair rule indicates that if the execution of an agent's plan (i.e., any plan that can be unified with the abstract plan expression) fails and the agent has a certain belief, then the failed plan should be replaced by another plan. A plan repair rule $\langle prrule \rangle$ has the following form: $\langle planvar \rangle$ "< –" $\langle belquery \rangle$ "|" $\langle planvar \rangle$.

A plan repair rule of an agent can thus be applied if 1) the execution of one of its plan fails, 2) the failed plan can be unified with the abstract plan expression in the head of the rule, and 3) the belief query expression is derivable from the agent's belief base. The satisfaction of these three conditions results in a substitution for the variables that occur in the abstract plan expression in the body of the rule. Note that some of these variables will be substituted with a part of the failed plan through the match between the abstract plan expression in the head of the rule and the failed plan. For example, if π, π_1, π_2 are plans and X is a plan variable, then the abstract plan $\pi_1; X; \pi_2$ can be unified with the failed plan $\pi_1; \pi; \pi_2$ resulting the substitution $X = \pi$. The resulted substitutions will be applied to the second abstract plan expression to generate the new (repaired) plan.

The following is an example of a plan repair rule. This rule indicates that if the execution of a plan that starts with @blockworld(east(),_);@blockworld(east(),_) fails, then the plan should be replaced by a plan in which the agent first goes one step to north, then makes two steps to east, and goes one step back to south. This repair can be done without a specific belief condition.

```
PR-rules:
   @blockworld(east(),_);@blockworld(east(),_);X <- true |
       { @blockworld(north(),_);@blockworld(east(),_);
         @blockworld(east(),_);@blockworld(south(),_);X }
```

Note the use of the variable X that indicates that any failed plan starting with external actions @blockworld(east(),_);@blockworld(east(),_) can be repaired by the same plan in which the external actions are replaced by four external actions.

The question is when the execution of a plan fails. We consider the execution of a plan as failed if the execution of its first action fails. When the execution of an action fails depends on the type of action. The execution of a belief update action fails if the pre-condition of the action is not derivable from the belief base or if the action is not specified, an abstract action if there is no applicable procedure call rule, an external action if the corresponding environment throws an ExternalActionFailedException or if the agent has no access to that environment or if the action is not defined in that environment, a test action if the test expression is not derivable from the belief and goal bases, a goal adopt action if the goal is already derivable from the belief base, and an atomic plan if one of its actions fails. The execution of all other actions are always successful. When the execution of an action fails, then the execution of the whole plan is stopped. The failed action will not be removed from the failed plan such that it can be repaired.

2.5   External Environment

An agent can perform actions in different external environments that are implemented by a programmer as Java classes. Any Java class that implements the *environment interface* can be used as a 2APL environment. The environment interface contains two methods, *addAgent(String name)* and *removeAgent(String name)* to add/remove an agent to/from the environment, respectively . The constructor of the environment must require exactly one parameter of the type *ExternalEventListener*. This object listens to external events.

The execution of action @Env($f(a_1, \ldots, a_n)$,R) calls a method with name f in environment Env with arguments $a_1, \ldots, a_n$. The first argument a_1 is assumed to be the identifier of the agent that executes the action. The environment needs to have this identifier, for example, to pass information back to the agent by means of events. The second parameter R of an external action is meant to pass information back to the *plan* in which the external action was executed. Note that the execution of a plan is blocked until the method f is ready and the return value is accessible to the rest of the plan.

Methods may throw an exception (ExternalActionFailedException). If they throw an exception, the corresponding external action is considered as failed. The following is an example of a method that can be called as external action.

```
public Term move(String agent, String direction)
   throws ExternalActionFailedException
{
   if (direction.equals("north") {moveNorth();}
   else if (direction.equals("east") {moveEast();}
   else if (direction.equals("south") {moveSouth();}
   else if (direction.equals("west") {moveWest();}
   else throw
    new ExternalActionFailedException("Unknown direction");
   return getPositionTerm();
}
```

2.6 Events and Exception

Information between agents and environments can be passed through *events* and *exceptions*. The main use of events is to pass information from environments to agents. When implementing a 2APL environment in Java, the programmer should decide when and which information from the environment should be passed to agents. This can be done by calling the method notifyEvent(AF event, String... agents) in the ExternalEventListener, which is an argument of the environments constructor. The first argument of this method may be any valid atomic formula. The rest of the arguments may be filled with strings that represents local names of agents. The events can be catched by agents whose name is included in the argument list to trigger one of their procedure call rules. If the programmer does not specify any agents in the argument list, all agents can catch the event. Such a mechanism of generating events by the environment and catching it by agents can be used to implement the agents' perceptual mechanism.

The exceptions in 2APL are used to apply plan repair rules. In fact, a plan repair rule is triggered when a plan execution fails. Exceptions are used to notify that the execution of a plan was not successful. The exception contains the identifier of the failed plan such that it can be determined which plan needs to be repaired. 2APL does not provide programming constructs to implement the generation and throwing of exceptions. In fact, exceptions are semantical entities that cannot be used by 2APL programmers.

3 2APL: Semantics

In the previous section, we described 2APL programming constructs and their intuitive meanings. In this section, we present the formal semantics of 2APL in terms of a transition system. A transition system is a set of derivation rules for deriving transitions. A transition is a transformation of one configuration into another and it corresponds to a single computation step. Because of the space limitation, we only present the configuration of 2APL agents, external actions, and characterizing 2APL constructs such as goal related constructs, atomic plan construct, and plan repair rules.

The configuration of an individual agent consists of its identifier, beliefs, goals, plans, specifications of belief update actions, reasoning rules, the substitutions resulted from queries to the belief and goal bases, and the received events. Since reasoning rules and the specification of belief update actions do not change during an agent's execution, we will not include them in the agent's configuration to keep the presentation as simple as possible. It should be noted that additional information is assigned to an agent's plan. In particular, an identifier is assigned to each plan which can be used to notify that the execution of the plan is failed. This is needed to identify and repair the plans the execution of which have failed. Moreover, the instantiation of the PG-rule through which a plan is generated is assigned to the plan. This information is used to avoid selecting a PG-rule to generate a plan if there is still a plan in the plan base that is generated by the same PG-rule and for the same goal.

Definition 1. *The configuration of a 2APL agent is defied as $A_\iota = \langle \iota, \sigma, \gamma, \Pi, \theta, \xi \rangle$ where ι is a string representing the agent's identifier, σ is a set of belief expressions $\langle belief \rangle$ representing the agent's belief base, γ is a list of goal expressions $\langle goal \rangle$ representing the agent's goal base, Π is a set of plan entries consisting of $\langle plan \rangle$, enriched with additional information, representing the agent's plan base, θ is a ground substitution that binds domain variables to ground terms, and ξ is the agent's event base. Each plan entry is a tuple (π, r, p) where π is the executing plan, r is the instantiation of the PG-rule through which π is generated, and p is the plan identifier. The agent's event base ξ is a tuple $\langle E, I, M \rangle$ where*

- *E is a set of events received from external environments. An event has the form event(A, S), where A is a ground atom passed by the environment S.*
- *I is a set of identifiers denoting failed plans. An identifier represents an exceptions thrown because of a plan execution failure.*
- *M is the set of messages sent to the agent. Each message is of the form message(s, p, l, o, φ), where s is the sender identifier, p is a performative, l is the communication language, o is the communication ontology, and φ is a ground atom representing the message content.*

In the rest of this paper, we use $\models$ as a first-order entailment relation (we use Prolog engine for the implementation of this relation).

The configuration of a multi-agents system is defined in terms of the configuration of individual agents in the multi-agent system and their shared external environments.

Definition 2. *Let A_i be the configuration of agent i and let χ be a set of external shared environments each of which is a set of atoms $\langle atom \rangle$. The configuration of a 2APL multi-agents system is defined as $\langle A_1, \ldots, A_n, \chi \rangle$.*

The idea of a test action is to check if the belief and goal queries within a $\langle test \rangle$ expression are entailed by the agent's belief and goal bases. Moreover, as some of the variables that occur in the belief and goal queries may already be bound by the substitution θ, we apply the substitution to the $\langle test \rangle$ expression before testing it against the belief and goal bases. After applying θ, the test expression can still contain unbound variables to bind next occurrences of the variable in the plan in which it occurs. Therefore, the test action results a substitution τ which will be added to θ.

Definition 3. *Let φ and φ' be $\langle test \rangle$ expressions, ϕ be a $\langle belquery \rangle$ expression, ψ be a $\langle goalquery \rangle$ expression, and $\models_t$ be the entailment relation that evaluates test expressions with respect to an agent's belief and goal bases (σ, γ).*

- $(\sigma, \gamma) \models_t B(\phi)\tau \iff \sigma \models \phi\tau$
- $(\sigma, \gamma) \models_t G(\psi)\tau \iff \exists \gamma_i \in \gamma : \gamma_i \models \psi\tau$
- $(\sigma, \gamma) \models_t (\varphi \ \& \ \varphi')\tau_1\tau_2 \iff (\sigma, \gamma) \models_t \varphi\tau_1 \text{ and } (\sigma, \gamma) \models_t \varphi'\tau_1\tau_2$

A test action φ can be executed successfully if φ is entailed by the agent's belief and goal bases and the goal associated to this action is entailed by the agent's goal base.

$$\frac{(\sigma, \gamma) \models_t \varphi\theta\tau}{\langle \iota, \sigma, \gamma, \{(\varphi, r, \_)\}, \theta, \_ \rangle \longrightarrow \langle \iota, \sigma, \gamma, \{\}, \theta \cup \{\tau\}, \_ \rangle}$$

A test action can fail if one or more of its involved query expressions are not entailed by the belief or goal bases. In such a case, the test action remains in the agent's plan base and an exception is generated to indicate the failure of this action.

$$\frac{\neg\exists\tau : (\sigma, \gamma) \models_t \varphi\theta\tau}{\langle \iota, \sigma, \gamma, \{(\varphi, r, id)\}, \theta, \langle E, I, M \rangle\rangle \longrightarrow \langle \iota, \sigma, \gamma, \{(\varphi, r, id)\}, \theta, \langle E, I \cup \{id\}, M \rangle\rangle}$$

The execution of an external action $@Env(\alpha(t_i, \ldots, t_n), V)$ has two different effects. The shared environments is changed and the variable V might be assigned to a term. To define the effect of an external action on the agent's state we define a function that returns a tuple containing the new state of the environments and the assignment for V. Let $F_{\alpha}^{Env}(t_1, \ldots, t_n, \chi)$ be the function that executes external action α with arguments $t_1, \ldots, t_n$ in the environment $Env \in \chi$ and returns a tuple (τ, χ'), where τ contains one substitution for the output variable V and χ' is the updated set of environments (a change in Env may change other environments in χ). A successful execution of an external action updates the agent's substitution θ and the set of shared environments χ. Note that because the environment is shared among agents, the transition for an external action of an individual agent is defined at the multi-agent level.

$$\frac{F_{\alpha}^{Env}(t_1\theta, \ldots, t_n\theta, \chi) = (t, \chi') \ \& \ t \neq \bot}{\langle A_1, \ldots, A_i, \ldots, A_n, \chi \rangle \longrightarrow \langle A_1, \ldots, A_i', \ldots, A_n, \chi' \rangle}$$

where
$A_i = \langle i, \sigma_i, \gamma_i, \{(@Env(\alpha(t_1, \ldots, t_n), V), r, id)\}, \theta, \xi \rangle$ &
$A_i' = \langle i, \sigma_i, \gamma_i, \{\}, \theta \cup \{[V/t]\}, \xi \rangle$

However, if the execution of an external action fails, then the environment Env generates an exception such that F_{α}^{Env} returns $(\bot, \chi')$. The failed action remains then in the plan base, the environments χ may be updated, and the event base ξ is updated to capture the failure exception.

$$\frac{F_\alpha^{Env}(t_1\theta,\ldots,t_n\theta,\chi) = (\bot,\chi')}{\langle A_1,\ldots,A_i,\ldots,A_n,\chi \rangle \longrightarrow \langle A_1,\ldots,A_i',\ldots,A_n,\chi' \rangle}$$

where

$A_i = \langle i,\sigma_i,\gamma_i,\{((@Env(\alpha(t_1,\ldots,t_n),V),r,id)\},\theta,\langle E,I,M \rangle \rangle$ &
$A_i' = \langle i,\sigma_i,\gamma_i,\{((@Env(\alpha(t_1,\ldots,t_n),V),r,id)\},\theta,\langle E,I \cup \{id\},M \rangle$

In order to achieve an agent's goal, plans should be generated and executed. The generation of plans is through application of planning goals rules. Applying PG-rules update only the plan base. Let $r = \kappa \leftarrow \beta \mid \pi$ be a PG-rule of the agent, P be the set of all possible plans, I be the set of all plan identifiers, $\gamma = [\gamma_1,\ldots,\gamma_i,\ldots,\gamma_n]$ be the agent's goal base, and $\kappa' \leftarrow \beta' \mid \pi'$ be a variant of r, i.e., all variables occurring in r are assumed to be fresh variables.

$$\frac{\gamma_i \models \kappa'\tau_1 \ \& \ \sigma \models \beta'\tau_1\tau_2 \ \& \ \neg\exists\pi^* \in P : (\pi^*, (\kappa'\tau_1 \leftarrow \beta \mid \pi), \_) \in \Pi}{\langle \iota,\sigma,\gamma,\Pi,\theta,\xi \rangle \longrightarrow \langle \iota,\sigma,\gamma,\Pi \cup \{(\pi'\tau_1\tau_2, \ \kappa'\tau_1 \leftarrow \beta \mid \pi, \ id)\},\theta,\xi \rangle}$$

where id is a fresh plan identifier. Note that it is checked that there is not already a plan in Π which is generated by the same planning rule for the same goal. Note also that κ can be true. In such a case, the applied PG-rule can be re-applied if the plan generated by it is completely executed and removed from the plan base.

Goals can be adopted and dropped from the goal base by means of specific adopt and drop goal actions. There are two actions to add goal g to the goal base: adopta(g) and adoptz(g).

$$\frac{\sigma \not\models g\theta \ \& \ \text{ground}(g\theta)}{\langle \iota,\sigma,\gamma,\{(\text{adoptX}(g),r,id)\},\theta,\xi \rangle \longrightarrow \langle \iota,\sigma,\gamma',\{\},\theta,\xi \rangle}$$

where $\text{ground}(g\theta)$ means that $g\theta$ is a ground formula, $\gamma' = g\theta \cdot \gamma$ if adoptX is adopta (i.e., the goal $g\theta$ is added to the begin of the list γ of goals) and $\gamma' = \gamma \cdot g\theta$ if adoptX is adoptz (i.e., the goal $g\theta$ is added to the end of γ).

The dropGoal(g) action drops all goals that are logical subgoals of g from the goal base.

$$\frac{\gamma' = \gamma \setminus \{f \mid g\theta \models f\}}{\langle \iota,\sigma,\gamma,\{(\text{dropGoal}(g),r,id)\},\theta,\xi \rangle \longrightarrow \langle \iota,\sigma,\gamma',\{\},\theta,\xi \rangle}$$

The transitions for dropSubGoal(g) and dropExactGoal(g) are similar except that $\gamma' = \gamma \setminus \{f \mid f \models g\theta\}$ and $\gamma' = \gamma \setminus \{f \mid f \equiv g\theta\}$, respectively. See section 2.2 for their intuitive meanings.

The execution of an atomic plan is the non-interleaved execution of the maximum number of actions of the plan. Let $[\alpha_1;\ldots;\alpha_n]$ be an atomic plan. We need to define a transition rule that allows the derivation of a transition from a configuration $A_1 = \langle \iota,\sigma_1,\gamma_1,\{([\alpha_1;\ldots;\alpha_n],r,id)\},\theta_1,\xi_1 \rangle$ to a configuration $A_m = \langle \iota,\sigma_m,\gamma_m,\Pi,\theta_m,\xi_m \rangle$ such that either $\Pi = \{([\alpha_k;\ldots;\alpha_n],r,id)\}$ and α_k is the first action whose execution fails, or all actions of the atomic plan are successfully executed, i.e., $\Pi = \{\}$. Let $A_i = \langle \iota,\sigma_i,\gamma_i,\{[(\pi,r,id)]\},\theta_i,\xi_i \rangle$ and $A_{i+1} = \langle \iota,\sigma_{i+1},\gamma_{i+1},\{[(\pi',r,id)]\},\theta_{i+1},\xi_{i+1} \rangle$. In order to specify the transition rule for atomic plans, we define $transition(A_i,A_{i+1})$ to indicate that the following one-step transition is derivable (the execution of one step of plan π results plan π')[1]:

$$A_i = \langle \iota, \sigma_i, \gamma_i, \{(\alpha; \pi, r, id)\}, \theta_i, \xi_i \rangle \longrightarrow \langle \iota, \sigma_{i+1}, \gamma_{i+1}, \{(\pi', r, id)\}, \theta_{i+1}, \xi_{i+1} \rangle = A_{i+1}$$

The following transition rule specifies the execution of atomic plan $[\alpha_1; \ldots; \alpha_n]$.

$$\frac{(\forall_i : 1 \leq i \leq m \rightarrow transition(A_i, A_{i+1})) \ \& \ \forall A : \neg transition(A_{m+1}, A)}{\langle \iota, \sigma_1, \gamma_1, \{([\alpha_1; \ldots; \alpha_n], r, id)\}, \theta_1, \xi_1 \rangle \longrightarrow \langle \iota, \sigma_{m+1}, \gamma_{m+1}, \Pi, \theta_{m+1}, \xi_{m+1} \rangle}$$

where $A_1 = \langle \iota, \sigma_1, \gamma_1, \{([\alpha_1; \ldots; \alpha_n], r, id)\}, \theta_1, \xi_1 \rangle$ and $A_{m+1} = \langle \iota, \sigma_{m+1}, \gamma_{m+1}, \Pi, \theta_{m+1},$ $\xi_{m+1} \rangle$. Note that the condition $\forall A : \neg transition(A_{m+1}, A)$ can hold for two reasons: either there is no action to execute or the execution of one of the involved action has failed. In the first case the resulting plan base Π contains an empty plan $([\epsilon], r, id)$ and in the second case a non-empty plan $([\pi_{m+1}], r, id)$.

Finally, the execution of the application of a plan repair rule is based on the received exceptions that identify failed plans. Let $\xi = \langle E, I, M \rangle$ be the event base of a 2APL agent and $\pi_1 \leftarrow \beta \mid \pi_2$ be a variant of a PR-rule. Suppose the execution of a plan $(\pi, r, id) \in \Pi$ fails such that $id \in I$. Then, the plan repair rule can be applied if the failed plan π matches the abstract plan expression π_1 in the head of the rule, and moreover, its belief condition is derivable from the belief base. The result is a substitution that will be applied to the abstract plan expression in the body of the rule to generate a new plan and to add it to the plan base. We assume a unification operator $U(\pi, \pi_1)$ that implements a prefix matching strategy for matching plan π with abstract plan expression π_1. Roughly speaking, a prefix matching strategy means that the abstract plan expression is matched with the prefix of the failed plan. The unification operator returns a tuple (τ_T, τ_P, π^*) where τ_T is a term substitution, τ_P is a plan substitution and π^* is the postfix of π that did not play a role in the match with π_1 (e.g., $U(\alpha(a); \alpha(b); \alpha(c)$, $X; \alpha(Y)) = ([Y/b], [X/\alpha(a)], \alpha(c)))$. Note the all substitutions are applied to the abstract plan expression from the body of the rule to generate a new plan.

$$\frac{U(\pi, \pi_1) = (\tau_T, \tau_P, \pi^*) \ \& \ \sigma \models \beta \tau_T \tau_2 \ \& \ id \in I}{\langle \iota, \sigma, \gamma, \{(\pi, r, id)\}, \theta, \langle E, I, M \rangle \rangle \longrightarrow \langle \iota, \sigma, \gamma, \{(\pi_2 \tau_T \tau_2 \tau_P; \pi^*, r, id)\}, \theta, \langle E, I \setminus \{id\}, M \rangle \rangle}$$

If no plan repair rule can be applied to the failed plan, then the exception is deleted from the event base and the failed plan remains in the plan base.

$$\frac{\forall (\pi_1 \leftarrow \beta \mid \pi_2) \in PR : (U(\pi, \pi_1) = \bot \text{ or } \sigma \not\models \beta) \ \& \ id \in I \ \& \ (\pi, r, id) \in \Pi}{\langle \iota, \sigma, \gamma, \Pi, \theta, \langle E, I, M \rangle \rangle \longrightarrow \langle \iota, \sigma, \gamma, \Pi, \theta, \langle E, I \setminus \{id\}, M \rangle \rangle}$$

4 Conclusion and Future Works

In this paper, we presented a BDI-based agent-oriented programming language that provides practical constructs for the implementation of cognitive agents. The complete syntax and the intuitive interpretation of the involved programming constructs are discussed. Unfortunately, because of the space limitation we could only present the transition semantics of some characterising programming constructs.

---

[1] Note that the execution of an abstract action in a plan can extend the plan.

We have implemented this semantics in the form of an interpreter that can execute 2APL programs (i.e., initial configuration of 2APL agents). The execution of agents is based on a deliberation cycle. Each cycle determines which transition in which order should take place. The 2APL interpreter starts with applying planning goal rules to generate plans for the agent's goals, selects and executes plans, checks for exceptions and repairs failed plans by applying plan repair rules, and finally checks for received messages and events to apply the procedural call rules. This interpreter is integrated in a 2APL platform that allows an agent programmer to load, edit, run, and debug a set of 2APL agents. This platform is built on top of the JADE platform in order to exploit all tools and facilities that are developed for the JADE platform. These include tools such as the Sniffer, Introspector, and RMA (Remote Agent management). We use also the JADE communication layer to implement the communication between agents. Note that the JADE platform aims to be complaint with the FIPA standards. Since the communication between 2APL agents are through the JADE platform, the 2APL interpreter inherits the objective of the JADE platform of being FIPA complaint.

We are working on various extensions of both 2APL language (e.g., adding constructs to implement organisations and coordination artifacts at the multi-agent level) as well as tools to be integrated in the 2APL platform (e.g., visual programming and debugging facilities). The current implementation of the 2APL platform together with some examples and documentation can be downloaded from the following 2APL web site.

$$http://www.cs.uu.nl/2apl/$$

References

1. Bellifemine, F., Bergenti, F., Caire, G., Poggi, A.: JADE - a java agent development framework. In: Multi-Agent Programming: Languages, Platforms and Applications, Kluwer, Dordrecht (2005)
2. Bordini, R., Hübner, J.F., Vieira, R.: Jason and the golden fleece of agent-oriented programming. In: Multi-Agent Programming: Languages, Platforms and Applications, Kluwer, Dordrecht (2005)
3. Dastani, M., van Riemsdijk, M., Meyer, J.-J.C.: Programming multi-agent systems in 3apl. In: Multi-Agent Programming: Languages, Platforms and Applications, Kluwer, Dordrecht (2005)
4. Dastani, M., van Riemsdijk, M.B., Meyer, J.-J.C.: Goal types in agent programming. In: Proceedings of the 17th European Conference on Artificial Intelligence (ECAI 2006) (2006)
5. Hindriks, K.V., Boer, F.S.D., Hoek, W.V.D., Meyer, J.-J.C.: Agent programming in 3apl. In: Autonomous Agents and Multi-Agent Systems, vol. 2(4), pp. 357–401 (1999)
6. Hindriks, K.V., de Boer, F.S., van der Hoek, W., Meyer, J.-J.C.: Agent Programming with Declarative Goals. In: Castelfranchi, C., Lespérance, Y. (eds.) ATAL 2000. LNCS (LNAI), vol. 1986, pp. 228–243. Springer, Heidelberg (2001)
7. Pokahr, A., Braubach, L., Lamersdorf, W.: Jadex: A BDI reasoning engine. In: Multi-Agent Programming: Languages, Platforms and Applications, Kluwer, Dordrecht (2005)
8. Winikoff, M.: JACK^{TM} intelligent agents: An industrial strength platform. In: Multi-Agent Programming: Languages, Platforms and Applications, Kluwer, Dordrecht (2005)

A Common Semantic Basis for BDI Languages[*]

Louise A. Dennis[1], Berndt Farwer[2], Rafael H. Bordini[2],
Michael Fisher[1], and Michael Wooldridge[1]

[1] Department of Computer Science, University of Liverpool, UK
[2] Department of Computer Science, University of Durham, UK
lad@csc.liv.ac.uk

Abstract. We describe the design of an intermediate language (AIL) for BDI-style programming languages. AIL is not intended as yet another programming language, but is meant to provide a common semantic basis for a number of BDI programming languages in order to support both formal verification and the transfer of concepts and developments. We examine some of the key features of AIL, unifying a wide variety of structures appearing in the operational semantics of BDI programming languages. In particular, we highlight issues in the treatment of events, goals, and intentions, which are central to the design of these languages.

1 Introduction

As the concept of an "agent" becomes more popular, so the variety of programming languages based upon this concept increases. These *agent-oriented* programming languages range from minimal extensions of JAVA through to logic-based languages for "intelligent" agents [1,15]. In our work, we are particularly concerned (at least initially) with approaches based on *rational agent theories* [28], primarily the *BDI theory* developed by Rao and Georgeff [23]. Such languages not only incorporate the autonomous behaviour required for the agent concept, but also provide sophisticated mechanisms for instigating, controlling, and reasoning about such behaviours.

Although programming languages based on the BDI approach (let us call these *BDI languages*) are increasingly popular, there are several problems, for example:

1. there are *too* many languages – consider all the varieties described in [1];
2. many of the languages are similar, yet subtly different – this makes it difficult for developers to learn more than one language, as they are not based on agreed notions/definitions; further, such differences make it difficult to identify precisely the general mechanisms and to transfer new techniques between languages; and
3. despite the fact that many BDI languages have logical semantics and utilise logical mechanisms, formal verification tools are rare.

This last aspect is particularly important, since BDI approaches are increasingly used in complex, critical applications such as space exploration [20,5,24].

In our work[1] we aim to design an intermediate language (called AIL– *Agent Infrastructure Layer*) for BDI-style programming languages. There are several motivations for this, including:

---

[*] Work supported by EPSRC grants EP/D054788 (Durham) and EP/D052548 (Liverpool).
[1] See http://www.csc.liv.ac.uk/~michael/mcapl06 for details.

M. Dastani et al.(Eds.): ProMAS 2007, LNAI 4908, pp. 124–139, 2008.
© Springer-Verlag Berlin Heidelberg 2008

- providing a common semantic basis for a number of BDI languages, thus clarifying issues and aiding further programming language development;
- supporting formal verification by developing a *model-checker* optimised for checking AIL programs – existing BDI languages can have language-specific compilers for AIL so as to take advantage of its associated model-checker; and
- providing, potentially, a high-level virtual machine for efficient and portable implementation.

Rather than attempting to cover all BDI languages from the start, we have initially tackled some of the most popular. Thus, we have principally referred to the variant of AgentSpeak [22] used in *Jason* [3] and 3APL [18,8] when designing the semantics for the AIL, but have also taken Jadex [21] and (Concurrent) METATEM [14] into account. However, we expect that a significant proportion of the existing programming languages for multi-agent systems will have mappings into AIL in the future.

The current design for AIL, in the form of an extensive operational semantics, can be found in [10]. For the sake of space, in this paper we only discuss the main aspects of AIL and introduce only the most important rules of the operational semantics. In order to model a particular language in AIL, it will be necessary to create a custom AIL compiler for that language. It may also be necessary to provide some custom JAVA classes for the language although these will, in general, be specific to a particular *interpreter* for the language rather than the language itself. We intend to provide such classes and compilers for AgentSpeak and 3APL, though this work remains to be done. The correctness of these compilers will then also need to be addressed. One of the reasons why AIL is to be implemented as a JAVA library is that we aim to use JPF[2] [26] as a target model checker for programs written in various BDI languages.

Sometimes it will prove possible to map only fragments of a given language into AIL. Our expectation is that large and useful fragments of most BDI-style agent programming languages will be translatable. In order to accommodate the main features of the main BDI languages, AIL has some components with overlapping functionality.

The structure of the remainder of this paper is as follows. In Section 2, we will describe the key similarities in the programming languages considered, which will in turn provide the basis for AIL. Section 3 then describes the core features and operational semantics of AIL. Within AIL, certain language design decisions were required; those related to plan revision in particular are highlighted in Section 4. Finally, in Section 5, we provide concluding remarks, outline future work, and point to aspects of AIL not covered in this paper.

2   General Similarities

There are some general concepts that are found in many BDI languages. We will review these similarities and discuss the design implications for AIL.

Formula Representation. 3APL, AgentSpeak, and METATEM all use minor variations on first order literals for the representation of beliefs, goals, actions, etc. Jadex uses an internal JAVA representation but fragments of this can be mapped into first order logic [4]. Therefore we have chosen first order literals as the basic representation.

---

[2] http://javapathfinder.sf.net

Beliefs. All these languages have the concept of a *belief base*, generally considered as a set of (belief) formulæ. A formula is considered to be believed if it is (unifiable with) a formula in this set. In some languages there is extra reasoning machinery on top of this. In both AgentSpeak and 3APL this additional machinery is a Prolog-style reasoning engine which we have therefore adopted for AIL.

Goals. All the BDI languages have the concept of goals – states of the world the agent is trying to bring about. The precise internal representation of goals differs but all the languages we have considered maintain sets of *outstanding goals*. In general, the languages (with the exception of METATEM) also maintain a stack (or set of stacks) of *deeds*[3] to be performed in order to achieve these goals – these deeds may include committing to the achievement of further sub-goals. Informally, an agent's reasoning cycle involves either adding new deeds to this stack (triggered by the creation of a sub-goal) or removing deeds from the stack (as actions are performed and goals achieved).

In [9], goals are categorised into four types: *achieve*, *perform*, *maintain* and *query*. When an achieve goal appears in a deed stack it must be believed before it can be removed. This contrasts with a perform goal which is removed as soon as new deeds are added to the stack as a result of generating an intention from a suitable plan. Query goals are used to query the belief base, usually in order to obtain instantiations for variables. Maintain goals only trigger plan execution if they cease to be believed.

Terminology and semantics in this area is quite subtle, sometimes also referring to *events* (AgentSpeak, 2APL [6]). In AgentSpeak, events refer both to commitment to achieving goals and changes perceived in the environment. There are also many ways of managing the relationship between (outstanding) goals, sub-goals, and the deeds associated with achieving them. Outstanding goals are those to which the agent has committed but not yet achieved. This places a design burden on AIL, as it must:

– allow outstanding goals to be identified;
– link a given outstanding goal with the sequence of deeds currently being pursued in order to achieve it;
– maintain sequences of deeds to be performed (including committing to new goals).

Actions. Actions are performed by an agent in the "outside world", i.e., the environment where the agent is situated. The only effect an action has on the working of AIL is that it may return a unifier for some variables (as this is allowed in some of the languages, but not all) and, of course, it may be deemed to have succeeded or failed. In some languages, actions have specific effects on the belief base (e.g., 3APL *capabilities*[4]); such actions can be modelled as plans (see next point).

Plans. The word 'plan' is overloaded among BDI languages and can be used to represent either something that a programmer writes to describe how particular goals should be tackled, or an agent's internal deed stack of pending actions. We have chosen to use *plans* for the first of these, and *deed stack* for the second.

---

[3] The term "deed" has not been used in the agent programming language literature, to our knowledge, but we have adopted it as a way to refer to the various types of formula one can typically have in the body of plans.

[4] A 3APL capability is an "internal" action which alters an agent's beliefs about the world.

BDI languages have plans which are triggered according to aspects of the agent's state, typically the existence of an outstanding goal. Such plans are of the form

(trigger,guard,body)

where the guard is some set of literals that should be believed for the plan to be deemed applicable. If a plan is selected, the plan body is placed on the relevant deed stack.

Jason also allows plans (and therefore deed stacks) to include belief update information and so this is also permitted in AIL. This allows us to model actions with side effects (and specifically 3APL capabilities) within our definition of plans.

It should be noted that we do not intend humans to write native AIL code, so we are able to ignore features which help a programmer conceptually differentiate between aspects of the language, as is the case with 3APL plans and capabilities.

As well as having plans triggered by outstanding goals, AgentSpeak allows plans to be triggered by changes in the belief base. 3APL allows *plan revision* rules/plans which match the prefix of the deed stack and replace it with some alternative. Jadex and METATEM have *constraint* rules/plans which are triggered by some specific configuration of the belief base alone. In order to represent these different types of plans within AIL, we need to make a number of generalisations. We assume a set of *intentions*, each composed, among other things, of a stack of *events* (such as outstanding goals and sub-goals or information about belief updates) and a stack of deeds. The structure of intentions will be further explained in Section 3.1 and later exemplified in Section 3.4. In this set, what some languages (such as AgentSpeak) call an "event" can be represented as an AIL intention with an empty deed stack. We assume that a *current intention*, thus also a *current event* and a *current deed stack*, has been selected from this set.

Each plan in the agent's plan library is represented by a tuple consisting of a trigger event, a deed stack (called the *prefix*), a stack of belief expressions (called the *guard stack*), and a (second) deed stack (called the *body*). The trigger must match the current event, and the prefix must match the prefix of the current deed stack for the plan to be deemed relevant. The belief expression at the top of the guard stack must also be believed by the agent. When this happens, the prefix is dropped from the current deed stack and replaced with the body. Each new deed is paired with the corresponding guard (i.e., belief expression) from the guard stack. Through the use variables in triggers and empty prefixes, this structure allows us to model many different types of plan.

We use a guard stack in order to model the different semantics for guards. Some languages (e.g., Jadex) have *invariant expressions* that must be checked at every stage during the execution of a deed stack, while others (e.g., AgentSpeak and 3APL) check guards only when a plan is to be adopted. When a plan does have an invariant expression, that expression is paired with every deed on the stack. For normal plans (i.e., those with only a guard and no invariants), only the first deed is paired with the guard expression; the remaining deeds are simply paired with $\top$ ('true', denoting an empty guard). Once again, since humans are not expected to write native AIL plans, the tedium of repeating the guard multiple times in order to represent a Jadex invariant is not an issue.

Applicable Plans. Most of the BDI languages employ the concept of determining an *applicable* plan for achieving an outstanding goal. This is based on matching the plan's trigger, or prefix (to determine *relevant plans*) and then checking the guard (to determine *applicable plans*). These BDI languages rely on user-defined methods used

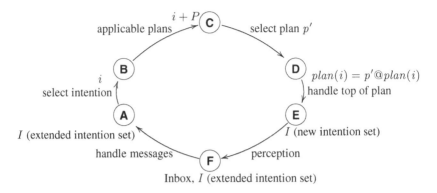

Fig. 1. AIL's reasoning cycle

by the interpreter to select *one* of the appropriate applicable plans, which then is used to generate a new deed stack. However, METATEM generates all possible next states (deed stacks). In particular, it instantiates all the relevant plans, in some cases generating several potential new deed stacks for a single plan, and then chooses between these based, among other things, on how many outstanding goals are achieved by each option. We adopt this as a more general solution.

3   Agent Infrastructure Layer

AIL's reasoning cycle may informally be viewed as shown in Figure 1.

In this cycle, starting at stage **A**, an *intention* – which includes a deed stack – is selected, leading to stage **B**. Using the agent's plan library and belief base, a set of applicable plans (P in Figure 1) is generated (stage **C**). From this, a single applicable plan is selected and its deed stack joined to the current deed stack (**D**). The top *deed* in this stack is then handled in the appropriate way (depending on the type of formula) and the set of intentions updated accordingly (**E**). Next, perception takes place, posting new events (i.e., belief updates), leading to stage **F**. At this final stage, agent communication messages are handled and the reasoning cycles restarts.

When events are generated from perception of the environment (from **E** to **F**), they are treated as intentions with empty plans. Agents have a message "inbox" where messages are placed. Any messages received during the last cycle are handled just before another reasoning cycle starts; this may also extend the intention set.

Since AIL is designed as a basis for efficient verification and not as a programming language to be used in developing agent-based systems, some parts of AIL programs are essentially syntax-less (e.g., plans are represented directly as data structures in AIL). We summarise AIL in the following sections.

3.1   Intentions: Events, Goals, and Deed Stacks

The concept of an *intention* is common in BDI languages and is used to represent the *intended means* for achieving goals – intentions include what we call a deed stack, but may also maintain information about the (sub-)goal they are intended to achieve or the event that triggered them.

In AIL, we treat intentions as a complex abstract data structure. This data structure aggregates the information about events, outstanding goals, and deed stacks used by the various BDI languages we have considered. As suggested above, we use the idea of events to represent outstanding goals (as, e.g., in AgentSpeak).

AIL intentions may most simply be viewed as a matrix structure consisting of four columns in which we record events, guards, deeds, and unifiers (respectively). These columns form an event stack, a guard stack, a deed stack, and a unifier stack. There are as many rows in the matrix as there are deeds (in the bodies of the plan instances that have become intentions) and events that have not been dealt with yet. Individual rows in the intention associate a particular deed with the event that has caused the deed to be placed on the intention, a guard, and a unifier; new events are associated with an empty deed. An example of the use of this data structure can be found in Section 3.4. The actual implementation of intentions is likely to be more compact than this – for instance the commitment to achieving a goal (i.e., an event) will generally cause a stack of deeds (the plan body) to be joined to the intention's deed stack, all of which will get associated with the same event; that is, each new deed generates a new row in the matrix and the event is repeated in all those rows some of this repetition can almost certainly be avoided. Information about outstanding goals can be extracted from the event stacks of all intentions, which record the agent's existing goals and the sequence of unachieved sub-goals generated in pursuit of these.

3.2 Interpreter Specifics

We already noted that many interpreters for BDI languages delegate plan selection to user-defined methods. *Jason* also defers intention selection to such methods. We have chosen to provide simple defaults for such functions (in each case the default selects the top of the stack) but allow them to be overridden. In some cases, such as METATEM, which has specific phases in which only certain plans are applicable, it will be necessary to override these defaults when theoretically modelling the language.

3.3 Operational Semantics

In this section we present a simplified outline of the operational semantics for AIL. The full semantics is available as a technical report (see [10]); we here focus on key issues and semantic rules.

We view an agent as a tuple consisting of an identifier ag, intentions (including a current intention), applicable plans, a belief base, plan library, and a tag indicating the current stage of the agent's reasoning cycle. For presentation reasons we will only show those parts of the state directly relevant to a rule.

Suppose we have already selected an intention (i.e., we are at stage **B** in Figure 1). We use the following rule to generate all applicable plans.

$$\frac{P' = \mathbf{filter}(appPlans(ag)) \quad P' \neq \emptyset}{< ag, P, \mathbf{B} > \rightarrow < ag, P', \mathbf{C} >} \tag{1}$$

In this rule, **filter** is an AIL function that, by default, is the identity mapping, but can be overridden by a particular interpreter to remove some of the plans which AIL considers applicable (e.g., ones which have already been attempted).

The AIL function $appPlans$ generates the union of two sets.

$$appPlans(ag) = match\_plans(ag) \cup continue(ag) \qquad (2)$$

Informally $match\_plans(ag)$ produces all the plans applicable to the current intention by inspection of the plan library. In contrast, $continue(ag)$ produces the plans which result from continuing to process the current deed stack. Typically the first set will be non-empty only when the top event in the intention has not yet been planned while the second will be non-empty only when it has been planned and there is an associated stack of deeds to process, however the existence of *plan revision rules* (See Section 4.1) means that it is possible for both sets to be non-empty in certain situations.

The plans generated by $appPlans$ are tuples consisting of the event, deed stack, guard stack, and unifier to be added to the current intention. However, they also include a number (n), representing a number of rows to be dropped from the current intention before this plan is added (typically, this number would be 1, to remove the ϵ "no plan yet" marker; see semantic rule (4)). The need for this is discussed further in Section 4.1.

The interpreter then selects one of these applicable plans, drops the specified number of rows from the current intention, and replaces them with a new row for each deed in the plan's deed stack (paired with the event, unifier, and appropriate guard as supplied by the plan). In the next semantic rule, the selection function '$\mathcal{S}_{plan}$' defaults to selecting the top plan in the stack but may be overridden if required by a particular application. We use 'i' to denote the current intention.

$$\frac{\mathcal{S}_{plan}(P) = (< e, ds, gs, \theta, n >)}{< ag, i, P, \mathbf{C} > \rightarrow < ag, (e, ds, gs, \theta) \, @ \, \mathtt{drop}(n, i)[\theta^{\mathtt{hd}}/\theta], [], \mathbf{D} >} \qquad (3)$$

The top n rows (as specified in the plans generated from $appPlans$) are dropped from the intention stack ($\mathtt{drop}(n, i)$), the top unifier on the unifier stack of this new intention[5] is replaced by θ ($[\theta^{\mathtt{hd}}/\theta]$) and the new intention segment (e, p, gs, θ) is joined to the front of the intention stack (@). The set of applicable plans is emptied. The plans provided to the agent by the programmer remain in its plan library.

Then the top of the plan is handled by a variety of rules. The following rule shows how to handle an (achieve) sub-goal not yet achieved. Recall from our discussion of $appPlans$ that 'ϵ' is a special symbol used to denote "no plan yet". In our semantics we use the syntax $+!_a g$ to signify the adoption of an achieve goal g (a for "achieve"). This is a deed when it appears in the deed stack of an intention and an event when it appears in the event stack – its type is determined by context. When $+!_a g$ appears in the event stack of an intention we may say that the agent has committed to achieving the goal. The full syntax for AIL can be found in [10].

$$\frac{ag \models gu, \qquad ag \not\models g}{< ag, (e, +!_a g, gu, \theta); i, \mathbf{D} > \rightarrow < ag, (+!_a g, \epsilon, \top, \theta); (e, +!_a g, gu, \theta); i, \mathbf{E} >} \qquad (4)$$

---

[5] see Section 3.1 for a description of the intention data structure.

The rule pushes "no plan yet" on top of the intention's deed stack. This is associated with the event $+!_a g$ (i.e., the commitment to achieving g) and an empty guard. Note that '$\models$' is used to represent the AIL belief checking process. Thus, "$ag \models gu$" asserts that the agent believes the guard to be true, while "$ag \not\models g$" asserts that the agent does not believe g, which can be interpreted as the agent not believing the goal has been achieved. Belief checking may cause the instantiation of variables.

If a goal is achieved, then we remove it from the top of the intention

$$\frac{ag \models gu, \quad ag \models g}{< ag, (e, +!_a g, gu, \theta); i, \mathbf{D} > \rightarrow < ag, i[\theta^{\mathrm{hd}(i)}/\theta \cup \theta^{\mathrm{hd}(i)}], \mathbf{E} >} \tag{5}$$

Because we want to preserve any decisions about unifiers, the unifier associated with $+!_a g$ is merged with the top unifier of i (the remainder of the intention).

It is worth noting here that AIL does not distinguish between *achieve* and *query* goals. Query goals are easily handled by (5), since '$\models$' instantiates variables. AgentSpeak even allows query goals to act as trigger events and match plans if they do not succeed, so (4) is also used. *Perform* goals can be handled by a simple modification to (4) which does not leave $+!_p g$ on the stack. Only *maintain* goals need to be treated entirely separately. In AIL, maintain goals insert a new constraint plan in the library which fires whenever the goal is no longer believed (details of this can be found in [10]).

Beliefs. All the languages we considered allow new beliefs to be inserted into, and removed from, the agent's belief base. However, some (e.g., AgentSpeak) also allow new plans to be placed in the plan library. We have therefore generalised the concept of belief to include many aspects of an agent's internal state, such as the plan library. Belief updates (i.e., the addition of new beliefs, or the deletion of old beliefs) are tagged by the relevant part of the state (e.g., $+b^{bb}$ is an instruction to add b to the belief base, while $+p^{pl}$ is an instruction to add p to the plan library). We have found by this mechanism that all such updates can be handled essentially by the same rule, the only difference being the state component that is selected. Rule (6) shows the special version of this general rule for adding a belief to the belief base[6].

$$\frac{ag \models gu}{\begin{array}{c} < ag, (e, +b^{bb}, gu, \theta); i, I, B, \mathbf{D} > \rightarrow \\ < ag, i[\theta^{\mathrm{hd}(i)}/\theta \cup \theta^{\mathrm{hd}(i)}], (+b^{bb}, [\epsilon], \top, \emptyset); I, B \cup \{b\}, \mathbf{E} > \end{array}} \tag{6}$$

This causes the top of the current intention to be removed as in rule (5), and also causes b to be added to the belief base. However, since a belief update may be a trigger for a plan, we also place a new intention on the intention stack $(+b^{bb}, [\epsilon], \top, \emptyset)$, which has a "no plan yet" deed stack. This, recall, is how events are represented in AIL.

3.4 Example

We now illustrate the operation of an AIL agent via a simple example. This is loosely based on a 3APL example available in its user guide[7]. A robot has a goal to clean rooms.

---

[6] AIL's actual semantics allows multiple belief updates of mixed types at once resulting in a rather complex rule but (6) captures the key idea applied to a single update.

[7] http://www.cs.uu.nl/3apl/download/java/userguide.pdf

When the robot believes a room is dirty, the plan is to go to that room and vacuum clean it. There is insufficient space here to discuss a translation from 3APL to AIL although we will briefly touch on some of the more interesting issues.

The robot possesses the following plans for cleaning rooms and changing locations.

PLAN 1:	
trigger	+!$_a$clean()
prefix	[ϵ]
guard stack	dirty(Room)
	TRUE
body	+!$_a$goto(Room)
	+!$_a$vacuum(Room)

PLAN 2:	
trigger	+!goto(R)
prefix	[ϵ]
guard stack	pos(P)
	TRUE
	TRUE
body	-pos(P)
	+pos(R)
	+goto(R)

We represent the robot's plans in table form showing the components introduced in Section 2. Since 3APL guards are only checked once, the guard is only associated with the top deed. Note that 3APL goals such as +!$_a$clean() are 'achieve' goals and it is expected that the truth of clean() will be established during execution. (In the sequel we assume all goals to be achieve goals so we can drop the subscripts.)

Plan 2 is derived from a 3APL capability. The semantics of capabilities is given in a Hoare-triple like format, for example: {pos(P)} goto(R) {NOT pos(P), pos(R)}. The plan shows how this is can be transformed into AIL.

Let us consider the execution of an AIL agent which starts out with the goal clean() and the beliefs pos(room3) and dirty(room1). We examine the intention stack since this is of the most use in understanding the execution of an AIL agent. We represent individual intentions as a matrix with four columns as discussed in Section 3.1.

Initially there is one intention, and this has one row to achieve the goal +!clean(). The event is the start of the program. The guard and unifier stacks are initially empty (left-hand table below). Since the agent does not believe clean(), ϵ is placed on top of the plan according to rule (5) with the trigger event noting the need to achieve clean().

trigger	deed	guard	unifier
start	+!clean()	$\top$	$\emptyset$

$\xrightarrow{(5)}$

trigger	deed	guard	unifier
+!clean()	ϵ	$\top$	$\emptyset$
start	+!clean()	$\top$	$\emptyset$

Plan 1 now matches the intention. The 'ϵ' is dropped (since it matches the prefix) and the plan's new deed stack is joined to the intention's remaining deed stack. All the deeds in this new stack are associated with the plan's trigger.

trigger	deed	guard	unifier
+!clean()	+!goto(Room)	dirty(Room)	Room = room1
+!clean()	+!vacuum(Room)	$\top$	Room = room1
start	+!clean()	$\top$	$\emptyset$

This process then repeats to plan goto:

trigger	deed	guard	unifier
`+!goto(R)`	`-pos(P)`	`pos(P)`	`Room = room1, P = room3, R = room1`
`+!goto(R)`	`+pos(room1)`	`⊤`	`Room = room1, P = room3, R = room1`
`+!goto(R)`	`+goto(room1)`	`⊤`	`Room = room1, P = room3, R = room1`
`+!clean()`	`+!goto(Room)`	`dirty(Room)`	`Room = room1`
⋮	⋮	⋮	⋮

AIL now performs the belief updates on the deed stack. These generate new intentions according to rule (6); let us assume these are not prioritised by the intention selection process so the intention stack becomes:

trigger	deed	guard	unifier
`+!goto(R)`	`+goto(R)`	`⊤`	`Room = room1, P = room3, R = room1`
`+!clean()`	`+!goto(Room)`	`dirty(Room)`	`Room = room1`
`+!clean()`	`+!vacuum(Room)`	`⊤`	`Room = room1`
start	`+!clean()`	`⊤`	`∅`
`-pos(room3)`	`ε`	`⊤`	`∅`
`+pos(room1)`	`ε`	`⊤`	`∅`

When we handle this last belief update the unifier is merged into the one for the top of the first sub-plan, preserving any unifications obtained.

trigger	deed	guard	unifier
`+!clean()`	`+!goto(Room)`	`dirty(Room)`	`Room = room1, P = room3, R = room1`
`+!clean()`	`+!vacuum(Room)`	`⊤`	`Room = room1`
start	`+!clean()`	`⊤`	`∅`
⋮	⋮	⋮	⋮

For lack of space we cannot expound on this example any further.

4   Plan Failure and Plan Revision

In most BDI languages, it is assumed, in general, that once an agent has committed to a goal, the goal is not abandoned. However, in reality, it is sometimes necessary to reconsider intentions. Unfortunately, the literature on agent programming languages is mostly vague about this process.

4.1   Plan Revision

3APL uses *plan revision rules* to replace the prefix of whole intentions with revisions. This influenced the design of AIL plans.

Consider an intention to give Jane a present, which has formed the deed stack: check what is in the Harrods department store, go to London, and purchase the gift. So our intention stack (ignoring guards) is represented as follows:

trigger	deed	unifier
`+!give(X1, Y1)`	`+!in_harrods(Y1)`	`X1 = jane, Y1 = X`
`+!give(X1, Y1)`	`gotolondon`	`X1 = jane, Y1 = X`
`+!give(X1, Y1)`	`purchase(Y1, harrods)`	`X1 = jane, Y1 = X`
start	`+!give(jane, X)`	`∅`

Let us suppose that achieving +!in_harrods(Y1) instantiates Y1 to 'computer' yielding the new intention stack:

trigger	deed	unifier
+!give(X1, Y1)	gotolondon	X1 = jane, Y1 = X, Y1 = computer
+!give(X1, Y1)	purchase(Y1, harrods)	X1 = jane, Y1 = X
start	+!give(jane, X)	∅

Suppose also that we have a plan revision rule that says that instead of going to London and buying a computer in Harrods we should, instead, purchase it from Dell:

PLAN 3:	
trigger	Any
prefix	gotolondon
	purchase(computer, harrods)
guard stack	TRUE
body	purchase(computer, dell)

The prefix is of length 2 so we drop two items from our intention. The last trigger of the dropped section is +!give(X1, Y1) so that unifies with Any and we replace the dropped parts of the stack with the new deed stack:

trigger	deed	unifier
Any	purchase(Y1, dell)	X1 = jane, Y1 = X, Y1 = computer, Any = +!give(X1, Y1)
start	+!give(jane, X)	∅

This has preserved the unifications already decided upon (e.g., that Y1 = computer)[8].

4.2   Plan Failure

The original AgentSpeak specification [23] includes a −!g construct in its syntax but its semantics has never been made clear and therefore it is often ignored in attempts to model the language. For instance [17], which embeds AgentSpeak in an early version of 3APL, ignores this aspect of the AgentSpeak semantics. The *Jason* interpreter [2] for AgentSpeak posts drop goal (−!g) events when a plan fails [19]. There are no default rules for handling these events but it is possible to write handlers as a plan, for instance:

$$-!g:true <- +!g$$

which forces backtracking[9], or other plans for handling failure. While there is no default backtracking behaviour in either AgentSpeak or 3APL, METATEM uses backtracking as a default revision procedure.

It seemed necessary to provide a mechanism by which the designer of an AIL compiler may define plan failure handling behaviour without providing unnecessary additions to the language. This meant that plan failure had to be defined by plans. We therefore needed to introduce a distinguished symbol 'backtrack' into our deed syntax which, if used, causes the execution of the AIL operational semantics rules to systematically retrace their steps attempting different instantiations and rules, as in traditional backtracking.

---

[8] This does mean that incautious use of plan revision can preserve unexpected unifications.

[9] Note that this backtracking only retries the goal – the programmer must enforce the use of a different plan or this could potentially cycle.

We adopt the *Jason* idea of posting a drop goal event when applicable plans cannot be found or actions fail. When this happens the current trigger event is selected and posted as a drop goal. A particular AIL interpreter need never select such events for handling. However, if a drop goal event *is* selected, then it is checked against *all* outstanding intentions to see if it unifies with an event (i.e., one of the goals or sub-goals to which the intention has committed). If it does, 'ϵ' is placed on top of the plan for that intention with $-!g$ as its trigger. We plan to extend the semantics to allow the option of modifying just one intention. This allows us to model 3APL's drop goal constructs[10].

Any plans available for dropping goals can then be applied at the applicable plan stage. Possible plans include:

PLAN: Actually drop a goal	
trigger	$-!g$
prefix	ϵ
guard stack	TRUE
body	$-!g$

PLAN: Retry a goal	
trigger	$-!g$
prefix	ϵ
guard stack	TRUE
body	$+!g$

PLAN: Traditional backtracking	
trigger	$-!g$
prefix	ϵ
guard stack	TRUE
body	backtrack

The first of these will place $-!g$ on top of the deed stack. We have specified the handling of a $-!g$ deed in AIL as dropping everything on the goal stack after that goal was first committed to. This also drops all unifiers allowing different plans to be used.

$$\frac{ag \models gu \qquad +!g = \texttt{events}(i)[n] \qquad \forall m > n.\neg(+!g = \texttt{events}(i)[m])}{< ag, (e, -!g, gu, \theta); i, \mathbf{D} >\rightarrow< ag, \texttt{drop}_e(n, i), \mathbf{E} >} \quad (7)$$

where $\texttt{events}(i)[n]$ is the nth trigger event on the intention stack.

Let us reconsider purchasing the present for Jane, suppose we are unable to get to London. The failure of the action `gotolondon` will post a new "drop goal" intention:

trigger	deed	unifier
`-!give(X1, Y1)`	ϵ	`X1 = jane, Y1 = X, Y1 = computer`
`+!give(X1, Y1)`	`gotolondon`	`X1 = jane, Y1 = X, Y1 = computer`
`+!give(X1, Y1)`	`purchase(Y1, harrods)`	`X1 = jane, Y1 = X`
start	`+!give(jane, X)`	$\emptyset$

Assuming this intention is selected, a new merged intention is generated:

trigger	deed	unifier
`-!give(X1, Y1)`	ϵ	`X1 = jane, Y1 = X, Y1 = computer`
`+!give(X1, Y1)`	`gotolondon`	`X1 = jane, Y1 = X, Y1 = computer`
`+!give(X1, Y1)`	`purchase(Y1, harrods)`	`X1 = jane, Y1 = X`
start	`+!give(jane, X)`	$\emptyset$

Upon using the plan "Actually drop a goal" above, we arrive at:

trigger	deed	unifier
`-!give(X1, Y1)`	`-!give(X1, Y1)`	`X1 = jane, Y1 = X, Y1 = computer`
`+!give(X1, Y1)`	`gotolondon`	`X1 = jane, Y1 = X, Y1 = computer`
`+!give(X1, Y1)`	`purchase(Y1, harrods)`	`X1 = jane, Y1 = X`
start	`+!give(jane, X)`	$\emptyset$

Now, (7) causes us to drop back to the first appearance of `+!give(X1, Y1)`:

---

[10] Mehdi Dastani, Personal Communication.

trigger	plan	unifier
start	+!give(jane, X)	$\emptyset$

We have lost our commitment to giving Jane a computer (since it is such commitments that may have caused failure).

5 Concluding Remarks

This paper provides an overview of our *Agent Infrastructure Layer* (AIL), capturing all major features of common BDI languages. The main purpose of AIL is to provide a common (operational) semantics for large fragments of these languages in order to aid the transfer of new ideas and techniques and to allow the development of common verification tools and technologies. The development of AIL has highlighted several subtle language design decisions, which we have described in the paper. In this way, AIL serves a valuable role in clarifying and formalising BDI language semantics.

In order to provide this semantics, we needed to characterise the shared concepts of beliefs, goals, actions, and plans as well as accounting for common variations such as the use of events and deed stacks. Thus, our semantics uses a complex data structure to represent intentions associating events (which include outstanding goals) with stacks of deeds (which include belief updates) to be performed. A generalised notion of a plan is developed to be used in this data structure which captures many of the notions of plans available in the literature.

While we have described aspects relating to goals, beliefs, plans, etc. *within* agents, AIL itself covers much more than we addressed in this paper [10]. Three important aspects that were omitted are mentioned briefly below.

Constraints. An additional construct within the agent's state is actually provided within AIL. *Constraints* describe pre-conditions that must hold before a given action may be performed or a goal adopted. These preconditions are checked just like the guards of plans and it is here that we particularly expect the extended notion of belief to become useful (so constraints may express that the agent has particular goals or particular plans in its library). It is important to note that whereas an agent selects *only one* applicable plan it must satisfy *all* relevant constraints. The generalised notion of constraint allows us to express a wide variety of permissions and prohibitions. If an action is *prohibited*, the pre-condition is simply $\bot$ (false), so it always fails and the action is never taken (or the goal never adopted). If certain actions are only permitted in certain situations, or to agents who have adopted certain roles, these can also easily be modelled (e.g., an agent can check if it is performing the appropriate role). The operational semantics of AIL, therefore, forces an agent to check if there are any constraints and, if so, to see that they hold before it takes an action or selects a plan.

Communication. Armed with constraints, we are able to describe a wide range of communication protocols. A common concept among BDI languages is that messages should contain both *content* and a *performative* (which determines what should be done with the content). Communication protocols are established by agreeing on constraints associated with these messages (e.g., which performatives can be used in a given stage of a communication protocol) and associating particular plans to be enacted on their receipt. Variations on these basic ideas are present in [27,3,13].

In this approach a communication protocol would consist of a selection of plans and constraints on send actions and received events. Sending messages is treated as an action by AIL, and constraints are checked in the same way as they are for any action. The last phase of the AIL reasoning cycle is dedicated to handling the receipt of messages.

$$\frac{I' = \{(+\texttt{received}(ag', ilf, \phi), [\epsilon], \top, \emptyset)|}{<ag', ilf, \phi> \in In \wedge check\_constraints(+\texttt{received}(ag', ilf, \phi)\}}{<ag, I, In, \mathbf{F}> \rightarrow <ag, I'@I, [], \mathbf{A}>} \quad (8)$$

In this rule, the intention stack, I, is extended with a set of +received events, one for each message in the inbox whose relevant constraints are satisfied. These events can then trigger appropriate plans for reacting to the message. The use of constraints allows AIL to filter out certain messages; this allows AIL to handle concepts such as the social acceptability of messages which are important, for example, in *Jason* [3].

Organisational Structures. We have designed AIL aiming, in future work, not only to be able to accommodate a variety of languages but also to account for future developments of the existing languages. For example, most languages currently concentrate on individual agents, so it is likely that those languages will be extended to include constructs to support the social level of multi-agent systems, particularly the notion of "organisations" [25]. Important common concepts in this area are the ability for agents to form groups which have and communicate goals, plans, permissions, and prohibitions. Furthermore, groups of agents need to be able to organise themselves into organisations, with specific roles within those organisations and specific relationships between roles. All of this implies that such groups adhere to certain communication protocols; [12,25,7] all describe variants which rely on these basic constructs as building blocks. Clearly any machinery for organisation and communication within AIL needed, at a minimum, to be able to express these notions and preferably needed to be customisable to allow variations on their basic forms.

AIL is therefore being designed with simple constructs which allow it to model many of the most obvious developments in this area. Of the BDI languages we have examined, only METATEM has any primitives for describing social organisations of agents (all other languages have messaging constructs and many are investigating frameworks for describing organisational structures). AIL's social organisations are currently based on METATEM's groups which flexibly allow the concepts of organisation and role to be captured [11,16]. In order to properly express permissions and prohibitions it was necessary to provide AIL with constraints as described above. We also needed to annotate aspects of the agent's internal state with sources of information/goals and define a concept of the relevance of a constraint or plan to a situation. The treatment of groups of agents as agents in their own right also provides a natural mechanism for introducing concepts of modularity into agent programs.

Space restrictions preclude further discussion of this important item, but we note that it forms a key part of our future work.

Future Work

As mentioned above, a key aim of this work is to provide a basis for the *formal verification* of programs written in BDI-based programming languages. AIL itself still requires refinement, in particular in the communication and organisation aspects mentioned above. Thus, deeper analysis of these aspects will be carried out, and appropriate high-level primitives will be developed.

Also in the short term, planned work revolves around the implementation of AIL (in JAVA) and the provision of compilers for, at least, significant fragments of AgentSpeak and 3APL. In the longer term, the correctness of these compilers needs to be addressed and verification tools for AIL developed. In particular, we aim to extend JPF [26] so that AIL classes are treated as internal classes of JPF, which should provide for efficient verification of agent programs written in various BDI languages.

An additional aim, within our future work, is to develop a subset of AIL, currently called AIL⁻, which: captures most *reasonable* BDI programs, has a very clear and straightforward semantics, and is easily implementable. Currently, AIL⁻ is conceived, in particular, as reducing the number of goal types available and the mechanisms for handling plan failure. It will also eliminate some of the flexibility of the current group structuring mechanisms. AIL⁻ would then provide the basis for a *lightweight, efficient,* and *verifiable* agent programming language.

References

1. Bordini, R.H., Dastani, M., Dix, J., El Fallah Seghrouchni, A. (eds.): Multi-Agent Programming: Languages, Platforms and Applications. Multiagent Systems, Artificial Societies, and Simulated Organizations, vol. 15, Springer, Heidelberg (2005)
2. Bordini, R.H., Hübner, J.F.: Jason: A Java-based interperter for an extended version of AgentSpeak (2006), http://jason.sourceforge.net
3. Bordini, R.H., Hübner, J.F., Wooldridge, M.: Programming Multi-agent Systems in AgentSpeak Using Jason. Wiley Series in Agent Technology, John Wiley & Sons, Chichester (2007)
4. Braubach, L., Pokahr, A., Farwer, B.: On Formalising Jadex. Personal Communication (January 2007)
5. Clancey, W., Sierhuis, M., Kaskiris, C., van Hoof, R.: Advantages of Brahms for Specifying and Implementing a Multiagent Human-Robotic Exploration System. In: Proc. 16th International Florida Artificial Intelligence Research Society Conference (FLAIRS), pp. 7–11. AAAI Press, Menlo Park (2003)
6. Dastani, M.: 2APL: A Practical Agent Programming Language. In: AAMAS conference PLDT-MAS Tutorial (2007)
7. Dastani, M., Dignum, V., Dignum, F.: Role-Assignment in Open Agent Societies. In: Proc. 2nd International Conference on Autonomous Agents and Multiagent Systems (AAMAS), ACM Press, New York (2003)
8. Dastani, M., van Riemsdijk, M.B., Meyer, J.-J.C.: Programming multi-agent systems in 3APL. In: Bordini et al, [1], ch. 2, pp. 39–67.
9. Dastani, M., van Riemsdijk, M.B., Meyer, J.-J.C.: Goal Types in Agent Programming. In: Proc. 17th European Conference on Artificial Intelligence (ECAI) (2006)
10. L. A. Dennis. Agent Infrastructure Layer (AIL): Design and Operational Semantics v1.0. Technical Report ULCS-07-001, Department of Computer Science, University of Liverpool (2007), http://www.csc.liv.ac.uk/research/techreports/

11. Dennis, L.A., Fisher, M., Hepple, A.: Language constructs for multi-agent programming. In: Proc. 8th Workshop on Computational Logic in Multi-Agent Systems (CLIMA) (2007)
12. Gutknecht, O., Ferber, J., Michel, F.: From Agents to Organizations: An Organizational View of Multi-agent Systems. In: Giorgini, P., Müller, J.P., Odell, J.J. (eds.) AOSE 2003. LNCS, vol. 2935, pp. 214–230. Springer, Heidelberg (2004)
13. FIPA. FIPA Communicative Act Library Specification. Technical Report FIPA00037, Foundation for Intelligent Physical Agents(2002)
14. Fisher, M.: MetateM: The story so far. In: Bordini, R.H., Dastani, M., Dix, J., Seghrouchni, A.E.F. (eds.) PROMAS 2005. LNCS (LNAI), vol. 3862, pp. 3–22. Springer, Heidelberg (2006)
15. Fisher, M., Bordini, R.H., Hirsch, B., Torroni, P.: Computational Logics and Agents — A Roadmap of Current Technologies and Future Trends. In: Computational Intelligence (in press)
16. Hepple, A., Dennis, L., Fisher, M.: A common basis for agent organisation in BDI languages. In: Languages, Methologies and Development tools for Multi-Agent Systems (LADS 2007) (2007)
17. Hindricks, K.V., Boer, F.S., van der Hoek, W., Meyer, J.-J.C.: A Formal Embedding of AgentSpeak(L) in 3APL. In: Antoniou, G., Slaney, J.K. (eds.) Canadian AI 1998. LNCS, vol. 1502, pp. 155–166. Springer, Heidelberg (1998)
18. Hindricks, K.V., de Boer, F.S., van der Hoek, W., Meyer, J.-J.C.: Agent Programming in 3APL. Autonomous Agents and Multi-Agent Systems, 2(4), 357–401 (1999)
19. Hübner, J.F., Bordini, R.H., Wooldridge, M.: Programming Declarative Goals using Plan Patterns. In: Proc. 4th International Workshop on Declarative Agent Languages and Technologies (DALT), Hakodate, Japan, pp. 65–81 (May 2006)
20. Muscettola, N., Nayak, P.P., Pell, B., Williams, B.: Remote Agent: To Boldly Go Where No AI System Has Gone Before. Artificial Intelligence 103(1-2), 5–48 (1998)
21. Pokahr, A., Braubach, L., Lamersdorf, W.: A Flexible BDI Architecture Supporting Extensibility. In: Proc. IEEE/WIC/ACM International Conference on Intelligent Agent Technology (IAT), pp. 379–385 (2005)
22. Rao, A.: AgentSpeak(L): BDI Agents Speak Out in a Logical Computable Language. In: Perram, J., Van de Velde, W. (eds.) MAAMAW 1996. LNCS, vol. 1038, pp. 42–55. Springer, Heidelberg (1996)
23. Rao, A.S., Georgeff, M.: BDI Agents: from theory to practice. In: Proc. 1st International Conference on Multi-Agent Systems (ICMAS), San Francisco, pp. 312–319 (1995)
24. Sierhuis, M.: Multiagent Modeling and Simulation in Human-Robot Mission Operations (2006), http://ic.arc.nasa.gov/ic/publications
25. Vázquez-Salceda, J., Dignum, V., Dignum, F.: Organizing multiagent systems. Technical Report UU-CS-2004-015, Institute of Information and Computing Sciences, Utrecht University (2004)
26. Visser, W., Havelund, K., Brat, G., Park, S.: Model checking programs. In: Proceedings of the Fifteenth International Conference on Automated Software Engineering (ASE 2000), Grenoble, France, September 11-15, pp. 3–12. IEEE Computer Society, Los Alamitos (2000)
27. Wooldridge, M., Fisher, M., Huget, M., Parsons, S.: Model Checking Multiagent Systems with MABLE. In: Proc. 1st International Conference on Autonomous Agents and Multi-Agent Systems (AAMAS) (July 2002)
28. Wooldridge, M., Rao, A. (eds.): Foundations of Rational Agency. Kluwer, Dordrecht (1999)

Adding Structure to Agent Programming Languages

Peter Novák and Jürgen Dix

Department of Informatics, Clausthal University of Technology, Germany
{novak,dix}@in.tu-clausthal.de

Abstract. There is a huge gap between agent programming languages used for industrial applications and those developed in academia. While the former are mostly extensions of mainstream programming languages (e.g. Java), the latter are often very specialized languages, based on reactive rules. These specialized languages enjoy clear semantics and come with a number of knowledge representation features, but lack important aspects such as *code re-use*, *modularity*, *encapsulation* etc.

We present a method to extend the syntax of existing specialized agent oriented programming languages to allow more efficient *hierarchical structuring of agent programs*. We illustrate our method through a simple language based on reactive rules. We then gradually extend the core language by several higher level syntactic constructs, thus improving the support for source code modularity and readability.

1 Introduction

While providing a clear and robust theoretical semantics and easy integration of powerful knowledge representation and reasoning techniques, an ideal specialized programming language for agents with mental states *must* also take into account *engineering aspects* of software development as equally important issues. We believe that an *easily readable* syntax of a programming language, allowing conceptual *encapsulation* on the source code level, and support for a program *modularization*, are crucial issues in design of programming languages for cognitive agents. *Such abstraction has to be both (1) a practical means for modular structuring of an agent program source code, as well as (2) a methodological tool guiding translation from an analytical model to a real source code implemented in a rule based programming language.*

In this paper, we demonstrate how the syntax of specialized agent oriented programming languages, based on reactive rules, can be carefully designed to approach the requirements of modern programmers. We understand this work as a work in progress towards development of high level abstract concepts for development of agents with mental states, rather than a proposal for an ultimate solution of this problem.

Our approach follows the tiered approach to programming language design [12] and focuses on introducing *purely syntactical* constructs, rather than making the semantics of the language more complicated. As a basis for further enrichment, we first propose a simple abstract programming language based on reactive rules (Section 2) together with an *interpreter* for it. The main focus of this paper is on gradually extending the core language by several higher level syntactic constructs (Section 3), thus improving the support for source code modularity and readability.

M. Dastani et al.(Eds.): ProMAS 2007, LNAI 4908, pp. 140–155, 2008.
© Springer-Verlag Berlin Heidelberg 2008

One of the main results in this paper is the introduction of a *mental state transformer* *(mst)*, an extension based on the functional view on an agent program. We propose a *compiler* transforming a program using the extended syntax into the core language. Discussion on related and future work (sections 4 and 5) conclude the paper.

2 Core Programming Language

The architecture of specialized programming languages for agents with mental states can be naturally decomposed in two parts. Firstly, the language has to provide means for *modeling the internal structure* of an agent's mental state. Secondly, it has to feature *control structures for encoding transitions* between these states. We are convinced, that these aspects of an agent oriented programming language should be studied separately. In this work, we focus on dynamic aspects of an agent programming language.

The starting point for the design of the core language is the approach applied in the *Modular BDI architecture* [15] and IMPACT [17], where authors abstract from the internal structure of agent's mental state. The structure of a mental state reduces to a black box providing only a query and update interface, while the programming language itself facilitates the control over mental state transitions.

An agent program in the core language consists of a set of reactive rules. Given a query, when a reactive rule evaluates to true in the current mental state, then an update operation is performed on this state. The semantics of a query and update operation is provided by abstract operators, specific to the internal structure of agent's mental states. We also abstract from the interface to agent's environment. It can be handled by queries (sensor interface) and updates (effector interface) integrated in the implementation of the mental state as well (see *Modular BDI architecture* presented in [15]).

The semantics of an agent system is then provided in terms of a transition system over a set of mental states. We give both operational and denotational views on the semantics of the core language. The operational semantics shows the execution of a single primitive construct of the language, while the denotational viewpoint provides a *functional* view on the semantics of an agent program. This view will later turn out to be crucial for modularizing the language. We conclude by detailing the interpreting algorithm and proposing a concrete syntax for the core programming language.

2.1 Abstract Syntax

We abstract from the internal structure of mental states by defining them as a theories in a given language $\mathcal{L}$. This abstraction keeps the concept of a mental state modular and allows to examine and update it by means of abstract *query* and *update* operations.

Definition 1 *(language, formula, query, update). Let $\mathcal{L}$ be a language of mental states. Then a mental state σ is a theory in this language and a formula $\varphi \in \sigma$ is called a mental state formula. Query and update languages $\mathcal{L}_Q$ and $\mathcal{L}_U$ are defined as follows:*

- *if $\varphi \in \mathcal{L}$, then $Q(\varphi) \in \mathcal{L}_Q$ and $U(\varphi) \in \mathcal{L}_U$,*
- *if $\phi_1, \phi_2 \in \mathcal{L}_Q$ then $\phi_1 \wedge \phi_2 \in \mathcal{L}_Q$, $\phi_1 \vee \phi_2 \in \mathcal{L}_Q$ and $\neg\phi_1 \in \mathcal{L}_Q$,*
- *$\top \in \mathcal{L}_Q, \perp \in \mathcal{L}_Q, nop \in \mathcal{L}_U$*

While update formulas are quite simple (a single update operation at a time) query formulas can be more complex. They can involve conjunctions, disjunctions and negations. Primitive constructs of the language are composed of query and update formulas.

Definition 2 *(transition rule, agent program).* *Let $\mathcal{L}_Q$ and $\mathcal{L}_U$ be query and update languages and $\phi \in \mathcal{L}_Q$, $\psi \in \mathcal{L}_U$ be formulas. We say that a rule of the form $\phi \longrightarrow \psi$ is a transition rule. An agent program is a set of rules*

$$\mathcal{P} = \{\phi \longrightarrow \psi | \ \phi \in \mathcal{L}_Q \ and \ \psi \in \mathcal{L}_U\}$$

composed of query and update formulas from the corresponding query and update languages $\mathcal{L}_Q$ and $\mathcal{L}_U$. We also say that $\mathcal{P}$ is an agent program in $\mathcal{L}$.

2.2 Semantics

Given an agent program, we show first how transition rules are interpreted as single transitions. Then, we also provide denotational semantics for a program to show a functional view of its meaning. The semantics of transition rules is defined in terms of abstract query and update operators. This makes the semantics of the core language modular and independent on the internal structure of agent's mental states.

Definition 3 *(abstract query/update operators).* *Let $\mathcal{L}$ be a language of mental states and $\sigma \subseteq \mathcal{L}$ be a mental state (theory) in that language. Let also $\varphi \in \mathcal{L}$ be a formula. An operator $Query_{\mathcal{L}}$ is a mapping*

$$Query_{\mathcal{L}} : \mathcal{L} \times 2^{\mathcal{L}} \to \{true, false\}; \langle \varphi, \sigma \rangle \mapsto Query_{\mathcal{L}}(\varphi, \sigma)$$

The corresponding update operator $Update_{\mathcal{L}}$ is a mapping

$$Update_{\mathcal{L}} : \mathcal{L} \times 2^{\mathcal{L}} \to 2^{\mathcal{L}}; \langle \varphi, \sigma \rangle \mapsto Update_{\mathcal{L}}(\varphi, \sigma)$$

We assume $Query_{\mathcal{L}}(\top, \sigma) = true$, $Query_{\mathcal{L}}(\bot, \sigma) = false$, $Update_{\mathcal{L}}(nop, \sigma) = \sigma$.

In the case of a query, the result is the truth value of φ w.r.t. σ. The result of an update operator application is a new mental state $\sigma' \subseteq \mathcal{L}$, which reflects an update φ on σ.

For practical purposes, query and update operators $Query_{\mathcal{L}}$ and $Update_{\mathcal{L}}$ should be computable procedures evaluating formula $\varphi \in \mathcal{L}$ against a theory $\sigma \subseteq \mathcal{L}$.

The semantics of transition rules is defined in terms of query and update operator evaluations. We relate formulas of the form $Q(\varphi)$ and $U(\varphi)$ to applications of corresponding abstract operators $Query_{\mathcal{L}}$ and $Update_{\mathcal{L}}$ to the actual mental state.

Definition 4 *(semantics of queries and updates).* *Let $\mathcal{L}$ be a mental state language and $\mathcal{L}_Q$ and $\mathcal{L}_U$ be query and update languages over $\mathcal{L}$. Let also σ be a mental state. Application of a query operator $Query_{\mathcal{L}}$ is denoted by $\models$ and $\oplus$ denotes an application of an update operator $Update_{\mathcal{L}}$ on a mental state. The semantics of a ground query formula $\phi \in \mathcal{L}_Q$ is defined as follows*

- *if $\phi = Q(\varphi)$ and $\varphi \in \mathcal{L}$, then $\sigma \models \phi$ iff $Query_{\mathcal{L}}(\varphi, \sigma) = true$, otherwise $\sigma \not\models \phi$ (i.e. $Query_{\mathcal{L}}(\varphi, \sigma) = false$),*

- if $\phi = \neg\phi'$ and $\phi' \in \mathcal{L}_Q$, then $\sigma \models \phi$ iff $\sigma \not\models \phi'$,
- if $\phi = \phi_1 \wedge \phi_2$ and $\phi_1, \phi_2 \in \mathcal{L}_Q$, then $\sigma \models \phi$ iff $\sigma \models \phi_1$ and $\sigma \models \phi_2$,
- if $\phi = \phi_1 \vee \phi_2$ and $\phi_1, \phi_2 \in \mathcal{L}_Q$, then $\sigma \models \phi$ iff $\sigma \models \phi_1$ or $\sigma \models \phi_2$

and for an update formula $\psi \in \mathcal{L}_U$:

- if $\psi = U(\varphi)$ and $\varphi \in \mathcal{L}$, then $\sigma \oplus \psi = \sigma'$ iff
  $Update_{\mathcal{L}}(\varphi, \sigma) = \sigma'$.

Note, that we do not define a more powerful notion of negation in query formulas (e.g. default negation): This would require a deeper insight in the structure of mental state. The interpreter of the language only needs to know whether a query is satisfied or not, regardless of the kind of specialized reasoning hidden behind the internal semantics of the query operator.

An agent system moves from one mental state to another by *applicable rules*.

Definition 5 *(agent system transition)*. *An agent system moves from σ to σ':*

$$\frac{\sigma \models \phi, \sigma \oplus \psi = \sigma'}{\sigma \longrightarrow \sigma'},$$

when $\phi \longrightarrow \psi$ is an applicable transition rule (i.e. $\sigma \models \phi$).

Finally, we specify a semantics of an agent program in terms of possible evolutions of within the transition system.

Definition 6 *(agent system: operational view)*. *A computation run $Comp(\sigma_0)$ of an agent system over a language of mental states $\mathcal{L}$, described by an agent program $\mathcal{P}$, is a possibly infinite sequence $\sigma_0, \ldots, \sigma_n, \ldots$ of mental states over $\mathcal{L}$ ($\forall i : \sigma_i \subseteq \mathcal{L}$), so that $\forall i \geq 0 : \sigma_i \longrightarrow \sigma_{i+1}$ is an agent system transition induced by some rule $r_i \in \mathcal{P}$.*

The agent system is then characterized by the set of all possible computation runs induced by the program $\mathcal{P}$.

The operational semantics offers a procedural view on the agent program as a specification of a problem subspace in terms of allowed computation runs. It gives a rather localized perspective on the meaning of a single transition rule w.r.t. to a given agent system evolution. But we can also see a single rule $\phi \longrightarrow \psi$ as a prescription of a transition between classes of mental states. The query part ϕ divides the space of mental states in two classes, according to the truth value of formula ϕ. When the system happens to be in one of the states in which ϕ evaluates to true, the update formula ψ specifies a *direction* in which it should move in the next step. The rule then prescribes a transition from the class of states in which ϕ holds to the set of states resulting from application of update formula ψ to it. This view inspires the alternative semantics of an agent system: *A set of transition rules is a partial function over mental states.*

Definition 7 *(agent system: denotational view)*. *Let $\mathcal{L}$ be a language of mental states and $\mathcal{P}$ an agent program in $\mathcal{L}$. The program $\mathcal{P}$ is characterized by a partial function*

$$\mathcal{F}_{\mathcal{P}} : 2^{\mathcal{L}} \times \mathcal{L}_U \longrightarrow 2^{\mathcal{L}}; \langle \sigma, \psi \rangle \longmapsto \sigma'$$

where $\sigma, \sigma' \subseteq \mathcal{L}$ are mental states and $\psi \in \mathcal{L}_U$ is an update formula. $\mathcal{F}_\mathcal{P}(\sigma, \psi) = \sigma'$ iff $\exists (\phi \longrightarrow \psi) \in \mathcal{P}$, such that $\sigma \longrightarrow \sigma'$ is a transition induced by this rule. We say that $\mathcal{P}$ is characterized by $\mathcal{F}_\mathcal{P}$. We also say that the set of states $\Sigma_{\mathcal{F}_\mathcal{P}}$ over which the partial function $\mathcal{F}_\mathcal{P}$ is defined is the application domain of $\mathcal{F}_\mathcal{P}$.

The function $\mathcal{F}_\mathcal{P}$ is a partial function defined only for those mental states in which some rule $r \in \mathcal{P}$ can be applied. I.e. those, in which a query formula of some rule from the program $\mathcal{P}$ is satisfied. It completely characterizes the agent system described by $\mathcal{P}$.

The operational semantics provides a view on an agent program as an explicit characterization of a problem subspace in terms of possible agent system evolutions. Complementary to that, the denotational semantics suggest a specification of the same problem space in terms of a specification of all the considered sets of mental states and all the allowed transitions between them. We stress here, that in essence both provided semantics allow formalization of a same system. They just reflect two different views on its specification. While the first shows how an existing agent program is interpreted, the second offers more methodological insight on how to analyze, create and organize such programs.

2.3 Concrete Syntax and Interpreter

To complete our core programming system definition we provide a concrete syntax and an interpreter algorithm for it. Our syntax proposal of the core language is straightforward. The EBNF of the core programming language is as follows (white space and string definitions are omitted):

```
<program> := <rules>
<rules>   := <rule> | <rule> <rules>
<rule>    := "when" <queries> "then" <update> ";"
<queries> := <query> | "not" <queries> |
             "(" <queries> "and" <queries> ")" |
             "(" <queries> "or" <queries> ")"
<query>   := "true" | "false" | "query" "[{" <qformula> "}]"
<update>  := "nop" | "update" "[{" <uformula> "}]"
```

`<qformula>` and `<uformula>` are well formed formulas from $\mathcal{L}_Q$ and $\mathcal{L}_U$ respectively. Query and update non-terminals are defined using quite complex bracket delimiters. This is because the syntax of `<string>` non-terminal can be arbitrarily complex and might involve various kinds of character combinations possibly including characters like {, or }[1].

We finally propose an extremely simple and straightforward interpreting algorithm following the generic scheme applied in other languages like e.g. 3APL. Algorithm 1 lists the detail pseudocode of the core language interpreter.

Given a current mental state, the interpreter first selects all the rules applicable in that state, then non-deterministically chooses one of them and applies its update formula to the actual mental state. The result of this update operation is a new mental state which

---

[1] In practice, probably additional handling of special character classes would be necessary.

becomes the current one in the subsequent interpreter iteration. In the case no rule is currently applicable, the interpreter loops and waits until the mental state changes by means of external events. The details of the interpreter algorithm can be found in [14].

Algorithm 1. run$(\sigma_0, \mathcal{P})$

$\sigma = \sigma_0$
loop
    $\rho = \{(\phi \longrightarrow \psi) \in \mathcal{P} | \sigma \models \phi\}$
    if $\rho \neq \emptyset$ **then**
        non-deterministically choose $(\phi \longrightarrow \psi) \in \rho$
        $\sigma = \sigma \oplus \psi$
    end if
end loop

We assume here, that the selection function which chooses the rule to be applied from the set of all applicable rules conforms to a *fairness* condition (inspired by a similar weak-fairness condition in GOAL [8]):

Condition 1 *(fairness condition). It is not the case that for a given computation run* $Comp(\sigma_0)$ *a rule* $r \in \mathcal{P}$ *is always applicable from some point in time on and never selected for the execution.*

An interpreter as described above is inherently non-deterministic. It is desirable to allow a programmer to secure a higher degree of determinism in the rule selection, when needed. To this end, we introduce in Subsection 3.1 a simple syntactic extension of the core language facilitating a finer grained control of the rule selection mechanism.

Note also, that our core language is intentionally oversimplified. For the sake of clarity, we did not introduce variables in transition rules and we also define only atomic updates without chaining of update formulas. Although these trivial extensions semantically enhance the language and in practice would be crucial for a practical use, they are not important within the scope of this paper. For introducing such language features we refer to [15], where we introduced them to a language similar to the one discussed here. We also discuss the problems following from introducing variables to the language in Section 5.

Example 1 **(stock exchange agent).** Consider an agent managing its user's stock portfolio. Given a mental state implementation in a Prolog-like language, a simplified program for buying the title MSFT might look like the following:

when *[{ wants(MSFT) }]* **and** *[{ price(MSFT)<avg(MSFT,12h) }]*
then *[{ act(issue_order(buy(MSFT,10))) }]* ;

when *[{ price(MSFT)<max(MSFT,180d) }]* **and** *[{ price(MSFT)<avg(MSFT,7d) }]*
then *[{ introduce_goal(wants(MSFT)) }]* ;

The agent buys the stock MSFT when it knows it wants it and its price falls under the last 12 hours average. Similarly, when the price of the stock is low, according to the agent's analysis, it introduces a desire to buy the stock.

3   Extensions

The core programming language as it is defined in the previous section is still quite rigid. It is hardly imaginable for a programmer to easily manipulate an unstructured and possibly huge set of reactive rules. Therefore, in this section we propose several extensions of the core language enhancing the flexibility in structuring the source code of an agent program.

To introduce various programming language extensions we follow the tiered approach to design a programming language [12]. This leads to a layered language processing structure: a *core language interpreter* and a *compiler* with integrated *macro preprocessor*. The compiler translates programs written in an extended language, using high level language features, into an equivalent program in the core language.

The tiered structure helps to maintain the simplicity and clarity of the programming language semantics and at the same time allows further extending of the language. The integration of a powerful macro language preprocessor allows a limited support for custom-made language extensions.

Firstly, we introduce the abstraction of *mental state transformer (mst)* inspired by the denotational view on an agent program. Then the *"when-then-else"* construct, extending the mental state transformer syntax, is defined. It facilitates structuring applicable and not applicable rules. For both of these extensions we provide a detailed translational semantics into the core programming language, which should serve as a basis for the language compiler implementation.

Secondly, we propose several extensions based on a *macro expansion mechanism*. The most important one is the construction of a *named mental state transformer*, which utilizes the previously introduced plain mental state transformer extension. Named mental state transformers provide a powerful means for agent program decomposition and modularization. To define the precise meaning of this construct, we also provide a translation to denotational semantics of standard mst's.

Finally, we mention several other, rather trivial, extensions based on macro expansion, which show the way how to further enrich and simplify the programming language syntax. More detailed description can be found in the extended version [14].

3.1   Core Language Extensions

Mental state transformers (mst). Denotational semantics of agent programs provides a functional view on sets of transition rules: Any set of rules can be considered an agent program of its own. Using this idea, we define a structural decomposition of an agent program in subunits and provide means for composing them into compound structures. According to Definition 7, a set of transition rules is a partial function, transforming a class of mental states to another class of mental states by means of performing updates on them. We call such a set of rules a *mental state transformer (mst)*[2].

Obviously, by unification of two mst's we obtain a new mst, which is defined over a larger class of mental states than the two original ones. Similarly, by specialization of all the query formulas of a set of transition rules, we again obtain a new mst defined

---

[2] The name *mental state transformer* is inspired by a feature of the language GOAL [8]: however, the semantics is different.

on a subclass of mental states of the original one. Hence the agent program source code can be hierarchically structured in terms of compound structures, mst's, which are combined by means of generalization and specialization.

Following the tiered specification approach, we first provide a modified syntax of agent program and subsequently define a translational semantics into the core language syntax, introduced in Subsection 2.3. For clarity, we also provide a constructive denotational semantics (using EBNF).

```
<program>       := <transformer>
<transformer> := <update> ";" |
        "{" <transformer>* "}" |
        "when" <queries> "then" <transformer> ";"
```

We get the extended programming language syntax by replacing the original definition of <program> and adding the definition of <transformer> to the syntax definition from Subsection 2.3. Obviously, the new syntax subsumes the old one. Definitions of <rules> and <rule> are obsolete and replaced by <transformer>.

Abstraction of mental state transformer provides a means for hierarchical nesting of transition rules of the core language. A primitive mst specifies a single update operation ψ. It is a shortcut for the fully expanded transition rule $\top \longrightarrow \psi$, however it helps translating the original syntax of transition rules to that of mst's.

Definition 8 *(mst: translational semantics). Let τ be a mental state transformer. Then τ is said to be an agent program with mental state transformers and the corresponding core language program $\mathcal{P}$ is constructed as follows[3]:*

1. *iff $r \in \tau$ is* <update>, *then* "when true then r" $\in \mathcal{P}$,
2. *iff $r \in \tau$ is a plain transition rule of the form* "when Q then U", *where Q and U are* <queries> *and* <update>, *then also $r \in \tau'$,*
3. *iff $r \in \tau$ is* "when Q then τ'" *where Q is* <queries> *and τ' is a plain set of transition rules, then for each rule $r \in \tau'$ of the form* "when Q' then U'" *a rule* "when Q and Q' then U'" $\in \mathcal{P}$. *Q and U are* <queries> *and* <update> *respectively.*

For multiply nested mst's, the transformation, specified by Item 3 should be performed bottom-up from the innermost nesting, which contains either a simple update, or a set of plain transition rules. A corresponding denotational semantics for mst's shows how the original notion of agent program is reconditioned.

Definition 9 *(mst: denotational semantics). Let $\mathcal{L}$ be a language of mental states. A mental state transformer τ is then characterized by a partial function over mental states $\mathcal{F}$ as follows*

1. *primitive mst $\tau = \{\phi \longrightarrow \psi\}$ is characterized by $\mathcal{F}(\sigma, \psi) = Update_{\mathcal{L}}(\psi, \sigma)$, where $\psi \in \mathcal{L}_U$, $\phi \in \mathcal{L}_Q$ and the rule $\phi \longrightarrow \psi$ is applicable in $\sigma \subseteq \mathcal{L}$. The application domain of $\mathcal{F}$ is $\Sigma_{\mathcal{F}} = \{\sigma | \sigma \models \phi\}$.*

---

[3] For better readability, we omit the syntactic sugar w.r.t. the language EBNF.

2. *if mst τ' is characterized by $\mathcal{F}'$ and $\phi \in \mathcal{L}_Q$ is a query formula, then mst $\tau = \{\phi \longrightarrow \tau'\}$ is characterized by partial function $\mathcal{F}(\sigma, \psi) = \mathcal{F}'(\sigma, \psi)$ with corresponding application domain $\Sigma_{\mathcal{F}} = \{\sigma | \sigma \in \Sigma_{\mathcal{F}'} \wedge \sigma \models \phi\}$.*

3. *if mst's τ' and τ'' are characterized by $\mathcal{F}'$ and $\mathcal{F}''$ correspondingly, then mst $\tau =$*

$$\tau' \cup \tau'' \text{ is characterized by } \mathcal{F}(\sigma, \psi) = \begin{cases} \mathcal{F}'(\sigma, \psi) & \text{if } \sigma \in \Sigma_{\mathcal{F}'} \\ \mathcal{F}''(\sigma, \psi) & \text{if } \sigma \in \Sigma_{\mathcal{F}''} \end{cases} \text{ with the corre-}$$

sponding application domain $\Sigma_{\mathcal{F}} = \Sigma_{\mathcal{F}'} \cup \Sigma_{\mathcal{F}''}$.

A simple rule is a *primitive* mst (Item 1). Primitive elements can be combined to *compound* mst's by means of *generalization* (Item 3) and *specialisation* (Item 2). Note, that according to Definition 8, Item 1, a simple update formula ψ serves as a shortcut for a trivial rule $\top \longrightarrow \psi$: a plain update formula is the most primitive mst.

An agent program is also a mst. The concept of mental state transformer provides a functional view on an agent program as composed of conceptually encapsulated subunits, which are again composed of lower level subunits (mst's) of the same type.

When-then-else. When in a given mental state several transition rules are applicable, the interpreter is supposed to non-deterministically choose one of them. A developer might need to restrict and narrow the choice of the interpreter's selection function. In the core language, this can be done by writing complex queries, so that the number of applicable rules in a certain mental state is minimized and in turn, the number of states in which a rule is applicable is minimized as well.

The abstraction of the mental state transformer introduced nested rules, allowing a developer to restrict the scope of applicability of the inner rule by the query of the outer one (*"when-then"* construct). As we already said above, according to its validity, a query divides a set of mental states to two classes. By a trivial extension of the *"when-then"* construct to handle also the *"-else"* branch, the programmer gets a means to specify mental state transformers for both of them. This helps to narrow the interpreter's choice using a compact syntax.

```
<transformer> := "when" <queries>
            "then" <transformer>
            "else" <transformer>
```

Definition 10 *(mst: translational semantics cont.)*

4. *iff $r \in \tau$ is "when Q then τ' else τ''", where Q is <queries> and τ', τ'' are plain sets of transition rules, then for each rule $r \in \tau'$ of the form "when Q' then U'" a rule "when Q and Q' then U'"$\in \mathcal{P}$. Similarly for each rule $r \in \tau''$ a rule "when $\neg Q$ and Q' then U'"$\in \mathcal{P}$. Q', U' are <queries> and <update> respectively.*

By introducing sequences of nested rules of the form "when Q_1 then τ_1 else when Q_2 then ... else when Q_n then τ_n ;" a programmer gradually restricts the choice of the interpreter using a compact syntax without annoying repetitions. An interesting consequence of using *"when-then-else"* construct is that the program can be read in a sequential way, although it is not sequential in nature.

Example 2 (**stock exchange cont.**). We modify the agent program from Example 1 to drop the goal to buy stock when there is a market turmoil going on. Otherwise it should behave as in Example 1.

when *[{ news('overtake')>2 }]* **and** *[{ avg(DOW,5h)<0.70∗avg(DOW,2d) }]*
then *[{ drop_goal(wants(MSFT)) }]*
else { *%% Example 1 code %%* } ;

Market turmoil is defined as a state, when at least two news about a company overtake arise and market index average in the last five hours falls more than 30% under the last two days average. Note, that in the core language, the equivalent program would require three separate transition rules.

3.2 Macro Extensions

As we already indicated at the beginning of this section, we propose integrating a macro language into the compiler. In the following, we introduce several extensions exploiting a macro expansion. In practice we have in mind employing a robust macro preprocessor like e.g. GNU M4[4].

Named mental state transformers. The concept of a plain mst introduced modularity into an agent program, however it does not allow an easy re-use of already defined mst's in different contexts of the agent program. The extension to a *named mental state transformer* provides a means to re-use previously defined mst's in different contexts of an agent program. A label (handle) of a named mst serves as a placeholder for it. It is expanded into a full-fledged code by a macro preprocessor.

Again, following the tiered approach, we first provide a syntactical specification followed by a detailed translation of named mst into the denotational semantics of plain mst. The syntax of the programming language is extended by the following EBNF:

```
<program>      := <trans_def>* <transformer>
<trans_def>    := "define" <identifier> <transformer>
<transformer>  := <identifier>
```

`<program>` is again redefined, and the rest of the definition extends the previous ones. `<identifier>` should be a unique label, distinct from the already introduced keywords like `query`, `update` etc. A straightforward denotational semantics of the extended definition of agent program in terms of simple mst's follows.

Definition 11 *(named mst: denotational semantics). A modified mst construct is defined by adding the following to Definition 9: Let τ be a mst and label is a unique identifier (`<identifier>`), then $(label, \tau)$ is a named mst definition.*

5. *If $(label, \tau')$ is a named mst definition and τ' is characterized by a partial function $\mathcal{F}'$, then mst $\tau = \{(label)\}$ is characterized by $\mathcal{F}(\sigma, \psi) = \mathcal{F}'(\sigma, \psi)$ with the application domain $\Sigma_{\mathcal{F}} = \Sigma_{\mathcal{F}'}$.*

---

[4] http://www.gnu.org/software/m4/

Note, that because the Definition 11 is an extension of the Definition 9 also mst of the form $\phi \longrightarrow (label)$ is a well formed mst defined as a specialisation of mst $(label)$ by the query formula ϕ.

Now we provide a translation of the extended mst construct to the plain mst as defined in Definition 9.

Definition 12 *(expanded mst). Let $\mathcal{L}$ be a language of mental states, Γ be a set of named mst definitions in $\mathcal{L}$ and τ be a mst. We define $Exp(\tau)$, the expansion operator:*

$$
Exp(\tau) = \begin{cases}
\tau & \text{if } \tau = \{\phi \longrightarrow \psi\}, \text{ where } \phi \in \mathcal{L}_Q, \psi \in \mathcal{L}_U \\
\{\phi \longrightarrow Exp(\tau')\} & \text{if } \tau = \{\phi \longrightarrow \tau'\}, \tau' \text{ is not primitive and } \phi \in \mathcal{L}_Q \\
\bigcup_{\tau' \in \tau} Exp(\tau') & \text{if } \tau \text{ is a union of several mst's} \\
Exp(\tau') & \text{if } \tau = (label) \text{ and } (label, \tau') \in \Gamma
\end{cases}
$$

Now the expansion fixed point is as usual: $Exp^0(\tau) = \tau$, and $Exp^{i+1}(\tau) = Exp(Exp^i(\tau))$. The expanded mst τ_e, corresponding to τ, is a fixed point of the Exp operator. I.e. such a mst τ_e, for which $\exists i \geq 0$, so that $\tau_e = Exp^i(\tau) = Exp^{i+1}(\tau)$.

The semantics of an agent program $\mathcal{P} = (\Gamma, \tau)$ with a set of named mst definitions Γ is that of the expanded mst τ_e corresponding to τ w.r.t. Γ.

The expansion operator Exp simply replaces all the labels by their corresponding content according to their definitions. For an agent program to expand correctly, each label, used as a placeholder for a mst, has to be previously defined in the agent program $\mathcal{P}$ as well. Recursive schemata of mst "calls" do not correctly expand into a simple program without labels, because the fixed point w.r.t. Exp operator, does not exist for them. Recursive applications of named mst's in the agent program, if allowed, would also lead to infinite query evaluation[5].

Note also, that due to uniqueness of labels of named mst's, there is *at most one* fixed point of Exp operator for any program $\mathcal{P} = (\Gamma, \tau)$. Obviously not all agent programs with syntax extended to named mst's have a semantics accroding to Exp expansion operator. This might happen when the program uses recursive application of a named mst, or when it uses a previously undefined mst w.r.t. given Γ.

Named queries, code templates and more. To conclude our tour through gradual extensions of the core programming language, we finally sketch several simple extensions, which further enrich the language and stand as an inspiration for implementation of the language compiler.

As we already mentioned several times above, queries in transition rules can be seen as mental state classifiers. It might be practical to re-use these classifiers in different contexts and specialize them in different parts of an agent program. For that, we can again use the macro expansion facility of the language compiler. A *named query* can be viewed as an abbreviation for a complex query formula:

---

[5] Except for external events, which we abstract from, a mental state cannot be changed unless an update is performed. In turn, this cannot happen either, because the interpreter cannot properly perform a query on it.

```
<query_def> := "defineq" <identifier> "{" <queries> "}"
<query>     := <identifier>
```

This definition again extends the definition of the core language syntax introduced in Subsection 2.3. We assume unique query abbreviation identifiers. A formal definition of named query expansion is similar to that of named mst: our comments w.r.t. recursive application and the existence of fixed points of the expansion operator apply as well.

Many more trivial extensions based on macro expansion can be introduced. We only briefly list some of those, which we believe contribute to improving the coding experience using a reactive rule based programming language, such as the one defined here. Named updates, or definition of re-usable modules, consisting of several named mst's, with features resembling name spaces, will further enhance modularization of an agent program. Parametrized macro definitions and their further extensions to syntactical constructs resembling lambda-calculus of Lisp will lead to implementation of re-usable code templates, similar to those of C++.

We conclude this section with an example sketching a part of an agent program using some of the features above.

Example 3 (**stock exchange cont.**). Parametrized mst definitions allow us to reformulate and modify the code from Example 2 to implement specific strategy w.r.t. certain stock title. Different variants of strategies for different stocks can be used in different situations. Use of a named query definition further improves the code readability as well.

define careful_strategy(TITLE) {
    when *[{ wants(TITLE) }]* **then** *[{ drop_goal(wants(TITLE)) }]* ;
}
define opportunistic_strategy(TITLE) {
    %% Adapted code from Example 1 %%
}
defineq market_turmoil {
    [{ news('overtake')>2 }] **and** *[{ avg(DOW,5h)<0.70∗avg(DOW,2d) }]*
}
. . .
when market_turmoil **then** {
    careful_strategy(APPL);
    careful_strategy(MSFT);
} **else** {
    opportunistic_strategy(APPL);
    opportunistic_strategy(MSFT);
}

The last rule clearly summarizes the meaning of the whole program in a very compact and easily readable statement.

4 Discussion and Related Work

Reactive planning is an important paradigm that led to implementations using reactive rules in languages like AgentSpeak(L) [16,2], 3APL [9,7], GOAL [8], or the one introduced here.

Interpreters of these languages in every step select a rule and then execute it w.r.t. semantics of the particular language. In general, in each cycle the interpreter considers a set of rules independently of the previously selected and executed rules (doing some bookkeeping within the internal structure of agent's mental state). The resulting agent system is then able to flexibly react to events and exceptional situations without reconsidering its previous actions.

However, designers of an agent oriented programming language face a very difficult problem: Such a reactive architecture of an agent program clashes with the traditional sequential and imperative view on the program code.

We argue, that the functional view on an agent program

1. can be appropriately represented by an abstraction called *mental state transformer*,
2. has a potential to become a basis for a powerful abstraction useful for conceptual decomposition of an agent program into functionally encapsulated subunits (higher level units "call" lower level ones, which allows structuring the agent program into several conceptually separated layers), and
3. is particularly appropriate in the context of programming languages for agents with mental states.

Instead of considering an agent program as a specification of all the paths along which the agent system is allowed to evolve within its transition system, this abstraction shifts the programming style to consider different contexts in which the agent might be in. Each such context forms a subspace of the agent's transition system and it might again consist of a number of smaller subspaces, in each of which the agent performs a different behaviour, i.e. different mental state update.

The concept of mental state transformer favours this subspace-nesting view on the specification of an agent system by nesting queries of transition rules, finally resulting in a mental state update. In the previous sections, we tried to demonstrate how this view can be used to conceptually decompose an agent program into functionally encapsulated subunits. We stress, that this work should be perceived more as a basis for further development of strong abstractions for agent oriented programming, rather then an ultimate solution of this problem.

Most probably, 3APL [9,7] is the rule based language which received the most attention w.r.t. agent program modularity. Recent works by Dastani et. al. [6] and by van Riemsdijk et. al. [18] introduce a semantically oriented modularity to 3APL. In [6] the authors formalize a notion of *role*, grouping together beliefs, goals, plans and reasoning rules of a BDI agent. A role can be enacted, or deacted at run-time. The whole process is handled by 3APL's deliberation cycle.

In [18], the authors introduce a concept of *goal oriented modularity* for 3APL. It is based on decomposition of a set of practical reasoning rules of a BDI agent into modules, according to goals they help to achieve. A module can be called within a rule to achieve a subgoal in the context of a plan. When the subgoal is achieved, the control returns back to the context from which the module was called. This resembles a stack of routine calls in procedural languages. Implementation of both of these 3APL extensions requires modification of 3APL's semantics and the language interpreter.

Both role and goal oriented approaches to modularize an agent program are based on particularities of the internal structure of agent's mental state, namely BDI architecture.

As our approach introduces a functional modularity, supported by *purely syntactic extensions* of the language, they can be seen as orthogonal to ours and, we believe, can be combined. A combination of modularization of practical reasoning rules, based on the abstraction of mst's, within the role, or a goal oriented module, can lead to a finer grained structuring of agent programs.

In [10] plan patterns for programming declarative goals in AgentSpeak(L) ([2]) are introduced. While their approach is similar to ours in that it exploits a macro preprocessor as well, in [10] the authors describe use of this mechanism only for implementation of code templates, similar to those we discuss in Subsection 3.2, for handling various types of goals. In this paper, we propose a *functional view of an agent program*, embodied in the concept of mental state transformer, which has an ambition to become a basis for further development of code templates implementing also agent's behaviours, or roles.

Finally, according to our personal communication with Koen V. Hindriks, there's an ongoing work on policy based modularization of GOAL [8].

We are not aware of any work introducing source code modularity into declarative approaches like e.g. MINERVA [11] and DALI [5]. These two languages exploit the strengths of declarative logic programming and the semantics of both of them is closely connected to logic program updates.

However, we believe that our approach can be adapted to introduce modularization in these languages as well (however, this is not straightforward for MINERVA and DALI, because their semantics is not just based on reactive rules).

A modularization based on the abstraction of *capabilities* was introduced in JACK [4] and further extended in Jadex [3]. Capability, similarly to a role in 3APL, encapsulates related beliefs, goals, plans and events. However, as both of these systems can be seen as extensions of Java, all the syntactically oriented modularity implemented in Java applies to them as well. Since our approach is oriented towards modularization of languages based on reactive rules, any direct comparison does not make sense.

IMPACT [17] and *Modular BDI architecture* [15] introduce a vertical modularity to agent programming. The programming language in which a developer encodes how an agent system should move from one mental state to another using updates, is in these approaches *independent of the internal structure* of agent's mental states. A programmer is free to choose a knowledge representation technique to employ and develop the agent's mental state representation in it. She can also agentize 3rd party legacy code like e.g. mainstream database systems. These two approaches inspired the design of our core programming language. It allowed us to study modularization of an agent program independently of intricacies of the architecture of an agent's mental state.

This paper is an attempt to engineer a practical syntax for the *Modular BDI architecture* introduced previously in [15]. A more thorough discussion on applicability of our approach to other agent oriented programming frameworks is given in [14].

5   Conclusion and Future Work

The contribution of this paper is an attempt to give an answer to the following question:

> *Given an (unstructured) agent language based mainly on reactive rules, how can the syntax be extended so that important features allowing code re-use, modularization and the like are available?*

To this end we introduced a *novel* abstraction: the *mental state transformer*.

We did not yet touch the important issue of *variables* in our language. Using variables broadens our approach significantly and enhances its applicability. The problem with allowing variables in the rules, is that the implementation of the notion of named mst using macros is not sufficient any more. In such an extended language the *name scope of variables* has to be considered, i.e. variables used in named mst, should be *local to that mst*. A *customized macro preprocessor*, which handles local variables has to be used in such a case. We are currently developing such preprocessor.

While we discussed in this paper only the theoretical basis, we are currently working on an implementation of an interpreter-compiler stack for the programming language similar to the one proposed here. We hope to refine some of the extensions of the language using macro expansion and to experiment with the resulting language, in order to put the abstraction of mst's to a test. As the structural decomposition, introduced in this paper, leads to a *new programming style*, it is necessary to prove the usefulness of the presented language in practice by developing a non-trivial agent system application.

Finally we would like to thank several anonymous referees for their careful reading. Their comments helped to improve this paper a lot.

References

1. Bordini, R.H., Dastani, M., Dix, J., El Fallah Seghrouchni, A.: Multi-Agent Programming Languages, Platforms and Applications. In: Multiagent Systems, Artificial Societies, and Simulated Organizations, vol. 15, Kluwer Academic Publishers, Dordrecht (2005)
2. Bordini, R.H., Hübner, J.F., Vieira, R.: Jason and the Golden Fleece of Agent-Oriented Programming. In: Multiagent Systems, Artificial Societies, and Simulated Organizations [1], ch. 1., vol. 15, pp. 3–37 (2005)
3. Braubach, L., Pokahr, A., Lamersdorf, W.: Extending the Capability Concept for Flexible BDI Agent Modularization. In: Bordini, R.H., Dastani, M., Dix, J., Seghrouchni, A.E.F. (eds.) PROMAS 2005. LNCS (LNAI), vol. 3862, pp. 139–155. Springer, Heidelberg (2006)
4. Busetta, P., Howden, N., Rönnquist, R., Hodgson, A.: Structuring BDI Agents in Functional Clusters. In: Jennings, N.R. (ed.) ATAL 1999. LNCS, vol. 1757, pp. 277–289. Springer, Heidelberg (2000)
5. Costantini, S., Tocchio, A.: A Logic Programming Language for Multi-agent Systems. In: Flesca, S., Greco, S., Leone, N., Ianni, G. (eds.) JELIA 2002. LNCS (LNAI), vol. 2424, pp. 1–13. Springer, Heidelberg (2002)
6. Dastani, M., van Riemsdijk, B., Hulstijn, J., Dignum, F., Meyer, J.-J.C.: Enacting and deacting roles in agent programming. In: Odell, J.J., Giorgini, P., Müller, J.P. (eds.) AOSE 2004. LNCS, vol. 3382, pp. 189–204. Springer, Heidelberg (2005)
7. Dastani, M., van Riemsdijk, M.B., Meyer, J.-J.: Programming Multi-Agent Systems in 3APL. In: Multiagent Systems, Artificial Societies, and Simulated Organizations [1], ch. 2, vol. 15 pp. 39–68, (2005)
8. de Boer, F.S., Hindriks, K.V., van der Hoek, W., Meyer, J.-J.C.: Agent programming with declarative goals. CoRR, cs.AI/0207008 (2002)

9. Hindriks, K.V., de Boer, F.S., van der Hoek, W., Meyer, J.-J.C.: Agent Programming in 3APL. Autonomous Agents and Multi-Agent Systems 2(4), 357–401 (1999)
10. Hübner, J.F., Bordini, R.H., Wooldridge, M.: Programming declarative goals using plan patterns. In: Baldoni, M., Endriss, U. (eds.) DALT 2006. LNCS (LNAI), vol. 4327, pp. 123–140. Springer, Heidelberg (2006)
11. Leite, J.A., Alferes, J.J., Pereira, L.M.: MINERVA - A Dynamic Logic Programming Agent Architecture. In: Meyer, J.-J.C., Tambe, M. (eds.) ATAL 2001. LNCS (LNAI), vol. 2333, pp. 141–157. Springer, Heidelberg (2002)
12. Meyer, B.: Introduction to the Theory of Programming Languages. Prentice-Hall, Englewood Cliffs (1990)
13. Nakashima, H., Wellman, M.P., Weiss, G., Stone, P. (eds.): 5th International Joint Conference on Autonomous Agents and Multiagent Systems (AAMAS 2006), Hakodate, Japan, May 8-12, 2006. ACM, New York (2006)
14. Novák, P., Dix, J.: Adding structure to agent programming languages. Technical Report IfI-06-12, Clausthal University of Technology (2006)
15. Novák, P., Dix, J.: Modular BDI architecture. In: Nakashima et al [13], pp. 1009–1015.
16. Rao, A.S.: AgentSpeak(L): BDI Agents Speak Out in a Logical Computable Language. In: Perram, J., Van de Velde, W. (eds.) MAAMAW 1996. LNCS, vol. 1038, pp. 42–55. Springer, Heidelberg (1996)
17. Subrahmanian, V.S., Bonatti, P.A., Dix, J., Eiter, T., Kraus, S., Ozcan, F., Ross, R.: Heterogenous Active Agents. MIT Press, Cambridge (2000)
18. van Riemsdijk, M.B., Dastani, M., Meyer, J.-J.C., de Boer, F.S.: Goal-oriented modularity in agent programming. In: Nakashima et al [13], pp. 1271–1278.

Modules as Policy-Based Intentions: Modular Agent Programming in GOAL

Koen Hindriks

EEMCS, Delft University of Technology, Delft, The Netherlands
k.v.hindriks@tudelft.nl

Abstract. Modular programming has the usual benefits associated with structured programming, information hiding and reusability, but also has additional benefits to offer when applied in agent programming. We argue that modules can be viewed as structures similar to that of policy-based intentions [2]. Modules perceived in this way are components within an agent that are triggered in a particular situation and combine the knowledge and skills to adequately pursue the goals of the agent in that situation. The context that triggers the activation of a module defines the interface of the module, which can be specified declaratively, in contrast to the usual functional interpretations of such interfaces. A feature that differentiates our notion of a module from plans is that modules provide an agent with a means to *focus* its attention on the relevant resources it needs to handle a situation. As a result, modules can be used to control or reduce the underspecification and inherent non-determinism that is typical of agent programs. In the paper, the proposed module concept is incorporated into the agent language GOAL and illustrated by means of a simple example.

1 Introduction

It has been argued by several authors that besides being able to decompose a complex system into multiple agents it is also important to be able to decompose single agents into structured units in agent programming languages. For various reasons, it is not always appropriate to provide this additional structure by decomposing a single agent into a group of yet smaller agents. An agent-based decomposition introduces additional communication overhead and requires duplication of knowledge and goals in those agents. This has motivated the introduction of *modularization* as a decomposition technique into various agent programming frameworks (cf. [3,4,17]).

Apart from the traditional motivations for modularization, we argue that there are also reasons more specifically related to rational agents for incorporating modules into agents. As in other programming paradigms, modularization provides the usual benefits associated with *structured programming*, *information hiding*, and *reusability*.

In agent programming, modules support the *encapsulation* of domain knowledge, basic actions and plans that are logically related and relevant for handling

M. Dastani et al.(Eds.): ProMAS 2007, LNAI 4908, pp. 156–171, 2008.
© Springer-Verlag Berlin Heidelberg 2008

particular situations. From a software engineering point of view, modules allow a programmer to focus on those skills that are required to handle a situation. As components of an agent program, modules can be viewed as specialized, dedicated units of control to realize particular goals of the agent. Modules in agent programming are also called *capabilities* sometimes in the literature (cf. [3,4]).

The main focus of this paper is on the dynamic control that module execution provides to a rational agent. As will be discussed below in more detail, modular agent programming also provides additional benefits which are not traditionally recognized or simply do not apply to other programming paradigms. One of the most important of these is the fact that *modules provide additional structure to control the inherent non-determinism of agent programs.* Agent programs typically do not specify for each situation that the agent may encounter a unique course of action that the agent should execute. In particular, often actions in parallel plans are interleaved non-deterministically, and various goal adoption rules and plan rules may be selected for execution at any time. As a result, agent programs in general *underspecify* the course of action that an agent takes.

This underspecification present in agent programs may result in suboptimal or even irrational behavior of an agent. Since an agent is supposed to "do the right thing", various proposals have been made to provide an agent with additional means to control the choices left open by the agent program. One particular strand of research has focused on defining control structures to achieve this objective. In the context of agent programming these are also called *deliberation cycles* (cf. [5,14]). Another interesting proposal has been to use decision-theoretic techniques (e.g. [1]). The proposal discussed in this paper is to use modules to provide *focus* in the selection of actions of an agent. It is argued that the concept of a module provides for a particularly flexible programming technique to reduce the underspecification typically present in agent programs.

A further advantage of introducing modules in agent programming is that the interface of a module can be provided with a natural and moreover completely declarative definition. This is a distinguishing feature of the module concept presented in this paper. Typically, the *interface* of a module that implements the information hiding is based on an explicit *importing* and *exporting* mechanism which is *not* declarative. As a result, such module interfaces do not provide a declarative specification of what they can be used for but instead only specify an accessibility mechanism that determines what is "visible" to the environment of the module. A declarative concept of module interfaces as proposed here, however, allows a programmer to read of the module's intended use from its interface without any additional inspection of the implementation details inside a module. The idea is that a declarative interface specifies in what circumstances a module can usefully be activated.

The declarative nature of module interfaces differentiates our proposal from those that are inspired by Prolog and Object Oriented concepts of modules such as [3,4] and is closer in spirit to the logic-based approach in [12]. In line with our conception of a module being specialized in handling specific situations it is natural to define a module interface as a condition that identifies that situation. The declarative interface of an agent module specifies *which situations* a module can handle well because it is designed to do just that. The internal structure of a module specifies *how* the situation specified by the interface is to be handled: it encapsulates the basic actions, knowledge, and plans that the agent needs to handle the situation, given its current goals.

This view of modules in agent programming provides for a natural and intuitive separation of concerns. On the one hand, the encapsulation of basic actions, domain knowledge and plans in a module facilitates the programmer in combining all relevant knowledge and skills that are needed to handle a particular situation. On the other hand, the declarative specification of a module interface entails that it can be defined more or less independently from other parts of the program: A module only has to provide a kind of plan to handle the situation as specified by the interface.

This concept of a module that focuses the attention of an agent in order to handle the situation at hand is incorporated in this paper in the agent programming language GOAL. Due to the additional structure that modules provide, the incorporation of modules into GOAL can also be viewed as an extension that makes available a structure similar to a *policy* or *plan* in GOAL. The paper is organized as follows. First, a brief overview of the GOAL programming language is presented. In section 3 GOAL is extended with modules. The semantics of modules is informally motivated and formally specified by providing an operational semantics. Section 4 compares with related work and concludes the paper.

2   The GOAL Language

GOAL, for Goal-Oriented Agent Language, is an agent programming language that incorporates declarative notions of beliefs and goals, and a mechanism for action selection based on these notions. That is, GOAL agents derive their choice of action from their beliefs and goals. For a detailed overview and discussion of the language see [7,10]. An example of an (incomplete) GOAL agent program that will be used throughout the paper for illustrative purposes is provided in Figure 1. This agent provides a specification for a delivery agent that delivers parcels to various clients. A GOAL agent program consists of four sections: (1) a set of initial beliefs, collectively called the (initial) *belief base* of the agent, (2) a set of initial goals, called the (initial) *goal base*, (3) a *program section* which consists of a set of conditional actions, and (4) an *action specification* that consists of a specification of the pre- and post-conditions of *basic actions* of the agent. To avoid confusion of the program section with the agent program itself, from now on, the agent program will simply be called *agent*. The term *agent* will be used both to refer to the program text itself as well as to the execution of such a program. It should be clear from the context which of the two senses is intended.

The program and action specification components of a GOAL agent are static and do not change at runtime. The agent's belief and goal bases are dynamic

```
:main:deliveryAgent
{
    :beliefs{ home(a).
        loc(p1,a). loc(p2,a). loc(p3,a). loc(p4,a). loc(truck,a).
        loc(c1,b). loc(c2,c). order(c1,[p1,p2]). order(c2,[p3,p4]).
        ordered(C,P) :- order(C,Y), member(P,Y).
        loaded_order(C) :- order(C,O), loaded(O).
        delivered_order(C) :- order(C,O), loc(C,X), loc(O,X), loc(truck,a).
        packed :- setOf(P,in(P,truck),L), size(L,2).
        empty :- setOf(P,in(P,truck),[]).
    }
    :goals{ delivered_order(c1). delivered_order(c2). ... }
    :program{
        if goal(delivered_order(C)), bel(ordered(C,P)), ∼bel(in(P,truck))
            then load(P).
        if goal(delivered_order(C)),
            bel(loc(truck,X), loaded_order(C), loc(C,Y)) then goto(Y).
        if goal(delivered_order(C)), bel(loc(truck,X), loc(C,X),
            in(P,truck), ordered(C,P)) then unload(P).
        if bel(loc(C, X), empty, home(Y)) then goto(Y).
        if bel(ordered(C,P), empty),∼bel(in(P,a)) then adopt(in(P,a)).
        ...
    }
    :action-spec{
        load(P){
            :pre{∼packed, loc(truck,X), loc(P,X)}
            :post{in(P,truck), ∼loc(P,X)} }
        goto(Y){
            :pre{loc(truck,X), X≠Y}
            :post{loc(truck,Y), ∼loc(truck,X)} }
        ...
    }
}
```

Fig. 1. Example of a GOAL agent program

and may vary over time. They change because of actions that are performed by the agent, which, apart from changing the agent's environment, also update and modify the beliefs and, indirectly, the agent's goals. Belief bases are typically denoted by Σ and goal bases by Γ. Together, the belief and goal base pair $\langle \Sigma, \Gamma \rangle$ are called the *mental state* of the agent, typically denoted by s. The language GOAL does not fix the representation of beliefs nor goals, but here we assume they are sentences from a first-order language, which in practice are suitably restricted to allow for an efficient implementation. Mental states are required to satisfy the following rationality constraints ($\models$ denotes first-order entailment):

(i)   Belief bases are consistent: $\Sigma \not\models \textbf{false}$,

(ii)   Individual goals are consistent: $\forall \gamma \in \Gamma: \not\models \neg\gamma$,

(iii)   Goals are not believed to be achieved: $\forall \gamma \in \Gamma: \Sigma \not\models \gamma$.

The beliefs of the agent in Figure 1 consist of facts about the current situation, in this case about parcel locations and clients and their orders, and a number of rules that represent the logical relations between these facts. For example, the rule for `delivered_order(C)` states that an order is delivered if all ordered parcels have been delivered at the client's site location and the truck is (back) at its home base `a`. (Due to space limitations, definitions of the `loc` and `loaded` predicates for lists and the `unload` action specification are not included, but the intended meaning should be clear. `setOf` is a standard Prolog predicate that returns a list of items satisfying the condition of its second argument.) Note that the example agent does not believe that it delivered an order and thus initially satisfies the constraint that goals are not believed by the agent.

The conditional actions in the program section of a GOAL agent define a mapping from states to actions, together specifying a non-deterministic policy or course of action. The condition of a conditional action is called a *mental state condition*. It determines the states in which the conditional action may be executed. Mental state conditions are boolean combinations of basic formulas **bel**(ϕ) or **goal**(ϕ) with ϕ a first-order formula. A prolog-like notation is used in examples, as in Figure 1: Literals in a conjunction are separated by means of a comma, and negation is written as $\sim$. (In the main text, however, we also use $\neg$ and $\wedge$ to denote negation and conjunction.) These conditions allow an agent to inspect its beliefs and goals. For example, in the program section of the agent in Figure 1, the first conjunct of the first condition, **goal**(`delivered_order(C)`), inspects the goal base and verifies whether the agent has a goal to deliver for some client `C`, and the second conjunct **bel**(`ordered(C,P)`) inspects the belief base and verifies whether client `C` ordered a parcel `P`. Free variables in mental state conditions are instantiated when the condition is evaluated at runtime.

Since mental state conditions need not be exclusive, multiple conditional actions may be simultaneously enabled. GOAL agents thus may underspecify the behavior of the agent resulting in a non-deterministic choice of action. In Figure 1, initially the first conditional action is enabled for each of the four parcels listed and the agent may load any of these parcels into the truck by executing a corresponding instantiation of the action `load(P)`. In such a case, the agent may non-deterministically choose any one of these actions for execution.

The fact that agents may be underspecified may provide benefits at design time, but it may also pose problems at runtime. In the example, the agent is supposed to deliver orders to various clients. In order to do so, the agent first needs to load the truck with the ordered items. However, since the agent has multiple orders to deal with and no priority on handling these orders has been specified, the agent may end up loading parcels into the truck that do not belong together. Since the load the truck can carry is also very limited, as a result, the agent may end up delivering no orders at all and end up in a deadlock situation. (Of course, a slightly smarter agent would start unloading parcels again, but this would not guarantee resolution of the problem. Other ways to resolve the problem in a principled way seem to require significant modification of the agent.) Note that in case the agent would have had only a single delivery goal to deal with, there would have been no problem, indicating that the example delivery agent is not an incorrect implementation per se. With the appropriate focus, the agent would have been able to deliver successfully. To provide agents with such focus is one of our motivations for introducing modules. Modules are introduced to provide a means to control the non-determinism inherent in agents and to provide agents with a focus of attention on some of their goals among the many others that they may have.

3   Modules as Policy-Based Intentions

In this section the use of modules conceived as policy-based intentions is illustrated using the example introduced in the previous section and the informal discussion of modules is complemented with a precise definition of the operational semantics of modules by means of a transition system (cf. [13]).

The concept of a module that is introduced here is inspired by the the concept of a *policy-based intention* in [2] and motivated by the fact that modules so viewed can be identified with plans or policies that guide the agent's action. Policy-based intentions are general policies and concern potentially recurring circumstances in the agent's life. Such policies shape an agent's plans in ways that may help achieve a range of different and potentially conflicting goals. They do so by providing a partial solution to the problems posed by the limited resources for deliberation by making a previously successfully tested strategy readily available to the agent. Policy-based intentions may be particular to an agent, coding the specific ways in which that agent typically handles a recurring circumstance.

Our notion of module incorporates the main ideas of such policy-based intentions. In particular, it incorporates the notion of a *circumstance-triggered* intention and a notion of *commitment* to executing the intention. A module viewed as a policy-based intention specifies these circumstances as a condition for activating the module. A module, additionally, can be used to structure and combine the relevant knowledge and skills needed to handle such circumstances in ways that help achieve the agent's goals. Modules do not only describe the capabilities that an agent has, but specify a policy or plan that an agent applies in particular situations to handle that situation.

The GOAL language allows for an elegant definition of modules that are circumstance-triggered, general policies for acting. Syntactically, GOAL modules are just GOAL agents with an additional *context section*. A module also has a name, which serves as a bookkeeping device and facilitates easy reference. An example GOAL agent with two modules named `deliverOrder` and `stockMngt` is provided in Figure 2. The example is a modified version of the agent in Figure 1 in which most of the program text has been placed inside the modules except for the facts in the belief base and the initial goals in the goal base (the ... refer to missing parts, which can be filled in partially by copying text from Figure 1). The context and program section of a module must be non-empty, but the belief and goal sections may be empty. Empty module sections can simply be left out, e.g. in our example the goals section of the first module might have been left out.

For ease of reference, below we write $m.section$ to refer to each of the different sections of a module named m. For example, `deliverOrder.context` refers to the context section of module `deliverOrder`.

Module Activation. Intuitively, a module is specialized in handling the situations that are specified by the context section. The context section of a module, which may be any mental state condition, determines its activation condition: A module may be *activated* when its context section is true. For example, the context section in Figure 2 of the module `deliverOrder` specifies that the module is specialized in achieving an instance of the goal `deliver_order(C)`. Context sections may also include conditions on the beliefs of an agent, to indicate in which circumstances a module may be used to achieve a goal, for example, a precondition for activating the `deliverOrder` module is that the ordered items are in stock. Note that context sections thus allow to define preconditions for executing composed activities, i.e. plans or polices, that are specified in the program section of a module. A module with a context section that consists of belief conditions only such as the `stockMngt` module is called a *reactive module*.

In order to present the formal operational semantics below a precise definition of the semantics of mental state conditions is required. A mental state condition is evaluated in a mental state $\langle \Sigma, \Gamma \rangle$. We overload the first-order entailment $\models$ and also use it to denote the truth conditions of mental state conditions.

Definition 1 (Mental State Condition Semantics)
The truth conditions for (closed) mental state formula, relative to a mental state $s = \langle \Sigma, \Gamma \rangle$*, are defined by the following four clauses:*

$$
\begin{aligned}
s &\models \mathbf{bel}(\phi) & \text{iff} \quad & \Sigma \models \phi, \\
s &\models \mathbf{goal}(\phi) & \text{iff} \quad & \text{there is a } \gamma \in \Gamma \text{ s.t. } \gamma \models \phi \text{ and } \Sigma \not\models \phi, \\
s &\models \neg\varphi & \text{iff} \quad & s \not\models \varphi, \\
s &\models \varphi_1 \wedge \varphi_2 & \text{iff} \quad & s \models \varphi_1 \text{ and } s \models \varphi_2.
\end{aligned}
$$

Like any mental state condition, a context φ may have free variables, denoted by $free(\varphi)$. Any free variables that occur in other sections of a module, with the exception of the program section, should also occur in the context section. (In the example agents, rules are assumed to be implicitly universally quantified.) Variables are instantiated at runtime when a module is activated. A module is instantiated when all its free variables have been instantiated. Formally, an instantiation of a module with free variables var in its context section is a substitution ρ such that $dom(\rho) = $ var and the range of ρ is a set of constants or closed terms. The application of a substitution ρ to a formula φ is written as usual as $\varphi\rho$. The composition of two substitutions ρ_1 and ρ_2 is written as $\rho_1 \circ \rho_2$.

The activation of a module requires that various items are recorded to facilitate a proper definition of the operational semantics, e.g. that module m has been activated, with what values ρ the free variables in the context of module m have been instantiated, and which goals are actively pursued. To this end, the notion of a *configuration* which extends a mental state with these items is introduced. Note that the static parts of a module, i.e. the domain knowledge,

```
:main:deliveryAgent
{
    :beliefs{ home(a).
      loc(p1,a). loc(p2,a). loc(p3,a). loc(p4,a). loc(truck,a).
      loc(c1,b). loc(c2,c). order(c1,[p1,p2]). order(c2,[p3,p4]).
    }
    :goals{ delivered_order(c1). delivered_order(c2). ... }
    :program{ ... }
    :action-spec{ ... }
    :module:deliverOrder{
    :context{ bel(order(C,O), in(O,a)), goal(delivered_order(C)) }
    :beliefs{
      ordered(C,P) :- order(C,Y), member(P,Y).
      ...
    }
    :goals{ }
    :program{
      if bel(ordered(C, P)), ~bel(in(P, truck)) then load(P).
      if bel(loc(truck, X), loaded_order(C), loc(C, Y)) then goto(Y).
      if bel(loc(truck,X), loc(C,X), in(P,truck), ordered(C,P))
         then unload(P).
      if bel(loc(C, X), empty, home(Y)) then goto(Y).
    }
    :action-spec{ ... }
    }
    :module:stockMngt{
    :context{ bel(ordered(C,P), empty), ~bel(in(P,a)) }
    :goals{ in(P,a) }
    :program{ ... }
    :action-spec{ ... }
    }
...
}
```

Fig. 2. Example of GOAL Agent with Modules

conditional actions in the program section, and the action specification need not be explicitly represented in a configuration. They can be retrieved when needed from the module and instantiated appropriately by applying the substitution which is recorded in a configuration. We write $\langle m, \rho, \Gamma_m, \langle \Sigma, \Gamma \rangle \rangle$ to represent a configuration in which a module m has been activated in a mental state $\langle \Sigma, \Gamma \rangle$, where Γ_m represents the associated set of goals handled by the module.

A module may be activated while another module has been activated. A configuration thus may consist of a stack of modules and in that case a more recently activated module is executed within the context of a previously activated module. For example, it may be that the former is activated because of additional subgoals or domain knowledge introduced by the latter module. It may also be the case, however, that a module is activated because of changes of the beliefs in the agent's belief base as e.g. the stockMngt module in the example. To allow for activation of a module when other modules have been activated and not yet terminated, we also write $\langle m_1, \rho_{m_1}, \Gamma_{m_1}, \ldots, \langle m_n, \rho_{m_n}, \Gamma_{m_n}, \langle \Sigma, \Gamma \rangle \rangle \ldots \rangle$ to indicate that module m_1 has been activated after modules m_n to m_2 (in that order) have been activated. We say that a ρ-*instantiation of module* m *has been activated* if the module name together with the substitution ρ occurs in the configuration $\langle m_1, \rho_{m_1}, \Gamma_{m_1}, \ldots, \langle m_n, \rho_{m_n}, \Gamma_{m_n}, \langle \Sigma, \Gamma \rangle \rangle \ldots \rangle$. Moreover, only the most recently activated module is called *active*.

The belief section of a module can be used to specify relevant domain knowledge for handling a situation. There is no restriction on the formulas allowed in the belief section of a module; it may contain both facts as well as rules, just like the belief base of the agent. When more than one module has been activated, we need to ensure that the domain knowledge of each activated module can be accessed by the agent. Each module is activated within a particular context and the information about this context, represented by the domain knowledge of previously activated modules, should still be available to the agent. To this end, we define the notion of *accessible beliefs in configuration* v as the set $\Sigma_{accessible}$ of the beliefs Σ combined with the domain knowledge $(m_i.beliefs)\rho_i$ of each activated module m_i, where any free variables have been instantiated by applying the substitution ρ_i. The accessible domain knowledge of all activated, properly instantiated modules is also denoted by Σ_{domain}. Σ_{domain} denotes all beliefs of all modules except for those in the global belief base Σ and we have that $\Sigma_{domain} \subseteq \Sigma_{accessible}$.

In the goal section of a module additional subgoals may be introduced for structuring the problem that needs to be dealt with, as is done e.g. in the stockMngt module. These goals are goals local to the module and are only pursued while the module is activated. Subgoals introduced by a module may trigger other modules again to achieve these subgoals.

Modules provide more focus by restricting the set of goals that the agent actively pursues. In our simple example agent, the module deliverOrder serves to provide a focus of attention on one of the delivery goals of the agent and to temporarily disregard any other goals that the agent may have. Upon activation of that module, the context is instantiated with either client c1 or client c2. Assuming that c1 is used, the set of active goals is restricted to the goal of delivering an order for c1 and the goal of delivering for c2 becomes passive. This provides the agent with the relevant focus to complete a delivery for a single client. The actions in a module thus will only be directed at achieving that goal and potential conflicts due to other goals are avoided.

Formally, the notion of *active goals in configuration* v is defined as the set of goals associated with the most recently activated module, i.e. $\Gamma_{active} = \Gamma_{m_1}$ where m_1 denotes that module. (Note that in this case no substitutions need to be applied since the goals in Γ_{m_1} have already been instantiated.) All other goals are called *passive* and the set of these goals can be defined as $\Gamma_{passive} = \Gamma \cup \Gamma_{m_2} \cup \ldots \cup \Gamma_{m_n}$ where Γ denotes the top-level goals of the agent and the

Γ_{m_i} denote the goals introduced and processed by previously activated modules m_i. Finally, $\Gamma_{all} = \Gamma_{active} \cup \Gamma_{passive}$, i.e. Γ_{all} is the set of all current goals.

When a module is activated, a filter is applied to the then active set of goals to select only those that triggered the activation. As a result, the agent will focus on those goals that entail the context of the module given the currently accessible beliefs. Informally, only those goals that the agent has adopted and make the context condition of the module true are considered after activation of that module in combination with those introduced by the module's goal section. The set of active goals is computed from the context section and the goal section. A context condition φ can be converted into disjunctive normal form, taking formulas of the form $\mathbf{bel}(\phi)$ and $\mathbf{goal}(\phi)$ as atoms. An occurrence of an atom of the form $\mathbf{bel}(\phi)$ or $\mathbf{goal}(\phi)$ is called a *positive literal* if it occurs unnegated in the normal form, otherwise it is called a *negative literal*. Assuming that a context condition φ is in disjunctive normal form, the function $filter(\varphi)$ extracts all positive literals of the form $\mathbf{goal}(\phi)$ from φ and removes the goal operator $\mathbf{goal}$. For example, if $\varphi = [\mathbf{bel}(p) \wedge \mathbf{goal}(q)] \vee [\mathbf{goal}(r) \wedge \neg\mathbf{goal}(p)]$, then $filter(\varphi) = \{q, r\}$. The focus of attention then is defined as those filtered atoms that are also currently active goals of the agent by the function $focus(\varphi, s) = \{\phi \in filter(\varphi) \mid s \models \mathbf{goal}(\phi)\}$, where s is a state defined by the accessible beliefs and active goals.

Definition 2 (Module Activation Rule)
Let $v = \langle m_1, \rho_{m_1}, \Gamma_{m_1}, \ldots \langle \Sigma, \Gamma \rangle \ldots \rangle$ be a configuration (possibly without module instantiations, i.e. $v = \langle \Sigma, \Gamma \rangle$), m be a module, and ρ be a substitution such that $dom(\rho) = free(m.context)$. Then the activation of module m is defined by:

$$\frac{\langle \Sigma_{accessible}, \Gamma_{active} \rangle \models (m.context)\rho \\ no\ \rho\text{-}instantiation\ of\ module\ m\ has\ been\ activated\ yet}{v \longrightarrow \langle m, \rho, focus((m.context)\rho, \langle \Sigma_{accessible}, \Gamma_{active} \rangle) \cup (m.goals)\rho, v \rangle}$$

The second condition in the rule avoids that the same instantiation of a module is activated twice. The activation of a module does not change the beliefs or goals in the mental state of the initial configuration v. Implicitly, however, the set of accessible beliefs $\Sigma_{accessible}$ is extended with the instantiated domain knowledge in the belief section (if any) of the module. Module activation also changes the set of active goals Γ_{active} to the set of goals that result from filtering the context of the module and computing the corresponding focus of attention combined with goals that result from instantiating the goal section of the module. As a consequence, other modules are only activated when they are relevant for achieving an active goal (with the exception possibly of reactive modules).

Action Execution. Once a module is activated execution is restricted to actions from the module's program section. This is a second way to structure and focus the behavior of an agent. For example, by excluding the first conditional action for adopting a goal to replenish stock from the module in Figure 2, any potential interference of actions to achieve this goal with the actions for delivering the ordered parcels is prevented. All actions that are relevant for delivering

an order are combined in the module which in this way facilitates the specification of a general policy for achieving this goal. In the `deliverOrder` module the
program section specifies that the context of the module is handled by loading
the truck with the items the client ordered, going to the client site, unloading
the ordered items, and returning to home base.

In order to define the semantics of action execution, a transition function
T is assumed to be given that captures the semantics of basic actions `a` and
is consistent with all the action specification sections (including those within
modules). Action specifications, moreover, are required to be consistent with
the domain knowledge stored in a module. That is, since it is assumed that
such knowledge does not change during the lifetime of an agent, an action is
not allowed to update this knowledge to avoid inconsistencies when a module is
activated. While in principle such beliefs can be added to the (global) belief base
Σ, encapsulating such knowledge in a module facilitates information hiding and
efficient execution. In the example agent of Figure 2 the rule for the predicate
`ordered` is used to represent fixed domain knowledge about the relation between
individual ordered items and the order of a client. Formally, this means that the
transition function should be defined in such a way that actions never update
knowledge stored in a module.

Constraint 1 (Domain Knowledge Not Updated)
*If a belief section in a module consists of a set of formulas D, then for any belief
base Σ and action a (including **skip**, i.e. the action without any effects) it must
be the case that $T(a, \Sigma \cup D) = \Sigma' \cup D$, such that $\Sigma' \cup D$ is consistent.*

Since the **skip** action does not change the configuration of an agent, it follows
that $T(\mathbf{skip}, \Sigma \cup D) = \Sigma \cup D$ must be consistent, which implies in particular that
the domain knowledge present in the various modules of an agent also should be
consistent with the initial beliefs of an agent.

An important aspect of modules concerns the encapsulation of the effects of
belief updates and goal updates. It is argued here that the beliefs in the mental
state of an agent (in contrast with the domain knowledge stored in modules),
and any updates on these beliefs, should *not* be encapsulated in a module. This
would make these beliefs "invisible" to other modules. The effects on the agent's
environment caused by executing a module, should be available for later reference
and therefore incorporated into the agent's belief base. For example, the updated
locations of parcels need to be stored in the belief base of the example agent.

It has already been argued that goals of an agent should be local to a module
in order to provide an agent with a focus on the goals relevant in a particular
situation. But even though the agent's focus is on achieving the active goals by
selecting appropriate actions, whenever either an active or passive goal has been
achieved such a goal is updated and removed from the set of all adopted goals.
It is considered irrational for an agent to invest any more time and resources in
a goal that has already been achieved.

The previous discussion is formally captured in the action execution rule for
modules. The rule restricts the choice of action to those that are available within

the program section of the most recently activated module. Modules thus may create focus and prevent unexpected or undesirable interference effects of other actions.

Definition 3 (Action Execution Rule: Modules)
*Let $v = \langle m_1, \rho_{m_1}, \Gamma_{m_1}, \dots \langle \Sigma, \Gamma \rangle \dots \rangle$ be a configuration, c be a conditional action of the form **if** φ **then** $a(t)$ in the program section of module m_1, ρ a substitution with $dom(\rho) = free(\varphi \rho_{m_1})$, and $\sigma = \rho_{m_1} \circ \rho$. Then the execution of the conditional action c is defined by:*

$$\frac{\langle \Sigma_{accessible}, \Gamma_{active} \rangle \models \varphi \sigma \text{ and } \Gamma_{active} \neq \emptyset}{v \longrightarrow \langle m_1, \rho_{m_1}, \Gamma'_{m_1}, \dots \langle \Sigma', \Gamma' \rangle \dots \rangle}$$

where:

- *$\Sigma' = \mathcal{T}(a(t)\sigma, \Sigma_{accessible}) \setminus \Sigma_{domain}$,*
- *$\Gamma'_{(i)} = \Gamma_{(i)} \setminus \{\psi \in \Gamma_{(i)} \mid \mathcal{T}(a(t)\sigma, \Sigma_{accessible}) \models \psi\}$, where $\Gamma_{(i)}$ denotes any of the sets Γ_i or the goal base Γ.*

Note that only the global beliefs in the belief base Σ of the agent's mental state are updated when an action is performed. The accessible domain knowledge stored in modules is not updated (and excluded from the result of applying the transition function to the set of all accessible beliefs). The definition of the updated beliefs Σ' based on the transition function $\mathcal{T}$ is correct provided that the constraint on updating knowledge stored in modules holds (cf. constraint 1).

Execution at the top-level (i.e. when no modules have been activated) is defined exactly the same as that for GOAL without modules (cf. [7]). In fact, it is a special case of the action execution rule for modules below since a GOAL agent can be viewed as a module without a context section.

Goal Update Actions. The action execution rule is not applicable to the goal update actions but only to basic actions $a(t)$. Different rules are needed for the goal update actions **drop** and **adopt**. Only the rule for **adopt**(ϕ) is provided here. The rule for **drop** can be derived from the rule provided in [7] and the action execution rule above. A **drop**(ϕ) action does not have any effect on the beliefs of an agent and simply removes all goals from the total set of goals which imply that ϕ is a (sub)goal of the agent, i.e. all active as well as passive goals that imply that ϕ is a (sub)goal of the agent are removed from the goal sets Γ_m in a configuration v, and from the top-level goal base Γ.

The rule for executing an **adopt**(ϕ) action requires the agent to check whether it is reasonable to add the goal ϕ, properly instantiated, to the set of adopted goals within the current context. A weak condition is used to verify whether adopting ϕ is reasonable: ϕ may be adopted if it is consistent and is not currently implied by any of the accessible beliefs of the agent. It is not required that ϕ is consistent with the domain knowledge of the agent, in order to avoid unnecessary complications. It is left to the programmer to verify that such consistency will always be maintained. The goal ϕ that is adopted is added to the set of active goals associated with the most recently activated module. The motivation for this is that newly adopted goals are only valid within the context of that module.

Definition 4 (Execution Rule for **adopt**: Modules)
Let $v = \langle m, \rho_m, \Gamma_m, \ldots \langle \Sigma, \Gamma \rangle \ldots \rangle$ be a configuration, c be a conditional action of the form **if** φ **then adopt**(ψ), ρ *be a substitution with* $dom(\rho) = free(\varphi \rho_m)$, *and* $\sigma = \rho_m \circ \rho$. *Then the adoption of a goal ϕ is defined by:*

$$\frac{\langle \Sigma_{accessible}, \Gamma_{active} \rangle \models \varphi \sigma \text{ and } \Gamma_{active} \neq \emptyset, \quad \Sigma_{accessible} \not\models \psi\sigma, \not\models \neg\psi\sigma}{v \longrightarrow \langle m, \rho_m, \Gamma_m \cup \{\psi\sigma\}, \ldots \langle \Sigma, \Gamma \rangle \ldots \rangle}$$

Module Termination: Intuitively, a module is terminated when its associated active goals are achieved. Upon module termination the module's name is removed from the stack along with the associated substitution and the (in this case empty) set of active goals related to the module. A module thus implements a commitment to the goals introduced by the module which can only be overridden by dropping goals using a **drop** action that is available within the module's program section.

Incidentally, this commitment of a module to achieving the associated goals also explains why the goal condition **goal(delivered_order(C))** in the mental state conditions of the conditional actions that were present in Figure 1 can be removed when they are placed inside the module: It may be assumed that this condition holds when the module is active, since the module itself does not introduce any new goals and because the appropriate instantiations for the variable C are used while the module is being executed (cf. also Definition 2 which introduces a substitution ρ to record variable instantiations).

The module **deliverOrder** of the example agent of Figure 2 is terminated after loading the truck with ordered items for a specific client, going to the client's site, unloading the ordered items at that location, and returning to home base. This achieves the goal condition of the context **goal(delivered_order(C))** since in that case the agent will believe that it delivered the order and a goal that is believed to be achieved is removed from the agent's goal base (cf. also Definition 2). At that moment, the context condition of the module no longer holds and the module is automatically terminated.

Definition 5 (Module Termination Rule)
Let $v = \langle m, \rho_m, \Gamma_m, \langle m_1, \rho_{m_1}, \Gamma_{m_1}, \ldots \langle \Sigma, \Gamma \rangle \ldots \rangle\rangle$ be a configuration, which contains at least one module instantiation and a set of active goals $\Gamma_{active} = \Gamma_m$. Then the rule for termination of the most recently activated module m is defined by:

$$\frac{\Gamma_{active} = \emptyset}{v \longrightarrow \langle m_1, \rho_{m_1}, \Gamma_{m_1}, \ldots \langle \Sigma, \Gamma \rangle \ldots \rangle}$$

After terminating the **deliverOrder** module, our example agent will resume execution at the top-level and may reenter the module to process another delivery order.

4   Conclusion

There are similarities between GOAL modules and plans in other agent programming languages (e.g. [6,8,15]). The plans referred to are typically part of a plan library that an agent is provided with during design. Both modules as well as such plans specify a condition called the *context* of the module or plan. Such context conditions specify the situation in which the module or plan can be put to good use. This context may in both cases also be used to bind variables through a substitution mechanism that instantiates variables in a module or plan body.

However, a 3APL [6] or AgentSpeak agent [15] that would implement our example agent, it seems, would have to face the same problem of dealing with the multiple goals for delivering orders. Typically, such agent programs trigger plans for achieving declarative goals and in the example discussed multiple plans would be introduced into the agent's plan base. As a result, similar interference effects are to be expected. The difference between GOAL modules and plans resides in the execution of a module and of a plan taken from a plan library. Once activated, a module becomes the *focus of execution* whereas a plan instead is added to the plan base of an agent and just is one of the current, "active" plans that an agent tries to complete.

The approach to incorporate modularization presented in [17] introduces an operator $m(\phi)$ that is applied to goals ϕ that is also motivated to control non-determinism. This operator may also be used to resolve the problem of our example agent. In contrast with the context sections of GOAL modules, however, this operator introduces a *non-declarative* mechanism for activating modules. Also, whereas the termination condition of GOAL modules is based on a commitment strategy that pursues goals until achieved, the termination of the modules in [17] is based on a strategy to try various plans once and in case of failure to quit. Moreover, in order to activate more than one module, calls to such modules need to be explicitly incorporated as steps in a plan. GOAL modules are not *called* by other modules nor by the agent's plans during run-time, but are *circumstance-triggered* and *focus the attention of the agent* on the situation for which the module provides a policy. In this sense, our notion of a module is similar to the notion of a policy-based intention in [2].

In this paper, several benefits of using modules in agent programming have been identified. In particular it has been argued that modules provide an elegant solution to *focus the execution* of an agent. Modules restrict both the goals that an agent takes into consideration in a given context as well as the conditional actions that the agent needs to choose from. Modules therefore can be used to reduce the inherent non-determinism present in agent programs. They also provide a tool to structure the flow of control in an agent.

Our module concept is related in various ways to other concepts presented in e.g. [3,4,11,12]. It shares with [12] the idea of relating modules to particular contexts. The idea of a "capability filter" in [11] to constrain adoption of goals is somewhat similar to our notion of a module acting as a context that filters out the active goals. Finally, it shares with [3,4] the idea of combining the relevant knowledge and skills (actions, plans) to achieve the agent's goals into a module. The main difference with the latter work is that it is based on events that trigger activation of a module. Although an event-based trigger may be used to realize similar behavior by means of a module encapsulating beliefs and goals of an agent, the purely declarative module interface proposed in this paper may provide a more expressive and explicit means to define the activation conditions of a module. As illustrated in this paper, it is for example quite easy to specify a precondition for activating a module given that specific goals are also present. Moreover, one of the contributions of this paper is that it provides a formal semantics of such module activation and execution.

Interestingly, modular approaches have also been investigated in the context of cognitive architectures, e.g. in SOAR [18]. A mechanism for context switching based on the fact that assumptions associated with modules, or problem spaces as they are called in SOAR, do not hold anymore is proposed in [18]. Although interesting, it is not quite clear how to incorporate such a mechanism into GOAL modules. An alternative could be to incorporate maintance goals in modules and use these as triggers for terminating a module.

Another related idea is to investigate how decision-theoretic notions can be combined with the module concept introduced here. Although GOAL modules provide a tool to qualitatively focus attention on a goal, they do not allow for the consideration of quantitative utilities that indicate preference over such goals. Adding utilities would not provide an agent with a focus on its goals per se, but adding utility-based preferences to GOAL modules may be useful in order to allow preference-based activation of modules as well as to allow an agent to compute optimal ways to execute the plan or policy coded in a module (cf. [1]). Another approach to deal with goal order might be to incorporate mechanisms that are able to deal with goal interference such as [16].

There are several other ideas for future research related to the proposal to view modules as policy-based intentions. In particular, one of the characteristics of such intentions is their *defeasibility* (cf. also [9]). In certain circumstances, the formation of such intentions (in the terminology introduced here, an active module) derived from generic policies (coded as modules here) are *blocked*. Another interesting aspect of policy-based intentions is time-related. The modules proposed and incorporated into GOAL do not allow to distinguish between the *time of adoption* of such an intention and the *time of execution* nor for a notion of *deadline*. It remains for future work to investigate how such extensions can be integrated into GOAL.

References

1. Boutilier, C., Reiter, R., Soutchanski, M., Thrun, S.: Decision-Theoretic, High-level Agent Programming in the Situation Calculus. In: Proceedings of the Seventeenth National Conference on Artificial Intelligence (AAAI-2000), pp. 355–362 (2000)
2. Bratman, M.E.: Intentions, Plans, and Practical Reasoning. Harvard University Press, Cambridge (1987)

3. Lamersdorf, W., Braubach, L., Pokahr, A.: Extending the Capability Concept for Flexible BDI Agent Modularization. In: Bordini, R.H., Dastani, M., Dix, J., Seghrouchni, A.E.F. (eds.) PROMAS 2005. LNCS (LNAI), vol. 3862, pp. 139–155. Springer, Heidelberg (2006)
4. Busetta, P., Howden, N., Ronnquist, R., Hodgson, A.: Structuring BDI Agents in Functional Clusters. In: Jennings, N., Lesperance, Y. (eds.) Intelligent Agents VI: Theories, Architectures and Languages, pp. 277–289 (2000)
5. Dastani, M., de Boer, F., Dignum, F., Meyer, J.-J.C.: Programming Agent Deliberation: An Approach Illustrated Using the 3APL Language. In: Proceedings of The Second Conference on Autonomous Agents and Multi-agent Systems (AAMAS 2003), pp. 97–104 (2003)
6. Dastani, M.M., van Riemsdijk, M.B., Dignum, F.P.M., Ch, J.-J.: A Programming Language for Cognitive Agents: Goal-Directed 3APL. In: Dastani, M., Dix, J., El Fallah-Seghrouchni, A. (eds.) PROMAS 2003. LNCS (LNAI), vol. 3067, pp. 111–130. Springer, Heidelberg (2004)
7. de Boer, F.S., Hindriks, K.V., van der Hoek, W., Meyer, J.-J.C.: A Verification Framework for Agent Programming with Declarative Goals. Journal of Applied Logic (2006) (In Press)
8. Georgeff, M.P., Lansky, A.L.: Reactive Reasoning and Planning. In: Proceedings of the Sixth National Conference on Artificial Intelligence, pp. 677–682. MIT Press, Cambridge (1987)
9. Governatori, G., Padmanabhan, V.: A defeasible logic of policy-based intention. In: Gedeon, T.D., Fung, L.C.C. (eds.) AI 2003. LNCS (LNAI), vol. 2903, pp. 414–426. Springer, Heidelberg (2003)
10. Hindriks, K.V., de Boer, F.S., van der Hoek, W., Meyer, J.-J.C.: Agent Programming with Declarative Goals. In: Castelfranchi, C., Lespérance, Y. (eds.) ATAL 2000. LNCS (LNAI), vol. 1986, pp. 228–243. Springer, Heidelberg (2001)
11. Padgham, L., Lambrix, P.: Formalisations of Capabilities for BDI-Agents. Autonomous Agents and Multi-Agent Systems 10, 249–271 (2005)
12. Parsons, S., Jennings, N.R., Sabater, J., Sierra, C.: Agent Specification Using Multi-Context Systems. In: Foundation and Applications of Multi-Agent Systems, pp. 205–226. Springer, Heidelberg (2002)
13. Plotkin, G.D.: A Structural Approach to Operational Semantics. Technical Report DAIMI FN-19, University of Aarhus (1981)
14. Pokahr, A., Braubach, L., Lamersdorf, W.: A Goal Deliberation Strategy for BDI Agent Systems. In: Eymann, T., Klügl, F., Lamersdorf, W., Klusch, M., Huhns, M.N. (eds.) MATES 2005. LNCS (LNAI), vol. 3550, pp. 82–93. Springer, Heidelberg (2005)
15. Rao, A.S.: AgentSpeak(L): BDI Agents Speak Out in a Logical Computable Language. In: van der Velde, W., Perram, J.W. (eds.) Agents Breaking Away, pp. 42–55. Springer, Heidelberg (1996)
16. Thangarajah, J., Padgham, L., Winikoff, M.: Detecting and avoiding interference between goals in intelligent agents. In: Proceedings of the 18th International Joint Conference on Artificial Intelligence (IJCAI 2003) (2003)
17. van Riemsdijk, M.B., Dastani, M., Meyer, J.-J.C., de Boer, F.S.: Goal-Oriented Modularity in Agent Programming. In: Birna van Riemsdijk, M. (ed.) Proceedings of the Fifth International Joint Conference on Autonomous Agents and Multiagent Systems (AAMAS 2006), pp. 1271–1278 (2006)
18. Wray, R.E., Laird, J.E.: An architectural approach to ensuring consistency in hierarchical execution. Journal of Artificial Intelligence Research 19, 355–398 (2003)

Specifying and Verifying a MAS:
The *Robots on Mars* Case Study

Bruno Mermet, Gaële Simon, Bruno Zanuttini, and Arnaud Saval

GREYC - UMR 6072

Abstract. This paper deals with the design of multi-agent systems. We demonstrate the goal-oriented agent model called Goal Decomposition Tree on an already studied multi-agent example, that of robots which must clean pieces of garbage on Mars. As we show, the model allows to prove that the agents' behaviour indeed achieves their goal. We then compare our approach to other ones.

1 Introduction

Goal Decomposition Trees (GDT) have been introduced by Simon *et al.* [19] as a model for specifying the behaviour of agents in a multi-agent system (MAS) together with a complete approach for the design of MAS. This approach consists in three steps:

1. an **agentification** step which helps the designer to determine the set of agents which must be used to implement a given system;
2. a **behaviour specification** step using an agent design model (GDT) which helps to design an agent behaviour that can be verified by a specific proof system;
3. an **implementation** step using an implementation model based on automata which can be automatically generated from the agent design model.

Thus the aim of this global approach is to provide a complete MAS design process starting from the problem specification and ending with an implementation. Central to this approach is the fact that it allows to produce verified implementations of agents' behaviours.

The goal of this paper is to present two important add-ons to the GDT model and to demonstrate the second point above and the associated proof step on an already studied example: two robots which must clean pieces of garbage on Mars. The main add-on consists in the introduction of *external goals* to the model: this is an important step to the verification of a whole multi-agent system. The second one allows to increase the power of the proof system thanks to the introduction of the *Guaranted Properties in case of Failure*. The scenario studied has been proposed by Bordini *et al.* [2] for demonstrating model checking of Rao's AgentSpeak language [16]. They have proposed agents' behaviours for this scenario and verified them using model checking. We have chosen this scenario because the goal of [2] (i.e. behaviour specification and proof) is very close to ours.

Thus this example allows us to compare the GDT model to the AgentSpeak one. We specify the agents' behaviour using the GDT model, mimicking as much as possible the behaviour specified by Bordini *et al.* in order to facilitate the comparison. It turns out

M. Dastani et al.(Eds.): ProMAS 2007, LNAI 4908, pp. 172–189, 2008.
© Springer-Verlag Berlin Heidelberg 2008

that the GDT model is as rich and concise as AgentSpeak, and allows more elements to be formally taken into account, especially (atomic) actions. Moreover, the GDT model also allows to prove the correctness of the agents' behaviours, whatever the number of pieces of garbage or the size of the grid modelling the surface of Mars. This is to be opposed to the model checking method presented by Bordini *et al.*, which only allows to verify the MAS on a finite number of grids in finite time (5×5 grids with 2 pieces of garbage in the paper).

The paper is organized as follows. In Sections 2 and 3 the GDT model, its new extensions and its proof system are specified. Then we present the Mars scenario, specify the behaviours of the agents using GDTs and verify their correctness (Section 4); in the light of this example, we compare our model to the AgentSpeak language in details. Then we compare our work to other approaches (Section 5), and finally we conclude.

2   Goal Decomposition Trees

In our approach, the behaviour of agents are represented by *Goal Decomposition Trees* (GDT). These are trees whose nodes are goals, defined by a satisfaction condition and associated either to atomic actions or to further decompositions into subgoals. The GDT of an agent specifies its whole behaviour, and the satisfaction condition of its root node is thus its main goal. GDT are presented in details in [19], but we give here the notions relevant to the paper.

Nodes. As already said, nodes (either leaves or internal nodes) correspond to the goals of the agent. To each node G a *satisfaction condition* (SC) is associated. Intuitively, a goal is satisfied if and only if its SC is made true. SCs are expressed over a restricted form of temporal logic, in which the states of variables used before and after trying to achieve the goal can be distinguished. For instance, if the SC of goal G is $x' > x \wedge x' \neq 0$, G is achieved if x has been incremented and is now nonnull.

Actions. The behaviour associated to a leaf goal (except external goals, detailed later) is described either by a list of assignments or by a *named action* (NA), i.e., an atomic action which consists in a name, a list of parameters, a precondition and a postcondition. Intuitively, the postcondition must entail the SC of the leaf goal.

Operators. Each internal node of a GDT is associated to a decomposition into subgoals, linked up with an operator. Eight such operators are defined in [18]. For instance, $SeqAnd$ is a classical lazy and ordered logical And operator, and $Iter$ allows to repeat a subgoal until the parent goal is achieved. Importantly, operators are associated to *automata composition patterns*, which are used incrementally to build the complete automaton which implements the behaviour specified by the GDT. For more details see [18].

In order to check the validity of our proof schemas, a formal semantics of our operators has been given in temporal logic. This is not the purpose of this article to describe this semantics, but here is an example for a not lazy node N decomposed in N_1 *seqand* N_2:

$$
\Box
\begin{pmatrix}
(\neg in_{N_1} \vee \neg in_{N_2}) \\
(in_{N_1} \vee in_{N_2} \to in_N) \\
(end_{N_1} \wedge sat_{N_1} \to \circ init_{N_2}) \\
(end_{N_1} \wedge \neg sat_{N_1} \to \circ end_N) \\
(end_{N_2} \wedge sat_{N_2} \to end_N \wedge sat_N) \\
(end_{N_2} \wedge \neg sat_{N_2} \to \circ end_N) \\
(init_N \to init_{N_1})
\end{pmatrix}
$$

where $init_A$, end_A and in_A are temporal variables that are respectively true when the resolution of goal A begins, ends and and during the whole execution of node A.

Typology of goals. In order to add flexibility to the specification and to take nondeterminism into account, goals have *types* according to two criteria. First of all, a goal (internal or leaf) can be *necessarily satisfiable* (NS) or not (NNS). In the former case, the decomposition into subgoals or the action associated to the goal always makes its SC true. In the latter case, the decomposition or action may fail to satisfy the goal. For instance, for an internal goal decomposed thanks to an AND operator, the father goal may fail if one of its subgoal fails. But if both subgoals succed, also does the father goal.

Orthogonally, goals can be *lazy* (L) or not (NL). When the agent has to achieve an L goal, it first checks whether its SC is true, and only in the negative executes the decomposition or action. On the contrary, the agent must always execute the decomposition or action of an NL goal. E.g., SCs which directly link the values of the variables before and after the goal execution, such as $x' > x$, can be associated to NL goals only.

Along with these two criteria, the types of each internal node in a GDT can be automatically determined by the types of its children together with the semantics of the decomposition operator. Consequently, if specified by the designer, types can be used to check the consistency of the specification.

External goals. External goals have been added to the model presented in [19]. Such a goal E in the GDT of an agent A is one which A cannot achieve (for instance because it depends on variables that A does not control). Thus an SC is as usual associated to E, but no action or decomposition, because another agent (verifying an *external property* P) is expected to make it true. Consequently, in this article, an external goal is an NS leaf goal together with a link to a goal G in another GDT. The semantics is that when it must achieve E, agent A waits until an agent with this latter GDT achieves its goal G, which will make the SC of E true.

External goals are a way to express dependencies between agents, that is to say collaborative agents. In particular, it can be seen as a specialization of "nonlocal tasks" of TAEMS (there is no contracting with our external goals). Moreover, an external goal as the left operand of a *SeqAnd* can be seen as a specification of an "enables" interrelationship in TAEMS. A more detaild comparison with TAEMS can be found in [19].

GDTs. A GDT is a tree built up from nodes as specified above. In addition, the following are associated to a GDT.

A set of variables specifies all environment variables together with a set of internal variables of the agent. All formulas are built upon this set. A *triggering context* (TC) specifies when the agent must execute its GDT (either the first or each time it becomes true, depending on the agent). A *precondition* ($PrecGDT$) is also given, which must be satisfied before the execution begins. In particular, a given *initialisation clause* achieves it when the agent is created, and for GDT executed several times, the precondition must be true again after each execution (in other words, before any GDT execution, $PrecGDT$ is true). Finally, an *invariant* describing the constraints of the problem is given, which must be preserved through the whole execution.

3   The Proof Process

Our aim is to prove the correctness of the GDT built for an agent (i.e., to prove that the behaviour specified by the tree always achieves the main goal of the agent). For each operator described in section 2, several *proof schemas* are defined according to types of goals. These schemas are intended to produce *Proof Obligations* that describe what must be proven in order to validate a goal decomposition. These schemas have been proven to be correct with respect to a semantics of GDTs in LTL not described here and under the assumption that actions are atomic and that parallelism can be represented by an interleaving model.

Since a future goal is to use a theorem prover to perform proofs, proof schemas are built in a rigorous manner to be automatized. Moreover, the compositional aspect of proofs makes proof simple, maximizing the success rate of an automatic theorem prover.

Applying these schemas to a GDT results in an agent's behaviour compositional proof. Each proof is performed using a context that can be computed by a *context propagation schema* associated to each operator that is not described here but that can be found in [13].

3.1   Notations

Variables. The set of environment variables is denoted by V_e, and the set of internal variables of a given agent by V_i. For each agent, we assume $V_i \cap V_e = \emptyset$, and whewe define $V = V_i \cup V_e$. Internal variables cannot be modified by another agent, while environment variables are variables that the agent can see and modify, but so can other agents or the environment itself.

Goals. The SC of a goal G is written SC_G. For the proof process, a *context* is also associated to G, which intuitively expresses what is known to be true when G is about to be attempted. In particular, the context of the main goal is $TC \wedge PrecGDT$ (defined in section 2), and the context of the other nodes is inferred from the GDT by *context propagation schemas* no detailed here. The context of G is written C_G. Finally, still for the proof process, something has to be known about the outcome of the resolution attempt of an NNS goal. This is expressed by a *Guaranted Property in case of Failure* (GPF). The semantics is that if the solving process of a goal fails (to satisfy its SC), then its GPF is still true. The GPF of a goal G is written GPF_G. Indeed, without GPFs, when a goal fails, no one property can be inferred from proof schema on the state after the goal execution.

GDTs. The triggering context of a GDT is written TC, its precondition is written $PrecGDT$, its initialisation clause (an assignement) is written `init` and its main goal is denoted MG. Its invariant is written $I = I_S \wedge I_A$, where I_S is the invariant of the system (over V_e) and I_A is that of the agent over V.

Temporal notation. In the SC of a goal G, the value of a variable x before and after executing the actions or decomposition associated to G are distinguished by primes: e.g., $x' < y$ means that the value of x after the agent has tried to achieve G is less than that of y was before this attempt.

However, if the SC does not relate both moments, only unprimed variables are used. This is for sake of consistency when considering the evaluation of the SC of a lazy goals, before any execution. For instance, if the goal is to set x to at least 2, then its SC is written $x \geq 2$. In the proof schemas we thus use a function, denoted T, such that for any goal G, primed variables in $T(SC_G)$ describe relations between the variables when G is achieved. Thus, for instance, $T((x' < y)) = (x' < y)$, while $T((x \geq 2)) = (x' \geq 2)$.

Substitution. We note $[x := y]P$ the syntactic substitution of any free occurence of x by y in P.

Transition between two goals solving process. When considering two goals G_1 and G_2 resolved sequentially (e.g., when proving a $SeqAnd$ decomposition), From the point of view of the agent, three states can be distinguished: S, the state right before the solving process of G_1, S^{tmp}, the state between the G_1 and G_2 solving processes, and S', the state right after the solving process of G_2. to unify variables v' after the G_1 solving process with the variables v before the G_2 solving process corresponding both to the value of variable v in state S^{tmp}, we replace them by variables v^{tmp} by the two following substitutions: $[v' := v^{tmp}]SC_{G_1}$ and $[v := v^{tmp}]SC_{G_2}$.

Projection. if F is a temporal logic formula and S_v a set of variables, we write F_{S_v} the projection of F to the variables of S_v. For instance, if $F = x < y \wedge x > 3$, $F_x = x > 3$. If $S_v = V_i$, we simply F_{V_i} by F_i.

3.2 Proof Schemas

In this section, a few proof schemas are detailed. The normal proof process requires to prove that the invariant is preserved by each goal of the GDT. However, when a GDT is fully specified, performing this proof for leaf goals is enough.

In addition, since most of the goals of R1 in the following case study are NS, we give proof schemas only for this kind of goals, and so GPFs are not involved. However, as one of the *Iter* operator in the example has an NNS subgoal, the *Iter* proof schema is given for this kind of subgoal.

Initialisation one must prove:

$$[\texttt{init}](PrecGDT \wedge I_A) \tag{1}$$

Moreover, for agents that can execute their GDT several times, the following property must also be proven:

$$I \wedge T(SC_{MG}) \wedge T(I) \Rightarrow T(PrecGDT) \tag{2}$$

SeqAnd: Proving $A \Leftarrow B\, SeqAnd\, C$ (when A is NL) requires to prove:

$$I \wedge C_A \Rightarrow \left(\left\{ \begin{matrix} [v' := v^{tmp}]\ T(SC_{B_i}) \\ [v := v^{tmp}]\ T(SC_C) \end{matrix} \right\} \Rightarrow T(SC_A) \wedge T(I) \right) \tag{3}$$

From the point of view of the agent, the state of its internal variables (and only them) after its attempt to achieve B is unchanged when it begins to try to achieve C; hence the substitutions of v' by v^{tmp} and of v by v^{tmp} and the projection SC_{B_i} onto the internal variables. Finaly, if A is lazy, the schema is the same, with $\neg\, SC_A$ as an additional hypothesis.

For instance, let consider the following example, where x is an internal variable of the agent:

$$I = x \in \mathbb{N} \qquad\qquad SC_A = x' = 2x + 2$$
$$C_A = true \qquad\qquad SC_B = x' = x + 1$$
$$SC_C = x' = 2x$$

The proof schema generate the following proof obligation:

$$x \in \mathbb{N} \wedge true \Rightarrow ((x^{tmp} = x + 1 \wedge x' = 2x^{tmp}) \Rightarrow (x' = 2x + 2 \wedge x' \in \mathbb{N}))$$

SyncSeqAnd$_{V_s}$: This operator is a synchronized version of the *SeqAnd* operator with a lock on a subset V_S of V_e. Its proof schema is similar to the *SeqAnd* one, but the projection onto internal variables V_i is replaced by a projection onto $V_i \cup V_s$.

Iter. To prove the decomposition $A \Leftarrow Iter(B, \mathcal{V})$, a variant $\mathcal{V}$ is needed. It corresponds to the formalisation of the *progress* notion in the resolution of the parent goal. Formally, a *variant* is a decreasing sequence defined on a well-founded structure. A *well-founded* structure is an ordered set such that each strictly decreasing sequence defined   on   this   set   has   a   lower   bound.   In   the following, we will denote the variant lower bound by $\mathcal{V}_0$. Thus proving that $A \Leftarrow IterB$ is correct requires proving that:

- if $\mathcal{V}$ reaches its lower bound, then A is achieved:
$$I \wedge (C_A \vee C_B) \wedge T(SC_B) \Rightarrow (T(\mathcal{V}) = \mathcal{V}_0 \Rightarrow T(SC_A)) \qquad (4)$$

- C_B is stable during the loop until A is achieved:
$$I \wedge (C_A \vee C_B) \wedge T(SC_B \vee GPF_B) \wedge \neg T(SC_A) \Rightarrow T(C_B) \qquad (5)$$

- the variant decreases: this may be proven whatever the success of B by proving:
$$I \wedge (C_A \vee C_B) \wedge \neg T(SC_A) \Rightarrow (T(SC_B \vee GPF_B) \Rightarrow T(\mathcal{V}) < \mathcal{V}) \qquad (6)$$

thanks to this last proof schema, the termination of A is guaranted, if B succeeds one or more time, or even if B never succeeds.

External Goals. The proof schema associated to external goals is quite different from the other ones. Let EG_A be an external goal of an agent A associated to an external property P and referencing a goal G_B of another agent B.

The proof consists in showing that:
- G_B is NS;
- achievement of G_B entails achievement of EG_A;
- when A waits for the achievement of EG_A, B will eventually achieve G_B.

The first item is a syntactic and trivial verification. The second one amounts to proving:

$$\left. \begin{array}{c} I_S \wedge I_A \wedge I_B \wedge C_{EG_A} \\ C_{G_B} \wedge P \end{array} \right\} \Rightarrow ([v := v_0]T(SC_{G_B}) \Rightarrow [v := v_1]T(SC_{EG_A})) \qquad (7)$$

where substitutions $[v := v_0]$ and $[v := v_1]$, replacing non-primed variables with free variables, allow to memorize the state of the system before the execution of goals EG_A and G_B.

Finally, the third verification is divided into two steps: identifying the set of goals S_B whose contexts are consistent with C_{EG_A} (and checking G_B is in this set) and then verifying for each trace corresponding to a behaviour of B that each time a state of B corresponds to the achievement of a goal in S_B then another state in the future corresponds to the achievement of G_B. The formalisation of this part of the proof schema is not detailed in this paper because it would require to expose the semantics of our operators in temporal logic, which is quite too long to be exposed here.

4   Application

In [2], a scenario with two agents that must collaborate is described. An implementation using Agentspeak and a verification based on model-checking are proposed. This case study has not been chosen to prove the applicability of our model to a real case, but to allow a comparison with another agent specification language and verification system. Using Bordini *et al.*'s description as a specification, we designed GDT models for the two agents of this scenario. In the following, some highlights of these GDTs and the associated proofs are presented. Finally, a comparison with the work exposed in [2] is detailed.

4.1 The Scenario

Agentspeak. The Agentspeak(L) language has been designed by Rao [16]. The goal of Agentspeak is to express the behaviour of BDI agents. An Agentspeak agent has a base of goals, a base of beliefs and a set of plans. A plan, in Agentspeak, is represented by a rule made of three parts: a triggering event (a goal or belief insertion or deletion), a context, and a list of actions. Agentspeak(L) allows to describe agents in a quite implementable way, but is not suitable to perform proofs by theorem proving for many reasons. For instance, goals are not described formally and most actions have to be implemented directly in the target language (Java for instance).

The Robots on Mars (RoM) scenario. The RoM scenario involves two robots that must remove garbage on Mars. Mars is represented by a rectangular grid on which pieces of garbage are randomly distributed. Each robot has different skills.

The first one, R1, moves on the grid to search for pieces of garbage. It can grab them only one by one. When it finds one, it picks it up (in at most three attempts), brings it to the position of R2, then drops it and finally goes back to its previous location and resumes its search. The second robot, R2, cannot move: it can only burn a piece of garbage situated in its cell. Of course, R1 does not grab garbage that are on R2's cell.

R1's behaviour can be summarized as follows (corresponding plans in the Agentspeak implementation are given):

1. it checks its position for a piece of garbage, if there is nothing, it goes to the next slot (plan p1);
2. otherwise (plan p2 to p7):

   (a) it tries to grab this garbage at most three times,
   (b) it brings the garbage to R2 and drops it,
   (c) it goes back and repeats (1).

For instance, plan p1 is the following:
```
+pos(R1,X1,Y1):checking(slots) & not(garbage(r1)) ← next(slot).
```

The behaviour of R2 is the following:

1. it waits for a piece of garbage to be in its cell,
2. it takes the new piece of garbage,
3. it burns it and repeats (1).

4.2 GDTs for the RoM Scenario

Add-ons to the initial specification. In [2], a few parts of the robots behaviour were unspecified or under-specified. So we had to make the following choices:

Garbage distribution. In Bordini *et al.*'s work, it is not specified whether each cell of the grid can contain at most one or more pieces of garbage. We decided that there is at most one piece of garbage in each cell.

Grabbing success. The informal specification states that a piece of garbage is grabbed by R1 in at most 3 attempts, but this is not explicit in the Agentspeak model. We made it explicit in our GDT.

Grid exploration. In [2], R1 explores the grid thanks to the `next(slot)` action, which is not specified. We chose to provide R1 only with actions allowing it to move one cell horizontally or vertically. This led us to specify its behaviour when moving, included for avoiding R2's cell (we chose to make it go through the grid row by row, from top to bottom, from left to right on odd lines and from right to left on even lines). Moreover, in [2], `next(slot)` seems to always succeed, but the action performed when R1 reaches the end of the grid is not specified. In the GDT presented here, R1 stops. We designed another GDT where R1 goes back to the first cell, but it is not presented here.

Synchronisation between R1 and R2. Since we specified that a cell cannot contain more than one piece of garbage, R1 cannot drop a new piece of garbage on R2's cell if R2 has not picked up the previous one yet. This synchronisation is not specified in [2]. Moreover, R2 is satisfied (and so cannot act before R1 has dropped a piece of garbage in its cell). So, there are two synchronisations:

- R1 waits for R2 to pick up the piece of garbage.
- R2 waits for R1 to drop a piece of garbage,

The first one is specified by an external goal in the GDT of R1 whereas the second one is specified thanks to the triggering context of the GDT of R2.

The environment. The environment is described by a variable G. $G(x,y)$ is true if there is a piece of garbage in the cell at position (x,y) and false otherwise. R2's position, which is constant, is also described by two environment variables x_{R2} and y_{R2}, and so are the minimum and maximum coordinates of the grid (variables $x_{min}, x_{max}, y_{min}, y_{max}$).

Robot R1. The goal of this robot is to clean the grid. To ensure it, it uses a variable named $clean$, which is a set of cells. This set is initially empty, and a cell can be added to it only by the action of picking a garbage or when it is observed to be clean. R1's main goal is $MG_{R1} = (clean = grid)$, where $grid$ is the set of all cells on the grid except R2's.

R1 also has variables x and y describing its position on the grid. Its other variables are not presented here.

To design the failure possibility of the arm grabing the garbage, we used an *Iter* operator where the subgoal describing the attempts is a NNS leaf one, so it can fail. In the proof, we show that the parent goal is achieved after, at most, three iterations.

The whole GDT of Robot R1 is presented figure 1. The satisfaction conditions of the nodes are not described here but we described informally the structure of the tree in the following.

The *iter* operator below node 1 correspond to the iteration on the set of the cells of the grid. So, node 2 correpond to the couple of actions "clear the current cell" (node 3) and go to the next cell different from R2's one (node 25).

In the left sub-tree, node 4 memorizes the fact that current cell is about to be cleaned. The sub-tree whis node 6 as root node correspond to the attempts of R1 to pick the piece of garbage on the current cell. The right subtree of node 5 is itself decomposed into two subtree: the first one, with node 11 as root node, makes R1 go to R2's and drop its garbage when R2's is empty (node 12 register the current cell: this is necessary so that R1 knows where to go back when it has brought a piece of garbage to R2). The second one makes R2 go back to the registered position. Each time a move must be performed, a *Case* operator allow an undeterministic choice between an horizontal and a vertical move (nodes 15, 22 and 28).

Robot R2. The GDT of R2 is simpler than R1's one. Its GDT correponds exactly to the behaviour described in [2]. It just picks up the garbage and burns it. So, its main goal is to be non busy and to have its cell clear: the satisfaction condition of its main goal is $SC_{MG_{R2}} = (\neg busy_{R2} \wedge \neg G(x_{R2}, y_{R2}))$. The synchronisation needed to ensure that R2 waits for a piece of garbage to burn is not directly expressed in the structure of the GDT but thanks to its triggering context $TC(R2) = G(x_{R2}, y_{R2})$. In fact, the GDT will be executed if and only if there is a piece of garbage at the position of R2. Let us notice that since R2 must not be busy before each of its executions, the property $\neg busy_{R2}$ is in the $PrecGDT_{R2}$ property.

4.3   Examples of Proofs

We now present three detailed local proofs of nodes in R1's GDT with, for each one, an informal description and the subtree associated to the parent goal. The full proof of the two GDTs can be found at [14].

SyncSeqAnd example. We first consider the part of the GDT where R1 drops a piece of garbage onto R2's cell (Figure 2 (a), where the rectangle denotes an external goal). R1 first waits for R2's cell to be empty (external goal B, "Empty cell", detailed below), then drops the piece of garbage it holds (leaf goal C, "Drop"). Variable $G(x, y)$ is synchronized in order to ensure that once R1 has observed the cell is empty, it stays so until R1 drops it garbage.

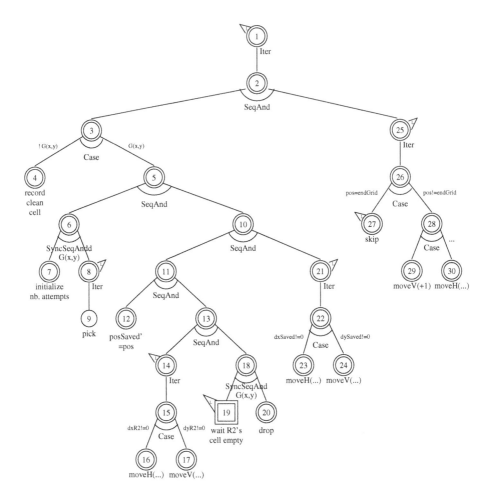

Fig. 1. GDT of robot R1

We have:

$$\begin{cases} C_A = (x,y) = (x_{R_2}, y_{R_2}) \wedge busy \\ SC_A = \neg busy' \wedge G'(x',y') \wedge (x',y') = (x,y) \\ SC_B = \neg G(x,y) \wedge busy \\ SC_C = \neg busy' \wedge G'(x',y') \end{cases}$$

Moreover, the parent Goal A is NL and NS. So, to prove the decomposition of A, according to the schema in Section 3 we have to prove:

$$I \wedge C_A \Rightarrow [v' := v^{tmp}]T(SC_{B_{i,G(x,y)}}) \wedge [v := v^{tmp}]T(SC_C) \Rightarrow T(SC_A)$$

That can be rewritten:

$$H \Rightarrow (\neg busy' \wedge G'(x',y') \wedge (x',y') = (x,y))$$

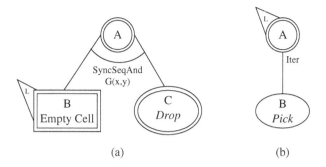

Fig. 2. Subtrees of R1's GDT

Conjuncts $\neg busy'$ and $G'(x', y')$ are entailed directly by $[v = v^{tmp}]T(SC_C)$. Now since variables x, y are internal and do not occur in SC_B and SC_C, we have $(x', y') = (x, y)$ and finally, $T(SC_A)$. Let Observe that synchronisation of $G(x, y)$ is not used in this proof; it is used only in the context propagation, for ensuring that the context of C entails $\neg G(x, y)$ as established by SC_B.

Iter example. We now consider the part of the GDT where R1 tries to pick up the piece of garbage on the current cell until success (Figure 2 (b)). R1 iterates over subgoal B, "Pick", which consists in applying the named action $\texttt{pick}$ (recall that this action may fail, but succeeds after at most three attempts).

Since this subtree ends up with picking a piece of garbage, variable $clean$ (set of positions R1 has cleaned or observed to be clean) is involved. In order to simplify the presentation, we however chose to remove it from the contexts and satisfaction conditions here, as well as condition $(x, y) \neq (x_{R_2}, y_{R_2})$, which is stable in this subtree.

The variant used in the proof involves variable $nbAttempts$; this variable counts the number of times R1 has already tried to pick up the piece of garbage. Moreover, the Guaranteed Property upon Failure (GPF) of an NNS goal is a formula which is true when the goal fails.

We have:

$$
\begin{cases}
C_A = G(x, y) \wedge \neg busy \wedge nbAttempts = 0 \\
C_B = G(x, y) \wedge \neg busy \wedge nbAttempts < 3 \\
SC_B = \neg G'(x', y') \wedge busy' \\
GPF_B = \begin{cases} G'(x', y') \wedge busy' = busy \\ \wedge\, nbAttempts' = nbAttempts + 1 \\ \wedge\, nbAttempts < 3 \end{cases}
\end{cases}
$$

Moreover, the parent node is lazy and NS, and its satisfaction condition is $SC_A = \neg G'(x', y') \wedge busy' = SC_B$.

Let $\mathcal{V} = (3 - nbAttempts)$ be the variant and let its lower bound be $\mathcal{V}_0 = 0$. $\mathcal{V}$ is well-defined because the invariant I of R1 entails $nbAttempts \leq 3$. According to the schema in Section 3, we have to prove:

$$\left.\begin{array}{r} I \wedge (C_A \vee C_B) \\ \neg SC_A \end{array}\right\} \Rightarrow \left\{\begin{array}{ll} T(SC_B) \Rightarrow T(\mathcal{V}) = \mathcal{V}_0 \Rightarrow T(SC_A) & (1) \\ \neg T(SC_A) \Rightarrow (T(SC_B) \vee T(GPF_B)) \Rightarrow T(\mathcal{V}) < \mathcal{V} & (2) \\ \neg T(SC_A) \Rightarrow (T(SC_B) \vee T(GPF_B)) \Rightarrow T(C_B) & (3) \end{array}\right.$$

Entailment (1) is obvious since $T(SC_B) = T(SC_A)$.

Entailment (2) holds when $T(SC_B)$ is true because in that case, $\neg T(SC_A)$ is false (as $SC_A = SC_B$). It also holds with $T(GPF_B)$ because $T(GPF_B)$ entails that $nbAttempts'$ $nbAttempts + 1$, which in turn entails $T(\mathcal{V}) < \mathcal{V}$ (as $\mathcal{V} = 3 - nbAttempts$ and $T(\mathcal{V}) = 3 - nbAttempts'$).

Entailment (3) holds when $T(SC_B)$ for the same reason as entailment (2). Finally, it also holds with $T(GPF_B)$ because $T(GPF_B)$ together with either C_A or C_B clearly entails $T(C_B)$.

External goal example. We finally consider the external node B on Figure 2 (a) in the GDT where R1 waits for R2's cell to be empty, in order to be allowed to drop the piece of garbage it holds onto it. Since R1 cannot empty this cell itself, it must wait for R2 to do it.

The goal of R2 achieving R1's desire is its main goal MG_{R2}. This goal is decomposed into two subgoals using a $SyncSeqAnd$ operator, namely goal "Pick" and goal "Burn". R2 has an internal variable $busy_{R_2}$ which is true if R_2 currently holds a piece of garbage and false otherwise.

As a consequence, we have:

$$\left\{\begin{array}{l} C_B = (x, y) = (x_{R_2}, y_{R_2}) \wedge busy \\ SC_{MG_{R2}} = \neg busy_{R_2} \wedge \neg G(x_{R_2}, y_{R_2}) \\ SC_B = \neg G(x, y) \wedge busy \end{array}\right.$$

According to the proof schema in Section 3, we first have to check that R2's goal MG_{R2} is NS, which is the case.

Now we have to check that the achievement of MG_{R2} entails the achievement of R1's goal B by applying proof schema 7, that can be here approximatively simplified in $C_B \wedge T(SC_{MG_{R2}}) \Rightarrow T(SC_B)$. Again, this is true since:

- $busy'$ in $T(SC_B)$ is entailed by $busy$ in C_B together with the fact that $busy$ being an internal variable of R1, $busy' = busy$,
- $\neg G'(x', y')$ in $T(SC_B)$ is entailed by $\neg G'(x_{R_2}, y_{R_2})$ in $T(SC_{MG_{R2}})$ together with $(x, y) = (x_{R_2}, y_{R_2})$ in C_B and the fact that x, y are internal variables of R1 and x_{R_2}, y_{R_2} are constants.

Finally, we have to check that every state of R2 which is compatible with C_B finally ends up with the achievement of MG_{R2}. When R1 waits for B to be satisfied, as B is lazy, we have:

$$C_B \wedge \neg SC_B$$

that is to say:

$$(x, y) = (x_{R2}, y_{R2}) \wedge busy \wedge \neg(\neg G(x, y) \wedge busy)$$

that can be rewritten:

$$(x, y) = (x_{R2}, y_{R2}) \wedge busy \wedge (G(x, y) \vee \neg busy)$$

that can be simplified:

$$(x, y) = (x_{R2}, y_{R2}) \wedge busy \wedge G(x_{R2}, y_{R2}) \tag{8}$$

As a consequence, the context of the *Burn* node of R2 entails $\neg G(x_{R2}, y_{R2})$, which is not compatible with equation 8. So the set of compatibles goals of R2 with B is $\{Pick, MG_{R2}\}$. If R2 is executing goal MG_{R2}, this goal is NS, and so will be achieved, implying that SC_B will be true. If R2 is executing goal $Pick$, as this goal is NS and is followed (thanks to a $SeqAnd$ operator) by another NS goal (Burn), the parent goal (which is MG_{R2}) will also be satisfied and so will be B.

Finally, we have to considered what happens if R2's GDT execution is ended. Recall that the triggering context of R2 defined in section 4.2 is $TC(R2) = G(x_{R2}, y_{R2})$. this is obviously entailed by equation 8 above. And so, R2, will reach the execution of its main goal, which satisfies goal B.

4.4   Comparison with Bordini et al.'s Work

Goal decomposition. The body of an Agentspeak plan is *"a sequence of basic actions or (sub)goals that the agent has to achieve (or test) when the plan is triggered"*. There are two kinds of such subgoals: the first kind must be achieved by other plans whereas the second one consists in beliefs additions or deletions. In a GDT, the first kind is specified by a goal decomposition and the second one corresponds to variable modifications inside leaf goals. So, there is a similarity between our goal decompositions and Agentspeak plans. However, as shown in the next section, the verification of behaviours is completely different.

Verification and proof. Verification in AgentSpeak is based on model-checking which takes place after the implementation step with JPF2. In [2], it has been made on an instance of this scenario where the size of the grid is 5x5 and with only 2 pieces of garbage. On the contrary, our proof is performed only once for all instances of this scenario without any constraint on the number of pieces of garbage, on the size of the grid and on the position of R2. Of course, when working with first-order logic, theorem proving is not decidable, leading some true properties unproved whereas model-checking can be automatically performed with a computable complexity. However, to obtain the same level of proof as ours on the RoM problem, it would be necessary to test an infinite number of situations, because the grid can be of any size.

Another interesting aspect of our proof process is that it helped us to find some problems in our first designs of GDTs before their implementation. Indeed, proof failures give local clues to solve inconsistencies or to highlight lacks in the specification. In that case, the compositional aspect of our proof process implies that required modifications of GDTs do not make the whole proof fail but only parts associated to goals involved in this modification. For instance, the presence of $\neg busy_{R2}$ in $PrecGDT_{R2}$ was not specified in a first version, generating a proof failure when R2 had to pick up a piece of garbage (he might have already been busy). Modifying this property also implied to modify the `init` clause of R2 to avoid a new proof failure.

Finally, model-checking performed on the RoM scenario can only be done on a complete implementation. For instance, an implementation of next(slot) must be provided in order to verify properties presented in [2]. Thanks to the compositional property of our proof process, the proof of the correctness of the behaviour of R1 can be made in two steps. In a first step, the correctness of the behaviour of R1 can be obtained under the assumption that $next\_cell$, the goal corresponding to the $next(slot)$ basic action, provides a behaviour ensuring that R1 moves to a never visited cell different from R2's. To do this, $next\_cell$ was specified by a goal with only a satisfaction condition but no subtree. In a second step, we have specified the $next\_cell$ goal by a subtree. The proof process has then allowed to prove the correctness of the subtree with respect to the $next\_cell$ satisfaction condition.

Expressiveness and conciseness. Since satisfaction conditions used in a GDT are based on sets theory, arithmetics and temporal logic, they are at least as expressive as Agentspeak and they allow to completely specify behaviours of BDI agents, the base of beliefs being represented by the set of the variables of the agent. For instance, we did not find any lack of expressiveness when we applied the model to the RoM scenario.

Another interesting comparison deals with the conciseness of Agentspeak and GDT. At first glance, Agentspeak seems quite more concise: the Agentspeak model for robot R1 is made of 9 plans whereas the GDT of R1 contains 30 nodes. However, the Agentspeak model uses unspecified actions (drop, grab, nextslot, etc.) that we fully specified in our GDT (since we wanted an automatic translation to an implementation). If these *implementation details* are removed from the GDT, its size becomes equal to 13 nodes with at most 2 subgoals each, which is comparable to the number of plans in the Agentspeak model, where each plan has up to 3 subgoals.

Finally, we wish to emphasize that our model allows to take into account the semantics of the actions, thanks to preconditions and postconditions. Every modification of a variable corresponding to an actuator which is used in the agent's goal can only be done through named actions.

5 Related Works

The GDT model of an agent behaviour and the associated proof system are differently connected to several different kinds of works. First of all, there are links with formal agent models like MetateM [9], Desire [4] or Gaïa [22]. These works are focused on agent models on which it is possible to reason which is necessary for analysis and especially for proof problems. A part of these formal models like [21,8,20] are focused on a declarative description of goals, which is exactly our point of view. A detailed comparison of these approaches with the GDT model can be found in [19]. There are also links between our proposal and agent programming languages like AgentSpeak [16], 3APL [7], ConGolog [10]. These languages allow to specify agents behaviours which can be directly executed which is one of the goals of the GDT model. However, 3APL does not allow to prove the specified behaviour and ConGolog is dedicated to situation calculus. Our approach can also be compared to goal oriented MAS development methods like Prometheus [12], MaSe [6], KAOS or Tropos. Indeed, our proposal is also intended to provide a complete MAS design process from the specification to the implementation. Moreover our approach takes place in the framework of "formal transformation systems" as defined in [6]. A detailed comparison of these works with the GDT model can be found in [19]. Last but not least, our proposal can be directly compared to SMA verification methods. Two subtypes can be distinguished: theorem proving based (like in PROSOCS) and model checking.

PROSOCS [3] agents are agents whose behaviour is described by goal decomposition rules *à la* Prolog. Rules are parameterised by time variables allowing to perform proofs about the evolution of the system state. Many characteristics of PROSOCS agents are very interesting for performing proofs, and a proof procedure has been implemented in Prolog. However, the system is limited to propositional logic formulas. The Goal [8] method also has a proof model, but is limited to propositional logic too.

Model checking is a verification method consisting in testing all the situations which may be encountered by the system. Two kinds of model checking can be distinguished: bounded model-checking [2] and unbounded-model checking [1,15,11]. However, with the two types of model-checking, proofs can only be performed on finite models or on models that can be considered as finite ones.

6   Conclusion

We have demonstrated the GDT model on an already studied example, and shown that it is as interesting as Agentspeak in terms of expressiveness and conciseness, but also allows to prove behaviours (as opposed to model checking or no verification at all).

Arguably, GDT are graphically rather complex to manipulate. This is why we have created an application, called `GdtEditor`, which allows to edit GDTs and all related information (satisfaction conditions, variables, actions...), and to export them in various formats. The application also automatically generates the implementation model (in Java), as is allowed by the model. This application is available at [17]. Current work aims at integrating it a theorem prover. Once the substitutions applied, our proof schemas generate proof obligations similar to those of the B method. As a consequence, using a prover of this method like krt [5] should be straightforward. Preliminary tests confirm this. An automatic connexion with this prover should be presented in a future article. A small percentage of the proofs of true properties may fail, but krt provides an interactive mode that allows to help the prover in these proofs.

Current work on the method aims at generalizing the model of external goals in order to allow specification and proof of more interactions, in particular when several other agents are needed to achieve an external goal. We are also working on parameterizing GDTs together with their proofs, so as to be able to factorize similar subtrees or more generally to reuse behaviours.

References

1. Alechina, N., Logan, B., Whitsey, M.: A complete and decidable logic for resource-bounded agents. In: Kudenko, D., Kazakov, D., Alonso, E. (eds.) AAMAS 2004. LNCS (LNAI), vol. 3394, Springer, Heidelberg (2005)
2. Wooldridge, M.J., Visser, W., Bordini, R.H., Fisher, M.: Verifiable Multi-agent Programs. In: Dastani, M., Dix, J., El Fallah-Seghrouchni, A. (eds.) PROMAS 2003. LNCS (LNAI), vol. 3067, pp. 72–89. Springer, Heidelberg (2004)
3. Bracciali, A., Endriss, U., Demetriou, N., Kakas, T., Lu, W., Stathis, K.: Crafting the mind of prosocs agents. In: Best of 'From Agent Theory to Agent Implementation 4' (to appear, 2004)
4. Brazier, F.M.T., van Eck, P.A.T., Treur, J.: Modelling a Society of Simple Agents: from Conceptual Specification to Experimentation. In: Simulating Social Phenomena, Lecture Notes in Economics and Mathematical Systems, vol 456., pp. 103–109 (1997)
5. Clear-Sy. B for free, http://www.b4free.com/public/resources.php
6. Deloach, S.A., Sparkman, C.H., Self, A.L.: Automated derivation of complex agent architectures from analysis specifications. In: Wooldridge, M.J., Weiß, G., Ciancarini, P. (eds.) AOSE 2001. LNCS, vol. 2222, Springer, Heidelberg (2002)
7. Dastani, M., de Boer, F., Dignum, F., Meyer, J.-J.: Programming agent deliberation: An approach illustrated using the 3apl language. In: Proceedings of the Second International Conference on Autonomous Agents and MultiAgent Systems (AAMAS 2003) (2003)
8. de Boer, F.S., Hindriks, K.V., van der Hoek, W., Meyer, J.-J.C.: Agent programming with declarative goals. In: 7th International Workshop on Intelligent Agents. Agent Theories Architectures and Language, pp. 228–243 (2000)
9. Fisher, M.: A survey of concurrent METATEM – the language and its applications. In: Gabbay, D.M., Ohlbach, H.J. (eds.) ICTL 1994. LNCS, vol. 827, pp. 480–505. Springer, Heidelberg (1994)
10. De Giacomo, G., Lesperance, Y., Levesque, H.J.: Congolog, a concurrent programming language based on the situation calculus. Artificial Intelligence 121(1-2), 109–169 (2000)
11. Kacprzak, M., Lomuscio, A., Penczek, W.: Verification of multiagent systems via unbounded model checking. In: Kudenko, D., Kazakov, D., Alonso, E. (eds.) AAMAS 2004. LNCS (LNAI), vol. 3394, Springer, Heidelberg (2005)
12. Khallouf, J., Winikoff, M.: Towards goal-oriented design of agent systems. In: Proceedings of ISEAT 2005 (2005)
13. Mermet, B., Fournier, D., Simon, G.: An agent compositional proof system. In: From Agent Theory to Agent Implementation (AT2AI 2006) (2006)
14. Mermet, B., Simon, G., Saval, A., Zanuttini, B.: GDTs and Proofs for Robots on Mars. Technical report, GREYC (2006),
http://scott.univ-lehavre.fr/~mermet/GDT/applications/proofRoM.p
15. Raimondi, F., Lomuscio, A.: Verification of multiagent systems via orderd binary decision diagrams: an algorithm and its implementation. In: Kudenko, D., Kazakov, D., Alonso, E. (eds.) AAMAS 2004. LNCS (LNAI), vol. 3394, Springer, Heidelberg (2005)
16. Rao, A.S.: AgentSpeak(L): BDI agents speak out in a logical computable language. In: Perram, J., Van de Velde, W. (eds.) MAAMAW 1996. LNCS, vol. 1038, Springer, Heidelberg (1996)
17. Saval, A.: Robots on mars: implementation (2006),
http://arnaud.saval.free.fr/backup/applet/page.html
18. Simon, G., Flouret, M.: Implementing Validated Agents Behaviours with Automata Based on Goal Decomposition Trees. In: Müller, J.P., Zambonelli, F. (eds.) AOSE 2005. LNCS, vol. 3950, pp. 124–138. Springer, Heidelberg (2006)

19. Simon, G., Mermet, B., Fournier, D.: Goal decomposition tree: An agent model to generate a validated agent behaviour. In: Baldoni, M., Endriss, U., Omicini, A., Torroni, P. (eds.) DALT 2005. LNCS (LNAI), vol. 3904, pp. 124–140. Springer, Heidelberg (2006)
20. van Riemsdijk, M.B., Dastani, M., Dignum, F., Meyer, J.-J.C.: Dynamics of declarative goals in agent programming. In: Leite, J.A., Omicini, A., Torroni, P., Yolum, p. (eds.) DALT 2004. LNCS (LNAI), vol. 3476, pp. 1–18. Springer, Heidelberg (2005)
21. Winikoff, M., Padgham, L., Harland, J., Thangarajah, J.: Declarative & procedural goals in intelligent agent systems. In: 8th International Conference on Principles of Knowledge Representation and Reasoning (KR 2002) (2003)
22. Wooldridge, M., Jennings, N.R., Kinny, D.: The gaia methodology for agent-oriented analysis and design. Journal of Autonomous Agents and Multi-Agent Systems 3(3), 285–312 (2000)

Tracking Causality by Visualization of Multi-Agent Interactions Using Causality Graphs

Guillermo Vigueras and Juan A. Botia

Departamento de Ingeniería de la Información y las Comunicaciones
Universidad de Murcia, Spain

Abstract. Programming multi-agent systems is a hard task and requires tools to assist in the process of testing, validation and verification of both MAS specifications and source code. In this paper, we propose the use of causality graphs, adapted to the context of debugging multi-agents systems, to track causality of events produced in interactions among agents in a group. We believe that simple sequence diagrams are not enough to visually track what are the predecessors or causes of a given new event (i.e. an unexpected message or the observation that a message did not came). We propose this kind of graph as an alternative. We redefine the concept of causality graph for this particular field and propose an algorithm for generation of such a graph.

1 Introduction

Multi-agent systems act in a coordinate fashion to achieve their individual and global goals with sufficient level of guarantee. Coordination is done, most of the time, through complex interactions which involves two or more agents. Programming multi-agent interactions is a delicate task because it is prone to errors due to, most of the times, the lack of tools which assist in the production of a verified and validated design and a correct and even automatic implementation of the interactions. Multi-agent systems interactions are instances of interaction protocols definitions. The definition of an interaction protocol is compound of three different parts. The first one is a specification of the possible sequence of messages exchanged between participants. The second one is the semantics of the performatives. The third one, although this part does not always appears in the definition, refers to the kind of content which could appear in the messages exchanged. We can find many examples of these definitions on FIPA-IEEE specifications[1]. In this paper, we rely on the first part of an interaction protocol definition, to assist in tracking the causality of a given communicative act. Causality of a concrete event (i.e. a message exchanged, an undesired result of the interaction studied, an unexpected conversation, etc.), in the context of multi-agent interactions, may be loosely defined as the cause which directly or indirectly leaded to generate the event. What we propose in this paper is the

---

[1] www.fipa.org

M. Dastani et al.(Eds.): ProMAS 2007, LNAI 4908, pp. 190–204, 2008.
© Springer-Verlag Berlin Heidelberg 2008

use of causality graphs to track causality messages inside multi-agent conversations. In order to do that, we propose the use of causality graphs adapted to the particularities of multi-agent systems, to follow the thread which starts on the event generation and goes back to the root cause of it. We define our own kind of causality graph, and algorithm for its creation, starting from a logically ordered set of messages exchanged, through logical clocks [11,8,13]. Events, as we consider them, refer only to sending and receiving messages. Only these two kinds of events are obvervable by an external entity. Events realted with the internals of the agents are not considered as the external entity does not have access to them.

The rest of the paper is organized as follows. Section 2 introduces the notion of causality in the context of a MAS interaction. Section 3 analyzes the problems of ordering events in a distributed system and gives a discussion about available techniques to solve this problem when messages in a MAS have to be ordered in some way. Section 4 introduces the technique we proposse to keep track of causality. Section 5 put this technique in the appropriate context and finally, section 6 enumerates most important conclusions and open issues.

2 Representing Causality through MAS Interactions

Testing multi-agent systems consists of the design, application and analysis of a set of test cases for multi-agent software, with the intention of finding errors in the code [14]. Verification has the intention of checking whether a MAS is correct with respect to its specification, e.g. the developer can check if some mental state properties are maintained by agents along system time execution [1]. Validation consists of checking whether a multi-agent system fulfills its designs requirements or not, i.e. to check whether the system works as the user expect or not [4]. In order to integrate testing, validation and verification in the MAS development cycle, is important to offer tools to perform these tasks in an easy way. This kind of tools should offer an abstract view of a MAS, which shows the performance of the system to detect errors in a easy and fast way, to reduce development costs and effort. In this paper, we propose an acyclic graph, which shows causality among messages sent by agents, extracted from conversations previously logged. An example of such a graph is presented in figure 1. In that graph, a multiparty conversation is represented, in which A_1 is the initiator agent (corresponds to the first and last nodes of the graph, if we read it from the upper to the bottom part) and $A_2, A_3, ..., A_n$ are participants. An example of a simple conversation inside the complex conversation, is the one between A_2 and A_4. As in both previous cases, agents $A_3, ..., A_n$ can interact using simple or multiparty conversations, with the rest of agents in the MAS, before they answer to A_1. The graph in figure 1, shows clearly that message m_1 is the cause that agent A_2 sends to A_4 the message m_{n+1}. Like this, if some sent message is not as expected or the agent does not receive an expected message, we can use a simple search inside the graph to locate the cause event, but also the developer will be able to analyze visually message trace that generate the wrong message, and find where the bug is.

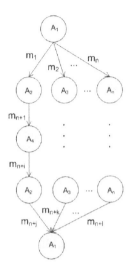

Fig. 1. Causality graph showing multiparty conversation among A_1 and $A_2, A_3, ..., A_n$

In order to generate a graph like the one which appears in figure 1, we need to have the whole set of messages exchanged by the agents of interest. Moreover, we need to have them ordered, in such a way that message m_j does not appear before message m_i if m_i actually occurred before m_j in the conversation, for any m_i, m_j in the whole set of messages sent. The rate of event occurrence can be very high in a multi-agent system. Reason why it will be virtually impossible to obtain the causal precedence relation among events, if physical clocks of each system element are not synchronized precisely. It is due to physical clocks precision is not accurate enough related with the high number of MAS events. Thus, for example, the Internet's Network Time Protocols, NTP for short, which maintains a time accurate to a few tens of milliseconds, are not adequate for capturing causality in distributed systems. For this reason, to order MAS events logically, different methods based on logical clocks [11], might be used instead of each agent's clock. Other approaches to do that rely on a priori assumptions like, for example, the existence of additional information inside messages which allow to recompose the mentioned order. This is the case for FIPA agents and the use of two slots in ACL messages which are `Reply-with` and `In-reply-to` which may be used for this purpose. But this option was discarded mainly for two reasons. The first one, and most important, is that FIPA slots mentioned above allow to establish a causal order only among messages which belongs to the same conversation, in this way, in the graph in figure 1, conversation between A_2 and A_4, generated as a consequence of the message sent by A_1 to A_2, will appear in another disconnected subgraph. Hence, keep track of causality among different disconnected subgraphs could be an unaffordable task. The second reason to avoid use FIPA slots is that FIPA specifications are not implemented by all agents platforms. Because our aim is to design a tool to be platform independent, we do not use this technique. Methods based on logical clocks are explained in following section.

3   Ordering Events in a Distributed System

There are two main types of methods to obtain an adequate logical order of events by means of logical clocks in a distributed system, depending on the information represented in each event [11,8,13], they are either vector or matrix based logical clocks.

Logical clock vectors [11], allow to determine causal precedence relation among events in a distributed system in which each process has synchronization problems. Problems that might made impossible to establish a precedence relation in the system.

A logical clock is a counter, one for each process or active entity in the distributed system, which keeps track of order of occurrence of events in processes. In a vector based logical clock, we have a counter for any single process in the distributed system which generates events of interest. Each event has a logical clock, which allows it to be ordered by means of a simple ordering relation. Given two vectors v_1 and v_2, both with n components, we say that $v_1 \leq v_2$ if $v_1[i] \leq v_2[i]$, $1 \leq i \leq n$. Also, we have $v_1 < v_2$ when they are $v_1 \leq v_2$ and there exist at least, an i such that $v_1[i] < v_2[i]$.

Using this simple relations, and an appropriate technique for updating the vector counters, we can order two events: given two events e_1 and e_2, stamped with vectors, v_{e_1} and v_{e_2}, respectively, if $v_{e_1} < v_{e_2}$, we can say that e_1 happened before than e_2. Details on the update process are out of the scope of this article.

As an alternative, we have logical clock matrix. In this case, instead of representing events with so n counters, being n the number of distributed entities, we use a $n \times n$ matrix. We store much more data but at the same time, we have much more information. For example, let $m[j, k]$ be a concrete counter of the matrix for the i-th distributed entity. This counter refers to the number of messages sent by entity j to entity k as the entity i knows it.

Logical clock matrix are useful in such cases in which a logical order has to be established among messages from a distributed system, but the order among messages is established on line, during the execution of the system, so in this way, each process can maintain an incomplete list of messages, which are already ordered. Using logical clock matrix method, each process can read the received messages in the correct order. In our problem, i.e. to build a causality graph, the algorithm that is in charge to order messages causally, works off line, i.e. the algorithm starts to order messages when the MAS stops running. So in such case, the algorithm will have all messages exchanged by agents in the system, and using the vector clock method is sufficient to our requirements.

4   Causality Graphs as a Means to Track Multi-Agent Interactions

Multiagent systems, are non-deterministic systems. The performance of each agent will depend on the efficiency to manage internal and external events, i.e. messages from other agents [10]. For this reason, analyzing agents interactions is an important issue and delivers powerful information to the developer. This information can be used to discover what is happening in the MAS. The most widely used graphical representation for multi-agent interaction protocols, UML sequence diagrams, shows the allowed sequence order among messages. However, due to the particularities of such kind of diagram, it is difficult to find visually any causal relation among messages.

To illustrate it, suppose a MAS, in which an agent delegates three tasks on other agents. Each one of these agents represents different organizations, and each one of them delegate tasks again to agents of their own organizations. To decide which agent will perform each task, a negotiation is made using FIPA Contract-net protocol [7]. If some agent reports a failure after performing some task, a new negotiation will start to perform the failed task. Lets think, for example, on A agent which delegates one task on B, C and D agents. After elaborating proposals, C agent will be in charge to perform task T1 and D is in charge to perform tasks T2 and T3. Suppose that C returns a failure when performing task T1. This event generates a new negotiation to find an agent to perform T1, among B, D and a recently created agent N. Figure 2 shows this

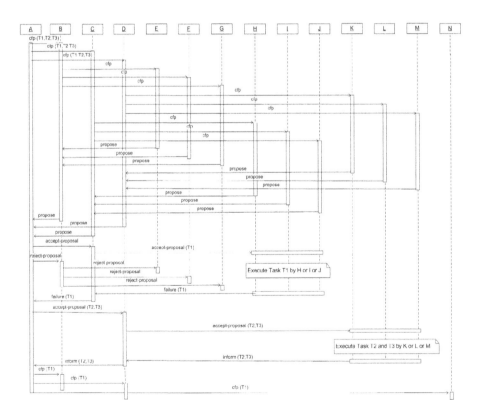

Fig. 2. UML sequence diagram which shows messages sent by agents. By means of this diagram is complex to find causality among messages.

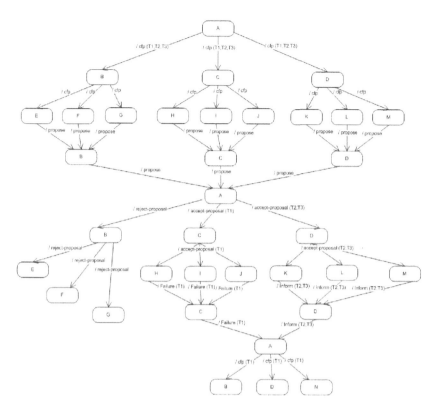

Fig. 3. Causality graph corresponding to the example MAS. Nodes are agents instances and edges are sent messages.

particular occurrence of the interaction protocol by means of a UML sequence diagram, and figure 3, shows the causality graph for the same conversation.

In the sequence diagram of figure 2, to find and follow the trace of each conversation among agents is not obvious. For this reason, finding the cause of any error or some wrong agent behavior, could be a non trivial task for the programmer. On the other hand, the diagram proposed in figure 3, is easier to analyze. Assisted by the causality graph in figure 3, a developer can find intuitively the cause why agent A rejects agent B proposal. Looking at the message trace, a developer will find that proposal sent by agent B, depends on proposals from agents E, F and G. In this way, to find the error, proposals from those agents should be analyzed.

4.1 Definition of the Causality Graph for Multi-Agent Interactions

In this section we will formalize the causality graph for multi-agent systems interactions. We will define, before interaction protocols, these other elements: logical clocks, conversations, messages and agents.

Let n be the number of agents in a MAS[2] and m the number of sent messages in a given MAS execution. Let also d be the number of conversations found and e the number of different interaction protocols of that set of conversations.

We will define a protocol as

$$P = \{p_1, p_2, ..., p_e \mid p_i = (Q, I, q_0, F, \delta)\},$$

where Q is the FSA's[3] states set, I is the input alphabet, composed by agents interaction performatives defined by FIPA [6], q_0 is the initial state, F is the final states set and $\delta : Q \times P \to Q$, is the transition function between states. We define also a set of logical clocks as

$$L = \{lc_1, ..., lc_m \mid lc_i = (x_1, ..., x_n) \ 1 \leq i \leq m \text{ and } x_j \in \mathbb{N}\}.$$

We need also to represent the whole set of agents involved in a MAS run, and we will denote it as $A = \{a_1, ..., a_n \mid n \in \mathbb{N}\}$. Agents belonging to this set will be involved in conversations in the run. Let

$$C = \{c_1, ..., c_d \mid c_j = (init, prot), init \in A, prot \in P\}$$

be the set of conversations. Agents that belong to the same conversation will use the same protocol. Each conversation has an initiator and one or many participants depending on whether protocol's conversation is simple or multiparty. Elements from this set will be pairs, containing conversation initiator and conversation protocol. Finally, we will refer to the set of messages of the studied run as M, where each element will be a 6-tuple as $(s, r, lc, conv, prot, perf)$. The first and second component reference, respectively, to message sender agent and receiver agent, the third component is the logic clock stamped in the message, fourth component is the conversation to which the message belongs to, fifth component is the protocol used in message conversation and the last component is the message performative.

Please, notice that cardinality of M and L sets will be the same, and between both sets there will be a biunivocal relation (i.e. for each message there will be only one logic clock and vice versa). Also, messages have been defined to build a causality graph which maintains independence from the MAS platform used. Thus, using examples of multi-agent platforms widely used like the ones that appear in [2], a developer will be able to send agents messages containing almost the 6-tuple related above. Another issue is that a messages set for a given MAS execution, is partially ordered using logical clocks. In this way, let m_1 be the first message in the message set, which is not caused by other message. After m_1, all messages caused by it will appear. After those messages, other message with no cause will appear denoted with m_n, and after m_n all messages caused

---

[2] We assume that the number of agents is known in advance as we are considering the case in which we are debugging the MAS, i.e. it is not in production mode. However, this assumption does not imply any loss of generality.

[3] We assume that any protocol might be formally defined with a Finite States Automaton.

by it. To understand it better, we refer to the messages order using the graph in figure 3. For that graph, the first message in set M will be the one sent by agent A to B with performative cfp. Following, messages sent by B to agents E, F and G with performatives cfp will be inserted, (order among this three messages is not important because they are concurrent). Following these three messages, messages caused by those three messages will be added, and so on until insert three reject-proposal messages sent by B to E, F and G. After those messages, message sent by A to C, with performative cfp, will be added, and after it, all messages caused by it, and so on until order all messages sent in the MAS. Order described above is established, because algorithm to build causality graph need to process MAS messages in sequential way. Thus, we finally define M as

$$M = \{m_1, ..., m_m | m_i = (s_i, r_i, lc_i, conv_i, prot_i, perf_i)\},$$

and we have $s_i, r_i \in A$, $lc_i \in L$, $conv_i \in C$, $prot_i \in P$ and $perf_i \in I$.

Now, we can define a causality graph for multi-agent systems interactions as a graph $G(V, E)$, where $V = \{(ag, inst) | ag \in A \land inst \in \mathbb{N}\}$ is the set of nodes and E is the set of edges with $E = \{(sr, tg, m) | sr, tg \in V$ and $m \in M\}$.

In multi-agent interactions causality graphs, there will be an edge for each message, and a node for each message sender and receiver. If the receiver and the sender of a message is the same agent, then both nodes will be joint in one. This process is explained in the following section. Elements from V are pairs, where the first component is an agent and the second component is a number to identify different nodes of the graph which refer to the same agent (i.e. the same agent sends different messages). Elements from set E, are 3-tuples. The first and the second component are the source node and target node, respectively. Third component is a label corresponding to the message sent.

4.2   Algorithm to Build the Graph

In this section we will define the algorithm to build a multi-agent interaction causality graph. To simplify notation used, we will access each element component from sets defined in previous section, by means of functions which have the same name as the component to get. Thus, for example, to get the sender of some message m we will use function $s(m)$.

In this algorithm, we will need a function that, given a concrete message, it delivers the cause message (i.e. the message which comes immediately before and whose occurrence generated this one). Let it be denoted with $Cause(m, M)$ for a message m and a subset of messages M in which the cause should be located at. It is possible that m does not have a cause (i.e. is the initial message of the conversation). In this case, the function will return $\bot$. To define the function, the subset M'' is explained. Given a message $m \in M'$, where M' is the messages set of already processed messages (see algorithm 1), let be $M'' \subseteq M'$, a messages subset so that, $m' \in M''$ iff $lc(m') < lc(m) \land r(m') = s(m)$. Using this set, $Cause$ function is defined:

$$
Cause(m, M'') = \begin{cases} \bot & M'' = \emptyset \\ m' & \exists m' \in M'' \mid \\ & lc\_s(m) - lc\_r(m') = \min_{m'' \in M''} \{lc\_s(m) - lc\_r(m'')\} \end{cases} ,
$$

where $lc\_s(m)$ and $lc\_r(m)$ return the counter of the logical clock of m for sender and receiver, respectively. Notice that this definition of $Cause()$ function does not consider explicitly that a message could have two messages or more as its root cause (e.g. in a contract net like protocol, the reason for sending reject/accept messages are the whole set of proposals received before). This is addressed in the algorithm. See also the example exposed in section 4.3.

Another functionality needed is that which says if two messages m and m' are equivalent. This means that, if we look at the DFA which defines the states of the protocol followed by the conversation, and interpret messages as tokens of the input alphabet of the automaton, m and m' generate transitions from the same source state (e.g. `accept-proposal` and `reject-proposal` messages are equivalent messages for the contract net protocol). Hence, it is defined as follows:

$$
Equivalent(m, m') = \begin{cases} true & prot(m) = prot(m') \wedge \exists q \in prot\_Q(m) \mid \\ & prot\_\delta(q, m) \in prot\_Q(m) \wedge \\ & prot\_\delta(q, m') \in prot\_Q(m') \\ \\ false & otherwise \end{cases} ,
$$

where $prot\_Q(m)$ and $prot\_\delta(q, m)$ return the set of states of the AFD which model the protocol of the conversation in which m appears and the next state starting from q and with m as input, respectively. These two functions are needed to generate the next state of the automaton to advance in the generation of the causality graph.

In a concrete situation of the algorithm (see algorithm 1), we will need the node which already exists in the partial graph constructed, representing the receiver of a message m'. This is needed when this message is the cause of another message which we want to transform into an edge in the graph. Hence, we define

$$
GetTargetInstance(m', E) = inst(tg(e)),
$$

provided that there exists $e \in E$ such that $m(e) = m$ and we use $m(e)$ to access the labeling message of arc e in the graph.

When the algorithm is building the graph, it starts from the most recent messages (i.e. whose order is provided by the logical clocks) to the older ones. New nodes of the graph means an agent sending and/or receiving a message. When we need to create a new node for an agent and a message or messages sent by it, we need the index of occurrence of the agent in the graph to correctly label the node. We use for that the $GetLastInstance()$ function, and we define it as

$$GetLastInstance(a, V) = \begin{cases} \max_{v=(a,i)\in V} \{inst(v)\} + 1 & \exists i | v = (a, i) \in V \\ \\ 0 & otherwise \end{cases},$$

given that a is the agent and V is the set of nodes already added to the algorithm. It will return 0 (the lowest index) if the agent was not already added.

When a new message has to be inserted in the graph, first thing we need to do is locating the node in the graph from which the new arc derived from the message will start. We will do this with $GetSender$ function. It returns the right occurrence of the agent which sends the message. It is defined for simple and multiparty conversations. In a multiparty conversation, the function joins, in the same source node, all messages with equivalent performatives. It will be defined as:

$$GetSender(m', m'', E, V) = \begin{cases} GetTargetInstance(m'', E) & m'' \neq \perp \wedge \exists e \in E \, | \\ & m(e) = m'' \\ inst(sr(e)) & \exists e \in E \, | \\ & Equivalent(m(e), m') \wedge \\ & s(m(e)) = s(m') \wedge \\ & conv(m(e)) = conv(m') \\ GetLastInstance(s(m'), V) & otherwise \end{cases}$$

where m' is the message to insert as an arc, m'' is the cause of m' and the pair E, V, correspond to the graph partially constructed. When we try to locate the right node in the graph to insert m', we will find one among three different situations. The first and most simple is that m' is the root message of a conversation, hence it has no cause, i.e. $m' = \perp$. In this case, we simply generate a new node. In the second case, m' also has no cause, but the root node has been generated before (by a previous call with another message equivalent to this, e.g. cfp messages in the beginning of a contract net conversation). The function returns the instance of the node. In the third case, the cause node exists, hence the function returns the node of the graph in which the arc corresponding to m'' ends.

If we need the target node of a message m' in the graph, we also need the source node of the same message. This is accomplished by $GetReceiver$. This function works with simple and multiparty conversations among agents. In a multiparty conversation, the function will join, in the same target node, all messages with equivalent performatives. Thus, the target node corresponding to message m', given as argument, will be a node that already exists in the graph. If that node does not exist, a new node will be created:

$$GetReceiver(m', E, V) = \begin{cases} inst(tg(e)) & \exists e \in E \, | \\ & Equivalent(m(e), m') \wedge \\ & r(m(e)) = r(m') \wedge \\ & conv(m(e)) = conv(m') \\ GetLastInstance(r(m'), V) & otherwise \end{cases}$$

Algorithm 1. Algorithm for the generation of a multi-agent interaction causality diagram

```
 1: Build_Graph(M,∅,∅); {Algorithm invocation}
 2: Build_Graph(M,V,E){ {Algorithm definition}
 3: M' ← ∅
 4: m ← next(M);
 5: while m ≠⊥ do
 6:    let m' be ∈ M∪{⊥}
 7:    let source,target be ∈ V
 8:    m' ← Cause(m,M');
 9:    if (init(conv(m)) = s(m)) then {m's sender is conversation's
       initiatior}
10:       source ← (s(m), GetSender(m,m',E,V));
11:       target ← (r(m), GetLastInstance(r(m),V));
          {Source and target node are created to the new edge that
          will be inserted, when s(m) is conversation's initiator}
12:    else {m's sender is conversation's participant}
13:       source ← (r(m'),GetTargetInstance(m',E));
14:       target ← (r(m), GetReceiver(m,E,V));
          {Source and target node are created to the new edge that
          will be inserted, when s(m) is conversation's participant}
15:    end if
16:    if source ∉ V then
17:       V ← V∪{source};
18:    end if
19:    if target ∉ V then
20:       V ← V∪{target};
21:    end if
22:    M ← M − m;
23:    M' ← M'∪{m};
24:    E ← E∪{(source,target,m)};
25:    m ← next(M);
26: end while
27: }
```

Finally, the global procedure is algorithm 1. Initially, E and V sets for arcs and nodes, respectively, are empty. M' is the set of messages, already added to the graph and, hence, can be cause of another message. The $next()$ function is used to obtain the next message of an ordered set of messages.

4.3 An Example

We will illustrate how the algorithm works with an example. Suppose that we execute a MAS, and from this run we obtain the list of ordered messages which appear in table 1. They correspond to a contract net based conversation

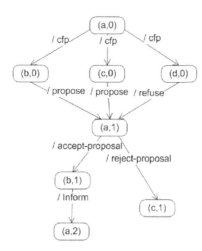

Fig. 4. Causality graph corresponding to messages set showed in table 1

Table 1. Messages set, for a conversation using contract-net protocol

Index (sender, receiver, clock, conv., protocol, performative)
1: $(a, b, [1, 0, 0, 0], c_1, p_1, cfp)$
2: $(a, c, [1, 0, 0, 0], c_1, p_1, cfp)$
3: $(a, d, [1, 0, 0, 0], c_1, p_1, cfp)$
4: $(b, a, [1, 1, 0, 0], c_1, p_1, propose)$
5: $(c, a, [1, 0, 1, 0], c_1, p_1, propose)$
6: $(d, a, [1, 0, 0, 1], c_1, p_1, refuse)$
7: $(a, b, [2, 1, 0, 0], c_1, p_1, accept - proposal)$
8: $(a, c, [2, 0, 1, 0], c_1, p_1, reject - proposal)$
9: $(b, a, [2, 2, 0, 0], c_1, p_1, inform)$

between agents a (the initiator) and b, c and d (the participants). For this list, the causality graph is shown in figure 4.

From now on, we will refer to each message using letter 'm' and the number of message , i.e. m_1 to message 1 and so on. Thus, firstly, m_1 is processed. Given that m_1 is the first, it does not have a cause, so a new node instance for agent a will be created (i.e. node $(a, 0)$). To get target node of m_1, a new instance of agent b will be created (node $(b, 0)$). After that, m_2 is processed, and it does not have a cause either, so a message with equivalent performative will be searched in already built graph. Because m_1 (which belongs to already built graph) has equivalent performative to m_2, the source node for both messages will be the same (node $(a, 0)$). The target node of m_2 will be a new node instance of agent c (node $(c, 0)$). For m_3, the same steps like for m_2 will be done. When m_4 is processed, the target node of its cause message (m_1) will be chosen as source node of m_4. The built process will choose m_1 as m_4's cause, because m_1 accomplish restrictions established by function *Cause* (see function *Cause* definition).To get the target node of m_4, a new instance of agent a (node $(a, 1)$)

will be created, because agent a did not receive messages yet. For m_5, the target node of its cause message (m_2) is selected as source node, but now the target node of m_5 will be the same like for m_4, because in both messages the receiver is initiator's conversation (agent a). The same steps like in the case of m_5 are done to find source and target nodes of m_6. The rest of the graph is built in a similar fashion.

This algorithm and the mechanism to get an ordered sequence of messages by logical clocks have been implemented and tested ACLAnalyser[4] [3]. Figure 5 is a capture (on the left of the figure) and a detail of the capture (on the right). It corresponds to the MAS example described in section 4. The detail includes

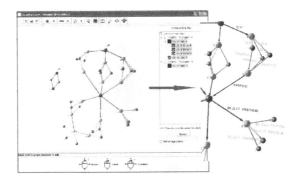

Fig. 5. Causality graph implemented in ACLAnalyser

a simple conversation among three agents. Looking at the detail, the developer can deduce the causes that agent B (node instance 2, i.e. B,2) has sent three `reject-proposal` to their interlocutors and that negotiation between A and B does not finish right. Tracking back in the graph, the developer can realize that B receives another `reject-proposal` from agent A. The cause of this rejection is the proposal sent by B to A, and the origin of this proposal is the set of three proposals received by agent B (node instance 1, i.e. B,1). So developer should review which are those proposals to know the reason why are rejected.

5   Related Works

Causality graphs were proposed more than a decade ago in the context of monitoring and debugging concurrency in distributed processes in a distributed operating system [5]. In the form it appears in that work, it is not very useful as it is, if we want to use it in the MAS debugging arena. We have extended the idea by incorporating the concept of interaction protocol, conversation and performative. Also, the algorithm to construct this different kind of causality graph is new.

---

[4] http://aclanalyser.sourceforge.net

Related with caused based graphs used in multi-agent systems, in [10] is proposed a graph in which, developer defines agent concepts and causal relation among those pre-defined concepts is shown (e.g. a believe created as a consequence of a received message). This work is complementary to our, because the caused graph is at intra-agent level an not inter-agent level.

Using visualization tools to assist in testing and debugging MAS software has been previously explored by the authors in previous works [9]. Simple communication graphs are used there, i.e. nodes are agents and arcs exits between nodes if they exchanged any message. However, when these communication graphs get so complex to be visualized (i.e. many agents and many arcs), a simplification process based on clustering is used to group agents. Different criteria are used to decide on the grouping.

An interesting work about visualizing multi-agent system is that done by Schroeder et al. [15]. It represents a multi-agent system in a 3D world, in which distances between agents are directly related with similarity. In this way, one can, at a glimpse, know which agents show a similar behavior (when they are near in the 3D space).

Keeping the attention on visualization tools for MAS, other interesting example is the one presented in [12]. In this case, the developer can use different kinds of visual diagrams. For example, Gantt diagrams show decomposition, dependency and ordering among agents tasks.

6   Conclusions

In this paper, a new visual element aimed to aid the developer in MAS testing, verification and validation tasks is proposed, showing an abstract view of the MAS, which allow a deeper and quick understanding of system behaviour. To build this kind of graph, we address the problem of logical ordering of events in a distributed system. Also, we propose an algorithm to build the whole graph. We show with examples that this kind of diagrams are easy to understand, even more than sequence diagrams when one wants to study causality relations. Details about performance and algorithm analysis will be provided elsewhere.

We keep working on different methods to obtain information about MAS through elaborated queries directed to the causality graph in order to reinforce visual validation and verification. To put it simple, to aid the developer to infer more conclusions about MAS behaviour. This will be useful in systems with many agents, in which trying to visualize any situation can be unaffordable.

Acknowledgements

This research work is supported by the Spanish Ministry of Education and Science in the scope of the Research Project TIN-2005-08501-C03-02.

References

1. Bordini, R., Fisher, M., Pardavila, C., Wooldridge, M.: Model checking agentspeak
2. Bordini, R.H., Dastani, M., Dix, J., EI Fallah-Seghrouchni, A. (eds.): Multi-Agent Programming: Languages, Platforms and Applications. In: Multiagent Systems, Artificial Societies, and Simulated Organizations, vol. 15. Springer, Heidelberg (2005)
3. Botia, J.A., Hernansaez, J.M., Gomez-Skarmeta, A.F.: Towards an approach for debugging mas through the analysis of acl messages. Computer Systems Science and Engineering (July 20, 2005)
4. De Wolf, T., Holvoet, T.: Towards a methodology for engineering self-organising emergent systems. Self-Organization and Autonomic Informatics 135, 18–34 (2005)
5. Dror Zernitk, M.S., Malki, D.: Using visualization tools to understand concurrency. IEEE Softw 9, 87–92 (1992)
6. FIPA. Fipa acl message structure specification. Technical report, FIPA (2002)
7. FIPA. Fipa contract net interaction protocol specication. Technical report, FIPA (2002)
8. Garg, V.K.: Concurrent and Distributed Computing in Java. Wiley, IEEE Press (2004)
9. Botia, J.M.H.J.A., Gomez-Skarmeta, A.F.: On the application of clustering techniques to support debugging large-scale multi-agent systems. In: Programming Multi-Agent Systems Workshop AAMAS, Hakodate, Japan (2006)
10. Lam, D.N., Barber, K.S.: Comprehending agent software. In: AAMAS 2005: Proceedings of the fourth international joint conference on Autonomous agents and multiagent systems, pp. 586–593. ACM Press, New York (2005)
11. Lamport, L.: Time, clocks, and the ordering of events in a distributed system. Commun. ACM 21(7), 558–565 (1978)
12. Ndumu, D.T., Nwana, H.S., Lee, L.C., Collis, J.C.: Visualising and debugging distributed multi-agent systems. In: ACM Press (ed.) AGENTS 1999: Proceedings of the third annual conference on Autonomous Agents, pp. 326–333 (1999)
13. Raynal, M., Singhal, M.: Logical time: Capturing causality in distributed systems. Computer 29(2), 49–56 (1996)
14. von Staa Roberta Coelho, A., Kulesza, U., Lucena, C.: Unit testing in multi-agent systems using mock agents and aspects. In: SELMAS 2006: Proceedings of the 2006 international workshop on Software engineering for large-scale multi-agent systems, pp. 83–90. ACM Press, New York (2006)
15. Schroeder, M., Noy, P.: Multi-agent visualisation based on multivariate data. In: Proceedings of the Fifth International Conference on Autonomous Agents, Montreal, Canada, ACM Press, New York (2001)

Hybrid Multiagent Systems with Timed Synchronization – Specification and Model Checking[*]

Ulrich Furbach[1], Jan Murray[1], Falk Schmidsberger[2], and Frieder Stolzenburg[2]

[1] Universität Koblenz-Landau, Artificial Intelligence Research Group, D-56070 Koblenz
{uli,murray}@uni-koblenz.de
[2] Hochschule Harz, Automation and Computer Sciences Department
D-38855 Wernigerode
{fschmidsberger,fstolzenburg}@hs-harz.de

Abstract. This paper shows how multiagent systems can be modeled by a combination of UML statecharts and hybrid automata. This allows formal system specification on different levels of abstraction on the one hand and expressing real-time system behavior with continuous variables on the other hand. It is shown, how multi-robot systems can be modeled by hybrid and hierarchical state machines and how model checking techniques for hybrid automata can be applied. An enhanced synchronization concept is introduced that allows synchronization taking time and avoids state explosion to a certain extent.

1 Multiagent Systems

Specifying behaviors for (physical) multiagent and multi-robot systems is a sophisticated and demanding task. Due to the high complexity of the interactions among agents and the dynamics of the environment the need for precise modeling arises. Since the behavior of agents usually can be understood as driven by external events and internal states, an obvious way of modeling multiagent systems is by state transition diagrams. Hierarchical state transition diagrams like statecharts are particularly well suited as they allow the specification of behaviors on different levels of abstraction [9]. They can directly be used as executable specifications for programming multiagent systems [1].

One important aspect of physical agents and robots is that they interact with a (possibly simulated) physical environment. Such interactions typically consist of continuous actions (e.g. the movement of a robot) and perceptions like the power status of a battery. Classical state transition diagrams are not well suited for modeling this, because the transitions between states are discrete. However, continuous extensions to these formalisms have been proposed, e.g. hybrid automata [6].

Especially for agents employed in safety critical environments, e.g. in rescue scenarios, behavior specification has to be done very carefully in order to avoid side effects that may have unwanted or even disastrous consequences. One approach to realizing

---

[*] This research is supported by the grants *Fu 263/8* and *Sto 421/2* from the German research foundation *DFG* within the special priority program 1125 on *Cooperating Teams of Mobile Robots in Dynamic Environments*.

M. Dastani et al.(Eds.): ProMAS 2007, LNAI 4908, pp. 205–220, 2008.
© Springer-Verlag Berlin Heidelberg 2008

the required clarity of a specification is the use of formal design methods. Fortunately, many state transition diagram dialects like hybrid automata are equipped with a formal semantics that makes them accessible to formal validation of the modeled behavior. Thus it becomes possible to (semi-)automatically prove desirable features and the absence of unwanted properties in the specified behaviors, e.g. with model checking methods.

2   Hybrid Hierarchical State Machines

In this section, we present the combination of two concepts: hierarchical statecharts and hybrid automata. As a running example, we use a scenario from the RoboCup rescue simulation league, which is shortly described in the following subsection. The RoboCup initiative (official homepage of the RoboCup Federation: www.robocup.org) aims at fostering research in robotics, artificial intelligence, and multiagent systems. As one example domain *robotic soccer* has been chosen, because soccer combines many interesting problems, e.g. dealing with uncertain and incomplete information, cooperation and coordination in a team of autonomous agents, decision support in multiagent systems, or planning and acting in a highly dynamic environment. Annual world competitions and a number of local events provide benchmarks and opportunity to present results of current research. RoboCup is divided into several leagues, which focus on different research aspects. The *simulation league* deals with aspects of situated multiagent systems like teamwork, spatial reasoning, decision making, and opponent modeling. There are also non-soccer leagues, e.g. the so-called rescue leagues (see next section).

2.1   Rescue Scenario

In the RoboCup rescue simulation league [19], a large scale disaster is simulated. The simulator models part of a city after an earthquake. Buildings may be collapsed or on fire, and roads are partially or completely blocked. A team of heterogeneous agents consisting of police forces, ambulance teams, a fire brigade, and their respective headquarters is deployed. The agents have two main tasks, namely finding and rescuing blocked civilians and extinguishing fires. An auxiliary task is clearing of obstructed roads, such that agents can move smoothly. As their abilities enable each type of agent to solve only *one* kind of task (e.g. fire brigades cannot clear roads or rescue civilians), the need for coordination and synchronization among agents is obvious.

Consider the following simple scenario. If a fire breaks out somewhere, a fire brigade agent is ordered by its headquarters to extinguish the fire. The fire brigade moves to the fire and begins to put it out. If the agent runs out of water it has to refill its tank at a supply station and return to the fire to complete its task. Once the fire is extinguished, the fire brigade agent is idle again. An additional task the agent has to execute is to report any injured civilians it discovers. Part of this scenario is modeled in Fig. 1 with the help of a hierarchical hybrid automaton [10]. In addition to the fire brigade agent the model should include a fire station, fire and civilians as part of the environment; all this will be explained in a subsequent section (cf. Fig. 2).

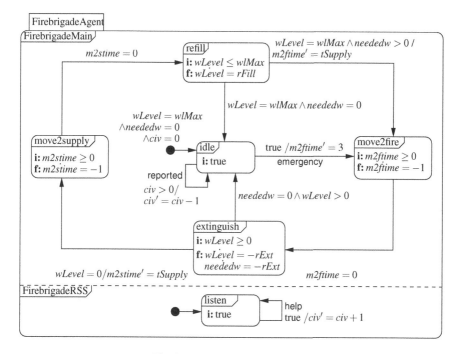

Fig. 1. A simple fire brigade agent

States are represented as rectangles with rounded corners and can be structured hierarchically. The specification of the fire brigade is a simple hierarchical chart, consisting of the main control structure (*FirebrigadeMain*) and a rescue sub-system (*FirebrigadeRSS*) which are supposed to run in parallel. The latter just records the detected civilians, which are not modeled in Fig. 1 (for this, see the sub-state *Civilians* in Fig. 2 later in the text). *FirebrigadeMain* consists of five sub-states corresponding to movements (*move2fire*, *move2supply*), extinguishing (*extinguish*), refilling the tank (*refill*), and an idle state (*idle*). The agent can report the discovered civilians when it is in its idle state. Details from this figure will be explained in the course of this section.

It should be obvious already in this stage, that even in this simple case with few components and a deterministic environment it is difficult to see if the agent behaves correctly. Important questions like "does the fire brigade try to extinguish without water?" or "will every discovered civilian (and *only* those) be reported eventually?" depend on the interaction of all components and cannot be answered without an analysis of the whole system. We will come back to these questions in Sect. 4.1.

2.2 State Hierarchies and Transitions

Statecharts are a part of UML [12,13] and a well accepted means to specify dynamic behavior of software systems. The main concept for statecharts is a state, which corresponds to an activity or behavior of a robot or agent. Statecharts can be described in a rigorously formal manner [1,14], allowing flexible specification, implementation and analysis of multiagent systems [9,18] which is required for robot behavior engineering and modeling and simulating complex robots.

Definition 1 (basic components). *The basic components of a* state machine *are the following disjoint sets:*

S: a finite set of states, which is partitioned into three disjoint sets: S_{simple}, S_{comp}, and S_{conc} — called simple, composite and concurrent states, containing one designated start state $s_0 \in S_{comp} \cup S_{conc}$, and
X: a finite set of (real-numbered) variables.

In our running example, *idle*, *extinguish* or *listen* are simple states, and *FirebrigadeAgent* is a concurrent state and *FirebrigadeMain* and *FirebrigadeRSS* are composite states, called regions in this case, which are separated by a dashed line. *m2ftime* and *wLevel* are examples for real-valued variables.

In statecharts, states are connected via *transitions* in $T \subseteq S \times S$, indicating that an agent in the first state will enter the second state. Transitions are drawn as arrows labeled with jump conditions over the variables in X together with actions. For example, the transition from *idle* to itself is labeled with $civ > 0 / civ' = civ - 1$, with the meaning: if the value of *civ* is greater 0, then the action $civ' = civ - 1$ is executed while performing the transition, i.e., the number of civilians that are found but not reported is decreased in this case.

The label reported at the same transition is used for synchronizing the transition with another automaton working in parallel, namely the one for *Firestation* (see Fig. 2). It is only legal for the combined system if both automata take the transition labeled reported at the same time. See [6] for details. In principle, the explicit use of events and actions as in UML statecharts is not needed, as both can be expressed with the help of variables. For example the occurrence of an external event can be represented by changing the value of the corresponding variable from 0 to 1.

Since hybrid automata [6] are akin to statecharts, it makes sense to combine the advantages of both models. Statecharts have the clear advantage of allowing hierarchical specification on several levels of abstraction, while hybrid automata enable the introduction of continuous variables and flow conditions. This extension of statecharts is done by the subsequent definition. Hybrid automata are widely used for the specification of embedded systems. By reachability analyses, diagnosis tasks can be solved. We will come back to this in Sect. 4.

Definition 2 (jump conditions, flows and invariants). *In addition to the variables in X, we introduce new variables $\dot{x}$ (first derivatives during continuous change) and x' (values at the conclusion of discrete change) for each $x \in X$, calling the corresponding variable sets $\dot{X}$ and X', respectively. Then, each transition in T may be labeled by a jump condition, that is a predicate whose free variables are from $X \cup X'$, which can be split into activation condition and effect. In addition, each state $s \in S$ is labeled with a flow condition (f:), whose free variables are from $X \cup \dot{X}$, and an invariant (i:), whose free variables are from X. Flow conditions may be empty and hence omitted, if nothing changes continuously in the respective state.*

In our example we use the dotted variable $w\dot{L}evel$ to denote the change of the water level in the state *refill*. A transition from this state to the state *move2fire* is performed, if the water level reached the maximum ($wLevel = wlMax$) and water is needed ($neededw >$ 0). During the transition the action $m2ftime' = tSupply$ is executed.

We will restrict our attention to linear conditions, i.e. linear equalities and inequalities among either ordinary variables in $X \cup X'$ or their first derivatives $\dot{X}$, because only then an exact reachability analysis (needed for model checking) is feasible [4,6]. Let us now have a closer look at states. Following the lines of [12,13], we define the hierarchical structure of statecharts as follows.

Definition 3 (state hierarchy). *Each state s is associated with zero, one or more* initial *states* $\alpha(s)$*: a simple state has zero, a composite state exactly one, and a concurrent state more than one initial state. Furthermore, each state* $s \in S \backslash \{s_0\}$ *belongs to* exactly one *state* $\beta(s)$ *different from s. It must hold* $\beta(s) \in S_{comp} \cup S_{conc}$*. If* $\beta(s) \in S_{conc}$*, then* $s \in S_{comp}$*, which implies that a concurrent state must not be directly contained in another concurrent state, as they could be merged into a single concurrent state in this case. s is called* region *of* $\beta(s)$ *then and may have a* cardinality *greater than one. We assume that transitions keep to the hierarchy, i.e., if* sTs' *holds, then* $\beta(s) = \beta(s')$*.*

In Fig. 1 we see that the start state s_0 is *FirebrigadeAgent*, a concurrent state. It represents the multiagent system, consisting of an agent *FirebrigadeMain* and *FirebrigadeRSS*. Both are realized as regions, which are separated by dashed lines (in the case of heterogenous agents), and each has cardinality one. The entire rescue scenario, which we will also use for model checking later on is depicted in Fig. 2; besides the fire brigade we additionally have concurrent regions with states for *Fire*, *Civilians* and *Firestation*.

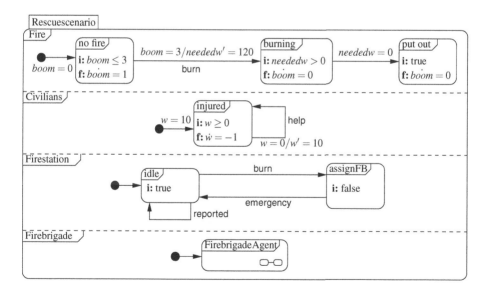

Fig. 2. A simple scenario from the RoboCup rescue simulation. The state *FirebrigadeAgent* corresponds to the one shown in Fig. 1. The icon ◯–◯ hints at the hidden sub-states.

2.3 State Trees and Configurations

The function β (see Def. 3) naturally induces a state tree with s_0 as root. This is shown for the running example in Fig. 3. Here, regions with cardinality greater than one must be treated as multiple composite states, which are distinguished by different indices. However, while processing, each region or composite state of the state machine contains only one active state. These states also form a tree, called configuration. A configuration of the given state machine, is indicated by the thick lines in Fig. 3. Let us now define the notion of configuration more formally.

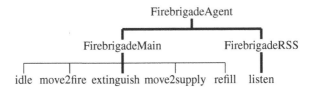

Fig. 3. State hierarchy and configuration tree (thick lines)

Definition 4 (configuration). *A configuration c is a rooted tree of states, where the root node is the topmost initial state of the overall state machine. Whenever a state s is an immediate predecessor of s' in c, it must hold $\beta(s') = s$.*

A configuration must be completed by applying the following procedure recursively as long as possible to leaf nodes: if there is a leaf node in c labeled with a state s, then introduce all $\alpha(s)$ as immediate successors of s.

3 Synchronization and Cooperation

The overall performance of programmed multiagent systems heavily depends on how cooperative agents behave. Cooperation and coordination of agents can be achieved by synchronization. Hence, it is essential to implement synchronization effectively. Synchronization means, that several actions must start or happen at the same time. In the rescue scenario (see Sect. 2), transition labels serve as triggers for synchronization in the formalism of hybrid automata, e.g., if an injured civilian cries for help, then the listening fire fighter hears this. However, if more complicated coordination and cooperation among agents has to be expressed, then this simple concept of synchronization may not suffice. In the following, we will therefore introduce an enhanced concept of synchronization (see [10,11]), which we motivate with an example from the robotic soccer domain.

3.1 An Example of Coordination in Robotic Soccer

Since (robotic) soccer is a team sport, cooperation of agents is essential. Clearly, it is not a good idea that all players try to get the ball at the same time. At best, exactly one player goes to the ball, while the others try to position themselves as good as possible on the pitch.

Fig. 4 shows the statechart for two players trying a coordinated behavior of going to the ball. To realize this behavior, the positions of two players, the ball, an opponent and the opponent goal are modeled. The positions are described as two-dimensional vectors $\mathbf{v} = \binom{x}{y}$. Components are accessed via the point notation, e.g. $v.x$. Constant names start with capital letters, variables with lower case letters. There are variables for the global, real ball position $\mathbf{bR}$ (initially $\binom{80}{60}$), the local ball position $\mathbf{b}$ measured by each player, global positions of the players 1 and 2 (initial values $\mathbf{p1} = \binom{0}{60}$, $\mathbf{p2} = \binom{0}{-60}$), the local position of the player $\mathbf{p}$ and his teammate $\mathbf{pT}$ and some constants for the global position of the (stationary) opponent $\mathbf{PO} = \binom{110}{-30}$, and the opponent goal $\mathbf{POG} = \binom{Field.x}{0}$. Additionally there is the field size $\mathbf{Field}$. The field reaches from $-\mathbf{Field}$ to $+\mathbf{Field}$. Further there is the measurement error $ME = 2$ of the players, the range $DHB = 5$ within which a player is assumed to be controlling the ball, and some scale factors $F01 = 0.1$, $F02 = 0.5$, $F03 = 0.3$, $F04 = 0.6$. To access a local value, the path over the states to the value is used. For instance, the local position of player 1 is soccer.teamplay.player1.$\mathbf{p}$ with the initial value $\mathbf{p1}$ and the local position of his teammate is soccer.teamplay.player1.$\mathbf{pT}$ with the initial value $\mathbf{p2}$.

The composite state *soccer* contains the concurrent state *teamplay* as initial state and the simple state *fail*. There is only one transition from *teamplay* to *fail*, and *fail* can only be entered, if the invariant of *teamplay* is false and the guard of the transition is true. In this case, the ball has to be out of the bounds of the field. Note that the synchronization variable *ball* and the invariant beside it belong to *teamplay*.

The behavior of the two players is modeled in the regions *player* inside of *teamplay*, which is a concurrent state with two regions: one for each of the two players. But since both players obey in principle the same specification, i.e., we have a homogeneous agent system, we express this by cardinality markers in the upper right corner of a region. If the cardinality is one, the marker may be omitted. The initial state of *player* is *free* (running freely) with the following behavior. The player moves to an optimal position related to $\mathbf{POG}$, $\mathbf{PO}$ and $\mathbf{pT}$ (state *walk*). If he is in an optimal position, he waits for the ball passed from the teammate (state *stand*). Otherwise he moves on. If the player is closer to the ball than his teammate, his state is changing from *free* to *gotoBall*. The flow condition inside *gotoBall* is modeling the movement of the player to reach the ball position. If his teammate gets closer to the ball, the player will fall back to the state *free*. Otherwise, if his distance to the ball becomes less than DHB, his state changes to *gotoWithBall*. Inside *gotoWithBall*, the following behavior is modeled. The player dribbles the ball to an optimal position related to $\mathbf{PO}$, $\mathbf{pT}$ and the center in front of the opponent goal (state *walk*). If he is in an optimal position, he waits (state *stand*) with the ball to pass to the teammate or to kick to the goal, otherwise he moves on. There are 3 transitions out of *gotoWithBall*. If the distance to the ball becomes greater than DHB, the player loses the ball (state *lostBall*) and changes further to *free*. If $\mathbf{p}$, $\mathbf{PO}$ and $\mathbf{pT}$ are optimal for a pass, the player will kick the ball to his teammate (state *kickToTeamMate*) and changes to free. If $\mathbf{p}$ and $\mathbf{PO}$ are optimal in front of the opponent goal, the player will kick the ball to the opponent goal (state *kickToGoal*) and afterwards he changes to free. The flow conditions of the last 3 states are omitted for a better clarity of the figure.

In this example, coordination is really important. Here, in contrast to simple synchronization mechanisms, coordination may take some time. The time between deciding to

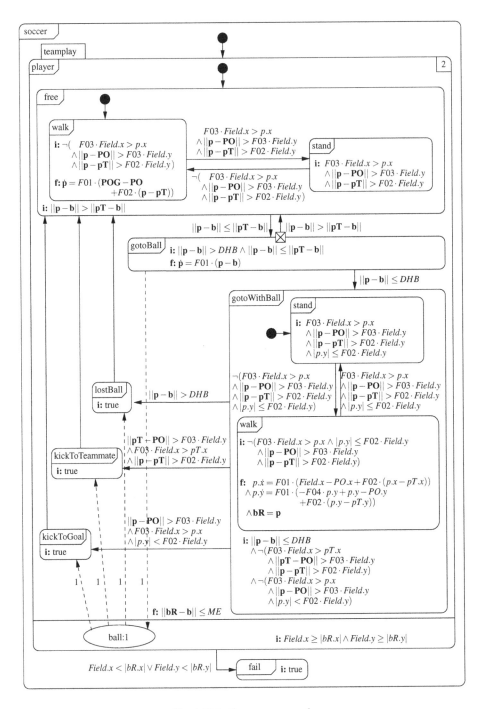

Fig. 4. Robotic soccer example

go to the ball and actually reaching it will almost always be greater than zero. Thus, we must be able to distinguish between the allocation and the occupation of a resource (e.g. the ball) in our specification formalism. In addition, since coordination may take some time, we associate the new synchronization method with states and not with transitions. All this is comprised in the concept of *timed synchronization* introduced next.

3.2   Timed Synchronization

Usually the so-called *synchrony hypothesis* is adopted for state machines, assuming that the system is infinitely faster than the environment and thus the response to an external stimulus (event) is always generated in the same step that the stimulus is introduced. However in practice, synchronization and coordination of actions cannot be done in zero time. In UML 1.5 [12], synchronization is present, but assumed to take zero time. In UML 2.0 [13] there does not seem to be a special synchronization mechanism available any longer except by join and fork transitions. Hence, it seems to be really worthwhile considering synchronization and coordination in more detail, because it is needed for multiagent systems. For this, we will introduce synchronization points which are associated with states, i.e. activities that last a certain time, and not with transitions (as in UML 1.5), because the transition from one state to another takes zero time according to the synchrony hypothesis.

Definition 5 (synchronization points). *A synchronization point (represented as oval) allows the coordinated treatment of common resources. It can be identified by special synchronization variables $x \in X_{synch} \subseteq X$ with a given maximal capacity $C(x) > 0$. Each such point may be connected with several states. We distinguish two relations: $R_+ \subseteq S \times X_{synch}$ and $R_- \subseteq X_{synch} \times S$, both represented by dashed arrows in the respective direction. Further, each connection in $R_+ \cup R_-$ is annotated with a number m with $0 < m \leq C(x)$.*

As just said, according to the previous definition, synchronization is connected to states and not to transitions as in UML 1.5. In consequence, it is now possible that synchronization may take some time as desired. The process of synchronization starts when a state s connected to a synchronization variable x is entered, and it ends only after some time when s is exited. Therefore, we distinguish the allocation of (added or subtracted) resources and their (later) actual occupation by additional variables x_+ and x_- (used during the allocation phase) in each synchronization point. Hence, for each $x \in X_{synch}$, x_+ and x_- must be added to X.

In the following, we write $\alpha^n(s)$ or $\beta^n(s)$ for the n-fold application of α or β to s, in particular, $\alpha^0(s) = \beta^0(s) = s$. Let us now have a closer look at variables. Variables $x \in X$ may be declared locally in a certain state $\gamma(x) \in S$. A variable $x \in X$ is *valid* in all states $s \in S$ with $\beta^n(s) = \gamma(x)$ for some $n \geq 0$, unless another variable with the same name overwrites it locally. All synchronization variables and their relatives are global in principle. Nevertheless, we associate synchronization points identified by the variable x with the state $\gamma(x)$ where it is declared; $\gamma(x)$ must be a concurrent state in this case. Therefore we assume, that for all states s connected to x, i.e. sR_+x or xR_-s, it must hold $\beta^n(s) = \gamma(x)$ for some $n \geq 0$, and all s' between s and $\gamma(x)$ in the state tree must be composite states.

Definition 6 (transition types). *Let x be a synchronization variable introduced at $\gamma(x)$ and s be a state connected with x. Then, $s_1 T s_2$ is called* incoming transition *for s iff $\alpha^n(s_2) = s$ for some $n \geq 0$. It is called* initializing, *if it is an incoming transition with $\alpha^n(s_2) = \gamma(x)$ for some $n \geq 0$. $s_1 T s_2$ is called an* outgoing transition *for s iff $s_1 = \beta^n(s)$ for some $n \geq 0$, where s_1 occurs in the actual configuration tree and x is valid in s. It is called* successful, *if it is an outgoing transition with $s = s_1$ and not marked with a crossed box $\boxtimes$; otherwise, it is called* failed.

Note that outgoing transitions cannot be characterized statically by the state hierarchy, but by the actual configuration tree. For the ease of presentation, we assume that there is a special *start transition* leading to s_0, annotated with a given *initial condition* of the whole state machine. For this, an artificial new start state may be introduced.

Definition 7 (synchronization constraints). *Synchronization points impose additional constraints to the transitions that are incident with states s, the synchronization variables x are connected to.*

1. *If sR_+x with annotation m, then*
   (a) *$x + x_+ + m \leq C(x)$ and $x'_+ = x_+ + m$ are added to all not initializing incoming transitions,*
   (b) *$x' = 0, x'_+ = 0, x'_- = 0$ are added to all initializing incoming transitions,*
   (c) *$x'_+ = x_+ - m$ is added to all outgoing transitions, and*
   (d) *$x' = x + m$ is added to all successful outgoing transitions supplementarily.*
2. *If xR_-s with annotation m, then*
   (a) *$x - (x_- + m) \geq 0$ and $x'_- = x_- + m$ are added to all not initializing incoming transitions,*
   (b) *$x' = 0, x'_+ = 0, x'_- = 0$ are added to all initializing incoming transitions,*
   (c) *$x'_- = x_- - m$ is added to all outgoing transitions, and*
   (d) *$x' = x - m$ is added to all successful outgoing transitions supplementarily.*

In Fig. 4, coordination is achieved by the synchronization variable *ball*. It has capacity 1, because obviously there is only one ball in a soccer game, and it is introduced in the concurrent state *teamplay*, i.e. $\gamma(ball) = teamplay$. The *gotoBall* state is positively connected to it, while the states *kickToGoal*, *kickToTeammate*, and *lostBall* are negatively connected to it. This means, that the ball resource is allocated during the *gotoBall* activity and deallocated after a kick. Concerning the *gotoBall* state, the transition annotated with $\|\mathbf{p} - \mathbf{b}\| \leq \|\mathbf{pT} - \mathbf{b}\|$ is an incoming transition. The transition marked with $\|\mathbf{p} - \mathbf{b}\| \leq DHB$ is successfully outgoing, while the transition marked with a crossed box is failed. Since the state *gotoBall* directly belongs to the region *player*, there are no other (indirect) incoming or outgoing transitions.

The method of timed synchronization is also applicable for the implementation of a commitment-strategy in BDI-agents [15]. There, parallel (partial) plans could be coordinated with a synchronization variable *execution*. At first, the agent has to revise his intentions, to select executable plans. Each plan is divided in three parts (states). The agent prepares the save plan execution in the first state. In the second state, the plan to reach the (partial) goal, is executed and in the last state concluding actions are possible. The synchronization variable is allocated during the execution of the first part of a plan and deallocated after the third part. After each (partial) plan execution, the agent has to revise his intentions and the next plan can be executed.

3.3 Operation of Hybrid State Machines

The state machine starts with the *initial configuration*, that is the completed topmost initial state of the overall state machine. In addition, an initial condition must be given, that is a predicate with free variables from $X \cup \dot{X}$. The current *situation* of the multiagent system can be characterized by a pair (c, v) where c is a configuration and v is a valuation, i.e. a mapping $v : X \cup \dot{X} \to \mathbb{R}$. The *initial situation* at time $t = 0$ is a situation (c, v) where c is the initial configuration and v satisfies the initial condition.

The behavior of a hybrid state machine can now be described by continuous and discrete state changes. Let (c, v) be the current situation, and $S(c)$ be the set of states occurring in the configuration tree c. As long as the conjunction of the invariants of all $s \in S(c)$ hold, the multiagent system evolves according to the conjunction of the flow conditions associated with all states $s \in S(c)$; we call this *continuous change*. Whenever after some time τ (chosen minimally) the invariants of one or more states do not hold any longer, then a discrete state change takes place, called micro-step:

Definition 8 (micro-step). *A micro-step from one configuration c of a state machine to a configuration c' by means of a transition sTs' with some jump condition in the current situation (written c → c') is possible iff:*

1. *c contains a node labeled with s whose invariant does not hold any longer,*
2. *the jump condition of the given transition holds in the actual situation (c, v),*
3. *c' is identical with c except that s together with its subtree in c is replaced by the completion of s', and*
4. *the variables in X' are set according to the jump condition.*

We assume, that hybrid state machines are deterministic automata, i.e., for each state s, the jump conditions of all transitions leaving s cannot hold at the same time. Nevertheless it might happen, that after some time τ several invariants become false simultaneously, then several micro-steps are performed in parallel for all respective states (called *macro-step* then). Conflicts may arise, if invariants of states on one and the same path in the configuration tree are involved. In this case, outer transitions are preferred over inner ones. The advantage of this procedure is that the agents are more reactive. In UML statecharts inner transitions have priority over outer transitions, while this is the other way round in [5]. State transitions are triggered by the invariants.

The pure state machine for discrete changes can easily be implemented in the declarative programming language Prolog [3]. Fig. 5 shows a meta-program realizing the state machine in Prolog. It mimics micro- and macro-steps in the predicate `step` and completion according to Def. 4 in the predicate `complete`. Configurations are encoded in Prolog lists, where the head of a list corresponds to the root of the respective configuration tree. The initial, completed configuration for the example in Fig. 1 e.g. can thus be represented as

`[firebrigadeagent,[firebrigademain,[idle]],[firebrigaderss,[listen]]].`

```
%%% step(+Config,-Next)
%%% perform transitions to next configuration
step([State|_],Tree) :-
        trans(State,Next), !,
        complete(Next,Tree).
step([Top|Sub],[Top|Tree]) :-
        maplist(step,Sub,Tree).
step([],[]).


%%% complete(+State,-Tree)
%%% build completed Tree below State
complete(State,[State|Complete]) :-
        init(State,Init),
        maplist(complete,Init,Complete).
```

Fig. 5. State machine in Prolog for discrete state changes

The Prolog code for the concrete specification (shown in Fig. 6) contains the fact start denoting the state s_0 and facts for the initial states (predicate init). The latter predicate is also used for simple states (in this case, the list of initial states is empty) and concurrent states (then this list contains more than one state, one for each region). The predicate trans realizes the transitions; it contains the jump conditions and actions of the respective transition in the body. This Prolog implementation technique has been applied successfully in the RoboCup 2D soccer simulation league (see [17, Appendix B]).

```
start(firebrigadeagent).

init(firebrigadeagent,[firebrigademain,firebrigaderss]).
init(firebrigademain,[idle]).
init(idle,[]).
init(move2fire,[]).
init(extinguish,[]).
init(move2supply,[]).
init(refill,[]).
init(firebrigaderss,[listen]).
init(listen,[]).
[...]
trans(move2supply,refill) :-
        set(m2stime,0).
[...]
```

Fig. 6. State hierarchy in Prolog for the example in Fig. 1

```
1  automaton Civilian
2    synclabs: help;
3    initially injured & w = -10;
4    loc injured:
5      while w<=0 wait {}
6      when w=0 sync help do {w' = -10} goto injured;
7  end

8  init_reach := reach forward from init endreach;
9  ext_error := loc[FirebrigadeMain] = extinguish & wLevel < 0;
10 if not empty(init_reach & ext_error)
11   then prints "Error: Tank empty!";
12 endif;
```

Fig. 7. Excerpt from the HYTECH code formalizing Fig. 2. Lines 1–7 model the civilian (sub-)automaton. Some analysis commands are shown in ll. 8–12.

4   Model Checking

As we already mentioned, hybrid automata are equipped with a formal semantics, which makes it possible to apply formal methods in order to prove certain properties of the specified systems, e.g. by model checking. However, in the context of hybrid automata the term *model checking* usually refers to *reachability* testing, i.e. the question whether some (unwanted) state is reachable from the initial configuration of the specified system. To this end, all states that can be reached by a discrete transition or evolving the continuous variables according to a flow condition are repeatedly added to the current configuration until a fixpoint R is reached. Then it can be tested, if unwanted states are reachable simply by intersecting the sets of reachable and unwanted states. However, for *rectangular* hybrid automata, a subclass of linear automata, even LTL model checking is decidable [8].

4.1   Examples with Standard Model Checkers

For the behavior specification shown in Figs. 1 and 2 we conducted several experiments with the standard model checkers HYTECH [7] and PHAVer [4]. Both model checkers are implemented for the analysis of linear hybrid automata. They take textual representations of hybrid automata like the one in Fig. 7 as input and perform reachability tests on the state space of the resulting product automaton. This is usually done by first computing all states reachable from the initial configuration, and then checking the resulting set for the needed properties. In the remainder of this section, we present some exemplary model checking tasks for the rescue scenario.

Is it possible to extinguish the fire? When the state of the automaton modeling the fire changes from *no fire* to *burning*, the variable *neededw* stores the amount of water needed for putting out the fire (*neededw* = 120 in the beginning). When the fire is put out, i.e. *neededw* = 0, the automaton enters the state *put out*. Thus the fire can be extinguished, iff there is a reachable configuration c_{out} where fire is in the state *put out*. It is easy to see from the specification, that this is indeed the case, as *neededw* is only decreased after the initial setting, and so the transition from *burning* to *put out* is eventually forced.

With the help of HYTECH's trace generation ability it is quite easy to solve the additional task of comparing different strategies, e.g. for refilling the water tanks. To this end, traces to c_{out} generated using the different strategies are compared. A shorter trace (w.r.t. time units, *not* discrete transitions) corresponds to a faster solving of the extinguishing task.

Does the agent try to extinguish with an empty water tank? The fact that the fire-brigade agent tries to put out the fire without water corresponds to the simple state *extinguish* being active while *wLevel* < 0. Note that we must not test for *wLevel* ≤ 0, because the state *extinguish* is only left when the water level is zero, so including a check for equality leads to false results.

Figure 7 shows how to check this property with HYTECH. The set of reachable states is collected in the variable `init_reach` (l. 8), and `ext_error` is assigned the set of illegal states (l. 9), i.e. all states where extinguish is active and the water level is below zero. Lines 10–12 finally show the actual test. If the intersection of reachable and illegal states in not empty (l. 10), an error message is printed (l. 11).

Does the agent report all discovered civilians? This question contains two properties to be checked:

(a) all discovered civilians are reported eventually, and
(b) the agent does not report more civilians than he found.

The discovery of a civilian is modeled by increasing the value of the variable *civ* by one. For each reported civilian one is subtracted from *civ*. From this it follows, that (b) holds, iff no configuration is reachable, where *civ* < 0. To show (a), one has to ensure that from all configurations with *civ* > 0 a configuration with *civ* $= 0$ will be reached eventually. Testing these properties with HYTECH reveals that (b) holds in the specification, i.e. for all reachable states *civ* ≥ 0.

However, the analysis also yields that (a) does not hold. As we stated earlier the fire fighter agent should report civilans when he is in the *idle* state. But as the invariant in this state (true) is never violated, the agent is not forced to take the self transition labeled reported, which corresponds to reporting a civilian. Thus, there is a legal run of the system, where no civilian is reported at all.

Concerning the robotic soccer example (Fig. 4), there are several questions, which can be answered with or without model checking. First of all, it is clear that because of the synchronization variable *ball* at most one agent will go to the ball. This can be seen by a careful inspection of the specification. However, the question whether always at least one agent goes to the ball, cannot be answered that easily. Therefore this is worthwhile to be model checked.

4.2   Effective Transformation of Multiagent Specifications

The original hybrid automata allow neither hierarchies nor concurrency. Hence, in order to be able to use standard hybrid model checkers, hierarchical hybrid automata as stated in this paper have to be flattened. For this, as states of the simple (flat) hybrid automaton we take the configurations c with invariants and flow conditions taken as the conjunction of the respective conditions in the states in $S(c)$. Thus, we define $flow(c) = \bigwedge_{s \in S(c)} flow(s)$ and $invariant(c) = \bigwedge_{s \in S(c)} invariant(s)$, respectively, for each configuration c. The transitions between configurations of the flat automaton can be defined as follows: there is a transition between c and c' iff a micro- or macro-step is possible. This means, there exist one or more transitions $s_1 T s_1', \dots, s_m T s_m'$ for $m \geq 1$ in the original automaton, annotated with the jump conditions $jump_1, \dots, jump_m$, respectively, such that $c \to c'$. Then, we simply annotate the transition from c to c' in the flat automaton with the conjunction $jump_1 \wedge \cdots \wedge jump_m$.

A problem during the transformation process is that some of the constraints, e.g. invariants, lead to heavily non-linear (in)equations, e.g. $\|\mathbf{p} - \mathbf{b}\| \geq DHB$. This cannot be dealt with standard model checkers for at least two reasons: they can neither deal practically nor even theoretically with them because of the appalling computational complexity. Therefore, the above-stated condition has to be reformulated. The Euclidean distance can be approximated by the Manhattan distance: $|p.x - b.x| + |p.y - b.y| \geq DHB$.

It should be remarked that synchronization points help us to reduce complexity. In order to see this, let us consider a multiple composite state with cardinality m containing k (simple) states. One of them, say s, is connected to a synchronization point with capacity C. Then there are in principle k^m different configurations, i.e. exponentially many. Since at most C agents can be in s, only $\sum_{l=0}^{C} \binom{m}{l}(k-1)^{m-l}$ configurations have to be considered. This is polynomial for $k = 2$. A naïve flattening of the example in Fig. 4 e.g. leads to $8 \cdot 8 + 1 = 65$ configurations, whereas taking synchronization into account leads to only $2 \cdot 2 + 2 \cdot 2 \cdot 6 + 1 = 29$ configuration states.

A translator that automatically converts hybrid hierarchical statecharts into simple flat hybrid automata has been implemented [2,16] (see `fstolzenburg.hs-harz.de/robocup/publications/`). This tool allows the text-based input of hybrid hierarchical automata specifications of multi-agent systems with synchronization, based on the procedure proposed in this paper. By means of different plug-ins, the translation into flat automata is performed, leading to executable code for Sony Aibo robot dogs on the one hand and code in PHAVer syntax for model checking tasks on the other hand. The former plug-in has been successfully applied in the RoboCup four-legged league within the team Harzer Rollers (see [16] and `robocup.hs-harz.de` for details).

5   Conclusions

In this paper, we demonstrated the use of hybrid hierarchical state machines for the specification of multiagent systems. We presented two application scenarios from the RoboCup, one from the rescue simulation and one from robotic soccer, and we demonstrated that state-of-the-art model checkers for hybrid automata can be used for proving properties of the specified systems. We exemplified this especially with an example from the RoboCup rescue scenario. The proposed method of treating synchronization avoids the state explosion problem to a certain extent, however, the growth of the number is still exponential. Model checking, i.e. reachability analysis helps us finding out possible paths, which could help in the pre-computation of multiagent system implementations. This point will be subject of future work.

References

1. Arai, T., Stolzenburg, F.: Multiagent systems specification by UML statecharts aiming at intelligent manufacturing. In: Proceedings of 1st International Joint Conference on Autonomous Agents & Multi-Agent Systems, pp. 11–18. ACM Press, New York (2002)
2. Bernstein, T., et al.: HAL – hybrid automaton language. Team project description (in German), Department of Automation and Computer Sciences, Hochschule Harz (2006)
3. Clocksin, W.F., Mellish, C.S.: Programming in Prolog, 4th edn. Springer, Berlin (1994)
4. Frehse, G.: PHAVer: Algorithmic verification of hybrid systems past HyTech. In: Morari, M., Thiele, L. (eds.) HSCC 2005. LNCS, vol. 3414, pp. 258–273. Springer, Heidelberg (2005)
5. Harel, D., Naamad, A.: The STATEMATE semantics of statecharts. ACM Transactions on Software Engineering and Methodology 5(4), 293–333 (1996)
6. Henzinger, T.: The theory of hybrid automata. In: Proceedings of the 11th Annual Symposium on Logic in Computer Science, pp. 278–292. IEEE Computer Society Press, Los Alamitos (1996)
7. Henzinger, T.A., Ho, P.-H., Wong-Toi, H.: HyTech: The Next Generation. In: IEEE Real-Time Systems Symposium, pp. 56–65 (1995)
8. Henzinger, T.A., Majumdar, R.: Symbolic model checking for rectangular hybrid systems. In: Tools and Algorithms for Construction and Analysis of Systems, pp. 142–156 (2000)
9. Murray, J.: Specifying agent behaviors with UML statecharts and StatEdit. In: Polani, D., Browning, B., Bonarini, A., Yoshida, K. (eds.) RoboCup 2003. LNCS (LNAI), vol. 3020, Springer, Heidelberg (2004)
10. Murray, J., Stolzenburg, F.: Hybrid state machines with timed synchronization for multi-robot system specification. In: Bento, C., et al. (eds.) Proceedings of 12th Portuguese Conference on Artificial Intelligence, pp. 236–241. IEEE Inc, Los Alamitos (2005)
11. Murray, J., Stolzenburg, F., Arai, T.: Hybrid state machines with timed synchronization for multi-robot system specification. KI 3/06, 45–50 (2006)
12. Object Management Group, Inc. UML Specification, Version 1.5 (March 2003)
13. Object Management Group, Inc. UML 2.0 Superstructure Specification (October 2004)
14. Pnueli, A., Shalev, M.: What is in a step: On the semantics of statecharts. In: Ito, T., Meyer, A.R. (eds.) TACS 1991. LNCS, vol. 526, pp. 244–264. Springer, Heidelberg (1991)
15. Rao, A.S., Georgeff, M.P.: BDI-agents: from theory to practice. In: Proceedings of the First Intl. Conference on Multiagent Systems, San Francisco (1995)
16. Ruh, F.: A translator for cooperative strategies of mobile agents for four-legged robots. Master thesis, Dept. of Automation and Computer Sciences, Hochschule Harz (2007)
17. Stolzenburg, F.: Multiagent systems and RoboCup: Specification, analysis, and theoretical results. Habilitation, Universität Koblenz-Landau, Koblenz, Reviewers: Armin Cremers, Ulrich Furbach, and Klaus Troitzsch (2005)
18. Stolzenburg, F., Arai, T.: From the specification of multiagent systems by statecharts to their formal analysis by model checking: Towards safety-critical applications. In: Schillo, M., Klusch, M., Müller, J., Tianfield, H. (eds.) MATES 2003. LNCS (LNAI), vol. 2831, pp. 131–143. Springer, Heidelberg (2003)
19. Tadokoro, S., et al.: The RoboCup-Rescue project: A robotic approach to the disaster mitigation problem. In: Proceedings of IEEE International Conference on Robotics and Automation (ICRA 2000), pp. 4089–4104 (2000)

Agent Contest Competition:
3rd Edition

Mehdi Dastani[1], Jürgen Dix[2], and Peter Novák[2]

[1]Utrecht University
P.O.Box 80.089, 3508 TB Utrecht, The Netherlands
mehdi@cs.uu.nl
[2]Clausthal University of Technology
Julius-Albert-Str. 4, 38678 Clausthal-Zellerfeld, Germany
{dix,peter.novak}@tu-clausthal.de

Abstract. This paper summarises the Agent Contest 2007 which was organized in association with ProMAS'07. The aim of this contest is to stimulate research in the area of multi-agent systems by identifying key problems and collecting suitable benchmarks that can serve as milestones for evaluating new tools, models, and techniques to develop multi-agent systems. The first two editions of this contest were organized in association with CLIMA conference series. Based on the experiences from the previous two editions ([8,9]), the contest scenario has been slightly extended to test the participating multi-agent systems on their abilities to *coordinate*, *cooperate*, and their *team work* and *team strategy* issues in a dynamic environment where teams compete for the same resources. Six groups from Germany, Brazil, England, Australia and The Netherlands did participate in this contest. The actual contest took place prior to the ProMAS'07 workshop and the winner, a group from the technical university of Berlin, was announced during ProMAS'07.

1 Introduction

Multi-agent systems are beginning to play an important role in today's software development. In the field of agent-oriented software engineering, various multi-agent system development methodologies have been proposed. Each methodology focuses on specific stages of the multi-agent system development. For example, Gaia [12] and Prometheus [10] focus on the specification and design stages assuming that other stages such as requirement and implementation are similar to corresponding stages of other software development paradigms. Therefore, software developers using Gaia and Prometheus propose models to specify and design multi-agent systems, while ignoring the implementation models.

Moreover, there is a growing number of agent-oriented programming languages and development platforms that are proposed to facilitate the implementation of multi-agent systems. These programming languages and platforms introduce programming constructs that can facilitate efficient and effective implementation and execution of multi-agent systems. The development of multi-agent systems

M. Dastani et al.(Eds.): ProMAS 2007, LNAI 4908, pp. 221 240, 2008.
© Springer-Verlag Berlin Heidelberg 2008

requires efficient and effective solutions for different problems which can be divided into three classes: 1) the problems related to the development of individual agents, 2) the problems related to the development of coordination and cooperation mechanisms to manage the interactions between individual agents, and 3) the problems related to the development of the shared environment in which agents perform their actions.

Typical problems related to individual agents are how to specify, design and implement issues such as *autonomy, pro-active/reactive behaviour, perception and update of information, reasoning and deliberation,* and *planning.* Typical problems related to the interaction of individual agents are how to specify, design and implement issues such as *communication, coordination, cooperation* and *negotiation.* Finally, typical problems related to the development of their environment are how to specify, design and implement issues such as *resources and services,* agents' access to *resources,* active and passive *sensing* of the environment, and realizing the *effects of actions.*

This competition is an attempt to stimulate research in the area of multi-agent systems by

1. *identifying key problems in developing multi-agent systems, and*
2. *evaluating state-of-the-art tools, models, and techniques in the field of multi-agent systems.*

While there already exist several competitions in various areas of artificial intelligence (theorem proving, planning, Robo-Cup, etc.) and, lately, also in specialized areas in agent systems (Trading Agent Competition (TAC) [1] and AgentCities competitions [2]), the emphasis of this contest is on the use of existing tools, models, and techniques that are proposed to develop multi-agent systems ([3,7,4]. In particular, we aim at evaluating existing approaches for the development of multi-agent systems where individual agents has to cooperate with each other to solve a task. In this respect, issues such as team working, team strategy, interaction with dynamic environment, modeling the environment, limited perception, uncertain action effects, reasoning and planning, and learning are essential.

The previous editions of this contest were organized in cooperation with CLIMA workshop series. The scenario from this year can be seen as an extension of the scenario from the CLIMA VII Contest 2006. The main differences include:

- perception now includes also the information about the number of gold items an agent carries,
- number of agents per team is 6, instead of 4 last year,
- agents can push each other,
- agents can collect and carry more gold items,
- each agent has to connect to the server from a separate IP address (this requirement might be a subject of change).

We believe that these extensions lead to a greater competitiveness of the scenario (the fun factor should not be underestimated) and put the participating multi-agent systems under a test w.r.t. coordination and cooperation issues in an environment where teams compete for the same resources.

2 Scenario Description

The competition task consisted of developing a multi-agent system to solve a cooperative task in a dynamically changing environment. The environment of the multi-agent system was a grid-like world where agents could move from one cell to a neighbouring cell. In this environment, gold could appear in the cells. Participating agent teams were expected to explore the environment, avoid obstacles and compete with another agent team for the gold. The agents of each team could coordinate their actions in order to collect as much gold as they could and to deliver it to the depot where the gold can be safely stored. Agents had only a local view on their environment, their perceptions could be incomplete, and their actions could fail. The agents were able to play different roles (such as explorer or collector), communicate and cooperate in order to find and collect gold in an efficient and effective way.

The idea was to divide participating agent teams randomly into groups before the tournament started. Each team from one group should then compete against all other teams in the same group in a series of matches. The winners from these groups should form a new group and each team in a new group should play against each other again. In the case of few participating teams, we had planned to form only one single group consisting of all teams. Because of the number of participants, we decided to form only one group for this edition of the agent contest. Each team competed against all other teams in a series of matches. Each match between two competing teams consisted of five simulations. A simulation between two teams was a competition between them with respect to a certain starting configuration of the environment. Winning a simulation yielded three points for the team, a draw was worth one point and a loss resulted in zero points. The winner of the whole tournament was evaluated on the basis of the overall number of collected points in the matches during the tournament. In the case of equal number of points, the winner should be decided on the basis of the absolute number of collected gold items. Details on the number of simulations per match and the exact structure of the competition was published prior to the Contest on the official Agent Contest 2007 website at `http://cig.in.tu-clausthal.de/AgentContest2007/`.

2.1 Technical Description of the Scenario

In the contest, the agents from each participating team were executed locally (on the participant's hardware) while the simulated environment, in which all agents from competing teams performed actions, was run on the remote contest simulation server run by the contest organizers. The interaction/communication between agents from one team were managed locally, but the interaction between individual agents and their environment (run on the simulation server) took place via Internet. Participating agents were connected to the simulation server that did provide the information about the environment. Each agent from each team connected to and communicated with the simulation server using TCP protocol and messages in XML format.

During the initial phase[1] agents from all competing teams connected to the simulation server, identified and authenticated themselves and got general match information. Each agent had to connect to the simulation server from a separate IP address. Teams not obeying this rule would have been disqualified and disconnected from the simulation server during the tournament. At the announced start time of the tournament, the simulation server was on-line and the agents from participating teams were able to connect to it. After a successful initial handshake during which agents identified themselves by their IDs and received acknowledgment from the server, they waited for the simulation start. The initial connecting phase took a reasonable amount of time in order to allow agents to be initialised and connected (15 minutes).

The simulation server controlled the competition by selecting the competing teams and managing the matches and simulations. In each simulation, the simulation server, in a cyclic fashion, provided sensory information about the environment to the participating agents and expected their reactions within a given time limit. Each agent reacted to the received sensory information by indicating which action (including the skip action) it wants to perform in the environment. If no reaction was received from the agent within the given time limit, the simulation server assumed that the agent performed the *skip* action. Agents had only a local view on their environment, their perceptions could be incomplete, and their actions could fail. After a finite number of steps the simulation server stopped the cycle and participating agents received a notification about the end of a simulation. Then the server started a new simulation possibly involving the same teams.

2.2 Team, Match, and Simulation

An agent team consisted of six software agents with distinct IDs. There were no restrictions on the implementation of agents, although we encouraged the use of approaches based on the state-of-the-art tools, methodologies and languages for programming agents and multi-agent systems, as well as the use of computational logic based approaches. The tournament consisted of a number of matches. A match was a sequence of simulations during which two teams of agents competed in several different settings of the environment. For each match, the server 1) picked two teams to play it and, subsequently, 2) started the first simulation of the match. Each simulation in a match started by notifying the agents from the participating teams and sending them the details of the simulation. These included for example the size of the grid, the depot position, the number of steps the simulation will perform, etc. A simulation consisted of a number of simulation

---

[1] The contest organizers contacted participants before the actual tournament and provided them the IDs necessary for identification of their agents for the tournament.

steps. Each step consisted of 1) sending a sensory information to agents (one or more) and 2) waiting for their actions. In the case that an agent did not respond within a timeout (specified at the beginning of the simulation) by a valid action, it was considered to perform the skip action in the given simulation step.

2.3 Environment Objects

The (simulated) environment was a rectangular grid consisting of cells. The size of the grid was specified at the start of each simulation and was variable. However, it was always at most 100x100 cells. The [0,0] coordinate of the grid was in the top-left corner (north-west). The simulated environment contained one depot, which served for both teams as a location of delivery of gold items. The environment did contain the following objects in its cells:

- an obstacle (a cell with an obstacle cannot be visited by an agent),
- gold (an item which can be picked from a cell) agent,
- an agent,
- the depot (a cell to which gold items are to be delivered in order to earn a point in a simulation),
- a marker (a string data with a maximum of 5 characters which can be read/written/rewritten/removed by an agent).

There could be only one object in a cell, except that an agent could enter cells containing gold, depot or mark. A gold item could be in a marked cell visited by an agent. At the beginning of a simulation the grid contained obstacles, gold items and agents of both teams. Distribution of obstacles, gold items and initial positions of agents was either hand crafted for the particular scenario, or completely random. During the simulation, gold items were appearing randomly in empty cells of the grid. The frequency and probability of gold generation was simulation specific, however not known to neither agents, nor participants. At the start of each simulation agents got the details of the environment (grid size, depot position, etc.). Agents also received information about their initial position in the perception information of the first simulation step.

Perception. Agents were located in the grid and the simulation server provided each agent with the following information:

- the absolute position of the agent in the grid,
- the content of the cells surrounding the agent and the content of the cell in which the agent currently stands in (9 cells in total),
- the number of gold items the agent currently holds.

If two agents were standing in each other's field of view, they were able to recognize whether they are enemies, or whether they belong to the same team. However an agent was not able to recognise whether the other agent carries a gold item or not. If there was a mark in a cell, within the agent's field of view, the agent also received the information about its content.

Actions. Agents were allowed to perform one action in a simulation step. The following actions were allowed:

- **skip:** The execution of the skip action had no influence on the local state of the environment around the agent (under the assumption that other agents did not change it). When an agent did not respond to a perception information provided by the simulation server within the given time limit, the agent was considered as performing the skip action.
- **movements (right, up, left, down):** An agent could move in four directions in the grid. These movement actions were specified as follows. The execution of move actions up, down, left and right changes the position of the agent one cell to the up, down, left, and right, respectively. A movement action succeeds only when the cell to which an agent is about to move does not contain an obstacle. In the case two agents stand in adjacent cells and one of them tries to step into the cell the second agent stands in while the second agent performs e.g. skip action, the second agent can be pushed away. The resulting local change of the environment amounts to the same situation as if the pushed agent performed a move action in the same direction as the pushing agent. The same constraints as for regular move actions apply, i.e. there cannot be another obstacle, or an agent standing in the way of the pushed agent. Only one agent can be pushed in one move. In the case both agents standing in the adjacent cells try to push each other, one of them will be randomly determined (with probability of 50%) as the pushing and the other as the pushed agent. A detailed specification of the action execution algorithm later in this paper describes further details of push action and its consequences. Moving to and from the depot cell were regulated by additional rules described later in this description.
- **pick, drop:** An agent could carry up to maximum of three gold items which it successfully picked up before. An agent could pick up a gold item if 1) the cell in which the agent stands in contains gold, and 2) the agent carries less than 3 gold items. An agent could drop gold item it carried only into the empty cell it stood in. The result of a successful pick action is that in the next simulation step the acting agent will be considered to carry one more gold item than before performing the pick action and the cell, it stands in, will not contain the gold item any more. The result of a drop action is that the acting agent is carrying one gold item less than before performing the drop action (given that the agent was carrying at least one gold item in that simulation step) and that the cell it stands in will contain the gold item in the next simulation step. Drop action performed in the depot cell results in dropping all the gold items the agent carries at once and increases the score of the agent's team by a number of points equal to the number of gold items the agent dropped in the depot cell. The depot cell never contains a gold item that can be picked by an agent.
- **mark, unmark:** An agent was allowed to mark a cell it stood in by a string data with a maximum of 5 characters. The result of a mark action is that the cell in which an agent is located, will contain a string in the next simulation

step. The depot cell, and cells containing an obstacle cannot be marked. By marking a previously marked cell, the old mark is removed and replaced by the new one. If the cell in which an agent is located, contains a mark, then the agent receives the string in the perception information from the simulation server. An agent was allowed to unmark the marked cell it stood in. The result of an unmark action is that the cell will not contain a mark in the next simulation step. Agents do not get immediate feedback on their actions, but can learn about the effects of their actions (and the actions of other agents) from the perception information that will be sent to them in the next simulation step.

Action Execution Algorithm. After the simulation engine collected the actions that the agents chose to execute in the next simulation step (or the simulation step timeout for agent's reaction elapsed), the next state of the environment was determined as follows:

1. all the agents' impossible actions were replaced by skip actions. An impossible action is:
   - the move action when the agent tries to step into an obstacle, or out of the grid boundary, or
   - the drop action when the cell already contains gold, or
   - the pick action when there's no gold contained in the cell, or
   - the unmark action when the cell does not contain a mark;
2. the simulation engine determined actions which will fail because of Fatigue (see description below) and replaces them with a skip action;
3. for each cell not containing an agent, or an obstacle, such that there's at least one agent indicating an intention to move into it, one of these agents was selected and moved to this cell. Actions of all the other considered agents were replaced with a skip action;
4. for each agent which can be pushed by more than one pushing agent (an agent can be pushed iff it is about to perform a skip action [after applying steps 1-3], the cell it is going to be pushed into is within the grid boundary and does not contain an agent, or an obstacle), one such pushing agent was selected, and both pushed and pushing agents were moved in the direction of the move of the pushing agent;
5. all other move actions which were not executed in steps 3 and 4 were replaced by skip action;
6. all the non-move actions were executed;
7. further internal changes and calculations of the environment, like e.g. gold generation, took place.

Depot cell. Strong conditions were imposed on the depot cell:

1. an agent not carrying a gold item was unable to enter the depot cell (the result of such an action is the same as if the depot was an obstacle);
2. agent which entered the depot cell should drop the gold item as the very next action it executed;

3. after dropping the gold item in a cell, an agent had to leave the cell in the first subsequent simulation step when it was able to move (i.e. when there was an empty cell at the time of agent's move action).

If an agent did not leave the depot in the first possible opportunity, or did not drop the gold item as the very next action after entering the depot, the simulation server punished it by "teleporting" it away (it was moved to a random cell not containing another agent, or obstacle in the grid by the environment simulator).

Timeout. The agents had to inform the simulation server which action they wanted to perform within a timeout specified at the beginning of the simulation. Timeouts were set reasonably high, so that even participants with a slow network connection and complex deliberation algorithms were able to communicate with the server in an efficient way. Simulation timeouts were not lower than two seconds and higher than 10 seconds per one simulation step.

A ping interface was provided by the server in order to allow participating agents to test the speed of their connection during the initial phase of the tournament. Note, that only a limited number of ping requests were processed from one agent in a certain time interval.

Fatigue (Information Distortion/Action Failure). Agents received incomplete information about the environment from the simulation server. The simulation server could omit information about particular environment cells, however, the server never provided incorrect information. Also, agent's action could fail. In such a case the simulation server evaluated the agent's action in the simulation step as a skip action.

Both the probability of sending an agent incomplete information (P_{inf}) and the probability of agent's action failure (P_{fail}) were constant and specific for each simulation, however not higher than 20%. Moreover, both probabilities increase in a linear fashion with respect to the number of gold items currently carried by the agent up to at most 50%. The equation regulating this relation was as follows:

$$p = P_{sim} + \frac{P_{max} - P_{sim}}{N_{itMax}} \times N_{it}$$

Here, P stands for the actual probability of action failure, or information distortion w.r.t. number of items the agent currently carries, P_{sim} is the probability of action failure/information distortion set as default for the current simulation (it is equal to the corresponding probability when agent does not carry a gold item). P_{max} and N_{itMax} are the maximal value of failure/information distortion probability (at most 50%) and maximal number of gold items the agent is allowed to carry (3 as specified above) respectively. These values, together with P_{sim} (at most 20%) are parameters of each current simulation. Finally N_{it} stands for the number of gold items the agent currently carries.

Below we list examples of two simulation settings together with tables of resulting probabilities for agent carrying 0, 1, 2 and 3 gold items:

$$P_{sim} = 10\% \quad P_{sim} = 5\%$$
$$P_{max} = 50\% \quad P_{max} = 40\%$$
$$N_{itMax} = 3 \quad N_{itMax} = 3$$

N_{it} - P	N_{it} - P
0 - 10.0%	0 - 5.0%
1 - 23.3%	1 - 16.6%
2 - 36.6%	2 - 28.3%
3 - 50.0%	3 - 40.0%

Simulation parameters P_{sim}, P_{max} are not known neither to agent team designers, nor to the agents during the simulation. As already mentioned above, N_{itMax} is a constant set to 3 for all simulations in the tournament.

Final Phase. In the final phase, the simulation server sent a message to each agent allowing them to disconnect from the server. By this, the tournament was over.

2.4   General Agent-2-Server Communication Principles

In this contest, the agents from each participating team were executed locally (on the participant's hardware) while the simulated environment, in which all agents from competing teams performed actions, was run on the remote contest simulation server. Agents communicated with the contest server using standard TCP/IP stack with socket session interface. The Internet coordinates (IP address and port) of the contest server (and a dedicated test server) were announced later via the official Contest mailing list. Agents communicated with the server by exchanging XML messages. Messages were well-formed XML documents, described later in this document. We recommended using standard XML parsers available for many programming languages for generation and processing of these XML messages.

Communication Protocol. The tournament consisted of a number of matches. A match is a sequence of simulations during which two teams of agents compete in several different settings of the environment. However, from the agent's point of view, the tournament consisted of a number of simulations in different environment settings and against different opponents.

The tournament was divided into three phases. During the initial phase, agents connected to the simulation server and identified themselves by username and password (AUTH-REQUEST message). Credentials for each agent were distributed in advance via e-mail. As a response, agents received the result of their authentication request (AUTH-RESPONSE message) which either succeeded, or failed. After successful authentication, agents waited until the first simulation of the tournament started.

At the beginning of each simulation, agents of the two participating teams were notified (SIM-START message) and received simulation specific information: simulation ID, opponent's ID, grid size, number of steps the simulation will last and the depot position.

In each simulation step an agent received a perception about its environment (REQUEST-ACTION message) and it responded by performing an action (ACTION message). Each request-action message contained information about nine neighboring cells around the agent (including the one agent stands on), its absolute position in the grid, simulation step number, number of gold items the agent carries and deadline for its response. The agent had to answer within the given deadline. The action message contained the identifier of the action, agent wants to perform, and action parameters, if required.

When the simulation was finished, participating agents received the notification about it (SIM-END message) which included the information about the number of gold items collected by the team agent belongs to and the information about the result of the simulation (whether the team won, or lost the simulation).

All agents which currently did not participate in a simulation had to wait until the simulation server notified them about either 1) the start of a simulation they are going to participate in, or 2) the end of the tournament.

At the end of the tournament, all agents received the notification (BYE message). Subsequently the simulation server terminated the connection to the agent.

Reconnection. When an agent lost connection to the simulation server, the tournament proceeded without disruption, only all the actions of the disconnected agent were considered to be empty (skip). Agents were responsible for maintaining the connection to the simulation server and in a case of connection disruption, they were allowed to reconnect.

An agent reconnected by performing the same sequence of steps as at the beginning of the tournament. After establishing the connection to the simulation server, it sent AUTH-REQUEST message and received AUTH-RESPONSE. After successful authentication, the server sent SIM-START message to an agent. If an agent participated in a currently running simulation, the SIM-START message was delivered immediately after AUTH-RESPONSE. Otherwise an agent had to wait until the next simulation in which it participates. In the next step when the agent was picked to perform an action, it received the standard REQUEST-ACTION message containing the perception of the agent at the current simulation step and simulation proceeded in a normal mode.

Ping Interface. The simulation server provided a ping interface in order to allow agents to test their connection to the simulation server. An agent can send a PING message containing a payload data (ASCII string up to 100 characters) and it received a PONG message with the same payload. As all messages contained a timestamp (see description of the message envelope below), an agent could also use the ping interface to synchronize its local time with the server.

XML Messages Description. XML messages exchanged between server and agents were zero terminated UTF-8 strings. Each XML message exchanged between the simulation server and agent consisted of three parts:

- Standard XML header: Contains the standard XML document header
  `<?xml version="1.0" encoding="UTF-8"?>`
- Message envelope: The root element of all XML messages was `<message>`.
  It has attributes: the timestamp and a message type identifier.
- Message separator: Each message is a UTF-8 zero terminated string. Messages are separated by null byte.

Timestamp is a numeric string containing the status of the simulation server's global timer at the time of message creation. The unit of the global timer is milliseconds and it is the result of standard system call "time" on the simulation server (measuring number of milliseconds from January 1, 1970 UTC). Message type identifier was one of the following values: auth-request, auth-response, sim-start, sim-end, bye, request-action, action, ping, pong.

Messages sent from the server to an agent contained all attributes of the root element. However, the timestamp attribute could be omitted in messages sent from an agent to the server. In the case it was included, server silently ignored it.

Example of a server-2-agent message:

```
<message timestamp="1138900997331" type="request-action">
    <!-- optional data -->
</message>
```

Example of an agent-2-server message:

```
<message type="auth-request">
    <!-- optional data -->
</message>
```

According to the message type, the root element `<message>` can contain simulation specific data. These simulation data are described and explained in the official contest webpage[2]

3   Submission

The participation in this contest consisted of two parts. Participants first submitted the description of analysis, design and implementation of a multi-agent system for the above application. Existing multi-agent system methodologies such as Gaia, Prometheus or Tropos can be used to describe the system. For the description of the implementation, it should be explained how the design is implemented. This can be done by explaining, for example, which programming language, platform, tools, and techniques are used to implement the multi-agent system. These submissions are included in this volume.

---

[2] http://cig.in.tu-clausthal.de/fileadmin/user_upload/_temp_/
ac07-protocol.txt

The second part of the contest is the actual participation in the tournament by means of an (executable) implementation of a multi-agent system. The agents from each participating systems (agent teams) were executed locally (on the participant's hardware) while the simulated environment, in which all agents from competing teams perform actions, was run on the remote contest simulation server. Interaction/communication between agents from one team has been managed locally, but the interaction between individual agents and their environment (run on the simulation server) was via Internet. Participating agents connected to the simulation server that provided the information about the environment. Each agent from each team connected and communicated to the simulation server using a TCP connection.

3.1   Received Submissions

We have received seven submissions for this edition of the contest from which one withdrew just before the start of the actual contest tournament. From the received submissions, which are included in this volume, three submissions used existing multi-agent development methodologies to specify and design their multi-agent systems. Other submissions used their own developed agent platforms and corresponding customised development methodologies. The withdrawn submission intended to use GoLog, a knowledge representation language based on logic. Unfortunately, one competitor in the contest could not provide a description of their team in this volume.

The submission by J.F. Hübner and R.H. Bordini was a collaboration between Durham University, UK, and Universidade Regional de Blumenau, Brazil. Like their submission to the previous edition of this contest, they use Prometheus [10] as the multi-agent system development methodology to specify and design their multi-agent system. Using this methodology, the multi-agent system is designed by means of a system overview Diagram that describes the interaction between miner and leader agents. Miners are the agents that interact with the contest simulator and the leader helps the coordination of some activities. These agents are subsequently specified and designed in terms agent overview diagrams describing their specific knowledge, goals and plans. Their designed system is then implemented in Jason [5], which is an interpreter of an extension of the agent programming language AgentSpeak [11]. As it was required by the contest, their multi-agent system consisted of six miner agents operating in the simulated environment. These agents follow a general strategy according to which each agent is responsible for one quadrant of the grid environment. The leader helps the miners to coordinate themselves in two ways. First, it allocates miners to quadrants, and second it coordinate the negotiation process that is started when a miner sees a piece of gold and is not able to collect it (because its container is full).

The second submission that uses existing multi-agent system development methodologies to specify and design their system is by L. Astefanoaei, C.P. Mol, M.P. Sindlar, and N.A.M. Tinnemeier from Utrecht University, Netherlands. They use a combination of Tropos and Moise$^+$ methodologies. They use Tropos to specify the multi-agent system in terms of system goal and subgoals and Moise$^+$ to specify the roles the agent cap play and the interaction between roles. In their system specification, an agent can play three different roles: leader, scout, and miner. Moreover, their system can have at most one leader, and zero to six players that can play the scout or miner role. The leader communicates with the scouts and the miners. The leader coordinate the behavior of scouts and miners by means of task ordering: first the scouts explore the wilderness, then the miners can gold-enrich the team. They use the 2APL programming language and its corresponding multi-agent platform to implement and execute their multi-agent system.

The third submission is by E. Tuguldur and M. Patzlaff from the DAI-Labor, Technische Universität Berlin, Germany. They develop a multi-agent system based on microJIAC agent definition and its corresponding Maven plug-in that supports the compilation and packaging process of agents. According to this definition, an agent consists of three components: connector, perceptor, and monitor. The connector maintains the connection to the contest server, the perceptor updates the agent's world model, and the monitor which provides a graphical user interface to display the world model of the agent (mainly for debug purposes). The microJIAC is a lightweight agent architecture targeted at devices with different capabilities. Each agent can be in either explorer or transporter mode. An agent in the explorer mode aims at collecting gold items up to the maximum amount of gold items that it can carry. When an agent changes its role to transporter mode, it aims at reaching the depot to drop all gold items. After dropping its gold items the transporter agent becomes an explorer again.

The fourth submission was by A. Hessler, B. Hirsch, and J. Keiser, also from the DAI-Labor, Technische Universität Berlin, Germany. They used the JIAC IV (Java Intelligent Agent Componentware) methodology and its corresponding framework to develop their multi-agent system participating in the agent contest. The JIAC methodology is based on the JIAC meta-model that has explicit notions of goal, rule, plan, service and protocol. The JIAC development process starts with collecting, structuring and prioritising domain vocabulary and requirements. Based on the requirements with the highest priority a multi-agent system architecture is designed by listing the agents. Plans, services and protocols are then implemented and plugged into agents. The application is then evaluated and, if necessary, the cycle is started until the desired quality of the multi-agent system is achieved. In their multi-agent system implementation agents cooperate by sharing their perceptions, states, and intentions as they may go for the same unknown field or to pick the same gold items. In their approach agent communication and cooperation is fully decentralised. There is neither a message broker nor a central instance which coordinates agents. Every agent builds its own world model from what it is told by the server and the other agents. Every agent also plans for itself, taking the states and intentions of other agents into account.

The fifth system, by Sebastian Sardina and Dave Scerri, from RMIT University, Australia, was mostly designed using the Prometheus [10] multi-agent system development methodology and implemented in the JACK BDI agent-oriented programming language [6] using its JDE development environment. In this system, there are two type of agents: player agents and one coordinator agent. The player agents are the ones that are able to interact with the game simulator; whereas the coordinator agent acts as an (information) proxy among the player agents, and instructs the players on some activities. At any point in time, a player agent can play either a "collector" role or an "explorer" role. These roles are assigned by the coordinator agent. As a collector, a player agent's main objective is to collect gold pieces and bring them to the depot location. In contrast, as an explorer, the objective of a player is to gather information about unknown areas of the world, and communicate such information to the coordinator. Collector players also have a set of quantitative parameters that influence the way it would behave. For example, an "exploration attitude" parameter determines how bias a collector agent is towards exploration. In that way, a collector can be bias to explore (or to avoid exploring) unknown areas of the grid while traveling to the depot location for gold deposition. Unfortunately, the JACK system was not able to sustain its participation throughout the whole contest, as the system communication infrastructure was not sufficiently robust and, as a result, the agents would very often lose communication with the contest simulator.

The final submission is by S. Schiffel, M. Thielscher, and D. Thu Trang from Dresden University of Technology, Germany. Like their submission in the previous edition of this contest, they do not use any specific multi-agent system development methodology. Instead, they use FLUX agents to design and implement their multi-agent system. Each FLUX agent is a logic program consisting of three modules: the fundamental reasoning facilities based on the fluent calculus, the specification of the effects of actions, and the strategy. Their implemented multi-agent system consists of six agents and a leader. The leader coordinates the behaviors of other agents by helping them to share their information about the environment. The action of an agent depends on the current intentions of that agent and the current state of the world. After an agent decides on its next action it sends its new information and its current intention to the leader. The leader sends information gathered by the other agents to the agent and might request the agent to change its intentions for coordinating the agents of the team. Conflicts between agents are resolved in two ways. First, the leader assigns areas to the agents for exploration. Second, small conflicts such as when several agents try to get into the same cell, are resolved using fixed priorities of the agents.

4   Technical Infrastructure

In the third edition of this Agent Contest, we re-used the technical infrastructure we developed for the second edition. Briefly, the server's architecture consists of

1. *simulation plug-in*: A replaceable module providing the logics of the environment simulation,

2. *agent session manager*: Responsible for holding the sessions between the server and individual agents and en/de-coding of XML messages of the protocol,
3. *visualization library*: It produced the SVG records from each time frame of the simulation environment state,
4. *contest webinterface*: Providing a public view and interface to the MASSim server, and
5. MASSim core module: Managing the tournament scheme and providing the connection between the simulation plug-in, agent session manager and web-interface.

A more detailed description of the system can be found in the report on the second edition of the Agent Contest [9]. The system is published on the official Contest website: http://cig.in.tu-clausthal.de/AgentContest/.

4.1   Contest Preparation

As in previous editions, before the tournament itself, the Contest organization went through several preparatory stages. We released the communication protocol for the 2007 Contest simulation scenario in February 2nd 2007 together with a template for system description submissions. The first protocol release contained a requirement that each agent has to run from a distinct IP address, however after a discussion with potential participants, we dropped this requirement later (February 23rd). The main reason was the variety of network infrastructures on the participants' side like e.g. NAT and various other IP masquerading technologies which render this requirement not enforceable.

Shortly before the system description submission deadline on March 10th 2007, we published the first release of the testing suite on March 6th, which was later followed by a precise description of the algorithm for calculating agent movements regarding various configurations of situations when agents push each other. The testing suite contained a testing version of the MASSim server configured to run the 2007 Contest simulation, together with a simple debugging tool (MASSim Debug Monitor) and vanilla agents compatible with the Contest scenario.

The Agent Contest 2007 testing phase was launched on March 27th 2007 and ran until the very Contest tournament launch on May 2nd 2007. During this period, which lasted more than one month, the participants could freely connect to the testing server and test their agents in a simulated match against our dummy *Bot* agent team. We did not allow different teams to compete against each other as this should happen only during the tournament itself. During the testing phase, few minor bugs in the scenario implementation were discovered and quickly fixed.

4.2   Tournament

The Agent Contest 2007 tournament itself was launched on Wednesday, May 2nd 2007 at 15:00 CEST (UTC/GMT+2). A few days in advance, the participants received the Internet coordinates of the tournament server together with credentials for their agents. The Contest was served on the tournament server `agentmaster.in.tu-clausthal.de` and it could be observed via a web-interface at the address `http://agentmaster.in.tu-clausthal.de/`. We provided also a chat space for participants, what in the course of the tournament itself turned out to be a vital and efficient communication tool.

The teams competed sequentially against each other so that the order of teams was fixed (decided randomly at the beginning of the tournament) and then 1st played against the 2nd, then 3rd, 4th, etc. and finally against the last in the row. Then the 2nd team played against the 3rd, 4th, etc. The participation order was:

1. microJiacteam,
2. FLUXteam,
3. JiacIVteam,
4. AC07bot,
5. JACKteam,
6. APLteam,
7. GOLOGteam,
8. Jasonteam.

Unfortunately, this approach caused the last team in a row (Jasonteam) to compete only at the end of every "cycle", which was also a reason for complaints raised by this team during the tournament.

The tournament itself ran for several days and officially finished only on Monday, May 7th 2007 in the early morning. However, its execution was disrupted by a simulation server failure on Saturday, May 5th in the late evening. The failure lasted for several hours and in the early morning on Sunday May 6th, the tournament was restarted and the remaining simulations were run to the end.

During the tournament, on Friday May 4th, because of technical and performance difficulties, the GOLOG team decided to withdraw from the tournament. The team was disconnected and to keep the tournament run consistently, replaced with a dummy bot team.

The tournament lasted for approximately 4 and a half days. The long tournament execution time was caused by the setup of the simulation scenarios and our own desire not to handicap deliberating approaches.

For illustration, for 8 participating teams, and 5 simulations, we get $7 \times 8 = 56$ matches, i.e. $56 \times 5 = 280$ simulations. Simulations had approximately 800 steps. Provided a timeout of approximately 4 seconds per simulation step, in the worst case (when each team fully uses the timeout for deliberation), we could have a tournament running for 248 hours, i.e. approximately 10 days. Therefore, in the next editions of the Contest we plan to approach this issue by a parallel execution of several simulations simultaneously.

All results, together with the SVG recordings of all the matches and the official DVD ISO image with a mirror-copy of the whole tournament website can be downloaded from `http://agentmaster.in.tu-clausthal.de/`.

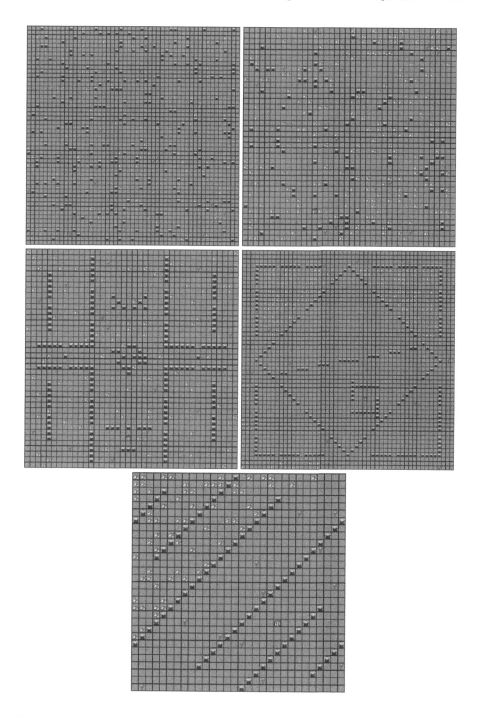

Fig. 1. Initial simulation scenarios *Park*, *Meadow*, *Semiramis*, *Fence* and *Overkill* (left → right, up → down)

4.3   Simulation Instances

The teams competed in matches each consisting of 5 different grid simulations with identifiers *Park*, *Meadow*, *Semiramis*, *Fence* and *Overkill* (Figure 1). The first two simulation scenarios *Park* and *Meadow* are randomly generated and differ only in the amount of gold items and trees. While the first features more trees and sparse gold, *Meadow* is configured to feature the opposite. Scenarios *Semiramis* and *Fence* are handcrafted labyrinths to challenge agent teams obstacle avoiding and communication approaches. Finally *Overkill* is a variation on the most difficult maze from the previous Contest 2006. The details of configuration properties of the scenarios is listed in Table 1.

Table 1. Simulation scenario configurations

simulation ID:	*Park*	*Meadow*	*Semiramis*	*Fence*	*Overkill*
grid size:	51x51	40x40	40x40	51x51	30x30
depot position:	random	random	(19,34)	(29,34)	(20,20)
number of obstacles:	250	95	175	235	76
initial number of gold items:	100	175	85	155	66
information distortion probability:	10%	10%	20%	5%	5%
action failure probability:	10-25%	5-33%	10-50%	10-50%	5-33%
gold generation frequency:	20 steps	10 steps	20 steps	20 steps	30 steps
number of generated gold items:	2	3	4	3	5
number of simulation steps:	1000	800	800	1000	700

5   Contest Results

The winner of the ProMAS'07 Agent Contest was the JIAC IV team from the DAI-Labor, Technische Universität Berlin, Germany. They gained the highest number of points: 63. The second team was microJIAC team, from the same institute, with 54 points followed by the Jason team with 49 points. The summary of the whole tournament is summarized in the Table 2.

Table 2. Final tournament results

Rank	Team	GoldScore	Points
1.	JIAC IV team	2824 : 1759	63
2.	microJiacteam	2680 : 1598	54
3.	Jasonteam	2563 : 1988	49
4.	FLUXteam	2514 : 1816	43
5.	APLteam	1246 : 2585	12

6   Conclusion

The main motivations behind this Agent Contest are the following:

- to foster the research and development of practically oriented approaches to programming multi-agent systems,
- to evaluate the state-of-the-art techniques in the field, and
- to identify key problems using these techniques.

The three editions of the Agent Contest have convinced us about its impact to the research in multi-agent system development. One important contribution is the great opportunity for the related research groups to participate in this contest in order to test and evaluate their developed agent development approaches. Participating in this contest helps them to discover bugs in their developed tools and technologies (e.g., multi-agent system methodology, agent programming language and their interpreters, agent platforms, etc.). The result is an improvement in the overall quality of the existing multi-agent system development approaches. Moreover, we notice that this contest helps research groups to deepen the understanding of practical aspects of using their approaches.

Another contribution of this contest is that different complementary multi-agent system development approaches are combined and aligned to develop multi-agent systems. For example, both Jason and 2APL teams use existing multi-agent system development methodologies to specify and design systems, which are subsequently implemented in their developed programming languages. Moreover, the implemented systems are then executed by their developed execution platforms. In this way, they can have a better understanding of problems related to the integration of different complementary approaches.

From the last three editions of the Contest we learned that the current scenario scheme does not enforce coordination and cooperation among the agent teams too much. Therefore, for the next edition of the Agent Contest we are planning to rethink the simulation scenarios so that participating agent teams will be required to have more advanced coordination mechanism. In particular this means that we need to introduce a higher level of dependency between the agents. I.e. 1) a single agent alone shouldn't be able to achieve a team goal, and 2) the environment itself has to have its own dynamics as if playing against the agent team.

As we already mentioned above, because of the extensive duration of the Contest tournament, we plan to modify the simulation server so, that it will be able to run multiple simulations simultaneously. To this end and to improve the simulation server reliability, we plan to migrate the existing software infrastructure to a computer with a higher processing power.

Of course, we also plan to improve the contest management, especially with respect to managing the contest infrastructure, mailing lists and contest schedule planning and announcements. The participating agent teams in the last edition of the contest advise us to have a scenario where there are few pieces of gold, so that good strategies to search for (scarce) gold can be evaluated. They also advised us to have more depots to avoid queues to deliver the gold. We are planning to organize the next edition of the Agent Contest again in association with the ProMAS workshop.

Acknowledgements

We are very thankful to the students for the Department of Informatics of Clausthal University of Technology. They worked hard in order to meet all the deadlines and deliver high-quality code. In particular, our thanks go this year to

- *Xavier Queralt Mateu* for the tournament server deployment, administration and maintenance, and
- *Slawomir Deren* for the simulation engine and scenarios development.

And of course we are thankful to *Bernd Fuhrmann, Michael Köster, David Mainzer* and *Dominik Steinborn* for the support when problems with the technical infrastructure occurred. We also thank all the contest participants who contributed to its success.

References

1. http://www.sics.se/tac
2. http://www.agentcities.org/EUNET/Competition
3. Bordini, R., Dastani, M., Dix, J., Fallah-Seghrouchni, A.E.: Multi-Agent Programming: Languages, Platforms, and Applications. In: MASA, vol. 15, Springer, Berlin (2005)
4. Bordini, R.H., Dastani, M., Dix, J., Seghrouchni, A.E.F. (eds.): PROMAS 2004. LNCS (LNAI), vol. 3346. Springer, Heidelberg (2005)
5. Bordini, R.H., Hübner, J.F.: BDI Agent Programming in AgentSpeak Using Jason (Tutorial Paper). In: Toni, F., Torroni, P. (eds.) CLIMA 2005. LNCS (LNAI), vol. 3900, pp. 143–164. Springer, Heidelberg (2006)
6. Busetta, P., Rönnquist, R., Hodgson, A., Lucas, A.: JACK Intelligent Agents: Components for intelligent agents in Java. AgentLink News Letter (January 1999)
7. Dastani, M., Dix, J., El Fallah-Seghrouchni, A. (eds.): PROMAS 2003. LNCS (LNAI), vol. 3067. Springer, Heidelberg (2004)
8. Dastani, M., Dix, J., Novák, P.: The First Contest on Multi-Agent Systems based on Computational Logic. In: Toni, F., Torroni, P. (eds.) CLIMA 2005. LNCS (LNAI), vol. 3900, pp. 373–384. Springer, Heidelberg (2006)
9. Dastani, M., Dix, J., Novák, P.: The second contest on multi-agent systems based on computational logic. In: Inoue, K., Satoh, K., Toni, F. (eds.) CLIMA 2006. LNCS (LNAI), vol. 4371, pp. 266–283. Springer, Heidelberg (2007)
10. Padgham, L., Winikoff, M.: Prometheus: A methodology for developing intelligent agents. In: Giunchiglia, F., Odell, J.J., Weiss, G. (eds.) AOSE 2002. LNCS, vol. 2585, Springer, Heidelberg (2003)
11. Rao, A.S.: AgentSpeak(L): BDI agents speak out in a logical computable language. In: Perram, J., Van de Velde, W. (eds.) MAAMAW 1996. LNCS, vol. 1038, pp. 42–55. Springer, Heidelberg (1996)
12. Zambonelli, F., Jennings, N.R., Wooldridge, M.: Developing multiagent systems: The Gaia methodology. ACM Transactions on Software Engineering and Methodology (TOSEM) 12(3), 317–370 (2003)

Developing a Team of Gold Miners Using *Jason*

Jomi F. Hübner[1] and Rafael H. Bordini[2]

[1] G2I – ENS Mines Saint-Etienne
158 Cours Fauriel
42023 Saint-Etienne Cedex, France
Jomi.Hubner@emse.fr
[2] Department of Computer Science
University of Durham
Durham DH1 3LE, UK
R.Bordini@durham.ac.uk

1 Introduction

This document gives an overview of a multi-agent system formed by a team of gold miners to compete in the Multi-Agent Programming Contest 2007 (the "gold miners" scenario). One of the main objectives has been to test and improve *Jason*, the interpreter for an agent programming language used to implement the MAS. *Jason* [2,4] is an agent platform based on an extension of an agent-oriented programming language called AgentSpeak(L) [6]. The language is inspired by the BDI architecture [7], hence based on notions such as beliefs, goals, plans, intentions, etc.

2 System Analysis and Design

One of the existing software engineering methodologies which we find particularly suitable for BDI agents is the Prometheus methodology [5]. Figures 1(a) and 1(b) are use the notation of that methodology to briefly give an idea of the overall system and the miner agent design, respectively. The analysis and design of the system is based on our previous team that won the CLIMA Contest in 2006 [3]. There are two kinds of agents in the team: miners and leader. Miners are the agents that interact with the contest simulator and the leader helps the coordination of some activities.

The leader helps the miners to coordinate themselves in two situations. It initially divides the grid representing the environment into four quadrants and then allocates miners to them; the miners will therefore look for gold in different places. Since we have six agents and only four quadrants, the two agents without a specific quadrant will search for gold anywhere in the grid, preferring the places least visited by the others. The second situation of coordination is the negotiation process that is started when a miner sees a piece of gold and is not able to collect it (because its container is full). This miner broadcasts the gold location to other miners who then send bids to the leader. The leader chooses the best offer and allocate the corresponding agent to collect that piece of gold (Figure 2). The protocol also states that whenever some agent decides to go to some gold location, it should announce it to others (so that they can reconsider their intentions). Similarly, they should announce whenever they collect a piece of gold.

All miners have the same individual goals:

M. Dastani et al.(Eds.): ProMAS 2007, LNAI 4908, pp. 241–245, 2008.
© Springer-Verlag Berlin Heidelberg 2008

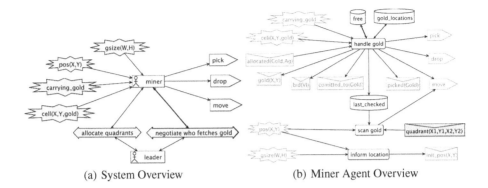

(a) System Overview   (b) Miner Agent Overview

Fig. 1. *Jason* Team Design Diagrams

search gold: search for gold in the environment. This goal is the initial goal of these agents and is also adopted when there is nothing else to do. Two strategies were used to achieve this goal. The first is used by agents that have a quadrant allocated to them and consists of scanning (i.e., searching systematically rather than randomly) for gold in the miner's quadrant. The second is used by "quadrant-less" agents and consists of always going the nearest least-visited location. For this latter strategy to work properly, all agents should inform the others about the places they are visiting.

fetch gold: go to the location of some known piece of gold and pick it up. This goal is adopted when the agent both has space in its container and knows of a "worthwhile" piece of gold. The piece of gold is known when the miner sees it or is informed about it by other miners (recall the gold negotiation protocol discussed above). The evaluation of the worth of a piece of gold is based on the path length from the agent to its location and that of the other agent possibly committed to the same piece. If there is no other agent committed, the piece is considered worthwhile. Otherwise, the distance to the piece, considering the agent's fatigue, must be less than the distance of the committed agent to the gold. This evaluation is also used to choose the gold to be fetched. To evaluate the other agents' distances to the gold, each agent should maintain the others informed of its location.

go to depot: go to the "depot" to drop there all pieces of gold being carried. This goal can only be adopted when the miner is carrying at least one piece of gold.

These goals are mutually exclusive and there is a preference relation between them: fetch > go to depot > search. To choose a goal to achieve at a certain moment in time, a miner follows this preference order, checking the adopt conditions for each of these alternative goals. Figure 4 shows an excerpt of the AgentSpeak code that implements the choice of a new goal, when that is necessary. The following events trigger the process of choosing a new goal to achieve: a new piece of gold is discovered through perception or communication; a piece of gold is allocated to the miner by the leader; some agent has picked or committed to a piece of gold the agent is currently fetching. Notice that to be allocated to fetch some gold does not necessarily imply that the agent will fetch that gold, it could be the case where the agent currently know that there is another better

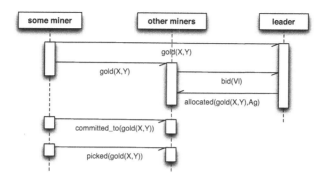

Fig. 2. Gold Allocation Protocol

piece of gold for it to fetch than the one just allocated. The above events thus only trigger the attempt to choose a new goal to achieve and are not directly related to a particular goal adoption.

3 Software Architecture

To implement our team, two features of *Jason* were specially useful: architecture customisation and internal actions (see Figure 3). A customisation of the agent architecture is used to interface between the agent and its environment. The environment for the Agent Contest is implemented in a remote server that simulates the mining field, sending perception to the agents and

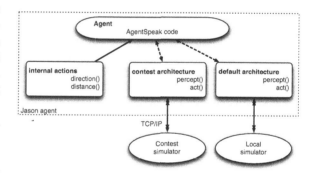

Fig. 3. Agent Architecture (reproduced from [2])

receiving requests for action execution. Therefore, when an agent attempts to perceive the environment, the customised architecture sends to the agent the information provided by the simulation server, and when the agent chooses an action to be performed, the architecture sends the action execution request also to the server. This architecture customisation also allow us to easily change between the contest simulation server and our (local) simulation by simply choosing another architecture; using a simulation running locally makes testing much faster and easier.

Although most of the agent code was written in AgentSpeak, some parts were implemented in Java, in this case because we wanted to use some legacy code. In particular, we already had a Java implementation of the A* search algorithm, which we use to find paths and calculate distances in the various scenarios of the competition. This algorithm

```
/* Plans to choose a new goal */
+!choose_goal
   :  container_has_space &             // I have space for more gold
      .findall(gold(X,Y),gold(X,Y),LG) & // LG is all known golds
      evaluate_golds(LG,LD) &           // Evaluate golds in LG
      .length(LD,LLD) & LLD > 0 &       // Is there a gold to fetch?
      .min(LD,d(D,NewG,_)) &            // Get the nearest
      worthwhile(NewG)
   <- .print("Gold options are ",LD,". Next gold is ",NewG);
      !change_to_fetch(NewG).
+!choose_goal                           // there is no worthwhile gold
   :  carrying_gold(N) & N > 0
   <- !change_to_goto_depot.
+!choose_goal             // not carrying gold, is "free" to search gold
   <- !change_to_search.

/* Plans to change the goal to fetching some gold */
+!change_to_fetch(G)                    // nothing to do,
   :  .desire(fetch_gold(G)).           // I am already fetching that gold
+!change_to_fetch(G)
   :  .desire(goto_depot)               // I am going to the depot
   <- .drop_desire(goto_depot);         // drop "goto_depot" first
      !change_to_fetch(G).
+!change_to_fetch(G)
   :  .desire(fetch_gold(OtherG))       // I am fetching another gold,
   <- .drop_desire(fetch_gold(OtherG)); // drop that goal
      !change_to_fetch(G).
+!change_to_fetch(G)                    // None of above conditions
   <- -free;                            // I am not free anymore
      !!fetch_gold(G).                  // Create the new goal fetch G
```

Fig. 4. Excerpt of AgentSpeak Code to Choose a New Goal to Achieve

was made accessible to the agents by means of *internal actions*. The more information (specially obstacles) about the scenario is available for A*, the better it performs. So when an agent sees an obstacle, it broadcasts this information to all agents so that they can update their world model accordingly (unlike in [3], we did *not* use shared memory for obstacle information in this implementation).

4 Discussion

The allocation protocol we used to assign new pieces of gold to agents is quite simple but efficient. All agents know all pieces of gold found by the team, who is committed to which gold, and the distance of the other agents to the gold locations. They can therefore calculate which is the best gold to fetch considering the others' options. Any novelty in the scenario may trigger the choice of a new (better) gold. Although this protocol requires a lot of information exchange, we did not note performance problems during the competition since the numbers of agents and golds are relatively small.

```
+!goto_depot
   <- ... plan to achieve
      the goal ...
-!goto_depot
   : <condition to repair>
   <- <actions to repair>;
      !goto_depot.
-!goto_depot
   <- !!choose_goal.
```

Fig. 5. Failure Handling

In this version of the team, we have emphasised the modelling and programming of the team by means of goals. This allows us to maintain a high abstraction level and a use good style in coding with the chosen programming language, as can be seen in the code shown in Figure 4. Regarding the set of goals, during the competition we noted that the preference order we have established is not ideal in all types of scenarios. Since the depot might be far from the agents, sometimes it is better to continue searching for gold instead of going to the depot (during this trip to the depot, the opponent team can discover more golds mines). We should evaluate this issue more carefully, taking the fatigue of the agent carrying the gold also into consideration.

The goal-based modelling we used also allows us to take advantage of the *Jason* features for handling plan failure. For instance, if the goal to go to depot fails for same reason, the agent may try to identify the problem and then chose another goal to achieve. Figure 5 contains a common pattern of code used to handle failures. Plans of the form $-!g$ in the figure are plans to handle a failure in achieving goal g.

5   Conclusion

The AgentSpeak code for the team of gold miners is, in our opinion, quite an elegant solution, being declarative, goal-based (based on the BDI architecture), and also adequately allowing agents to have long-term goals while reacting to changes in the environment. The *Jason* interpreter provided good support for high-level (speech-act based) communication, transparent integration with the contest server, and for use of existing Java code (e.g., for the A* algorithm). Although not a "purely" declarative, logic-based approach, the combination of both declarative and legacy code was quite efficient without compromising the declarative level (i.e., the agent's practical reasoning, the level for which AgentSpeak is an appropriate language).

On the other hand, using a new programming paradigm [1] is never easy, and *Jason* being a relatively new platform, some features had never been thoroughly tested before. The development of the *Jason* team was a good opportunity for experimenting with multi-agent programming and the improvements of the *Jason* platform that ensued.

References

1. Bordini, R.H., Dastani, M., Dix, J., El Fallah Seghrouchni, A. (eds.): Multi-Agent Programming: Languages, Platforms and Applications. Springer, Heidelberg (2005)
2. Bordini, R.H., Hübner, J.F., Wooldrige, M.: Programming Multi-Agent Systems in AgentSpeak using Jason. Wiley, Chichester (2007)
3. Bordini, R.H., Hübner, J.F., Tralamazza, D.M.: Using *Jason* to implement a team of gold miners. In: Inoue, K., Satoh, K., Toni, F. (eds.) CLIMA 2006. LNCS (LNAI), vol. 4371, pp. 304–313. Springer, Heidelberg (2007)
4. Bordini, R.H., Hübner, J.F., Vieira, R.: Jason and the golden fleece of agent-oriented programming. In: Bordini, et al. (eds.) [1], ch. 1, pp. 3–37.
5. Padgham, L., Winikoff, M.: Developing Intelligent Agent Systems: A Practical Guide. John Wiley and Sons, Chichester (2004)
6. Rao, A.S.: AgentSpeak(L): BDI agents speak out in a logical computable language. In: Perram, J., Van de Velde, W. (eds.) MAAMAW 1996. LNCS, vol. 1038, pp. 42–55. Springer, Heidelberg (1996)
7. Rao, A.S., Georgeff, M.P.: BDI agents: From theory to practice. In: Proc. of ICMAS 1995, AAAI Press / MIT Press (1995)

Going for Gold with 2APL

L. Astefanoaei, C.P. Mol, M.P. Sindlar, and N.A.M. Tinnemeier

Utrecht University
Department of Information and Computing Sciences
P.O. Box 80.089, 3508 TB Utrecht, The Netherlands
{astefano,christian,michal,nick}@cs.uu.nl

Abstract. This paper describes our approach to the Multi-Agent Programming Contest in coordination with ProMAS and AAMAS 2007. The object of the contest is to mine as much gold as possible in competition with other teams in a multi-agent goldrush scenario. Our agents are implemented in 2APL, a BDI-based agent-oriented programming language. As required by the contest, we designed and specified our approach using a multi-agent methodology. Several methodologies were evaluated, and eventually we chose a combination of $\mathcal{M}$oise$^+$ and Tropos.

1 System Analysis and Design

Before implementing the multi-agent system, we analyzed and designed our case of study by specifying it with the help of existing methodologies. For this purpose, we chose Tropos [1] combined with $\mathcal{M}$oise$^+$[2], rather than using Gaia [3] or Prometheus [4], as this is more suitable for our application. Gaia was deemed to be focused too much on the specification of organizational structure, without giving any guidelines for the implementation. Furthermore, it only vaguely defines notions such as goals and plans. Also, the lack of a specific notation was considered a significant drawback. Prometheus details the implementation phase at a finer grain, and provides a precisely specified notational technique. Where it comes to identifying and describing the system's functionalities, Prometheus was found to be quite helpful. However, the small-scaleness of the contest scenario, and the fact that specifics which would normally have been decided through using the methodology (such as the number of agents) are known from the start makes it superfluous.

In the following we present our specification, combining Tropos and $\mathcal{M}$oise$^+$. Designing our system in Tropos consists of four phases. The first one, Early Requirements Analysis (Figure 1), describes the main scenario. Each player has its own private instance of the map. Scouts that explore the map inform the leader about what they have seen. As soon as the leader has gathered enough information about the map, he sends a map update to all players who require it. The leader also keeps track of locations where gold has been spotted and the positions of the players that roam the map. It is the task of the miners, that harvest the gold, to inform the leader about locations of gold. They only send these locations in case they are not able to carry it themselves. The leader

M. Dastani et al.(Eds.): ProMAS 2007, LNAI 4908, pp. 246–250, 2008.
© Springer-Verlag Berlin Heidelberg 2008

then assigns the gold to the nearest available `player`. In this phase we decide the dependence relations: `scouts` and `miners` rely on the `leader` for map updates, and he depends on the `miners` and `scouts` for information resources.

Figure 1 can be separated into two distinct diagrams (Figures 2 and 3) by means of $\mathcal{M}oise^+$ concepts.

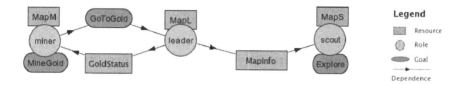

Fig. 1. Tropos: Early Requirement Analysis

Fig. 2. $\mathcal{M}oise^+$: Goal Decomposition Tree

As follows from the Goal Decomposition Tree in Figure 2, the ultimate goal of our "greedy" team is to be the richest. In order to achieve this goal, we decompose it into three subgoals: updating the gold locations, exploring the map, and mining the gold. Furthermore, goals can be either performative goals (update gold location), or achievement goals (exploring region, collecting gold).

Roles, and the relation between them, are specified in $\mathcal{M}oise^+$ at the structural level. An agent, in our model, can play three different roles: `leader`, `scout`, and `miner`. From Figure 3 it follows that our team can have at most one `leader`, and zero to six `players`, who can have the role of either `scout` or `miner`. The `leader` communicates both with the `scouts` and the `miners`. A large part of the coordination is thus inherently within the `leader`. Coordination takes place in terms of task ordering: first the `scouts` explore the wilderness, then the `miners` can gold-enrich the team.

At the deontic level, we couple roles and goals in terms of commitments and responsibilities. The `leader` is responsible of assigning to-be-mined regions to `players`. When such a player is in the role of `scout`, he switches to the role of `miner`. The `leader` can thus influence when a `player` should change its role.

Having a more accurate vision on roles and goals, we can return to the second specification phase in Tropos. This is the Late Requirement Analysis, which takes each actor as a system and describes its functions. For example, in our case, this means that the `leader` has to consult the map before sending a `miner` on mission. Every `scout` can have its own strategies when exploring an unknown

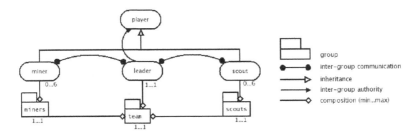

Fig. 3. $\mathcal{M}$oise$^+$: Role Diagram

territory. As for `miners`, their task is to mine the gold. Our agents depend on the `leader`, but can also perform their tasks themselves, thus preserving their autonomy.

How the team interacts with the environment is specified in the Architectural Design phase. The environment, by definition, provides information for our team, and furthermore the `players` act upon the environment. We can specify how the data is communicated at the Detailed Design level. In the next section, we describe how the specification connects to the implementation phase.

2   Software Architecture

Our agents are implemented in the BDI-based programming language 2APL [5]. The following gives an overview of the language in general, and, more specifically, to our approach for this contest.

2.1   2APL

2APL (`http://www.cs.uu.nl/2apl`), the successor to 3APL, is an agent-oriented programming language that facilitates the implementation of multi-agent systems. At the multi-agent level, it provides programming constructs to specify a multi-agent system in terms of a set of individual agents, and a set of environments in which they can perform actions. Multiple agents can run together in a single instance of the 2APL platform, each with its own thread of control. The platform also allows communication among agents, and can run on several machines connected in a network.

At the individual agent level, 2APL provides programming constructs to implement cognitive agents based on the BDI architecture. In particular, one can implement an agent's beliefs, goals, plans, actions (such as belief updates, external actions, or communication actions), events, and a set of rules through which the agent can decide which actions to perform. 2APL supports the implementation of both reactive and proactive agents. The next subsection sketches how those concepts can be used to implement the design as discussed in section 1.

2.2   An implementation in 2APL

In the analysis phase we identified a `leader` and a `player`. Each `player` performs either the `miner` or `scout` role, but not both at the same time. Three 2APL files define the player: `player.2apl`, which specifies behavior common to all players, and `scout.2apl` and `miner.2apl`, for role-specific behavior. The role of `leader` is implemented by a file `agent007.2apl`.

Each `leader` and `player` has *beliefs* and *goals* which may change during the agent's execution. A `scout`, for instance, has beliefs about the cells it has explored, and `miners` have a belief about the maximum amount of gold they can carry. Updating beliefs in 2APL is realized by performing belief updates like the ones specified below:

```
BeliefUpdates:
  { role(X) }  Enact(Y)    { not role(X), role(Y) }
  { true }     Seen(X,Y)   { seen(X,Y) }
```

For example, when an agents executes `Enact(Y)`, then the precondition is that he currently believes `role(X)`, and the postcondition specifies that after the belief update he will be believe to be enacting `role(Y)`, and not `role(X)`. Notice that, in this rule, X and Y can denote the same role.

The goals of a 2APL agent consist of a list of ground conjunctions each of which denotes a situation the agent wants to realize (not necessary all at once). Goals are the highest-level construct for governing agents' behavior. In our implementation, `scouts` have a performative goal of exploring the map, and an achievement goal of having explored specific cells. The `miners` have an overall goal of having mined gold, which is achieved when they carry no gold, and are not aware of any gold locations to mine. At this point, they switch back to the `scout` role in order to find more gold.

In addition to actions to manipulate the belief base, the `players` and `leader` use communication actions to communicate with other agents, external actions to act upon the environment (moving, picking up gold, etc.), actions to test their belief and goal bases, and actions to add and drop goals. All of these are provided by 2APL.

In 2APL, so-called `PG`-rules can be used to specify that an agent should generate a plan if it has certain goals and beliefs:

```
PG-rules:
  explored(REGION) <- role(scout) | { ...  }
```

The body of the rule, which is omitted, would state that the agent should first go to the region to be explored, and then specifies a particular heuristic for exploring the region. For general path planning we use the A*-algorithm. Having a clear distinction between `miner` and `scout` roles enabled us to implement a role-dependent A* in which `scouts`, whose primary goal is to explore new regions, prefer to travel over cells that are marked as unexplored, whereas `miners`, whose perception deteriorates as they carry more gold, prefer already explored cells over unexplored ones to travel over.

During their execution, `players` receive messages from the `leader` requesting them to mine a certain gold locations, or informing them about updates to the map. In 2APL, so-called PC-rules generate plans as a response to such messages and events. For example, we use the following PC-rule to deal with a request from the `leader` to mine a certain gold location.

```
PC-rules:
  message( agent007,request,mine(GX,GY) ) <- role(R) | {...}
```

2APL is built on JADE [6] framework, which allows for running instances of the platform in a distributed fashion on multiple machines. We exploited this feature by running our agents on different machines, in order to ensure maximum stability. If any of the agents crashed for some reason, and came back online during a match, it received the necessary information, such as the most recent copy of the map, from the `leader`.

2APL has a well-defined API for creating custom Java environments. The following piece of code shows the update of a specific cell in the contest environment map with the information that it contains an obstacle.

```
@goldworld( updateCell(X, Y, obstacle), L )
```

3   Conclusion

We have presented our approach for programming a multi-agent system for the gold-mining contest in 2APL. It involved two phases; first we specified our system using Tropos and $\mathcal{M}oise^+$, and then we implemented it. We found that having a formal description can simplify design and implementation. In this sense, the possibility of mapping a specification automatically to 2APL code would be an interesting and useful object of study, and is indeed part of our future work.

References

1. Bresciani, P., Perini, A., Giorgini, P., Giunchiglia, F., Mylopoulos, J.: Tropos: An agent-oriented software development methodology (2004)
2. Hübner, J.F., Sichman, J.S., Boissier, O.: Moise$^+$: Towards a structural, functional, and deontic model for MAS organization. In: Proc. of AAMAS 2002, pp. 501–502 (2002)
3. Wooldridge, M., Jennings, N.R., Kinny, D.: The Gaia methodology for agent-oriented analysis and design. Autonomous Agents and Multi-Agent Systems 3(3), 285–312 (2000)
4. Padgham, L., Winikoff, M.: Developing Intelligent Agent Systems. John Wiley & Sons Ltd, Chichester (2004)
5. Dastani, M., Hobo, D., Meyer, J.J.C.: Practical extensions in agent programming languages. In: Proc. of AAMAS 2007 (2007)
6. Bellifemine, F., Bergenti, F., Caire, G., Poggi, A.: JADE - A Java Agent Development Framework. In: Multi-Agent Programming, pp. 125–147 (2005)

Collecting Gold:
MicroJIAC Agents in Multi-Agent Programming Contest

Erdene-Ochir Tuguldur and Marcel Patzlaff

DAI-Labor, Technische Universität Berlin, Germany
tuguldur.erdene-ochir@dai-labor.de
marcel.patzlaff@dai-labor.de

Abstract. This paper describes our contribution to the Multi-Agent Programming Contest organised as part of the ProMAS 2007 workshop. The objective of this contribution was the evaluation of a new lightweight agent architecture targeted at devices with different capabilities. Therefore, the agents developed in this work can run on mobile devices that makes our approach different from the other contributions to the competition.

1 Introduction

For the contest, we implemented a multi agent system that is capable of running on mobile devices. We used a lightweight agent architecture targeted at devices with different capabilities. This framework was the result of a diploma thesis [1] written at DAI-Labor of the Technische Universität Berlin. The motivation to participate in the contest was to test the functionality and usability of this framework. Since the problem left enough space to experiment, a solution was found that fits in the framework's agent model and exploits most of its capabilities. All test results were evaluated within the scope of the aforementioned diploma thesis to draw conclusions and to propose future development of the framework.

2 System Analysis and Design

This contribution to the contest implements a multi agent system whose agents are reactive and autonomous. These agents consist of three main components (see Figure 1).

1. Connector

   The connector maintains the connection to the competition server. It parses the messages received from the server and creates perceptions from them. These perceptions are forwarded to all other agents and also to the current agent's own perceptor. Thus, the connector is essential for the communication and coordination between the agents. At last, it delegates the actions from the current agent to the server.

M. Dastani et al.(Eds.): ProMAS 2007, LNAI 4908, pp. 251–255, 2008.
© Springer-Verlag Berlin Heidelberg 2008

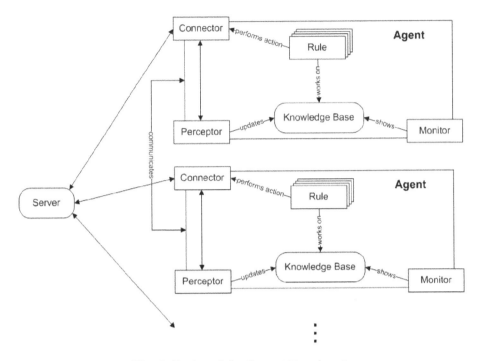

Fig. 1. Design of the Competition Agents

2. Perceptor
   It updates the world model, the associated monitor and fires notification events to trigger the rules.
3. Monitor
   It provides a graphical user interface which displays the world model of the agent. This is used mainly for debug purposes.

Furthermore, each agent has a set of rules which are associated to specific world model states. Depending on the state, the rules trigger actions for the agent.

Through the Connector each agent receives its own feedback from the competition server. This feedback is evaluated by the Perceptor updating the current agent's world model. The perception is also forwarded by the connector to all other agents in the team to share the knowledge of the surroundings. Thus, each agent has the same world model state. With this state, each agent calculates the next target and communicates it to its teammates. This is part of the coordination concept which ensures that a location is not target of more than one agent.

All agents are identical, meaning that there are no experts in the team, and are able to change their roles dynamically: they can act as explorer or transporter.

3   Software Architecture

The system is realised using the microJIAC framework [1] which is a lightweight agent architecture targeted at devices with different capabilities. It can be used on both: resource-constrained devices (i.e. cell phones and PDAs) and desktop computers. It is implemented in the Java programming language. At the moment, a full implementation for CLDC[1] devices is available, which is the most restricted J2ME[2] configuration that is supported.

MicroJIAC's agent definition is adapted from [2]. Thus, the framework is also split into environment and agents. The environment is the abstraction layer between the device and agents. It defines lifecycle management and communication functionalities. These functionalities include a communication channel through which the agents send their messages.

Agents are created through a combination of different elements. In the contest implementation, we use only three of the predefined element types: Consumers, Producers and Rules. Consumers and Producers are the interface between the agent and the environment. The former resemble actuators through which the agent manipulates the environment — they consume data from the agent. The latter instead resemble sensors through which the agent gains knowledge from its surroundings — they produce data for the agent. Rules specify reactive behaviour. All elements are strictly decoupled from each other and are thus exchangeable. Only Consumers are allowed to define handles through which other elements may communicate with them. These handles are derived from the Connection interface of the GCF [3]

In contrast to JIAC IV [3], which is used by the other contribution of our institute, microJIAC does not use an ontology or agent programming language such as JADL [4]. Furthermore, agent migration is restricted to Java configurations which support custom class loaders and reflection. It should not be left unmentioned that beside the similarity in the names both architectures are targeted at different fields of application and have different development histories. Of course, it is planned to use a common communication infrastructure to enable information exchange between each others agents.

3.1 Tools

The standard build tool for microJIAC is Maven[4] which eases the dependency and project management. Maven is based on a component architecture implemented in Java and is extensible through plug-ins. MicroJIAC comes with its own Maven plug-in which supports the compilation and packaging process of agents targeted at CLDC devices. This is needed to generate several classes which circumvent the absence of Java reflection. Furthermore, it can reduce the size of byte code by using the ProGuard[5] obfuscator.

---

[1] Connected Limited Device Configuration http://java.sun.com/products/cldc/

[2] Java 2 Platform Micro Edition http://java.sun.com/javame/index.jsp

[3] Generic Connection Framework
http://developers.sun.com/techtopics/mobility/midp/articles/
genericframework/

[4] Maven http://maven.apache.org/

[5] ProGuard Obfuscator http://proguard.sourceforge.net/

3.2 Implementation

As mentioned before, each agent consists of three main components and a set of rules. The rules are implemented using the IRule interface where the main components are realised as follows:

1. Connector

   The connector consumes data from the rules and therefore implements the IConsumer interface. Furthermore, we introduced a reconnection timer that is triggered if the connection to the server could not be established. So this component also implements the IRule interface to react on the timer events.

2. Perceptor

   The perceptor consumes the server responses that are received by the connector. So it also implements IConsumer. Moreover, it processes the message from the other agents in the team and thus need to implement IRule. At least it implements IProducer to fire a rule processing event.

3. Monitor

   The monitor displays the world model in some graphical user interface. It receives its data from the perceptor and therefore implements the IConsumer interface. For the Wireless Toolkit, it looks like depicted in Figure 2.

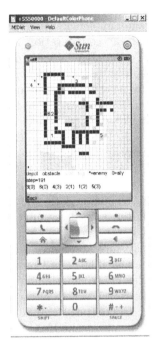

Fig. 2. An agent runs on SUN Wireless Toolkit

4 Agent Team Strategy

Each agent is either in explorer or transporter mode. The explorer guides its steps to unknown territory or nearby nuggets and collect gold items it steps over. If the agent carries a certain amount of gold items, it changes its role and switch to transporter mode. Hereby the amount of gold items to trigger this mode transition depends on the maximum amount an agent can carry, the simulation step and the size of the grid. After reaching the depot and dropping all gold items, the transporter agent becomes an explorer again.

At each step, all explorer agents recalculate their targets. These computed targets are communicated among the team to avoid two or more explorer heading for the same target.

After an agent has calculated its target, which can be a gold item, an unexplored cell or the depot, the agent computes the shortest path to it with the A* algorithm. Hereby enemy agents next to the computing agent are treated as obstacles. So collisions with these enemy agents are avoided but the distance to the target cell increases due to this detour.

Whenever the connection between an agent and the server breaks during the simulation, the agent tries to reconnect. It is the only implemented recovery mechanism that each agent has.

5 Discussion

In the end, we reached a good result with this implementation. Nevertheless, we had several problems to overcome or to compensate. First of all, our agents slowed down while games progressed. Especially the A* calculations grow in time and we still do not know why. We know that if the grid world grows in the next contest, as we expect it will, we have to detach the computation from the main thread of each agent and also to reduce the amount of computations. Another problem is the complexity of the communication. As you might have deduced, there are

$$6 \cdot 5p + 6 \cdot 5a = 60$$

messages floating through the network between two simulation steps. So the current communication approach does not scale in the slightest w.r.t. the number of agents in a team. Especially the fixed amount of overhead (message headers) leads to a bad payload:header ratio in a message. What we can do here is to reduce the number of messages while increasing their payload.

And at least these insights in our architecture justified the additional workload in participating in the contest. Also if the contest, due to the very special task, might not allow the deduction of the over-all quality of the MAS, it is a good testbed for increasing system performance and, of course, for finding bugs and other unwanted "features".

6 Conclusion

In this contribution, we evaluated our agent framework microJIAC. The second place this approach earned in the contest demonstrates its potential. We look forward to participate in the next contest and meanwhile improving our system.

References

1. Patzlaff, M.: Development of a Scalable Agent Architecture for Constrained Devices. Master's thesis, Technische Universität Berlin (2007)
2. Russel, S., Norvig, P.: Artificial Intelligence: A Modern Approach, 2nd edn. Prentice-Hall, Englewood Cliffs (2003)
3. Sesseler, R.: Eine modulare Architektur für dienstbasierte Interaktionen zwischen Agenten. PhD thesis, Technische Universität Berlin (2002)
4. Konnerth, T., Hirsch, B., Albayrak, S.: JADL - an Agent Description Language for Smart Agents. In: Baldoni, M., Endriss, U. (eds.) DALT 2006. LNCS (LNAI), vol. 4327, pp. 141–155. Springer, Heidelberg (2006)

JIAC IV in Multi-Agent Programming Contest 2007

Axel Hessler, Benjamin Hirsch, and Jan Keiser

DAI-Labor, Technische Universität Berlin, Germany
{axel.hessler,benjamin.hirsch,jan.keiser}@dai-labor.de

Abstract. A competition always shows the performance of the participants. We have developed the JIAC IV agent framework over years now and took this as a chance to see where we stand. This paper describes our approach to the contest scenario from a software engineering point of view, i. e. how we would solve similar problems of complex and distributed nature.

1 Introduction

The JIAC IV agent team has been prepared by members of the *Competence Center Agent Core Technologies* of DAI-Labor at Technische Universität Berlin. We use the JIAC IV agent framework with accompanying toolkit, which have been created in the course of several projects at DAI Labor, intended for telecommunications and telematics services to be implemented quickly and effectively, and to be administered reliably.

2 System Analysis and Design

The Java Intelligent Agent Componentware agent framework (JIAC IV) comes with its own customised methodology and a number of tools integrated in the Eclipse IDE.

As shown in Figure 1, the development process starts with collecting domain vocabulary and requirements, which then are structured and prioritised. Second, we take the requirements with the highest priority and derive a MAS architecture by listing the agents and create a user interface prototype. The MAS architecture then is detailed by creating a role model, showing the design concerning functionalities and interactions. We then implement plans, services and protocols, which are plugged into agents during integration. Agents are deployed to (one or more) agent platforms and the application is ready to be evaluated. Depending on the evaluation we align and amend requirements and start the cycle again with eliminating bugs and enhancing and adding features until we reach the desired quality of the agent-based application.

The JIAC methodology is based on the JIAC meta-model. JIAC has explicit notions of goal, rule, plan, service and protocol. Knowledge written in JADL and AgentBeans written in Java constitute agentroles, which are plugged into

M. Dastani et al.(Eds.): ProMAS 2007, LNAI 4908, pp. 256–260, 2008.
© Springer-Verlag Berlin Heidelberg 2008

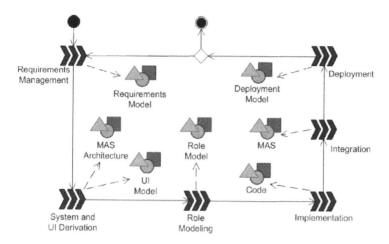

Fig. 1. JIAC methodology - iterative and incremental process model in SPEM [1] notation

standard JIAC agents. The standard JIAC agent is already capable of finding other JIAC agents and their services, using infrastructure services and provides a number of security and management features.

For any part of the JIAC meta-model we provide an editor (source code as well as visual editor) in the JIAC IDE for easy agent and application development. Reuse is supported by a plugin that allows search and retrieval of components and solutions. A context sensitive help and a number of interactive tutorials complete the JIAC IV toolbox.

3   Single Agent Behaviour

We started collecting the simulation domain vocabulary and created the ontology containing such concepts as nuggets, gold-digger, grid cells, and so on. Listing 1.1 shows the *GoldDigger* category with its attributes. Furthermore, basic features such as the ability to communicate with the simulation server and a simple path-finding algorithm have been created.

```
(cat GoldDigger (ext TemporalGridObject)
  (name string)
  (currentPosY int (init -1))
  (currentPosX int (init -1))
  (teammate bool)
  (carriesGold int (init 0))
  (intention Intention))
```

Listing 1.1. Extract from GoldWorld ontology

In a further iteration, some higher level plans have been designed, embodied into special roles such as *Explorer* or *Transporter*. In particular, we created behaviours for finding gold, moving to a certain position, picking up gold, and scoring. The explorer role had capabilities to systematically search the terrain for gold, the transporter role brings the gold to the depot. Listing 1.2 shows the `makePoint` plan of the transporter role.

```
(act makePoint (var ?score:int ?self:GoldDigger ?x:int ?y:int ?world:GridWorld)
  (pre (and
    (att score SIMULATION (fun Int_DAI_1.sub ?score 1))
    (att self SIMULATION ?self)
    (att currentPosX ?self ?x)
    (att currentPosY ?self ?y)
    (att world SIMULATION ?world)
    (att hasGold (fun getCellFromGridWorld ?world ?x ?y) true)))
  (eff (att score SIMULATION ?score))
  (script (var ?depot:GridCell ?depotX:int ?depotY:int)
    (seq
      // pick gold
      (goal (and (att self SIMULATION ?self) (att carriesGold ?self true)))
      // goto depot
      (eval (and (att depot SIMULATION ?depot) (att posX ?depot ?depotX) (att posY ?depot ?
          depotY)))
      (goal (and (att self SIMULATION ?self) (att currentPosX ?self ?depotX) (att
          currentPosY ?self ?depotY)))
      // drop gold
      (goal (and (att self SIMULATION ?self) (att carriesGold ?self false)))
) ) )
```

Listing 1.2. Higher-level plan "makePoint"

Furthermore, we exchanged our path finding capability with a generic A* implementation as our local search path finding algorithm did not work in labyrinths. In Figure 2 the principle control flow of a single agent is shown, which worked well with the simulation environment.

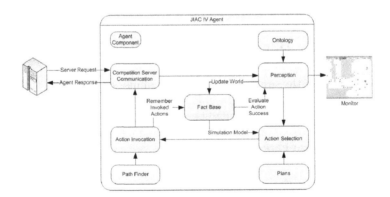

Fig. 2. Customising the JIAC IV standard agent for the contest

4   Software Architecture

JIAC is based upon the CASA BDI architecture described in [2]. It combines a scalable component framework, a knowledge representation toolkit, a control architecture, and an agent infrastructure. Additional features are a runtime environment, system agents, tools, and libraries [3].

JIAC provides the JADL (JIAC Agent Description Language) programming language. Based on three-valued logic, it incorporates ontologies, FIPA-based speech acts, a (procedural) scripting part for (complex) actions, and allows to define protocols and service based communication. Rather than only relying on a library of plans, the framework also allows agents to plan from first principles [4].

5   Agent Team Strategy

When dealing with MAS we always assume that the MAS must be worth more than the sum of its parts. We addressed this in a number of iterations dealing with communication, coordination, and cooperation.

Agents cooperate on a number of levels. First, they share their perception. Next, we enabled our agents to share their agent state (e.g. that the agent carries no gold items) and intentions (such as "I plan to pick gold at X,Y") as they may choose to go to the same unknown field or to pick the same gold item. Now every agent can appraise from what it knows if it will be better to leave the team member alone or to take the intention as its own when its more promising.

Our approach to communication and cooperation is fully decentralised. Each agent has the capability for finding the other agent on the network. It then directly tells every agent about its perception, agent state and intentions. There is neither a message broker nor a central instance which coordinates the contest agents. Every agent builds its own world model from what it is told by the server and the other agents. Every agent also plans for itself, taking the states and intentions of its teammates into account.

6   Discussion

There are still issues left. Our agents behaved fair, in that they gave way for other agents even if they are opponents. We also assume that the current approach to coordination does not scale very well as it takes $n * (n - 1)$ connections with n the number of agents in the team. Observation of opponents would be a possible extension as well as to guess what they plan and then to crisscross it. There is evidence that this can be solved with some more iterations following the methodology.

Although the scenario of the contest seems quite simple we have found that it is not trivial to design and implement a well performing solution even using the agent-oriented approach, the agent framework and tools. The contest has shown that a practical comparison sometimes provides results that are not as obvious from theoretical deliberations.

7   Conclusion

We have shown that it is very easy and effective to solve the simulation problem using the JIAC IV agent framework. We first collect the domain vocabulary and basic requirements from the scenario description, derive a monitor GUI and basic agent architecture. Then we gather basic capabilities and interactions in roles and implement them. Implemented roles are plugged into the agents and deployed on the agent platform. After evaluating the performance of our agents we collect new requirements, bugs and feature enhancements and start a new iteration.

References

1. Group, O.: Software Process Engineering Metamodel (SPEM) Specification. Version 1.1. Object Management Group, Inc (2005)
2. Sesseler, R.: Eine modulare Architektur für dienstbasierte Interaktionen zwischen Agenten. PhD thesis, Technische Universität Berlin (2002)
3. Fricke, S., Bsufka, K., Keiser, J., Schmidt, T., Sesseler, R., Albayrak, S.: A Toolkit for the Realization of Agent-based Telematic Services and Telecommunication Applications. Communications of the ACM 44(4), 43–48 (2001)
4. Konnerth, T., Hirsch, B., Albayrak, S.: JADL — an agent description language for smart agents. In: Baldoni, M., Endriss, U. (eds.) DALT 2006. LNCS (LNAI), vol. 4327, pp. 141–155. Springer, Heidelberg (2006)

An Agent Team Based on FLUX
for the ProMAS Contest 2007

Stephan Schiffel, Michael Thielscher, and Doan Thu Trang

Dresden University of Technology
Dresden, Germany
{stephan.schiffel,mit}@inf.tu-dresden.de
tieuyen@gmail.com

Abstract. FLUX is a constraint logic programming system based on a general calculus for reasoning about actions. FLUX supports the development of agents that base their decisions on their own knowledge state and update this state in accordance with a declarative specification of their primitive actions and sensing capabilities. This is the second time we participate in the Multi-Agent Programming Contest with a team of FLUX agents, and in this paper we describe an improved system architecture for competing in the Gold Mining Domain.

1 Introduction

Intelligent agents have the ability to generate actions based on their own knowledge about the environment that they inhabit. Since last year, the Multi-Agent Programming Contest provides the research community with an opportunity to apply and compare different approaches and methodologies for the design of intelligent agents. This is the second time we participate in the contest with a team of FLUX agents, and in this paper we describe an improved system architecture for competing in the Gold Mining Domain.

FLUX [1] is a constraint logic programming system based on a general calculus for reasoning about actions. It supports the development of agents that base their decisions on their own knowledge state and update this state in accordance with a declarative specification of their primitive actions and sensing capabilities. A FLUX agent is a logic program consisting of three parts. A general *kernel* provides the basic reasoning facilities by means of an encoding of the foundational axioms of the action formalism known as fluent calculus [2]. The domain-specific *background theory* is used to maintain the internal knowledge state of an agent. It consists of a declarative specification of the actions and sensing capabilities of an individual agent. Finally, the *strategy* part of a FLUX program guides the behavior of the agent. The quality of a team of agents is crucially dependent on the quality of the strategy of each individual agent and how these work together.

This paper is organized as follows. Following this introductory section, we give an overview of the System Design, where we show how the three parts of

M. Dastani et al.(Eds.): ProMAS 2007, LNAI 4908, pp. 261–265, 2008.
© Springer-Verlag Berlin Heidelberg 2008

each FLUX agent are constructed, including the strategy of the whole team as well as of each individual agent. Thereafter, we give details about our software architecture, describing the tools and environment that are being used for the FLUX agent team with which we participate in the Multi-Agent Programming Contest 2007.

2   System Analysis and Design

As described above, an agent developed using the FLUX framework is a logic program consisting of three modules: the fundamental reasoning facilities based on the fluent calculus, the specification of the effects of actions, and the strategy. Since the first part is application-independent and is therefore provided by the general FLUX system, developing a FLUX agent amounts to programming the latter two modules. In what follows, we give an overview of these modules of the FLUX agents for the Gold Mining Domain.

FLUX Agent Team. Our FLUX agent team consists of six agents and a leader. The role of the leader is to help the other agents in sharing information about the environment and to coordinate the other agents. To reduce communication complexity, the agents do not communicate directly with each other. Instead, the leader collects and distributes all new information among the agents.

Each agent has intentions that change over time based on sensor information and executed actions. The next action of an agent depends on the current intentions of that agent and the current state of the world.

In order for the agents to cooperate, after an agent decides on its next action it sends new information it got and its current intention to the leader. In return the

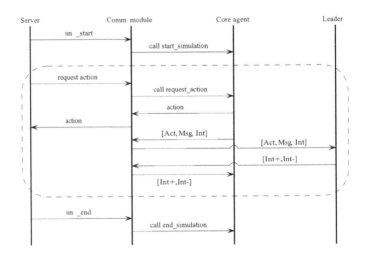

Fig. 1. Messages within Flux Agents

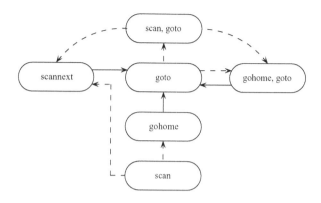

Fig. 2. Intentions of agents

leader sends information gathered by the other agents to the agent. Additionally the leader might request the agent to change its intentions for coordinating the agents of the team. Figure 1 shows how the agents of the FLUX Team exchange messages with each other.

Figure 2 shows how intentions of agents are changed. The solid arrows indicate the modifications of intentions that are decided by the leader, and the broken arrows mean that the transitions are done by the agents themselves. The main intentions of an agent are to scan an area of the grid, to go to some location either for scanning the area around it or for collecting a gold item, or to go home, i.e., go to the depot. The intentions can change when gold is picked up or dropped or an area was scanned completely. The intentions are sometimes changed upon request of the leader in order to assign areas to the agents for exploration or to resolve conflicts between the agents' intentions.

Knowledge Update. Depending on the type, each member of the FLUX agent team behaves differently when updating its own knowledge about the environment. A knowledge update for the leader is triggered whenever an agent sends new information. The information that the leader receives contains all new information that the agent learned as well as the agent's intentions and action. Based on this, the leader updates its current knowledge of the grid as well as of the states of the agents. A knowledge update for an agent, on the other hand, is done whenever it executed an action. The knowledge state of an agent is updated using a FLUX implementation of a so-called Knowledge Update Axiom in the fluent calculus. To deal with the nondeterministic nature of actions due to random action failures it is sufficient to check whether the position of the agent and the number of nuggets it carries differs from the expectation. The Knowledge Update Axiom incorporates all sensor information about the contents of the cells surrounding the agent into its state.

3   Software Architecture

Each agent of the team of agents consists of two processes communicating via streams. One process runs a Java program responsible for communicating with the contest server and the other agents. The other process executes the actual strategy of the agent. The latter is implemented in (ECLiPSe)-Prolog using the FLUX framework. The agents of a team communicate with asynchronous messages using a simple self-implemented communication framework based on sockets. This architecture has a couple of advantages. It allows the individual agents to run on different computers across a network. All the other agents remain functional if one the agents crashes. Only failure of the leader agent will result in a less efficient strategy because of the coordination of the agents is missing. The system can be used easily for different numbers of agents.

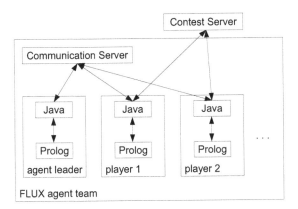

Fig. 3. Software Architecture

4   Agent Team Strategy

The goal of the team is to collect as much gold as possible in a match. However, given the complexity and nondeterministic nature of the domain, it is difficult to come up with a plan for each agent of the team which maximizes the overall score of the team taking the unpredictable and widely hidden activities of the opponent team into account. Therefore, the agents mostly act greedily. Competing interests of exploration and predictable and fast traveling are only rudimentarily incorporated into the path planning algorithm. Conflicts between the agents of our team are resolved in two ways. First, the leader coordinates the agents by assigning areas to the agents for exploration. Second, small scale conflicts such as when several agents try to get into the same cell, are resolved using fixed priorities of the agents without the direct help of the leader. In order for the agents to be able to cooperate, it is necessary that the individual goals and intentions of the agents are communicated between each other. To keep the communication complexity low, there is no peer-to-peer communication between the agents. Instead all information is collected and distributed by the leader agent. Apart from the communication with the simulation server each agent (except for the leader) sends and retrieves just one message per step. The obvious weak point in this setup is the leader agent. The complexity of the leader agent and computation power of the computer also limit the maximal number of agents that can be added to the system.

5   Discussion

Our successful participation in the ProMAS Contest 2007 has shown that FLUX - originally designed as a single agent framework - can be used as a basis for true multi-agent systems. The only weak spot we discovered was that FLUX lacks an integrated mechanism for communication between the agents.

The contest provides a useful testbed for multi-agent systems. However, it doesn't cover all aspects of uncertainty which agents normally have to face in an environment. In particular, the nondeterministic nature of the actions is easily resolved using the sensor information in the next step of the simulation. As a consequence, several important features of agent programming systems, like the support for nondeterministic actions, were not covered by the ProMAS Contest.

6   Conclusion

We have given an overview of an approach to the design of intelligent agents that participate in the ProMAS Contest 2007. In comparison with our contribution to the previous competition [3], the FLUX team has been significantly improved in the way the agents communicate with each other in order not to just follow their individual strategy but to also build a joint strategy for the entire team. The behavior of each agent is written in Prolog while the communication module has been implemented in Java. Thanks to the interface between Java and Prolog supported by ECLiPSe Prolog, single agents developed using the FLUX methodology can be easily joined in a team for multi-agent settings.

References

1. Thielscher, M.: FLUX: A logic programming method for reasoning agents. Theory and Practice of Logic Programming 5, 533–565 (2005)
2. Thielscher, M.: From situation calculus to fluent calculus: State update axioms as a solution to the inferential frame problem. Artificial Intelligence 111, 277–299 (1999)
3. Schiffel, S., Thielscher, M.: Multi-agent FLUX for the gold mining domain (system description). In: Inoue, K., Satoh, K., Toni, F. (eds.) CLIMA 2006. LNCS (LNAI), vol. 4371, pp. 294–303. Springer, Heidelberg (2007)

Author Index

Lecture Notes in Artificial Intelligence (LNAI)

Vol. 4953: N.T. Nguyen, G.S. Jo, R.J. Howlett, L.C. Jain (Eds.), Agent and Multi-Agent Systems: Technologies and Applications. XX, 909 pages. 2008.

Vol. 4946: I. Rahwan, S. Parsons, C. Reed (Eds.), Argumentation in Multi-Agent Systems. X, 235 pages. 2008.

Vol. 4938: T. Tokunaga, A. Ortega (Eds.), Large-Scale Knowledge Resources. IX, 367 pages. 2008.

Vol. 4933: R. Medina, S. Obiedkov (Eds.), Formal Concept Analysis. XII, 325 pages. 2008.

Vol. 4930: I. Wachsmuth, G. Knoblich (Eds.), Modeling Communication with Robots and Virtual Humans. X, 337 pages. 2008.

Vol. 4929: M. Helmert, Understanding Planning Tasks. XIV, 270 pages. 2008.

Vol. 4924: D. Riaño (Ed.), Knowledge Management for Health Care Procedures. X, 161 pages. 2008.

Vol. 4923: S.B. Yahia, E.M. Nguifo, R. Belohlavek (Eds.), Concept Lattices and Their Applications. XII, 283 pages. 2008.

Vol. 4914: K. Satoh, A. Inokuchi, K. Nagao, T. Kawamura (Eds.), New Frontiers in Artificial Intelligence. X, 404 pages. 2008.

Vol. 4911: L. De Raedt, P. Frasconi, K. Kersting, S. Muggleton (Eds.), Probabilistic Inductive Logic Programming. VIII, 341 pages. 2008.

Vol. 4908: M. Dastani, A. El Fallah Seghrouchni, A. Ricci, M. Winikoff (Eds.), Programming Multi-Agent Systems. XII, 267 pages. 2008.

Vol. 4898: M. Kolp, B. Henderson-Sellers, H. Mouratidis, A. Garcia, A.K. Ghose, P. Bresciani (Eds.), Agent-Oriented Information Systems IV. X, 292 pages. 2008.

Vol. 4897: M. Baldoni, T.C. Son, M.B. van Riemsdijk, M. Winikoff (Eds.), Declarative Agent Languages and Technologies V. X, 245 pages. 2008.

Vol. 4894: H. Blockeel, J. Ramon, J. Shavlik, P. Tadepalli (Eds.), Inductive Logic Programming. XI, 307 pages. 2008.

Vol. 4885: M. Chetouani, A. Hussain, B. Gas, M. Milgram, J.-L. Zarader (Eds.), Advances in Nonlinear Speech Processing. XI, 284 pages. 2007.

Vol. 4874: J. Neves, M.F. Santos, J.M. Machado (Eds.), Progress in Artificial Intelligence. XVIII, 704 pages. 2007.

Vol. 4870: J.S. Sichman, J.A. Padget, S. Ossowski, P. Noriega (Eds.), Coordination, Organizations, Institutions, and Norms in Agent Systems III. XII, 331 pages. 2008.

Vol. 4869: F. Botana, T. Recio (Eds.), Automated Deduction in Geometry. X, 213 pages. 2007.

Vol. 4865: K. Tuyls, A. Nowe, Z. Guessoum, D. Kudenko (Eds.), Adaptive Agents and Multi-Agent Systems III. VIII, 255 pages. 2008.

Vol. 4850: M. Lungarella, F. Iida, J.C. Bongard, R. Pfeifer (Eds.), 50 Years of Artificial Intelligence. X, 399 pages. 2007.

Vol. 4845: N. Zhong, J. Liu, Y. Yao, J. Wu, S. Lu, K. Li (Eds.), Web Intelligence Meets Brain Informatics. XI, 516 pages. 2007.

Vol. 4840: L. Paletta, E. Rome (Eds.), Attention in Cognitive Systems. XI, 497 pages. 2007.

Vol. 4830: M.A. Orgun, J. Thornton (Eds.), AI 2007: Advances in Artificial Intelligence. XIX, 841 pages. 2007.

Vol. 4828: M. Randall, H.A. Abbass, J. Wiles (Eds.), Progress in Artificial Life. XII, 402 pages. 2007.

Vol. 4827: A. Gelbukh, Á.F. Kuri Morales (Eds.), MICAI 2007: Advances in Artificial Intelligence. XXIV, 1234 pages. 2007.

Vol. 4826: P. Perner, O. Salvetti (Eds.), Advances in Mass Data Analysis of Signals and Images in Medicine, Biotechnology and Chemistry. X, 183 pages. 2007.

Vol. 4819: T. Washio, Z.-H. Zhou, J.Z. Huang, X. Hu, J. Li, C. Xie, J. He, D. Zou, K.-C. Li, M.M. Freire (Eds.), Emerging Technologies in Knowledge Discovery and Data Mining. XIV, 675 pages. 2007.

Vol. 4811: O. Nasraoui, M. Spiliopoulou, J. Srivastava, B. Mobasher, B. Masand (Eds.), Advances in Web Mining and Web Usage Analysis. XII, 247 pages. 2007.

Vol. 4798: Z. Zhang, J.H. Siekmann (Eds.), Knowledge Science, Engineering and Management. XVI, 669 pages. 2007.

Vol. 4795: F. Schilder, G. Katz, J. Pustejovsky (Eds.), Annotating, Extracting and Reasoning about Time and Events. VII, 141 pages. 2007.

Vol. 4790: N. Dershowitz, A. Voronkov (Eds.), Logic for Programming, Artificial Intelligence, and Reasoning. XIII, 562 pages. 2007.

Vol. 4788: D. Borrajo, L. Castillo, J.M. Corchado (Eds.), Current Topics in Artificial Intelligence. XI, 280 pages. 2007.

Vol. 4775: A. Esposito, M. Faundez-Zanuy, E. Keller, M. Marinaro (Eds.), Verbal and Nonverbal Communication Behaviours. XII, 325 pages. 2007.

Vol. 4772: H. Prade, V.S. Subrahmanian (Eds.), Scalable Uncertainty Management. X, 277 pages. 2007.

Vol. 4766: N. Maudet, S. Parsons, I. Rahwan (Eds.), Argumentation in Multi-Agent Systems. XII, 211 pages. 2007.

Lecture Notes in Artificial Intelligence (LNAI)

Vol. 4760: E. Rome, J. Hertzberg, G. Dorffner (Eds.), Towards Affordance-Based Robot Control. IX, 211 pages. 2008.

Vol. 4755: V. Corruble, M. Takeda, E. Suzuki (Eds.), Discovery Science. XI, 298 pages. 2007.

Vol. 4754: M. Hutter, R.A. Servedio, E. Takimoto (Eds.), Algorithmic Learning Theory. XI, 403 pages. 2007.

Vol. 4737: B. Berendt, A. Hotho, D. Mladenic, G. Semeraro (Eds.), From Web to Social Web: Discovering and Deploying User and Content Profiles. XI, 161 pages. 2007.

Vol. 4733: R. Basili, M.T. Pazienza (Eds.), AI*IA 2007: Artificial Intelligence and Human-Oriented Computing. XVII, 858 pages. 2007.

Vol. 4724: K. Mellouli (Ed.), Symbolic and Quantitative Approaches to Reasoning with Uncertainty. XV, 914 pages. 2007.

Vol. 4722: C. Pelachaud, J.-C. Martin, E. André, G. Chollet, K. Karpouzis, D. Pelé (Eds.), Intelligent Virtual Agents. XV, 425 pages. 2007.

Vol. 4720: B. Konev, F. Wolter (Eds.), Frontiers of Combining Systems. X, 283 pages. 2007.

Vol. 4702: J.N. Kok, J. Koronacki, R. Lopez de Mantaras, S. Matwin, D. Mladenič, A. Skowron (Eds.), Knowledge Discovery in Databases: PKDD 2007. XXIV, 640 pages. 2007.

Vol. 4701: J.N. Kok, J. Koronacki, R. Lopez de Mantaras, S. Matwin, D. Mladenič, A. Skowron (Eds.), Machine Learning: ECML 2007. XXII, 809 pages. 2007.

Vol. 4696: H.-D. Burkhard, G. Lindemann, R. Verbrugge, L.Z. Varga (Eds.), Multi-Agent Systems and Applications V. XIII, 350 pages. 2007.

Vol. 4694: B. Apolloni, R.J. Howlett, L. Jain (Eds.), Knowledge-Based Intelligent Information and Engineering Systems, Part III. XXIX, 1126 pages. 2007.

Vol. 4693: B. Apolloni, R.J. Howlett, L. Jain (Eds.), Knowledge-Based Intelligent Information and Engineering Systems, Part II. XXXII, 1380 pages. 2007.

Vol. 4692: B. Apolloni, R.J. Howlett, L. Jain (Eds.), Knowledge-Based Intelligent Information and Engineering Systems, Part I. LV, 882 pages. 2007.

Vol. 4687: P. Petta, J.P. Müller, M. Klusch, M. Georgeff (Eds.), Multiagent System Technologies. X, 207 pages. 2007.

Vol. 4682: D.-S. Huang, L. Heutte, M. Loog (Eds.), Advanced Intelligent Computing Theories and Applications. XXVII, 1373 pages. 2007.

Vol. 4676: M. Klusch, K.V. Hindriks, M.P. Papazoglou, L. Sterling (Eds.), Cooperative Information Agents XI. XI, 361 pages. 2007.

Vol. 4667: J. Hertzberg, M. Beetz, R. Englert (Eds.), KI 2007: Advances in Artificial Intelligence. IX, 516 pages. 2007.

Vol. 4660: S. Džeroski, L. Todorovski (Eds.), Computational Discovery of Scientific Knowledge. X, 327 pages. 2007.

Vol. 4659: V. Mařík, V. Vyatkin, A.W. Colombo (Eds.), Holonic and Multi-Agent Systems for Manufacturing. VIII, 456 pages. 2007.

Vol. 4651: F. Azevedo, P. Barahona, F. Fages, F. Rossi (Eds.), Recent Advances in Constraints. VIII, 185 pages. 2007.

Vol. 4648: F. Almeida e Costa, L.M. Rocha, E. Costa, I. Harvey, A. Coutinho (Eds.), Advances in Artificial Life. XVIII, 1215 pages. 2007.

Vol. 4635: B. Kokinov, D.C. Richardson, T.R. Roth-Berghofer, L. Vieu (Eds.), Modeling and Using Context. XIV, 574 pages. 2007.

Vol. 4632: R. Alhajj, H. Gao, X. Li, J. Li, O.R. Zaïane (Eds.), Advanced Data Mining and Applications. XV, 634 pages. 2007.

Vol. 4629: V. Matoušek, P. Mautner (Eds.), Text, Speech and Dialogue. XVII, 663 pages. 2007.

Vol. 4626: R.O. Weber, M.M. Richter (Eds.), Case-Based Reasoning Research and Development. XIII, 534 pages. 2007.

Vol. 4617: V. Torra, Y. Narukawa, Y. Yoshida (Eds.), Modeling Decisions for Artificial Intelligence. XII, 502 pages. 2007.

Vol. 4612: I. Miguel, W. Ruml (Eds.), Abstraction, Reformulation, and Approximation. XI, 418 pages. 2007.

Vol. 4604: U. Priss, S. Polovina, R. Hill (Eds.), Conceptual Structures: Knowledge Architectures for Smart Applications. XII, 514 pages. 2007.

Vol. 4603: F. Pfenning (Ed.), Automated Deduction – CADE-21. XII, 522 pages. 2007.

Vol. 4597: P. Perner (Ed.), Advances in Data Mining. XI, 353 pages. 2007.

Vol. 4594: R. Bellazzi, A. Abu-Hanna, J. Hunter (Eds.), Artificial Intelligence in Medicine. XVI, 509 pages. 2007.

Vol. 4585: M. Kryszkiewicz, J.F. Peters, H. Rybinski, A. Skowron (Eds.), Rough Sets and Intelligent Systems Paradigms. XIX, 836 pages. 2007.

Vol. 4578: F. Masulli, S. Mitra, G. Pasi (Eds.), Applications of Fuzzy Sets Theory. XVIII, 693 pages. 2007.

Vol. 4573: M. Kauers, M. Kerber, R. Miner, W. Windsteiger (Eds.), Towards Mechanized Mathematical Assistants. XIII, 407 pages. 2007.

Vol. 4571: P. Perner (Ed.), Machine Learning and Data Mining in Pattern Recognition. XIV, 913 pages. 2007.

Vol. 4570: H.G. Okuno, M. Ali (Eds.), New Trends in Applied Artificial Intelligence. XXI, 1194 pages. 2007.

Vol. 4565: D.D. Schmorrow, L.M. Reeves (Eds.), Foundations of Augmented Cognition. XIX, 450 pages. 2007.

Vol. 4562: D. Harris (Ed.), Engineering Psychology and Cognitive Ergonomics. XXIII, 879 pages. 2007.

Vol. 4548: N. Olivetti (Ed.), Automated Reasoning with Analytic Tableaux and Related Methods. X, 245 pages. 2007.

Vol. 4539: N.H. Bshouty, C. Gentile (Eds.), Learning Theory. XII, 634 pages. 2007.

Vol. 4529: P. Melin, O. Castillo, L.T. Aguilar, J. Kacprzyk, W. Pedrycz (Eds.), Foundations of Fuzzy Logic and Soft Computing. XIX, 830 pages. 2007.